SEX REWARDED, SEX PUNISHED

A STUDY OF THE STATUS "FEMALE SLAVE" IN EARLY JEWISH LAW

DIANE KRIGER

Judaism and Jewish Life

Geoffrey Alderman (University of Buckingham, England)
Meir Bar-Ilan (Bar-Ilan University, Israel)
Herbert Basser (Queen's University, Canada)
Donatella Ester Di Cesare (Universita La Sapienza, Italy)
Simcha Fishbane (Touro College, New York), Series Editor
Andreas Nachama (Touro College, Berlin)
Ira Robinson (Concordia University, Montreal)
Nissan Rubin (Bar-Ilan University, Israel)
Susan Starr Sered (Suffolk University, Boston)
Reeva Spector Simon (Yeshiva University, New York)

ACADEMIC
STUDIES
PRESS

SEX REWARDED SEX PUNISHED

A STUDY OF THE STATUS "FEMALE SLAVE" IN EARLY JEWISH LAW

DIANE KRIGER

(final editing and preparation for publication by Tirzah Meacham leBeit Yoreh)

Boston
2011

Library of Congress Cataloging-in-Publication Data

Kriger, Diane.
Sex rewarded, sex punished : a study of the status 'female slave' in early Jewish law / Diane Kriger.
p. cm. -- (Judaism and Jewish life)
Includes bibliographical references and index.
ISBN 978-1-934843-48-2 (hardback)
1. Women (Jewish law) 2. Women slaves (Jewish law) 3. Women in the Bible. I. Title.
KBM526.K75 2011
296.086'25--dc22

2010054363

ISBN 978-1-934843-48-2

Book design by Olga Grabovsky

On the cover: *Abraham Sends Hagar and Ishmael Away*, by Gustave Doré, 1866.

Published by Academic Studies Press in 2011
28 Montfern Avenue
Brighton, MA 02135, USA
press@academicstudiespress.com
www.academicstudiespress.com

I wish to dedicate this work to the memories of three individuals who have also inspired me with their courage:

Imi Shirley Rachel Movshovitz Kriger, ז"ל*, bat Mordechai and Chanah*

Judith Leah Ain, ז"ל*, bat Avraham and Malkah*

Lynne Mary Wheller, B.A., 1961-1996

ACKNOWLEDGMENTS

I find it most interesting that a fourteen-year study on the minutiae of slavery and marginalization, combined with a good hard fight against cancer, have rendered me now very aware of those who go above and beyond the call of duty in rendering *tikkun olam*. To those who have assisted me in this way, I hope to acknowledge here the gratitude I feel:

— to my thesis supervisors, Prof. H. Fox and Prof. T. Meacham of the Department of Near and Middle Eastern Civilizations at the University of Toronto, for their example of extreme devotion and encouragement to their students; and to Prof. A. K. Grayson and the staff of the Department, especially for their generous assistance in the use of the Royal Inscriptions of Mesopotamia Project Library,

— to Dr. H. Offman, and to Dr. Rashida Haq and the staff and nurses of the Medical Daycare Department at St. Mike's Hospital,Toronto,

— to the Social Sciences and Humanities Research Council of Canada, for their financial assistance,

— to my mentors Dr. Cindy Nimchuk and Dr. Jennifer Hellum, and to my friends Forrest Ann Lenney, Dr. Alison Barclay, Dr. Rhona Singer, Heather Resnick, Pearl Elman, Brenda Saunders, Cheryl Tallan, Laliv Clenman, and Morris Burshtyn, an amazing conclave of affective and intellectual sustenance,

— to Dr. Paul Heger, for his many discussions on plurality in Jewish law,

— to Linda Charyk Rosenfeld, my first editor, and the most creative and generous of individuals,

and finally, to the members of my family/caregivers (David, Susan, Judy, Akiva, Shirley, Sarah and Debra). May your continued selflessness be returned in kind.

Ottawa, Ontario

IN MEMORIAM

My dear daughter Diane, of blessed memory, was born in October 1951, two days after Rosh Hashanah, during the *yamim nora'im*, the Days of Awe, which indeed seemed to me to be words that could be applied to the days of her academic career—awesome days!

From top grades through the eight years of Hillel Academy Day School in Ottawa and through Ottawa high schools, an Honours B.A. (Magna cum Laude) at Queen's University in Kingston, continuing through L.L.B. and L.L.L. degrees at the University of Ottawa, an M.B.A. at York University in Toronto, and an M.A. and Ph.D. in Near Eastern Studies at the University of Toronto—all this to the rest of her family and friends: totally awesome.

Diane was modest about her achievements. When awarding Diane the prize for first year Greek at Queen's University, her professor told her, "You are a remarkable student." She commented later, "Well, it was only for first year Greek—'baby' Greek!"

Diane lived her life

> ... yearning in desire
> To follow knowledge like a sinking star,
> Beyond the utmost bound of human thought.

This book is the culmination of my daughter's love of Jewish text and her love of Jewish law and justice.

צדק צדק תרדף

Akiva Kriger
Ottawa, 2009

CONTENTS

FOREWORD xv
NOTES ON SOURCES, TRANSLITERATIONS AND TRANSLATIONS xvii
LIST OF ABBREVIATIONS xix

INTRODUCTION
The Construction of Status 1
What is a "Slave"? 3
Sex Right as a Status Marker 4
Sex Rewarded: Marriage and the Matrilineal Principle 6
Sex Punished: Adultery as Property Crime or Sex Crime? 10
Methodological Issues 14
I. A Word on "Representativity": Are We Dealing With Legal Texts? 14
II. Philology and Functional Equivalence 15
III. The Use of a Pluralistic Model 17
Slave Status in Biblical Law: A "Common Law"? 20
Slave Status in Postbiblical Law: A Unified Tradition? 26
Chapter Summary 32

CHAPTER 1
What is a "Female Slave"? Context and Comparison 35
1.1 The *amah* and the *shifḥah*: Breeder, Drudge, Concubine or Wife? 36
1.1.1 The Terms are Biblical Synonyms Indicating a Servile Status 40
1.1.2 North-East Semitic Versus North-West Semitic? 45
1.1.2.A The *amah* as a Secondary Wife 48
1.1.3 Conclusion: On the Slave-Wife Continuum 52
1.1.4 Conclusion 52
1.2 Are There Biblical Terms for Second Generation Slaves? 53
1.2.1 *ben amah* 53
1.2.1.A Ishmael 54
1.2.1.B Avimelekh 57
1.2.1.C As Parallel to *eved* in Psalms and Sabbath Law 59
1.2.1.D Conclusion 62

1.2.2 *yelid bayit* - Houseborn Slave? 62
1.2.2.A The Form and Meaning of *yelid* and the Akkadian *wilid bītim* 68
1.2.2.B Other Akkadian Equivalents 72
1.2.2.C Post-Biblical Occurrences 74
1.2.2.D Conclusion 78
1.2.3 *ben bayit* 78
1.2.3.A Akkadian *mār bīti* 81
1.2.3.B Post-Biblical Sources 82
1.2.3.C Conclusion 87

CHAPTER 2
The *pilegesh*: Status or Topos? 89
2.1 On the Wife-Slave Continuum? 91
2.2 Foreign Loanword? 96
2.3 The *pilegesh* as a Literary Topos? 99
2.4 Biblical Examples of Three Instances of *pilegesh* as Topos 101
2.4.A The Male *pilagshim* of Ezekiel 23:20 101
2.4.B Genesis 35:22: Bilhah as *pilegesh* 104
2.4.C The *ishah pilegesh* of Judges 19 111
2.5 Conclusion 119

CHAPTER 3
The *amah* of Exodus 21:2-11 121
3.1 Exodus 21:2-11 and its Relation to Other Manumission Rules 121
3.1.1 The Significance of the Different *amah* Rules 127
3.2 An Analysis of Exodus 21:2-11 132
3.2.1 Is the Passage to be Read as a Unity? 132
3.2.2 Akkadian Parallels 137
3.2.3 Specific Textual Issues in Exodus 21:7-11 141
3.2.3.A *Ketiv* (לא) Versus *qere* (לו) in Verse 8
and the Significance of *bQiddushin* 18ab 141
3.2.3.B "If He Takes Another" (אם אחרת יקח לו) in Verse 10 148
3.2.3.C "These Three Things" (שלש אלה) in Verse 11 149
3.3 Conclusion 150

CHAPTER 4
The *shifḥah neḥerefet* of Leviticus 19:20-22 151
4.1 Treason and Trespass 151
4.2 The Issue: Mixed Ownership 156
4.3 The Relationship: The Meaning of *neḥerefet la-ish* 159
4.3.1 Prior Opinions 159
4.3.2 The Semantic Range of the Biblical *ḤRP I* 163
4.3.3 A Possible Akkadian Cognate 166
4.3.4 Proposed Meaning of *neḥerefet la-ish* 168
4.4 The Outcome: The Phrase *biqqoret tihyeh* 171

4.4.1 Prior Opinions 172
4.4.2 Biblical Instances of *BQR* as "Claim for Trespass" 175
4.4.3 *BQR/PQR* as "Claim" in Akkadian Sources 178
4.4.3.A San Nicolo's Study of *BQR* in Old Babylonian Sources 178
4.4.3.B The Scholarly Debate on the Relationship of *biqqoret* to Akkadian *BQR/PQR* 181
4.4.3.C "Non-Narrow" Uses of *BQR/PQR* in Process Documents and Warranties 185
4.4.3.D Conclusion 190
4.4.4 *BQR/PQR* as "Claim" in Postbiblical Hebrew 191
4.4.4.A The *iggeret biqqoret* 193
4.4.4.B Sanctified Property and *biqqoret*: *Tosefta Arakhin* 4:3 210
4.4.4.C *PQR* in Other Formulary Documents 211
4.4.4.D The Association of *hevqer/hefqer* with "Claim" 212
4.4.4.E The Proposed Meaning of *biqqoret* 216
4.5 Conclusion 217

CHAPTER 5
The "Inheritance" of Slavery in Rabbinic Law:
The Non-Linearity of the Matrilineal Principle 219
5.1 Introduction 219
5.2 The Freeing of the Hebrew *amah* at Puberty 220
5.2.1 Pentateuchal Rules on the Acquisition and Manumission of Slaves 220
5.2.2 The Mishnaic Manumission Scheme for Hebrew Females 222
5.2.3 The "Manumission List" in Midreshei Halakhah 225
5.2.4 The Manumission List in *bQiddushin* 18a 230
5.2.4.A. "Against His/Her Will" (בעל כרחו - בעל כרחה) 231
5.2.4.B Diminution of Purchase Price (גרעון) or Death of Master (מיתת האדון) 235
5.2.5 Conclusion 236
5.3 The Interaction of Slavery and Nationality 237
5.3.1 Levitucus 25 and the "Ethnic" Differentiation of Slaves 237
5.3.2 *Sifra Behar parshah* 6 and its Parallels 240
5.3.3 Conclusion 245
5.4 *Tosefta Qiddushin* 5:11: "Symmetrical" Inheritance of *Mamzerut*? 245
5.5 Variability in Genealogical Thinking 250

CHAPTER 6
Rabbinic Interpretations of Leviticus 19:20-22 251
6.1 The Significance of Parallel Baraitot 251
6.2 *Mishnah Kereitot* 2:4b-6 252
6.3 *Tosefta Kereitot* 1:16-18 256
6.4 *Sifra Qedoshim pereq* 5 260
6.4.1 Overview of the Text 260
6.4.2 *Sifra's* Interpretation of Leviticus 19:20 262

6.4.2.A The Age of the Parties 262
6.4.2.B The Nature of the Offence 264
6.4.2.C The Identity of the *shifḥah neḥerefet* (the "Intermarriage Baraita") 265
6.4.2.D The Creation of a "Half-Slave" 272
6.4.2.E The Punishment of the Woman 279
6.4.2.F The Necessity of a Deed of Manumission 279
6.4.2.G The Punishment of the Male 283
6.4.2.H Further Specification of the Nature of the Offence 283
6.4.2.I The Summary Section 286
6.5 Assessing the Parallel Texts 290
6.5.1 General Considerations Between Mishnah and Tosefta 291
6.5.2 General Considerations between *Sifra* and Tosefta 294
6.5.3 The "Intermarriage" Pericope 295
6.5.4 The Priority of the Tosefta Passage 304
6.5.5 Conclusion 304
6.6 Excursus: The Existence of a Half-Slave, Half-Free Status 305

CHAPTER 7
Literature in Support of Law: The Problem of Bilhah and Zilpah 313
7.1 The Dilemma 313
7.2 Biblical References to Bilhah and Zilpah 314
7.3 Early Postbiblical References 317
7.3.1 לחנה in Onkelos as a Cognate of the Akkadian *laḫḫi/anatu*, "Female Subordinate" 318
7.3.2 The Relationship between Targum Onkelos and Josephus 324
7.4 Bilhah and Zilpah as "Matriarchs" 326
7.5 The Genealogy of Bilhah and Zilpah 333
7.5.1 The *Aḥiyot* Tradition 334
7.5.1.A The Naming Speech 339
7.5.1.B Channels of Transmission 340
7.5.2 The Lavan Tradition 343
7.6 Conclusion 344

CONCLUSION 345

BIBLIOGRAPHY 353

CITATIONS INDEX 385

FOREWORD

In November 2008, three weeks before Diane Kriger passed away, I visited her in Ottawa. I believe we both knew that it was our last face-to-face visit, but it was filled with family news, updates on students and colleagues, discussion of her book, my research projects, conferences, the academic scene in Israel, the new feminist commentary to the Talmud project, and laughter—much laughter. It was only then, that close to the end, that she was willing to let go of her book. That night she signed the contract for this book, something I had been urging her to do for several months. It was essentially complete—she needed to finish her conclusion, which she sent to me a few days later. We over-optimistically set a date for submission early in 2009. But books take longer to get all the details right. She quoted several languages, including Hebrew, Aramaic, Greek, Latin, Akkadian (thankfully in transliteration) as well as German and French. Unfortunately, all foreign alphabets and diacritical marks disappeared in the transfer of material to me. Even with the help of computer technicians we were unable to recover the original languages. With the help of a scanner, nearly all lost material was keyed in very accurately by Yael Richardson, to whom I am most grateful. Nevertheless, everything needed to be checked, the notes renumbered, the bibliography finalized, and many other details with which only editors and publishers are concerned needed to be addressed. Diane had been the person who helped me with this work in my books and articles. She was an expert and I am a novice. I have tried very hard to fulfill my promise to her that we would "do her proud" in getting her book out, but I am responsible for the many delays. I had no Diane with whom to consult with my questions, only the loss of Diane with which I had to come to terms while immersed in her thoughts and ideas. Readers will see the density with which she writes, both in the difficulty of concepts and in the terseness of presentation. I have made some modifications for the sake of clarity, remaining as faithful as possible to her ideas as I understood them. I have streamlined her presentation of variant readings of rabbinic texts, divided one chapter into two, and filled in her conclusions. This was for the sake of clarity only; I changed nothing of the content of her thoughts. I have also prepared the indices which depended on pagination and added a few notes marked [TM].

I am grateful to Harry Fox (leBeit Yoreh) with whom I regularly consulted, to Paul Heger for his support, to Yael Richardson for her help in restoring the lost texts, to Matt Iannucci for his help with the bibliography and to my colleagues P.A. Beaulieu and Doug Frayne for their help with the Akkadian references. I feel Diane's absence every day and the loss of her talents for the academic world, for those seeking justice, and for her family and friends. I hope the final outcome of my efforts would be acceptable to Diane. May her memory be blessed.

Tirzah Meacham (leBeit Yoreh)
ל"ג בעומר תשס"ע

NOTES ON SOURCES, TRANSLITERATIONS AND TRANSLATIONS

1. Citations of Mishnah, Talmud and aggadic works are from standard printed editions, most of which have been downloaded from the Bar Ilan Responsa Project Data Base. If there are significant variants, the text may be presented according to a particular manuscript as noted and variants from other witnesses may be presented in an apparatus or in a note. Occasionally line numbers and punctuation are added. Tosefta citations are from Lieberman where available and otherwise from Zuckermandel.
2. Citations from Targum Onkelos and the Targumim to the Prophets and the Hagiographa are from the Yemenite Tag' (תאג'). Citations from Targum Pseudo-Jonathan are from E. G. Clarke, 1984. Citations from Targum Neofiti are from A. Diez Macho, 1970. Citations from the Samaritan Targum are from A. Tal, 1988.
3. Hebrew transliteration is based on the "non-technical" system cited in *Encyclopedia Judaica*, 1972, Vol. 1. Exceptions are made for some commonly used words, particularly names (e.g. Moses, Akiva, etc.). When a vowel combination is not a diphthong but two separate syllables, I have indicated such by use of an apostrophe. I have also included a dot under the "h" (ḥ) to indicate the letter ח.
4. Transliterations of the Mesopotamian law collections are taken from M. Roth, 1995. Akkadian transliteration uses the Thames font developed by Dr. J. Hoch of the Department of Near and Middle Eastern Civilizations at the University of Toronto. Cunieform texts

from Babylonian tablets are cited using the abbreviations in W. von Soden (cited as *AHW*) and the *Chicago Assyrian Dictionary* (cited as *CAD*).

5. Unless otherwise indicated, English translations of Hebrew, Aramaic, and Akkadian texts are my own.
6. Citations from the Septuagint are taken from the Göttingen edition where available. English translations of the Septuagint passages are taken from L. Brenton, 1986. Quotations from the work of Philo and Josephus and translations thereof are taken from the Loeb Classical Library editions.

D.K.

LIST OF ABBREVIATIONS

ABL = Assyrian and Babylonian Letters (Harper)
ADD = Assyrian Documents and Deeds (Johns)
Arakh. = Tractate *Arakhin*
b, *B*, BT = Bavli, Babylonian Talmud
B.Bat. = Tractate *Baba Batra*
BE = Babylonian Expedition of Univ. of Pennsylvania, Series A: CT
Bikk. = Tractate *Bikkurim*
B.Metz. = Tractate *Baba Metzia*
BU = British Museum (Signature Budge)
B.Qam. = Tractate *Baba Qama*
CH = Code of Hammurapi
CIS = Corpus Inscriptionum Semiticarum
CT = Cunieform Texts
D = Deuteronomist Editor
Dar = Darius
E = Elohist Editor
Eruv. = Tractate *Eruvin*
Gitt. = Tractate *Gittin*
GPA = Governor's Palace Archives
H = Holiness Code Editor
Hil. = *Hilkhot*
Hor. = Tractate *Horai'ot*
HSS = Harvard Semitic Series
J = Yahwist Editor

JEN = Joint Expedition at Nuzi
K = Kouyunjik Collections of the British Museum
Ker. = Tractate *Kereitot*
Ki = King's Excavations (L.W. King Collection of British Museum)
LB = Late Babylonian
LE = Laws of Eshnunna
LH = Laws of Hammurapi
LL = Laws of Lipit Ishtar
LU = Laws of Ur-Namma
LXX = Septuagint
m, M = Mishnah
MAL = Middle Assyrian Laws
Ma'as.Sh. = Ma'aser Sheni
MB = Middle Babylonian
MishTor = Mishneh Torah
MS, MSS = Manuscript, Manuscripts
MSL = Materials for the Sumerian Lexicon
MT = Masoretic Text
N = Nuzi (according to Saarisalo, 1934)
NA = Neo-Assyrian
NB = Neo-Babylonian
NRVU = *Neubabylonische Rechts- und Verwaltungsurkunden* (M. San Nicolo and A. Ungnad, 1929)
NT = New Testament
OA = Old Assyrian
OB = Old Babylonian
P = Priestly Editor
PBP = *pisqa ba'emtza pasuq*
Qidd. = Tractate *Qiddushin*
RCAE = *Royal Correspondence of the Assyrian Empire*
SAA = State Archives of Assyria
San. = Tractate *Sanhedrin*
Shabb. = Tractate *Shabbat*
SP = Samaritan Pentateuch
t, T = Tosefta
Ta'an. = Tractate *Ta'anit*

TCL = Textes cunéiforms du Louvre
TK = S. Lieberman, *Tosefta KiFeshutah*
TY = Targum Yonatan (Pseudo-Jonathan) to the Pentateuch
UAZP = *Urkunden des Altbabylonischen Zivil- und Prozessrechts* (M. Schorr, 1913)
VAB = Vorderasiatische Bibliothek
VAS = Vorderasiatische Schriftdenkmäler
y, *Y*, YT = Yerushalmi, Jerusalem Talmud
YBT = Yale Babylonian Texts
Yev. = Tractate *Yevamot*
Zev. = Tractate *Zevaḥim*

Manuscript Abbreviations

MISHNAH
פ = Parma De Rossi 138 (Mishnah)
ק = Kaufmann A50 (Mishnah)
ר = Rambam Autograph (Mishnah)
ל = Cambridge Add. 470.1 (Mishnah)
ג = Various geniza fragments noted *in situ*
ד = Napoli Edition of Mishnah 1492

TOSEFTA
ע = Erfurt (Tosefta)
ב = Vienna Cod. Hebr. 20 (Tosefta)

SIFRA
א = Assemani 66 (Sifra)
ר = Vatican 31 (Sifra)
ב = Breslau (Sifra)
ג = Parma (Sifra)
ד = Venice Edition (Sifra)
ה = Oxford (Sifra)
ל = London (Sifra)

TALMUD

י = Leiden MS of Yerushalmi

ג = geniza fragment Cambridge TSE II 88 (*bKer.*)

ז = Vatican Ebr. 113 (*mKet.*)

ו = Vatican Ebr. 119 (*mKer., bKer.*)

ט = Vatican Ebr. 130 (*mKet.*)

מ = Munich 95 MS (BT)

F = Firenze Nationale Central Biblioteca II.1.7 (*bKer.*)

L = London British Museum Add. 25, 717 (*bKer.*)

V^{120} = Vatican Ebr. 120 (*bKer.*)

MIDRASH AND TARGUM

מ = Midrash HaGadol

ח = Midrash Ḥakhamim

ש = Yalqut Shimoni

Sa = Targum to Samaritan Pentateuch, MS A

Sj = Targum to Samaritan Pentateuch, MS J

SIGLA FOR CRITICAL APPARATUS

∩ = sign for homeoteleuton in critical apparatus

[= sign for end of lemma and start of variants

° = correction in MS

°° = correction in MS in a different hand (when it can be determined)

˜ = sign for marginal note in MS

* = most MSS have given reading

*̲ = most MSS have given reading - some minor variation in orthography/ abbreviation

<>= secondary and tertiary witnesses

{ } = text not readable in base text but completed by other MSS

Abbreviations used in the bibliography:

AHW	*Akkadisches Handworterbuch*
AJS Review	*Association for Jewish Studies Review*
AOS	American Oriental Series
ARSP	*Archiv für Rechts- und Sozialphilosophie*
BiOr	*Bibliotheca Orientalis*
BZAW	Beihefte zur Zeitschrift für die alttestamentliche Wissenschaft
CAD	*Chicago Assyrian Dictionary*
COD	*Canadian Oxford Dictionary*
DJD	*Discoveries in the Judean Desert*
DSD	*Dead Sea Discoveries*
EM	*Encyclopedia Miqrait (Encyclopedia of Bible)*
IEJ	*Israel Exploration Journal*
JAOS	*Journal of the American Oriental Society*
JBL	*Journal of Biblical Literature*
JCS	*Journal of Cuneiform Studies*
JHCS	*Journal of Halakhah and Contemporary Society*
JJS	*Journal of Jewish Studies*
JNES	*Journal of Near Eastern Studies*
JQR	*Jewish Quarterly Review*
JSOT	*Journal for the Study of the Old Testament*
JSS	*Journal of Semitic Studies*
JTSA	Jewish Theological Seminary of America
OED	*Shorter Oxford English Dictionary*
PAAJS	*Proceedings of the American Association of Jewish Studies*
RA	*Revue d'assyriologie*
RAI	*Rencontre assyriologique internationale*
RIDA	*Revue internationale des droits de l'antinquité*
SAAS	State Archives of Assyria Studies
TWOT	*Theological Wordbook of the Old Testament* (from 2006 version)
VT	*Vetus Testamentum*
ZA	*Zeitschrift für der Assyriologie und verwandte Gebiete*
ZAW	*Zeitschrift für die alttestamentliche Wissenschaft*

INTRODUCTION

The Construction of Status

Several years ago, an article in the *Journal of Halakhah and Contemporary Society* proposed the following argument:[1] Since neither the State of Israel nor its political predecessors have ever passed any legislation banning slavery, it would still be possible to acquire in Israel a *shifḥah kena'anit* (a non-Jewish female slave) for use under the provisions of *mQidd.* 3:13. The purpose of such a transaction would be to "cure" the descendants of a *mamzer* (a male outcast[2]), who would have limited marrying capacity within the Jewish community, by having the *mamzer* produce offspring with the slave woman.[3] The children would be slaves, like their mother,[4] and could then be freed, untainted by any outcast status. The slave would presumably be someone willing to accept her assignment in return for a monetary reward, and she could be "freed" after she had produced the child or children. Manumission constitutes conversion, so that the slave who became obligated in the negative commandments when acquired becomes a full Jew at manumission.

Should we question such transactions in legally marginal statuses, even

1 David Katz, "The *Mamzer* and the *Shifcha*," *JHCS* 28 (1994): 73-104.

2 In *mYev.* 4:13 there are various definitions of a *mamzer*; in general it may be said that it is the offspring of a woman with whom one is forbidden to have a sexual union. A point to note is that the term is narrower in meaning than English "bastard," which generally connotes any offspring of unmarried parents.

3 *MQidd.* 3:13 states in part: "R. Tarfon says: *mamzerim* can clear themselves [of disqualification from marrying Israelites]. How? A *mamzer* who married a *shifḥah* — the offspring is a slave. If he [his father] freed him, the son is thereby a free man."

4 A dissenting opinion of R. Eliezer in *mQidd.* 3:13 holds that the offspring would be both a slave and a *mamzer*.

if the proposed transactions are (at least to some extent) symbolic? In my opinion, the answer is yes, because such transactions bring us too near the "slippery slope" between word and deed.[5] Where, in fact, would the women in such transactions be found? We may be lulled into a belief that female slaves who are associated with the widespread violence, kidnapping, and abuse associated with plantation slavery are a phenomenon limited to particular areas of the third world. Marginalization of humans, however, particularly the physical trafficking in and economic exploitation of females, is a worldwide phenomenon, though its victims may be hidden behind such labels as "prostitute" and "illegal immigrant."[6] It is far too easy to assume that such marginalized statuses are what mishnaic law had in mind by "female non-Jewish slave."

Further, the uncritical maintenance of such vague terms allows us to forget that such categories are not "natural or inevitable."[7] "Slavery" and "slaves" are constructs, supported by particular legal, political, economic, and social definitions.

In this case, we may question why marginal statuses arise in the first place in legal systems, and why they remain. Are they simply enforcing an existing social hierarchy? Can their development be explained by theories of evolution (some variation of the status-contract progression, for instance, or overactive analogy, i.e., the logical extension of a limited term to wider categories), or by theories of diffusion (borrowing from foreign sources, for instance), by political or economic changes (such as the development of Diaspora Judaism or the waning of an agricultural society), or by some dynamic, multivariate model?[8]

---

5 Martin J. Burke, *The Conundrum of Class* (Chicago: University of Chicago Press, 1995), xvi: words both register ideas and give effect to them.

6 For three among many summaries that show the variety of transactions that may be included under the term "slavery," see Bryan Welch, "Putting a Stop to Slave Labor: A Moral Solution to Illegal Immigration," *UTNE Reader*, March-April 2007, 42-44; Thomas S. Axworthy, "Sexual Slavery Seen as World's Greatest Crime," *The Toronto Star*, 25 September, 2005, A-17; Barry Came, "Freeing the Slaves of Sudan," *Maclean's*, 10 April, 2000, 20-27.

7 Barry Came, "Freeing the Slaves of Sudan," 22. Martha Minow, *Making All the Difference: Inclusion, Exclusion, and American Law* (Ithaca, N.Y.: Cornell University Press, 1990), also notes that such categories can become "reified," leading to "levels of abstraction remote from actual experience" (114).

8 For a summary of and comments on various evolutionary and diffusionist models, see, e.g., Bernard S. Jackson, "On the Problem of Roman Influence on the Halakhah and

I wish to contribute to this discussion by examining the status of "female slave" in early Jewish law. I conclude that there is a "leap" between biblical and postbiblical meanings of this term. The "female slave" envisioned in the Bible, though clearly dependent, was valued for her reproductive capability, and the Bible's concern was to place her within a family continuum. In the Mishnah, she is already a marginalized entity, sex with whom is either forbidden or made legally insignificant.

What is a "Slave"?

Before beginning a discussion of the changes in female slave status, it is well to note that the concepts of "slave" and "free" in biblical and postbiblical documents differ from our modern understanding of these terms. Modern notions of "slave" as a specific status distinct from "free" probably did not apply in the Bible. Certain scholars have argued that the ancient Near East was in fact unfamiliar with the modern notion of "freedom," and the overall ideology was one of a hierarchy of dependence.[9] The ideal, in other words, was a notion of belonging. One theory in fact proposes that slaves in Mesopotamia were simply household members who were acquired by means other than birth or marriage, but who otherwise simply took their place as part of an overall dependence continuum.[10]

Certainly, dependence is also presented as an ideal in the Bible; as one of many examples, see Lev. 25:55: "For to me the children of Israel are slaves; they are my slaves whom I have taken out of the land of Egypt; I am

Normative Self-Definition in Judaism," in *Aspects of Judaism in the Graeco-Roman Period*, vol. 2 of *Jewish and Christian Self-Definition* (ed. E. P. Sanders *et al.*; Philadelphia: Fortress, 1981), 158-59. In "History, Dogmatics and Halakhah," in *Jewish Law in Legal History and the Modern World*, (Leiden: Brill,1980), 17-22, Jackson proposes a multivariate approach to legal development that takes into account both innate and external factors (including foreign influence). He proposes that the relative importance of each factor will vary according to the type of legal phenomenon studied — that is, whether it relates to form (e.g., classificatory divisions) or content (e.g., rules or notarial practice). This model will be discussed further below. Alan Watson has argued in contrast that, at least in the Western world, borrowing has been the usual process of development: Alan Watson, *Legal Transplants: An Approach to Comparative Law* (Edinburgh: Scottish Academic Press, 1974), 7.

9 See Orlando Patterson, *Freedom* (New York: Basic Books, 1991), 1:33-41.

10 Patterson, *Freedom*, 34-37.

the Lord your God." (One might argue that Eden itself represents the ideal biblical hierarchy, conditional upon each element of creation maintaining its assigned place.) Further, the biblical term *ḥofshi*, usually translated as "free," seems to have more the sense of "apart," and is not necessarily an ideal state.[11] And there are certainly hints throughout the Bible that slaves would be on the lower end of any such hierarchy; "world-upside-down" depictions such as that found in Prov. 30:21-23 (the *eved* who reigns and the *shifḥah* who inherits) suggest that the opposite was the ideal. It is in the Mishnah, with its introduction of a new term for "free" in *ben ḥorin*, as well as the introduction of the status of a freedman, *meshuḥrar,* that we seem to come closer to the notions of slavery found in Greek and Roman law. In the Bible, the slave is a dependent creature. In postbiblical works, the slave is a truly marginalized creature.

Sex Right as a Status Marker

If the notions of dependence versus marginalization are sufficient in general to differentiate biblical from postbiblical slaves, why study female slaves in particular? Female slaves have not yet been the subject of particular study, as I will discuss in more detail below. Prior studies have tended to subsume females within the more general principles derived with respect to male slaves. This scholarly marginalization, however, has also obscured the important fact that female slaves have reproductive capacity; as such, I argue that the female slave is better compared to the *ishah*, "wife," than to the male slave. Certainly, some scholars have attempted to rank various biblical females, particularly the *amah*, *shifḥah*, and *pilegesh* (the word usually translated "concubine") in relation to the *ishah*. One of the most detailed hierarchies was proposed by Epstein, who suggested that the "oriental" type of extended family structure might have included the chief wife, the concubine (assumed to be a wife of lower rank with the same legal strictures regarding inheritance, adultery, and incest), the freedwoman (though this term is not mentioned in the Bible), the captive wife, the slave wife, and the female slave; these were associated legal

---

11 One must therefore question whether Exod. 21:26-27, which purports to give the injured slave his or her "freedom," was actually beneficial to the slave.

statuses of descending rank.[12] In these studies we find perfect examples of the tendency to rank females first and foremost according to "sex right" — that is, in terms of the degree of sexual access permitted to a female and the consequences of such access. As Pateman has suggested, sex is divided into separate areas of significance— compartmentalized — according to the woman involved.[13]

In this concept of sex right separating women into categories, I believe we have an appropriate status "marker" that may be used to trace the way in which female slaves were differentiated from wives and other women as Jewish law developed. Using the notion of sex right, I trace the meaning of the Hebrew terms *amah* and *shifḥah* (the usual terms used for female slave)[14] as it is represented in texts within the Jewish legal canon, primarily the Hebrew Bible, Mishnah, midreshei halakhah, and baraitot within the Talmudim. The method of study will include both philological analysis of specific terms relating to slavery and a functional comparison to rules and attitudes found in certain documents contemporary with or antecedent to the primary texts.[15] The study also addresses issues regarding the

---

12 Louis Epstein, "The Institution of Concubinage Among the Jews," *PAAJS* 6 (1934-1935): 154, 156.

13 Carol Pateman, *The Sexual Contract* (Stanford: Stanford University Press, 1988), 224. Pateman's own study also focused on the idea that "wives," "slaves," and "serfs," among others, may all be seen as part of a continuum of dependence. Thus in fact they share certain disabilities in law. In her review of the implications of coverture in English common law, she notes the loss of identity that has been common to both "slave" and "wife":

> To be a slave or wife was, so to speak, to be in a perpetual nonage that wives have not yet entirely cast off. Adult male slaves were called "boys" and adult married women were — and still are — called "girls." As befitted civilly dead beings, the slave was brought to life by being given a name by his master.... When a woman becomes a wife, her status was/is singled out by the title "Mrs." A wife was included under her husband's name and, still today, can be called "Mrs. John Smith." (p. 21)

It is thus not surprising to find similar mishnaic terminology regarding the acquisition of wives and slaves (the language of *qinyan*, in *mQidd.* chapter 1), and the use of a *get* (either a writ of divorce or a writ of manumission) to sever both the marriage and the slave relationship.

14 It is the biblical terms *eved* for a male and *amah* and *shifḥah* for a female that are generally taken to refer to slaves.

15 These include the Mesopotamian law collections, Mesopotamian contractual evidence, Qumran documents, apocryphal and pseudepigraphic texts, the Tosefta, and midreshei

relative priority of different slave laws in Mishnah, Tosefta, and talmudic baraitot.

How is sex right manifested in a legal system? I focus on two types of provisions that I believe are significant for explicating this topic: the use of legal marriage and correlative ideas about the legitimacy of children as a means of differentiating class; and the extent to which adultery provisions are used to protect a man's sex right to a particular woman.

I thus use certain repercussions of sexual activity as a "marker" of legal status. "Status" here is used in the modern legal sense of an abnormality or difference in legal condition from some presumed norm, which cannot be acquired, changed, or divested at will.[16] This definition is intended to emphasize the idea that status in a legal system is not an inherent condition, but one assigned by the system according to characteristics it deems relevant at particular times. By the use of differentials in the legal provisions on sexual activity, formal legal recognition thus tends toward status inequality.

I shall explain these two facets of sex right in more detail.

Sex Rewarded: Marriage and the Matrilineal Principle

Various studies of social stratification have noted the way that prohibitions against intermarriage between different groups serve as a means of delineating class structure.[17] The stratification is further maintained by making a child's status — its "legitimacy" for community membership, domicile, inheritance, or other purposes — dependent upon whether its mother has entered into a "valid" marriage. That is, where the woman's options and roles are limited and feature as a major element the bearing of children, such conditions on her offspring's legitimacy act as a strong incentive to enter into a "valid" marriage."

---

aggadah. Certain mediaeval Jewish texts will also be examined.

16 This definition is based on R. H. Graveson, *Status in the Common Law* (London: Athlone, 1953), chap. 1. Though this is an older work, it is useful in setting out the nature of the modern Western idea of status, as opposed to other concepts of status. In particular, Graveson notes the distinction between this idea and the concept of status in Roman law, which connoted the legal condition of the "normal" person, or Sir Henry Maine's concept of status as deriving from one's position in the family (4, 34).

17 See, e.g., Joseph Schumpeter, "The Problem of Classes," in *Class, Status and Power* (2nd ed.; ed. R. Bendix and S. M. Lipset; New York: Free Press, 1966), 42-46, at 43.

Not surprisingly, a common feature of many slave systems is to deny slaves, particularly female slaves, the ability to engage in such legally valid marriages, and as a corollary to make the slave status of a child interdependent with its mother's marital status.[18] These two elements, a restriction on legal marriage and the interdependence of a child's status with that of its mother, are termed in this work the "matrilineal principle."[19]

The economic benefits to the slave master of such a principle are obvious: slave women, unlike other women, do not have their status changed by intercourse, whether with their master or other males; their offspring, in turn, add to the master's supply of slaves.[20] These benefits to the master were expressed succinctly by Frederick Douglass, describing his own experience as a slave in the United States:

> The whisper that my master was my father, may or may not be true; and, true or false, it is of but little consequence to my purpose whilst the fact remains, in all its glaring odiousness, that slaveholders have ordained, and by law established, that the children of slave women shall in all cases follow the condition of their mothers; and this is done too obviously to administer to their own lusts, and make a gratification of their wicked desires profitable as well as pleasurable; for by this cunning arrangement, the slaveholder, in cases not a few, sustains to his slaves the double relation of master and father.[21]

---

18 The interdependence of the child's status and the mother's marital status is also a common feature of modern legal systems. We may note, for instance, that Canadian law, like many common law jurisdictions, held (until 1968) that a child's domicile followed that of its mother, unless the mother was validly married.

19 The term "matrilineal" is used in this work in its general meaning of "deriving from the mother," rather than in any technical, anthropological sense.

20 It is still seems to be a matter of debate, however, whether "breeding" was ever an economically viable way of increasing the supply of slaves, and whether the matrilineal principle may be related to such use of breeding. Claude Meillassoux's classic study of certain African societies posited circumstances in which it was more economical to have all slaves engage in production of goods that could be exchanged for more slaves: Claude Meillassoux, *Anthropologie de l'esclavage. Le ventre de fer et d'argent* (Paris: Presses Universitaires de France, 1986), 292-93. Meillassoux argued (302) that the greater the trend toward this kind of production, the greater the *déféminisation* of female slaves (and the less price differential between them and male slaves).

21 Frederick Douglass, "Narrative of the Life of Frederick Douglass, an American Slave," in *Autobiographies* (New York: Library Classics of the United States, 1994), 1:16-17. Douglass goes on to remark that in his experience such children, being a "constant offence" to the master's (white) wife, suffered greater hardships, and were more likely to be sold away.

A legal rule connecting the status of the child to that of its mother is also deemed by some to be simply a matter of common sense; as Watson notes, a rule that made a child's status dependent on that of its father would give rise to "endless problems of proof."[22]

Given the economic and other benefits of a matrilineal principle, it is not at first glance surprising to find such a principle in mishnaic law. The Mishnah in fact uses it to define the status of children in two types of "intermarriage": Jewish-gentile and free-slave. The principle finds expression in the Mishnah in two apparently asymmetrical parts. *MQidd.* 3:12 deals with a case in which the mother is a gentile or slave woman: the child of the gentile mother is a gentile; the child of a slave mother is a slave.[23] Both results are based on the idea that neither the slave woman nor the gentile woman is capable of entering a legal marriage (*qiddushin*). *MYev.* 7:5 deals with a case in which the mother is an Israelite and it is the father who is a gentile or slave;[24] the offspring in both cases is a *mamzer*.[25]

---

22 Alan Watson, *Roman Slave Law* (Baltimore: Johns Hopkins University Press, 1987), 10.

23 This Mishnah reads:

וכל מי שאין לה לא עליו ולא על אחרים קדושין הולד כמותה ואיזה זה ולד שפחה ונכרית

And whoever does not have *qiddushin* with him or with others — the offspring is like her. And which is this? The offspring of a slave or a gentile.

24 This Mishnah reads:

העבד פוסל משום ביאה ואינו פוסל משום זרע כיצד בת ישראל לכהן בת כהן לישראל וילדה הימנו בן והלך הבן ונכבש על השפחה וילדה הימנו בן הרי זה עבד היתה אם אביו בת ישראל לכהן לא תאכל בתרומה בת כהן לישראל תאכל בתרומה ממזר פוסל ומאכיל כיצד בת ישראל לכהן ובת כהן לישראל וילדה הימנו בת והלכה הבת ונישאת לעבד או לגוי וילדה הימנו בן הרי זה ממזר היתה אם אמו בת ישראל לכהן תאכל בתרומה בת כהן לישראל לא תאכל בתרומה.

The slave disqualifies because of intercourse but he does not disqualify because of offspring. How? The daughter of an Israelite [married] to a priest, [or] the daughter of a priest [married] to an Israelite, and she bore to him a son, and the son went and had intercourse with a slave woman and she bore him a son — he is a slave. [If] his father's mother were the daughter of an Israelite [married] to a priest — she may not eat *terumah*; [if his father's mother were] the daughter of a priest [married] to an Israelite — she may eat *terumah*. A *mamzer* disqualifies and gives the privilege to eat. How? The daughter of an Israelite [married] to a priest or the daughter of a priest [married] to an Israelite who bore to him a daughter and the daughter was married to a slave or to a gentile and she bore to him a son — he is a *mamzer*. [If] his mother's mother were the daughter of an Israelite [married] to a priest — she may eat *terumah*; [if his mother's mother were the] daughter of a priest [married] to an Israelite — she may not eat *terumah*.

25 In later law there was a trend to declare the offspring of a gentile or slave father *kasher* (valid)

The role of this principle with respect to children who have one gentile parent has recently been debated quite extensively, particularly regarding the idea that the principle is of postbiblical, possibly Roman, origin.[26] The question of slaves' children is, however, mentioned only incidentally.

At a second glance, the presence of a matrilineal rule for slaves in the Mishnah rule is puzzling.

First, there is the great "leap" between the biblical status of slaves' children and the mishnaic rules. Despite the use of Exod. 21:4 in legal midrash as the basis for arguing the existence of a matrilineal principle in the Bible, I demonstrate that there is in the Bible no conclusive evidence of a prohibition of legal marriage for female slaves or of an automatic inheritance of slave status from a parent. Second, if the purpose of the mishnaic principle were simply to prevent ethnic intermarriage, gentile slaves would be covered by the general rule regarding the status of gentile children; why add them separately? Put another way, we may ask: What is the commonality between slavery and religious status that would justify

rather than a *mamzer:* see, e.g., the statement of Ravina in *bYev.* 23a and Maimonides, *MishTor Hil. Issure Biyah* 15:4.

26 An extensive discussion of the issue took place following the proposal by American Reform Judaism to also recognize as Jewish the child of a Jewish father, even if its mother was gentile. A collection of such arguments appears in *Judaism* 34/1 (1985). Much of the argument that took place at the time of the Reform proposal was concerned with tracing the origin of the precise rule that the child of a gentile woman should follow the status of its mother. Such arguments about origin followed two main trends. One line of thought suggested that the rule connecting the gentile mother and her child was an innate development in Jewish law, a logical outgrowth of such biblical passages as Ezra 10:2-3 (attesting to the covenant made by the returning exiles to put aside the wives taken from "the peoples of the land" as well as their children) and Neḥ. 13:23-24 (noting that the children born of wives from Ashdod, Ammon, and Moav could speak only the mother's language). For an example of this viewpoint see Lawrence Schiffman, "Jewish Identity and Jewish Descent," *Judaism* 34/1 (1985): 78-84, esp. 81. Another line of thought, exemplified in particular by Shaye Cohen, suggested that this rule actually originated in the postbiblical period. Noting that biblical attitudes favored a patrilineal principle, Cohen argued that the development of a matrilineal principle might have been actuated by external factors (particularly Roman law), but might also have been an organic development from the biblical concern with forbidden mixtures; see his extended article: Shaye D. Cohen, "The Origins of the Matrilineal Principle in Rabbinic Law," *AJS Review* 10/1 (1985): 19-53. For a recent critique of Cohen's position, see Ranon Katzoff, "The Children of Intermarriage: Roman and Jewish Conceptions," in *Rabbinic Law in its Roman and Near Eastern Context* (ed. Catherine Hezser; Tübingen: Mohr Siebeck, 2003), 276-86.

their association under the same matrilineal principle? Further, there is an asymmetry in the rule: the fate of children of these "mixed" unions differs depending on whether the male or female parent was the slave. S. Cohen has suggested that this asymmetry is evidence that the Mishnah did not know of a unified matrilineal principle.[27] I demonstrate that there were a variety of ideas regarding the inheritance of slave status even in postbiblical literature, so that there is no ground for arguing for a linear development of the matrilineal principle in early Jewish law. The evidence in my opinion is consistent with the overall difference between dependence and marginalization in biblical and postbiblical texts.

Sex Punished: Adultery as Property Crime or Sex Crime?

Given that wives and female slaves existed on the same sexual continuum, what separated one from the other? Certainly different expectations as to work obligations, dowries, and inheritance came into play. There is also, however, the question of the degree to which the husband's or master's sexual access to a woman was protected, and here the concept of adultery is pivotal. Leviticus 19:20-21 addresses the question of a female slave who is bound sexually in some way to a male (the *shifḥah neḥerefet*) and seems to state that such a woman is incapable of adultery due to her unfree condition. Does this section reflect a conflict between sex right and some sort of property right, with the resolution in favor of the latter?

Certainly the conceptualization of slaves, both male and female, as "property" as opposed to "person" is often treated as a given in the study of slave systems. This distinction is far from straightforward, however;[28]

---

27 Shaye J.D. Cohen, *The Beginnings of Jewishness: Boundaries, Varieties, Uncertainties* (Berkeley: University of California Press, 1999), 278.

28 For a brief idea of the range of opinion on this complex topic, we may note the view of Guillaume Cardascia, "Le concept babylonien de la propriété," *RIDA* (3e serie) 6 (1959): 19-32, at 25, who argued that Babylonian sources reflect only an undifferentiated concept of ownership, a direct relationship between person and object, without the type of constitutive elements that were recognized in the Roman system, and without a clear differentiation between ownership of an item and possession of it; and the view of Paul Koschaker who argued that the Laws of Hammurapi [=LH] consist of various layers, some layers reflecting more "primitive" ideas of ownership. See Paul Koschaker, *Rechtsvergleichende Studien zur Geseztgebung Hammurapis, Königs von Babylon* (Leipzig:

further, concepts of property and person often collide, resulting in widely inconsistent treatment of slaves within the same legal system.[29]

One such juncture of property and person is the prominent pattern in certain ancient legal systems of assigning different punishments for an offense, depending on the status of the perpetrator, and different remedies, depending on the status of the victim. In Athenian law, for instance, offenders who were slaves were often subjected to corporal punishment, while free citizens who committed the same offense might receive only a fine; the apparent physical inviolability of the latter possibly emphasized the degradation of the former.[30]

And so it is that one of the most explicit of such differential remedies in both biblical and Mesopotamian law is the use of the *lex talionis* in the case of injury or death.[31] As has been noted long ago by

---

Von Veit, 1917). Koschaker argued specifically that the slave warranty in s. 279 seems to presuppose that a claim to the slave might be asserted by some third party, without it being alleged that the vendor or buyer was a thief; this stands in contrast to LH ss. 9-13, where the mere presence of a third party claim seems to put the onus on buyer and seller to prove their contractual right to the item (p. 51). He also argued (p. 46) that while the warranty in s. 279 assumes that a third party could trace an item into the hands of the current possessor, LH 125, the case of goods stolen while on deposit, appears to assume that an owner who has parted with possession of an item, in this case the "depositor," must look for satisfaction only to the person to whom he has ceded possession, the "depositee," if the goods are stolen; he may not, therefore, follow the goods into the hands of the thief or the current possessor. In the latter situation Koschaker found a parallel to the concept of *Hand wahre Hand* in early Germanic law, by which someone who voluntarily gave up possession of an item, without actually conveying it (such as in a deposit), retained only the right to claim it back from the depositee.

29 Paul Virgil McCracken Flesher, *Oxen, Women or Citizens? Slaves in the System of the Mishnah* (Brown Judaic Studies 143; Atlanta: Scholars Press, 1988), makes this point about mishnaic law. Flesher's arguments will be discussed in more detail below.

30 Virginia Hunter, "Status Distinctions in Athenian Law" (paper presented at "Law and Social Status in Classical Athens" conference, University of Toronto, April 1997).

31 This vast topic is the subject of much scholarly discussion, particularly regarding the conceptual development of the law and whether it was ever actually carried out in practice. I shall simply suggest here certain topics related to status differentials that I think should be investigated further. There are various theories that *talion* is "primitive" and is eventually replaced by a system of compensation as the concept of "like penalty" is extended to a concept of "equivalent penalty" (e.g., G. R. Driver and J. C. Miles, *Babylonian Laws* [Oxford: Clarendon, 1952], vol. 1). In my opinion, however, this is contradicted (at least in Mesopotamia) by the fact that *talion* appears in the LH but not in any of the earlier law collections, where compensation is the main remedy for injury or death. One must also note that the scheme of payments and *talion* in the LH is not complete or necessarily

Driver and Miles,[32] *talion* in the Law of Hammurapi [= LH] is restricted to injury or death of an *awīlu* (full citizen); compensation for injury or death to a *muškēnu* (commoner) or a slave is monetary. There are very close parallels between LH and the talionic rules in Exodus 21.[33] The Bible, however, introduces a particular facet of the slave as victim of death or physical injury: the case in which the slave is killed or injured by his or

---

logically consistent; in my opinion this suggests an attempt to impose a talionic concept (perhaps western Semitic?) on an existing (eastern Semitic) compensation scheme. Cf. E. Grace, "Status Distinctions in the Draconian Law," *Eirene* (*Studia Graeca et Latina*) 11 (1973): 5-30, who argues (p. 8) that the gaps in status specifications with respect to either perpetrator or victim in the Draconian law reflects the fact that status inequalities at this time were still largely internal to the individual household. For a summary of *talion* theories regarding the ancient Near East, see Raymond Westbrook, *Studies in Biblical and Cuneiform Law* (Paris: J. Gabalda, 1988). Westbrook himself argues that both *talion* and compensation always coexisted as alternatives. See also J. J. Finkelstein, *The Ox That Gored* (Transactions of the American Philosophical Society 71/2; Philadelphia: The American Philosophical Society, 1981), who argues that *talion* is a later development, marking the "elevation" of injuries and death to public crimes, as opposed to private wrongs remedied only through self-help.

32 Driver and Miles, *Babylonian Laws*, 1:420.

33 To briefly summarize the relevant texts:

Exod. 21:12, 20-21, 23-27:

v. 12: If a man strikes a man and he dies, he shall surely die.

v. 20: If a man strikes his *eved* or his *amah* with a rod and he/she dies under his hand, he shall surely be avenged.

v. 21: But if he lingers a day or two, he will not be avenged, as it is his money.

v. 23: ...you will give life for life,

v. 24: eye for eye, tooth for tooth, hand for hand, foot for foot,

v. 25: burning for burning, wound for wound, bruise for bruise.

v. 26: If a man strikes the eye of his *eved* or the eye of his *amah* and puts it out, he shall send him/her free for his/her eye.

v. 27: And if he knocks out the tooth of his *eved* or the tooth of his *amah*, he shall send him/her free for his/her tooth.

Laws of Hammurapi (trans. M.Roth), sections 196-201:

s. 196: If an *awīlu* should blind the eye of another *awīlu* they shall blind his eye.

s. 197: If he should break the bone of another *awīlu*, they shall break his bone.

s. 198: If he should blind the eye of a commoner or break the bone of a commoner, he shall weigh and deliver 60 shekels of silver.

s. 199: If he should blind the eye of an *awīlu*'s slave or break the bone of an *awīlu*'s slave, he shall weigh and deliver one-half his value (in silver).

s. 200: If an *awīlu* should knock out the tooth of another *awīlu* of his own rank, they shall knock out his tooth.

s. 201: If he should knock out the tooth of a commoner, he shall weigh and deliver 20 shekels of silver.

her own master. Remarkable here is the fact that slave is provided with a remedy that seems to be meant as equivalent to but not the same as *talion*: the ambiguous "he shall surely be avenged" in Exod. 21:20 and the freeing of the slave in verses 26-27, which in effect give the slave back his own body.

Such provisions raise questions as to whether the Bible did view slaves as solely property, so that injury to them was simply an economic loss to the master.[34] I propose that the stylistically difficult text of the *shifḥah neḥerefet* law in Lev. 19:20-21 is to be resolved not by assuming that the female slave as property could not commit adultery, but by viewing adultery in the biblical scheme as an upset of the dependence hierarchy, punishable here as elsewhere by death.[35] This model is also consistent with the various prophetic portrayals of Israel's betrayal of God metaphorically as a wife's sexual betrayal of her husband.[36] And just as Israel's betrayal of God is a type of "treason," I would argue that a wife's betrayal of a husband is also a type of "treason, in this case warranting the death penalty."[37] (Interestingly, we may also note that LH 129 seems to juxtapose a wife's adultery with treason against the king; if the husband, here called the "master," allows his wife to live, the king may allow the male transgressor to live.)

Leviticus 19:20-21 argues, however, that a female slave is incapable of treason given the conditions of coercion under which she exists; this, I will argue, is the meaning of the *hapax neḥerefet* in Lev. 19:20. Either the sexual line created between master and slave is not strong enough, given the coercion, to create a marriage bond protected by the laws of adultery,[38] or the lack of freedom prevents the slave woman from "crying out" against

---

34 A related question, which I also will not discuss here, is whether different concepts of slaves as "property" is behind the apparent distinction, in the matter of physical treatment, between different types of slaves: for the slave called *aḥ* (brother) in Lev. 25:39, the master is admonished לא תרדה בו בפרך (You shall not rule over him harshly, Lev. 25:43).

35 See, e.g., J. J. Finkelstein's discussion of the death penalty with respect to the goring ox of Exod. 21 as punishment for a breach in the hierarchy (*The Ox That Gored,* 19).

36 See, e.g., Ezek. 16 and 23.

37 One is put in mind of the English law of "petit treason," which would apply to the murder of a husband by a wife or of a master by a slave. Such murder of a superior was considered more serious than "ordinary" murder and punished accordingly.

38 In postbiblical law, we may note that a female slave, unlike a wife, cannot be acquired simply by sexual relations (*mQidd.* 1:2-3).

her adulterer. There has been no breach of the hierarchy warranting the death penalty, but there is still some form of relationship that would warrant a claim of trespass, with its vaguely proprietary sense, against the third party; this is the meaning of the *hapax biqqoret* in Lev. 19:20. Again, the question of the slave as property in the Bible is only vaguely suggested.

In the postbiblical period, as has been argued by B. Cohen, Flesher, and Hezser, among others, Jewish law came into contact with Greco-Roman law and its more precise distinctions between persons and property. In the movement toward emphasis on the individual, the notion of a dependence hierarchy becomes irrelevant. How is Lev. 19:20-21 to be interpreted against this background? The sages' reaction was to compartmentalize this biblical provision through exegesis into a completely novel crime whose conditions were likely too tenuous to be put into practice, including the unusual notion of "half slave, half free." The female slave was no longer within a dependence hierarchy and was taken outside any suggestion of kinship or other relationship. Again we see a movement away from dependence and toward marginalization.

Before outlining each chapter in detail, I would like to focus on certain methodological issues and assumptions that inform this study.

Methodological Issues

I. A Word on "Representativity":[39] Are We Dealing With Legal Texts?

Since this study focuses on concepts I have termed "legal," I believe it is appropriate to make the case that the biblical and postbiblical sources to be used in this study may be studied in this way. These materials, like the Mesopotamian law collections, can be considered "internormative," that is, containing rules that share variable frontiers among moral, ethical, and religious norms, civil and economic regulations, or political goals. Given

39 This term is used by Josine Blok, "Sexual Asymmetry: A Historiographical Essay," in *Sexual Asymmetry: Studies in Ancient Society* (ed. J. Blok and P. Mason; Amsterdam: J. C. Gieben, 1987), 1-57 at 43, to describe the extent to which source material represents a specific historical condition.

this "framing" or context, scholars have questioned whether these texts can be approached with methodology appropriate to civil or secular legal material.[40] I accept an anthropological definition of "law" as a complex phenomenon rather than a discrete set of rules, a function of the discourse, practices, and beliefs of a particular society that are deemed essential to that society's existence, and which are protected through "juridicization," or codification, in some form.[41] That is, one need not view "law" in the modern, Western sense of a self-contained sector of society, parallel to but separate from "economics" or "politics" or "religion."[42] Thus while B. Levinson and others are correct to point out that these internormative texts are not "statute" law in the modern sense,[43] the texts are still capable of reflecting legal phenomena.

II. Philology and Functional Equivalence

I propose to use both diachronic philological examinations and comparisons to terms and provisions of other legal systems.

By a philological approach, I mean a study of particular words and phrases in their contexts in a variety of texts, so as to ascertain the development of the concepts reflected in these terms. It may be noted that scholars differ on just how closely such concepts mirror actual events or social reality. An aggressive view of this connection is expressed by Burke:

> [T]he investigation of changes in semantic meaning requires the examination of a broad sample of formal texts and other sources over extended periods of time. The concepts located in these sources are more than simple reflections

40 Various scholars question the use of such an approach to such texts. See, e.g., Bernard Levinson, "The Case for Revision and Interpolation within the Biblical Legal Corpora," in *Theory and Method in Biblical and Cuneiform Law: Revision, Interpolation and Development* (JSOT Supplement Series 181; Sheffield Academic Press, 1994), 37-59, esp. 49, 53-54, who raises this point with respect to the Bible.

41 N. Rouland, *Legal Anthropology* (trans. P. Planel; London: Athlone, 1994), 129.

42 Rouland, *Legal Anthropology*, 91.

43 Bernard S. Jackson, *Essays in Jewish and Comparative Legal History* (Leiden: Brill, 1975), esp. 2, 16, does in fact argue that while the Bible and the Mishnah were not necessarily drafted as statute law, they came to be regarded as such after being written down. The correctness or incorrectness of this opinion does not affect my point that in any event such texts can be the subject of a legal study.

> of other, more basic transformations. These concepts both registered historical change and gave shape to its outcomes.[44]

Watson, commenting on the relationship between a society and the legal rules that operate within it, suggests that while legal rules are ultimately rooted in social values, such rules may take on a life of their own.[45] We may assume that if we find such terms as *amah*, *shifḥah*, and *eved* in the texts, some distinction was imputed to such persons. Beyond this assumption, however, I shall make no attempt to describe the connection between the legal texts and the social or historical "reality" they may reflect, and I propose this study as a history of concepts only.

I shall also make use in some cases of comparisons between Hebrew and Akkadian terms. While such a comparison makes no assumption regarding the specific historical relationship between these languages or the extent of borrowing between them, it is reasonable to assume that where terms in these languages seem to be cognate, nuances of meaning in one language may suggest similar nuances in the other.

In certain cases I shall attempt to explain particular slave laws by a comparison with "functionally equivalent" acts and remedies from other legal systems. This technique, a basic method of comparative law,[46] involves in essence a comparison of how different legal systems seem to have solved a particular problem. The use of this type of comparison is not without difficulty. First, the assessment of "functional equivalence" is largely subjective. However, given the fruitfulness of this method in generating hypotheses regarding explanations for particular rules, this subjectivity seems to be justified.[47] A second difficulty is the scholarly tendency to confuse issues of comparison with issues of linkage — the assumption, for instance, that one must show an actual connection between particular legal systems before comparisons can be made between them, or, conversely, the

44 Burke, *Conundrum of Class*, xvi.

45 Alan Watson, *The Evolution of Law* (Baltimore: Johns Hopkins University Press, 1985), 68-70. Watson notes in particular a tendency for lawmaking to become concentrated in the hands of elites, who treat law as existing for its own sake (p. 72).

46 See, e.g., K. Zweigert, "Methodological Problems in Comparative Law," *Israel Law Review* 7 (1972): 465-74, at 466.

47 This point was noted by Jackson, *Essays*, 12.

assumption that such connection exists when the legal systems seem to contain close parallels. I do not think that it is necessary to demonstrate linkage before arguing for functional equivalence.[48]

III. The Use of a Pluralistic Model

As summarized above, my analysis will show that the halakhic construction of "female slave" status was neither consistent nor linear, and that historical causes offer at least a partial explanation of why particular principles became dominant. I accept, therefore, a multi-factor model of halakhic development, of the type that is proposed by B. Jackson,[49] which allows for roles for both historical causes and inherent logical development in the analysis of any decision. I offer no opinion here, however, on whether my findings support Jackson's use of a structuralist model of legal development, particularly the idea that there is "a [universal] sequential development in the cognitive capacity" of a legal system.[50] In particular, while it is plausible that the appearance of particular types of logical reasoning (such as the use of propositional logic) may appear in a regular diachronic sequence in the development of any legal system, I wish to focus instead on the use of different reasoning methods by sages operating within the same general time frame. This would include, for instance, the question of whether a particular

48 This point has been amply demonstrated by many scholars. G. R. Driver and J. C. Miles used comparisons to English common law to explain aspects of Babylonian and Assyrian law (see, e.g., *Babylonian Laws*, 1:48, 56). Koschaker compared aspects of the Laws of Hammurapi to early Germanic law (see, e.g., Koschaker, *Rechstvergleichende Studien*, 46, and the discussion in chap. 5 n. 87); Asher Gulak, *The Documents in the Talmud in Light of the Greek Papyri from Egypt and in Light of Greek and Roman Law* [in Hebrew] (rev. and trans. from German [1935]; Jerusalem: Magnes, 1994), compared talmudic law with Greco-Egyptian papyri; Boaz Cohen used comparisons between tannaitic and Roman law (see, e.g., Boaz Cohen, *Jewish and Roman Law: A Comparative Study* [New York: JTSA, 1966], 1:xii); and Reuven Yaron compared terms and concepts from the Aramaic papyri from Elephantine with demotic sources (see, e.g., Reuven Yaron, *Introduction to the Law of the Aramaic Papyri* [Oxford: Clarendon, 1961], 126).

49 As Jackson summarizes in "History, Dogmatics and Halakhah," 15: "Neither the innate [capacity for logical consistency] nor the environmental can be viewed as sufficient causes."

50 Bernard S. Jackson, "History, Dogmatics and Halakhah," 24-25. See also idem, "Towards a Structuralist Theory of Law," *Liverpool L. Rev.* 2 (1980): 5-30, esp. 17, 29-30.

halakhic midrash was the source of a sage's halakhic decision[51] or an *ex-post-facto* rationalization of it, and the question of whether different referents were used by different sages in their construction of analogies.[52] In my opinion, the pluralistic model of P. Heger provides a more nuanced view of halakhic development, in that it imputes to each decision maker a combination of individual influences, both logical and environmental, in tension with a deep belief in the immutability of the Torah.[53] Such an approach acknowledges the productive use of "legal fiction" in allowing a legal system to adapt to changing circumstances while still maintaining a sense of continuity;[54] it allows for a role for such historical factors as custom, foreign influence, and personal motives in assessing each halakhic decision, side-by-side with an analysis of the "logical" factors inherent in the decision.

I thus disagree with any positivist model of halakhah that demands or assumes logical consistency throughout the Jewish legal canon. D. Novak, for instance, uses such a monolithic approach in claiming that there are "deep differences of gender that permeate the Jewish tradition from its very beginnings in Scripture and forever after," and that this is the reason why women are religiously unequal and must stay that way.[55] Aside from the faulty assumption that "difference" necessarily implies "inequality" in the legal sense, such a view fails to recognize the many disparate opinions regarding women's status that are found throughout the Jewish sources as well as the explicit rejection of earlier opinions.[56]

---

51 For summaries of the various opinions regarding the relative priority of Mishnah and midrash, see, e.g., D. Weiss Halivni, *Midrash, Mishnah and Gemara: The Jewish Predilection for Justified Law* (Cambridge: Oxford University Press, 1986), 18-21 and M. Halbertal, *Interpretive Revolutions in the Making* [in Hebrew] (Jerusalem: Magnes, 1997), 13-15.

52 See, e.g., Cees W. Maris, "Milking the Meter," in *Legal Knowledge and Analogy: Fragments of Legal Epistemology, Hermeneutics, and Linguistics* (ed. P. Nerhot; Dordrecht: Kluwer Academic Publishers, 1991), 74-102, esp. 97, who argues that the process of determining what is similar and different in the process of analogy-creation is culturally conditioned; Bernard S. Jackson, "Analogy in Legal Science: Some Comparative Observations," in *Legal Knowledge and Analogy,* 148-64, esp. 164, who suggests that such determination may be based on "social-experiential narrative grounds" rather than abstract legal concepts.

53 Paul Heger, *The Pluralistic Halakhah: Legal Innovation in the Late Second Commonwealth and Rabbinic Periods* (Studia Judaica 22; Berlin: De Gruyter, 2003). See, e.g., his description of this tension at 19-26.

54 Heger, *The Pluralistic Halakhah*, 102.

55 D. Novak, *Natural Law in Judaism* (Cambridge: Cambridge University Press, 1998), 202.

56 An example of such non-linearity of opinion follows. Novak (*Natural Law in Judaism*, 202 n.

One may also question attempts to render traditional halakhah immune from historical criticism. I. Englard, for instance, argues: "The dogmatic exclusion of historical inquiry is achieved by the notion of authority ... the authority of a scholar as accepted as absolutely binding by tradition."[57] But what exactly is binding? If, as I am arguing, the meaning of legal concepts changes over time, it seems that historical inquiry must be linked to any dogmatic inquiry into a particular trend of reasoning.[58] Further, if one acknowledges the crucial role played by authority, does this not necessitate as well an inquiry into the motives of and influences on that authority? J. Roth, though he too would restrict the relevance of history in halakhic decision making,[59] does seem to acknowledge, at least implicitly, the importance of individual motives in decision making, given the broad role he assigns to judicial discretion within the halakhic process.[60]

---

69) argues that the *locus classicus* for gender inequality lies in the principle in *mQidd.* 1:7 that women are exempt from time-bound *mitzvot*. Though studying Torah is not time-bound, one view in a mishnaic dispute in *mSotah* 3:4 claims that women are not only exempt from such study but are actually prohibited from being taught Torah: "Ben Azai says: A man is obligated to teach his daughter Torah.... R. Eliezer says: Anyone who teaches his daughter Torah, it is as if he teaches her frivolity/obscenity [*tiflut*]..." Though *bSotah* 21b acknowledges that this issue is a matter of dispute, Maimonides claims that the prohibition is commanded, based on some rather specious reasoning (*MishTor*, *Hil. Talmud Torah* 1:13):

> A woman who studies Torah has merit, but not like the merit of a man, because she is not commanded [to do so] ... Even though she has merit, the Sages commanded that a man not teach his daughter Torah, because the minds of most women are not directed toward being taught, and they find the words of Torah like words of indifference because of the poverty of their intellect.

Menachem Elon, *Jewish Law: History, Sources and Principles* (Philadelphia: Jewish Publication Society, 1994), 4:1799-1802, quotes more modern sources which are quite willing to view such an attitude as belonging firmly in the past.

57 I. Englard, "Research in Jewish Law," in *Modern Research in Jewish Law* (ed. B. Jackson; Leiden: Brill, 1980), 21-65, at 36.

58 Jackson, "History, Dogmatics and Halakhah," 10 n. 27, argues that the traditional division of approaches to the study of law into dogmatic, historical, comparative, and ethical is "conceptually incoherent." E. E. Urbach has demonstrated that legal terms/concepts in the tannaitic period have undergone changes by the late amoraic period, a matter of a few generations. See one of several examples in *The Halakha: Its Sources and Development* (Givatayim, Israel: Yad Le-talmud, 1984), 124-26.

59 Roth argues that the historical origin of a halakhic norm becomes irrelevant to decision-making once the norm becomes "established" or ceases to be the *raison d'être* of the norm: Joel Roth, *The Halakhic Process: A Systemic Analysis* (New York: JTSA, 1986), 11, 243.

60 Roth, *The Halakhic Process*, 84, 160. This discretion includes the ability to abrogate Torah

Based on such evidence of pluralism, I also disagree with approaches that preclude comparison between texts on the ground that each text is a logical entity unto itself. While I agree with both H. Fox and J. Neusner[61] that any provision in a text needs first to be instantiated within the overall context of that text, I disagree with Neusner's assertion that this precludes any detailed comparison of provisions within a text or between texts. Neusner's "macro" approach takes place at a high level of abstraction (perhaps so abstract as to exist only in the redactor's unconscious[62]) and does not preclude analysis at a more "micro" level.[63] This allows, in my opinion, for the attribution of significance to inconsistencies — whether logical inconsistencies or differences in wording in texts that are supposedly parallel to each other. One need not conclude, in other words, that because a text is fixed it is also internally consistent.

As these approaches run directly counter to other techniques that have been used by scholars in elucidating slavery in biblical and postbiblical texts, I shall briefly review some of these approaches and explain how my assumptions differ.

Slave Status in Biblical Law: A "Common Law"?

The three best-known, or at least most studied, biblical provisions on slavery have to do with manumission of slaves, and each provision is different.[64] Not surprisingly, the differences in the Hebrew terms for

law. Roth suggests that the *rishonim* in fact favored the retention of broad judicial discretion (103).

61 Harry Fox, "Textual, Intratextual and Intertextual Studies," in *Introducing Tosefta: Textual, Intratextual and Intertextual Studies* (ed. H. Fox [leBeit Yoreh] and T. Meacham [leBeit Yoreh]; Ktav Publishing House, 1999), 27-28; Jacob Neusner, *Wrong Ways and Right Ways in the Study of Formative Judaism* (Brown Judaic Studies 145; Atlanta: Scholars Press, 1988) 59 n. 29.

62 For a discussion of implied and implicit levels in writing, see Jackson, "History, Dogmatics, and Halakhah," 12.

63 For the same reason I believe one may question the approach of Haym Soloveitchik, who argues that one may not attribute "extraneous influence" to a particular literary work (in his case, Tosafot) unless the thinking involved is "atypical" of this literature. See Haym Soloveitchik, "Halakhah, Hermeneutics, and Martyrdom in Medieval Ashkenaz (Pt I of II)," *JQR* 94/1 (2004): 77-108, esp. 77. Yet Tosafot is a multi-authored work; can it be perceived as a single literary work with a "typical" mode of thought?

64 To summarize: Exod. 21:2-6 speaks of Hebrew slave (*eved ivri*), whose term of service is

slaves, the period of service, and the treatment of females, among many other issues, have led to many scholarly conjectures, particularly as to the possible historical contexts within which each provision was promulgated. These provisions have been particularly fruitful as bases for source criticism and for determining the relative priority of the E, P, and D strata. Many of these conjectures take an evolutionary model as a starting point and assume a close connection between some of the biblical material and Mesopotamian documents.

Thus I. Mendelsohn proposed a legal and economic history of slavery in biblical Israel based on both comparative philology and explicit "gap-filling" — supplementing apparent gaps in the biblical records of slavery with evidence from Mesopotamian documents on the assumption of the existence of a "common law" within these societies.[65] He concluded that while slaves were legally chattel, the boundaries between slave and "free" were quite fluid.

Mendelsohn suggested that large-scale slavery existed only in the "public" (state and temple) sectors;[66] in the "private" sector, however, despite occasional references to war captives, foreign or native (e.g., 2 Chr 28:8-10), he concluded that the major source of slaves in ancient Israel was native-born debtors.[67] Mendelsohn emphasized particularly the apparent lack of recognition of a slave's family bonds as evidence of the slave's treatment as chattel.[68] This was especially true, in his opinion, with

limited to six years, and who may become a "permanent" slave (*eved olam*) if he wishes to remain with a woman given to him as a wife by his master; in contrast, an *amah* sold by her father must be espoused or set free (Exod. 21:7-11). Lev. 25:39-46 speaks of an *aḥ* (brother), presumably a fellow Israelite, who has sold himself under economic coercion. His term is limited to fifty years or to the next Jubilee, whichever comes first. In contrast, the slave acquired from the surrounding peoples may be kept forever and passed on as heritable property. Deut. 15:12-18 again speaks of an *eved* and *amah*; in this case the term of both is limited to six years unless each chooses to remain as an *eved olam* with the master.

65 Isaac Mendelsohn, *Slavery in the Ancient Near East* (New York: Oxford University Press, 1949), v.

66 Permanent slaves were taken from foreign prisoners or subject nations, to whom reference is found in such biblical terms as *mas eved* and *avde shlomoh*, and would presumably have been part of corvées used for large public works undertaken by the kings (Mendelsohn, *Slavery,* 96-98).

67 Mendelsohn, *Slavery,* 23.

68 Mendelsohn, *Slavery,* 64, 122.

respect to women: he interpreted Exod. 21:7-11, based on a presumed parallel with Nuzi contracts providing for the "conditional sale" of women, as allowing female slaves to be mated successively with different people, and he took Lev. 19:20 as referring to a betrothed woman who was left as a debt pledge in the creditor's household and then leased out as a prostitute.[69] He characterized such women, as well as the slave women in Genesis married to the patriarchs, as half slave, half free — part "maid" and part slave-bearing mother. Based on such imprecise categories, Mendelsohn concluded that despite chattel-like treatment there was no sharp boundary between slave and "free"; slavery was thus not a caste (other than the hereditary *netinim* class), but rather an economically dependent class based on wealth.[70]

To arrive at his conclusions, Mendelsohn assumed a common law prevalent throughout the ancient Near East, on the basis of which one may interpret "gaps" in the biblical record by looking to Mesopotamian law collections. This assumption has also been used by other scholars, based on the strong parallels between certain biblical and cuneiform rules. R. Westbrook, for instance,[71] argues for the existence of a common, and fairly static, customary law throughout the entire Near East for a period of at least 1500 years. On this basis he proposes that the individual cases in both the biblical and cuneiform law collections may be interpreted by reference to cases in the other collections. Thus the specific cases within each document do not represent more abstract principles and are not "code specific."

One primary objection to this approach is the assumption of a static law over some 3000 years or more of Near Eastern civilization. Reason alone would preclude a legal system remaining static over this amount of time. In fact, Koschaker argues convincingly for different theories even within Hammurapi's laws, showing a development in legal concepts.[72] E. E. Urbach has demonstrated that legal terms/concepts in the tannaitic period have undergone changes by the late amoraic period, a matter of

69 Mendelsohn, *Slavery,* 10-14, 55.

70 Mendelsohn, *Slavery,* 119-20; cf. ibid., 76-77.

71 Raymond Westbrook, "What is the Covenant Code?" in *Theory and Method in Biblical and Cuneiform Law: Revision, Interpolation and Development* (JSOT Supplement Series 181; ed. B. Levinson; Sheffield Academic Press, 1994), 15-36, esp. 31, 33.

72 See, e.g., Koschaker, *Rechtsvergleichende Studien.*

a few generations.[73] Another difficulty of this synchronous approach is the failure to posit the mechanisms by which this "common law" became so widespread. In other words, what were the channels of transmission by which these parallel rules entered each culture? J. J. Finkelstein, in his analysis of the goring ox provisions in Exodus 21 and the Eshnuna and Hammurapi law collections, rejects any *a priori* assumptions of a common law or custom, yet he acknowledges the quandary here: given the closeness of this and other parallels, both in the choice of a particular case out of all possible areas of human behavior and in the wording and style, any explanation other than an "organic linkage" between the two groups of sources is precluded; yet such linkage, in his opinion, cannot be independently established.[74] It must be noted that Finkelstein specifically rejects any notion of oral transmission, though he proposes a gap of only several hundred years between the cessation of cuneiform use in Palestine (13th century B.C.E.) and the earliest redaction of the Covenant Code (10th century B.C.E.).[75] A solution to this quandary is the assumption of a common "school tradition" and the existence of a scribal connection between eastern and western Semites. I adopt this assumption but do not suggest that it must lead inevitably to assuming the existence of a common law throughout the ancient Near East. Finkelstein and Heger, among others, have argued that biblical law, though likely facing the same problems as other legal systems, contains particular solutions to such problems that are consistent with its own theology.[76]

Further, this type of "synchronous" interpretation becomes even more tenuous when the parallels are less clear, which I suggest is the case with respect to Mendelsohn's interpretation of Exod. 21:7-11 and Lev. 19:20 based on comparisons with Nuzi.[77] I think there is "functional

---

73 See Urbach, *Halakhah*, 123-38.

74 Finkelstein, *The Ox That Gored*, 19.

75 Finkelstein, *The Ox That Gored*, 19-20.

76 Finkelstein, *The Ox That Gored*, 25-31, 36-39, 42-41; Heger, *The Pluralistic Halakhah*, 37-38.

77 The issue of channels of transmission raises a particular stumbling block in questions of comparison between the *masoret*ic and Nuzi texts; the usual channel, moving from east to west, is considered to be the people known as *hapiru*. For a recent summary of the controversy regarding this term, see Gregory C. Chirichigno, *Debt-Slavery in Israel and the Ancient Near East* (JSOT Supplement Series 141; Sheffield: JSOT Press, 1993), 205-18;

equivalence" between the Nuzi examples and the biblical law in these cases; as I shall discuss in Part I, both attempt to address the question of conflicting claims of ownership of a female slave. This does not, however, warrant the assumption of successive mating in Exodus 21 or prostitution in Lev. 19:20.[78]

G. Chirichigno has made use of both the assumption of a common scribal tradition and the technique of comparison with Mesopotamian law in his examination of the biblical manumission laws. [79] While some scholarly opinions suggest that the differences between these laws reflect chronological development, Chirichigno proposes that all were part of a comprehensive social welfare scheme designed to deal with debt slavery and its consequences. Based on Old Babylonian [=OB] parallels and extensive structural and philological analysis of the biblical rules, he concludes that the three manumission laws (like their OB counterparts) were part of a single scheme. This provided for the periodic release of debt slaves (Exod. and Deut.); remission of debts (Deut. 15:1-3, similar to the function of OB *mīšarum* edicts); and the provision of interest-free loans and endowments (Exod. and Deut) that would be of assistance to poor farmers.[80] Like Mendelsohn, he argues that Leviticus attempts to ameliorate the more serious case of someone forced to sell himself (and his family) into slavery in order to survive by preventing permanent slavery and alienation of patrimonial land; further, this type of person was to be treated like a day laborer, since he was not paying off a debt. Consequently, Chirichigno posits that the biblical manumission laws could all have been operative at the same period. Deuteronomy thus does not repeal Exodus, but simply

---

Chirichigno rejects any connection between *ivri* and *hapiru*.

78 I would also question Mendelsohn's assumption that the presence of subject populations or a large labor force for public works projects necessarily implies that these people were "slaves." For instance, Mendelsohn assumes that slave labor was used for large mining projects in the Aravah, citing Nelson Glueck's evidence in this regard. Glueck, however, does not offer precise evidence of the use of slave labor. In his discussion of the site of a copper mine at Khirbet Nahas in the Negev (*Rivers in the Desert: A History of the Negev* [Philadelphia: Jewish Publication Society of America, 1959], 155-56), he describes the exploitative conditions presumed to have prevailed at this site; he then assumes that the mine must consequently have been worked by an expendable labor force and that this must necessarily have consisted of slaves.

79 Chirichigno, *Debt-Slavery,* 28.

80 Chirichigno, *Debt-Slavery,* 142-44.

addresses a different aspect of debt slavery; in particular, Exodus is said to address the marital rights of debt slaves, while Deuteronomy discusses the case of a woman sold for non-sexual labor.

Chirichigno's case is based in part on a particular model of economic evolution. It may be noted that other scholars, using different models of linguistic or social evolution, analyze the relationship among the three manumission passages differently. Weinfeld, for instance, sees a progressive social development from E to P to D,[81] while Van Seters, in contrast, has posited that E is the latest stratum and argues that the manumission rules of Exodus 21 support this conclusion.[82] It may also be noted that those scholars who have used economic models in their analyses of ancient Near Eastern slavery have differed in their evolutionary assumptions. In his portrayal of the rise of the landholding class, Diakonoff relies on a specifically Marxist theory of the development of slaveholding societies; Gelb similarly relies on an anthropological assumption regarding the formation of centralized states.[83] M. Dandamaev, in his study of slave documents in the Neo- and Late-Babylonian periods, is critical of this tendency of early researchers to use the cuneiform sources and the biblical text to support such *a priori* theories. From his own research, he concludes that slaves need not all have possessed a similar distance from the means of production. The documents he reviews appear to show slaves owning other slaves and possessing rights in a peculium-like pension; thus he concludes that slaves, at least in these later periods, did not constitute a single economic class but rather what he termed "an hereditary estate."[84]

Aside from the lack of agreement on the appropriate model, one major difficulty with such evolutionary approaches is that they tend in their broad outlines to obscure the specific differences that relate to females. I

81 Moshe Weinfeld, *Deuteronomy and the Deuteronomic School* (Oxford: Clarendon, 1972), 282.

82 J. Van Seters, "The Law of the Hebrew Slave," *ZAW* 108 (1996): 534-46, esp. 540-41.

83 See, e.g., I. M. Diakonoff, "Slaves, Helots and Serfs in Early Antiquity," in *Wirtschaft und Gesellschaft im alten Vorderasien* (ed. J. Harmatta and G. Komoróczy; Budapest: Akadémiai Kiadó, 1976), 45-78, esp. 46; I. Gelb, "From Slavery to Freedom," *RAI* 18 (1972): 81-92, esp. 81.

84 M. Dandamaev, *Slavery in Babylonia: From Nabopolassar to Alexander the Great (626-331 BC)*, (ed. and rev. M. Powell; trans. V. Powell; DeKalb: Northern Illinois University Press, 1984), 656, 658.

believe an examination of functional equivalence may serve as a corrective in this respect, allowing a focus on the problem that a specific rule was intended to address and enabling modern scholars to compare how such problems were addressed in different sources.

Slave Status in Postbiblical Law: A Unified Tradition?

There is an evident "leap" from the biblical provisions to those found in the Mishnah. The terms *eved*, *amah*, and *shifḥah* remain in the Mishnah; however, there is a distinction in some provisions between "Hebrew" (*ivri*) and "Canaanite" slaves (the latter term appears nowhere in the Bible). The term for "free person" is not *ḥofshi*, but *ben ḥorin*; and there now appears a separate status of "freedman," the *meshuḥrar*. Further, there are many mishnaic rules regarding slavery that have no explicit biblical source, and there are a number of biblical rules that have been modified or are altogether absent from the Mishnah. One example, as noted above, is *mQidd.* 1:2, which speaks of a Hebrew female slave being released once she shows signs puberty.

This "leap" has also led to various proposals regarding the connection between the Bible and postbiblical canonical documents, particularly the Mishnah. Traditionally, the midreshei halakhah attempt to explain (often not clearly) the biblical hooks upon which the mishnaic provisions depend. Modern scholars take radically different approaches. At one end of the continuum there are scholars who accept the traditional assumption of a linear connection between Bible and Mishnah. [85] At the other extreme are scholars such as J. Neusner who argue that the Bible and rabbinic works are to be treated as self-contained, mono-thematic works and cannot be compared except at this "macro" level; in particular, Neusner argues that the Mishnah reflects a type of utopian or "imaginary" system and is not reflective of actual historical conditions.[86]

---

85 E.g., David Halivni, *Peshat and Derash: Plain and Applied Meaning in Rabbinic Exegesis* (Oxford: Oxford University Press, 1991), 7-9.

86 See, e.g., Jacob Neusner, "The Mishnah in Historical and Religious Context," in *The Mishnah in Contemporary Perspective, Part Two* (ed. A. J. Avery-Peck and J. Neusner; Leiden: Brill, 2002), 81-109, and "The Synoptic Problem in Rabbinic Literature: The Cases of the Mishna, Tosepta, Sipra and Leviticus Rabba," *JBL* 105 (1986): 499-500, 503.

Between these two extremes lie the arguments of E. E. Urbach.[87] Surveying the slave rules in Mishnah and the Talmudim, his approach is to delineate the differences and logical contradictions among the various slave rules, to posit that these reflected different historical layers, and then to hypothesize the conditions which gave rise to each layer. He thus develops an outline of Jewish slavery from the Second Temple period to the 4th century C.E., concluding that Hebrew slaves would have been most prevalent in the period following Neḥemiah, while non-Hebrews became the major source of slaves following the Maccabean wars and Hasmonean conquests. Though useful in noting the contradictions and distinctions in rabbinic slave law, no consistent methodology is proposed to accurately date the various layers, nor is proof in many cases offered for the hypothesized context.[88]

---

87 E. E. Urbach, "The Laws Regarding Slavery as a Source for Social History of the Period of the Second Temple, the Mishnah and Talmud," in *Papers of the Institute of Jewish Studies, London* (ed. J. G. Weiss; Jerusalem: Magnes, 1964), 1:1-94.

88 As one example of the difficulties in this method, we may note Urbach's comments on the following baraita in *bQidd.* 14b, which discusses *mQidd.* 1:2 on the acquisition and manumission of the Hebrew slave. The issue is the apparent differences in the manumission laws of Exod. and Deut. regarding the term of slavery, the creation of a permanent slave, the maintenance given to the slave who is set free, and whether a woman is provided to a male slave. In one tanna's opinion, the difference is between one who has sold himself into slavery and one sold by a Beit Din, presumably for theft:

> [1] This [regarding the author of a preceding opinion] is the tanna who teaches: If one sells himself, he is sold for six years or more than six years; if the Beit Din sells him, he is sold for only six years. If one sells himself, [his ear] is not pierced [as a permanent slave]; if the Beit Din sells him, [his ear] is pierced. If one sells himself, he is not given maintenance [on his release]; if the Beit Din sells him, he is given maintenance. If one sells himself, his master does not give him a Canaanite *shifḥah;* if the Bet Din sells him, his master gives him a Canaanite *shifḥah.*
>
> [2] R. Elazar says: Both are sold only for six years; both have the ear pierced; and both are given maintenance; and the master gives both a Canaanite *shifḥah.*

This distinction between the slave who has sold himself and one sold by a Beit Din is found neither in *mQidd.* 1:2 nor, as Urbach notes, in any of the biblical manumission provisions. Urbach concludes:

> Now it happens that there is extant a piece of exegesis that fits R. Eleazar's view exactly... [citing *Mekhilta deR. Shimon Bar Yoḥai*, Epstein-Melamed, 59]. As against this, it is difficult to find any exegetical point corresponding to the line first taken in the baraita, and it would seem that the *halakhah* which limits

P. Flesher is a follower of the Neusner method of systemic analysis and objects specifically to the use of the "philological" approach practiced by Urbach.[89] He focuses on slave rules in the Mishnah, and in particular on two of the anomalies found therein:

1) Slaves seem to be classed with property in some cases and with humans in others.
2) An "ethnic" distinction is in some cases made between Hebrew and Canaanite slaves.[90]

In using Neusner's systemic approach, Flesher compares the Mishnah's system (or systems) of slavery to the Bible's system of slavery, deriving the latter by also treating the Bible's "legal" provisions as a systemic whole (as it is assumed the postbiblical sages would have done). Any differences between the biblical and mishnaic systems are then assumed to have been initiated by the sages.[91] He concludes that the Bible's system of slavery is ordered upon a genealogical criterion, a distinction between Israelites and non-Israelites. The former are really indentured servants serving for a limited period and then returning to their former place in Israelite society. The latter are chattel slaves who lose their former identity and find a (lowly) place in Israelite society solely through their dependence on the master.[92] This conclusion would seem to be based primarily on the provisions of Leviticus 25, which do make a clear distinction between the treatment of *aḥim* (brethren) and the treatment of the "surrounding nations"; but it is assumed in Flesher's analysis that the slavery provisions in Exodus and

---

> the laws of a Hebrew enslaved to fellow Jews represents the *halakhah* as it was actually applied.

In other words, Urbach has detected two different traditions here, only one of which can be traced explicitly to the biblical sources. To conclude, however, that the other tradition must therefore represent halakhah in practice is too far a leap without further evidence.

89 See Flesher, *Oxen, Women or Citizens?* x-xiv.

90 As noted above, though the term *ivri* is applied to slaves in the biblical text (e.g., Exod. 21: 2), the "Canaanite slave" (*shifḥah kena'anit* or *eved kena'ani*) is nowhere found in the biblical text. Further, this distinction is made in the Mishnah in less than 10% of its slave provisions. Flesher (*Oxen, Women or Citizens?* Appendix) notes some 129 mishnaic passages that refer to the *eved* or *shifḥah*, of which six have this ethnic distinction: *mArakh.* 8:4-5; *mB.Metz..* 1:5; *mB.Qam.* 8:3 and 8:5; *mEruv.* 7:6; *mMa'as.Sh.* 4:4; *mQidd.* 1:2-3.

91 Flesher, *Oxen, Women or Citizens?* 11-15.

92 Ibid., 26, 54-59.

Deuteronomy also make this distinction, presumably since the word *ivri* (Hebrew) is found in these provisions.

The Mishnah carries through the Bible's genealogical distinction between Hebrew slaves and non-Hebrew slaves (in the Mishnah called "Canaanite" slaves), but in only six of its provisions. The Mishnah's primary system of slavery, Flesher argues, instead defines slavery in terms of the control exercised by the male Israelite householder over the slave, regardless of the latter's ethnic background.[93] The slave is located on the boundary between inanimate objects (called "property") and human beings; he can be classed in some cases with property such as oxen, in some cases with other dependent household members such as women, and in some cases with householder-citizens, depending on the nature of the householder's control.[94] In this system the slave's ethnic background is irrelevant; the slave is contrasted instead with the freedman. The term "slave" in this system is also assumed to be gender-neutral. Flesher attributes this change in systemic outlook completely to the Sages, whose system of classification, in his view, was intended to reflect their understanding of the proper hierarchical relationship to the Deity; humans are both objects to be classified and classifying agents, with the householder able to prevent others from fully exercising their power of classification.[95] Flesher explains the existence of a separate "ethnic system" simply by positing that certain matters cannot be explained without a distinction between Hebrew and Canaanite slaves.[96]

Flesher has identified an interesting pattern in these rules based on the nature of the householder's control. Yet in his concern to place all slave provisions within this one "system," many nuances and contradictions are overlooked which cannot be described or explained by means of the concept of householder control. I would particularly note that he makes no special case for female slaves. Flesher argues that the *amah* and *shifḥah* of Exod. 21:7-11 and Lev. 19:20 are to be left out of the biblical system of slavery because they are "concubines" rather than merely slaves; this is shown by their use as sex objects in these verses. The *amah* of Deuteronomy, on the

93 Ibid., 43-45, 62-63.

94 Ibid., 7-8, 171-72.

95 Ibid., 30-32, 61-62, 67-71.

96 Ibid., 54-59.

other hand, is simply the female counterpart of the *eved*. For the Mishnah's primary system of slavery, however, he argues that females likely belonged more to the category of "slaves" than to the category of "women."[97] They merely possessed the added "attribute" of sexual use.

Yet this distinction is not trivial or without legal significance; we need merely look to the different "halves" of the matrilineal principle for male and female slaves in *mYev.* 7:5 and *mQidd.* 3:12. This distinction is not easily explained by differences in householder control. Further, despite Flesher's suggestion that the proposed primary and ethnic slavery systems are complementary, this is not so with respect to female slaves: the subject matter in this case not only overlaps, but is treated differently. In the "non-ethnic" system (which would presumably cover both Hebrew and non-Hebrew slaves), there are several provisions referring to the *shifḥah* who gives birth (e.g., *mQidd.* 3:12). In the ethnic system, on the other hand, *mQidd.* 1:2 provides that the Hebrew female slave is to be manumitted when she shows signs of puberty; in other words, she would be manumitted before she could ever give birth.[98] Again, it is difficult to explain these differences in terms of householder control; other principles seem to be at work, as I shall explain in the course of this work.[99]

97 See Flesher, *Oxen, Women or Citizens?* 17 n. 17. J. R. Wegner, in her comprehensive study of women in the Mishnah, also excluded female slaves, referring the reader to Flesher's study. See Judith Romney Wegner, *Chattel or Person? The Status of Women in the Mishnah* (New York: Oxford University Press, 1988), 220, n. 19.

98 It is also difficult to reconcile *mQidd.* 1:2 with such passages as *mB.Metz.* 7:6, which speaks of adult female slaves in general.

99 We may note briefly here two other nuances in the mishnaic slavery rules that are not explained by the notion of householder control. First, it is necessary to account for the fact that slaves in the Mishnah are not simply classed as "property"; in some cases they appear to be classed with so-called "personal" property (i.e., movable goods and chattels, as in *mB.Qam.* 9:2 with respect to depreciation and *mB.Bat.* 3:1 with respect to conditions of sale); and in other cases with "real" property (immovables such as land and buildings, as in *mQidd.* 1:3, in which the modes of acquisition for Canaanite slaves parallel those for land in *mQidd.* 1:5; *mB.Metz..* 4:9 with respect to overreaching; *mB.Bat.* 3:1 with respect to adverse possession; *mSheb.* 6:5 with respect to oaths). This distinction was in fact already noted by the Sages in *yQidd.* 1:3 60a.

Second, Flesher posits that the concept of the "freedman" (*meshuḥrar*) was developed by the sages as a contrast to the idea of the slave; that is, someone who, unlike the slave, is no longer under a householder's control, but who, like the slave lacks a legitimate genealogy. There are several instances, however, in which one would expect the lack of genealogy to be relevant, but which have no mention of the freedman (e.g., *mBikk.* 1:5). Connected

This failure to address these nuances stems, in my opinion, from certain assumptions underlying Flesher's systemic approach. This approach emphasizes that the relevant context against which to measure the Mishnah's rules (or those of any document) is first and foremost the document itself; the document reflects the worldview (or partial view) of a "clearly defined social group."[100] Thus an analysis of such matters as what was included and excluded and the methods of ordering is said to reveal the principles underlying the document.

This argument, however, tends to assume that the Mishnah in particular is a homogeneous "code," a complete description of the utopian society proposed by its redactors. It may be argued that the Mishnah is rather a collection of specific rules, ordered in some pattern, but not intended as a complete codification in the modern sense. Further, as shown by Urbach and others, the Mishnah and other documents are layered, which makes it doubtful that such documents represent a consistent worldview. Thus, to describe such a set of rules as a system does not inevitably mean that there are a limited number of fundamental principles underlying it.[101] There is arguably a difficulty in attempting to derive such principles at the macro level. I think it is reasonable, however, to assume that the documents do have "micro-contexts" (as perhaps legal systems have "local unities"[102]). As one example, the positioning of several rules next to each other may be based on some common theme underlying the rules that can be derived through contextual analysis. Such "positional analogy," as Jackson notes, was not only utilized by the sages in their hermeneutical methods, but was

with this issue is the meaning of the term *ḥetzyo eved veḥetzyo ben ḥorin*. Though Flesher interprets this expression (as used in *mPesaḥ.* 8:1) as "half bondman, half freedman," it is not clear that *ben ḥorin* equals *meshuḥrar*; further, *ben ḥorin* is itself a postbiblical term of uncertain meaning, possibly but not certainly equivalent to the biblical *ḥofshi*.

100 Jacob Neusner, *First Principles of Systemic Analysis* (Lanham: University Press of America, 1987), 57.

101 This type of question has been posed for "law" in general: is positive law as a whole to be conceived as a unified, rational system based on certain fundamental principles (Maris, "Milking the Meter," 79)? Jackson poses the question from another angle: Does "law" as a semiotic system derive from an innate system of fundamental norms or duties, similar to the universal grammar of Chomsky's language theory ("Can One Speak of the 'Deep Structure' of Law?" in *Theory and Systems of Legal Philosophy* [ARSP Supplement 3; ed. S. Panow et al.; Stuttgart: Franz Steiner, 1988], 250-61, esp. 250ff.)?

102 Maris, "Milking the Meter," 79.

actually used in practice even in the biblical codes.[103] There may in fact be a disjunction between a principle derived at the "macro" level and those reflected at the "micro" levels.

Thus while Flesher is right to approach the Mishnah first as a whole, the results of this approach reveal not unified patterns but many inconsistencies. I make the assumption that these differences do not necessarily reflect different editorial viewpoints, but can reflect different school traditions, and thus can be profitably compared to and contrasted with provisions in other canonical texts. I will argue in particular that the differences in the construction of female slave status between Mishnah provisions and supposed parallels in other tannaitic works, particularly the Tosefta,[104] actually reflect a multiplicity of halakhic viewpoints. I thus accept Urbach's appreciation for the layers implied by these various inconsistencies, while rejecting the *Sitz im Leben* he proposes for them.

Finally, Hezser compares rabbinic and Roman laws regarding slavery as an extended functional analysis between the two systems.[105] This presents an in-depth synchronic analysis of postbiblical slavery. Although the current study differs in that it focuses on an individual diachronic analysis of a particular aspect of slavery, sex right, to analyze its evolution from its ancient Near Eastern to its Greco-Roman context, I believe that in fact the two approaches complement each other.

Chapter Summary

Based on assumptions that:

1) biblical provisions need not be explained by a Near Eastern common law, and that there is a gap in the case at hand between biblical and postbiblical law; and

103 Jackson, "Analogy in Legal Science," 162-63. Jackson also notes, however, that it is difficult to tell in ancient texts whether the underlying themes are based on "social-experiential narrative frames" rather than abstract legal concepts.

104 For a compilation of recent scholarly studies on the relationship between the Mishnah and Tosefta, see Fox and Meacham, eds., *Introducing Tosefta*.

105 See Catherine Hezser, *Jewish Slavery in Antiquity* (Oxford: Oxford University Press, 2005).

2) postbiblical law reflects a variety of principles and influences, justifying a pluralistic method of study,

this work proceeds as follows:

Chapters 1-4 examine biblical provisions relating to the female slave, the matrilineal principle, and adultery, to establish the biblical understanding of the status of female slave as measured by these notions. Chapter 1 examines: i) the biblical female slave terms *amah* and *shifḥah*; ii) the biblical terms *ben amah*, *ben bayit*, and *yelid bayit*, suggestive of the type of description that would be used for a second-generation slave. I argue that the terms *ben amah*, *ben bayit*, and *yelid bayit* were not restricted to slaves, but were intended to emphasize the inclusion of these individuals, as dependents or otherwise, within the family unit.

Chapter 2 examines the biblical term *pilegesh*, usually translated as "concubine." I conclude that while the sexual utility of the female slave, including for breeding purposes, was recognized, this sexual role was placed within some sort of family structure. In contrast to the sexuality of slaves as part of the dependency continuum, the sexuality of the concubine was that of a dangerous outsider to the family.

Chapter 3 examines Exod. 21:2-11 within its ancient Near Eastern context, concluding that this passage was concerned with the question of ownership of a slave woman as between father, husband, and master, and that some of the provisions can be seen as functional equivalents of the Akkadian "fitting out" contracts.[106] Again, there is confirmation of a desire to ensure that the female slave, and particularly her children, are placed within some sort of familial context. Contrary to the traditional rabbinic interpretation, Exod. 21:4 does not serve as support for a biblical matrilineal principle based on a prohibition of slave-free intermarriage.

Chapter 4 focuses on Lev. 19:20-21 and its various *hapax*es. Using philological and functional comparison, it is argued that the key to the provision is the meaning of the *hapax neḥerefet* as "sexually coerced." The *hapax biqqoret* is taken to mean "a claim for trespass," based in part on a comparison to Akkadian *BQR/PQR* terms in slave warranties. I shall add

106 That is, contracts under which a father with limited means sold his daughter to a third party, who was to "fit her out" for marriage and receive the bride-price.

to this much-discussed argument by exploring the trespass idea in relation to these warranties, as providing some general insight into the development of property law.

Having confirmed in chapters 1-4 that female slave status in the Bible must be seen as attempting to fit the slave's reproductive capacity within a dependence hierarchy, chapters 5 and 6 examine the development of female slave status in postbiblical texts. Chapter 5 argues that there were principles other than matriliny that were debated with regard to the inheritance of slave status and suggests that the mishnaic matrilineal principle became prominent in response to Greco-Roman administrative rules, particularly the need to define "slaves" for tax purposes. Chapter 6 illustrates the exegetical development of Lev. 19:20-21 into an exoteric and vague ruling, likely not related to *realia*. This exegesis is seen particularly in several superficially parallel baraitot in the Mishnah, Tosefta, and *Sifra*, which, it will be argued, actually contain some significant differences. This allows us to study the relationship between these three sources with respect this case and to speculate on the forces of development influencing their particular differences.

In Chapter 7 I also examine some non-legal sources discussing the case of Bilhah and Zilpah, the slave-wives of Jacob. By the mishnaic matrilineal principle, their offspring, Dan, Naftali, Gad, and Asher, would have been slaves. Tracing the attitudes toward Bilhah and Zilpah in the various sources gives further evidence that the development of the matrilineal idea was not straightforward. In particular, there are two "genealogical" traditions that can be followed through Targumim, Qumran, and mediaeval sources that argue against Bilhah and Zilpah's slave origins; further, certain midrashim appear to have ignored their origins and considered them "matriarchs."

Conclusions contains a summary of the conclusions in the first seven chapters and poses the question of why the construct "female slave" changed from biblical to postbiblical law, at least with regard to sex right, and concludes that this was due to a combination of adaptation to external forces and internal halakhic development. Finally, it is argued that it should be legitimate within common halakhic principles to "vacate" this halakhic category based on evidence that some of its major underlying defining points are no longer morally relevant or applicable.

CHAPTER 1

WHAT IS A "FEMALE SLAVE"? CONTEXT AND COMPARISON

"Slavery," as M. I. Finley noted, is an institution fraught with ambiguity and contradiction.[1] How does one define a female slave, as opposed, for instance, to a wife, a servant (indentured or otherwise), an employee, a dependent relative or hanger-on, a nursemaid, a lady-in-waiting, a concubine, a mistress? In fact, a female slave may have partaken of all these roles.

There is much literature on the origins and definitions of slavery in both ancient and modern slave systems. As we have noted in the introductory chapter: 1) in the case of the ancient Near East, such theories often depend on the particular economic or political ideology assumed by the scholar; 2) definitions of slavery in Mesopotamia are also complicated by the theory that dependence, versus "freedom", was the ideal state; and 3) finally, female slaves tend to be either simply assimilated with male slaves, or assumed to have been only concubines or breeders.

I shall argue that a contextual and etymological analysis of the terms for female slaves assign them to the same continuum of dependence which wives inhabited. Their reproductive capabilities were certainly valued, but with a role sought for them within a family or kinship structure. There is nothing biblically to indicate that marriage with female slaves was prohibited, or that the children of female slaves were automatically slaves. Finally it will be argued that it was actually the concubine, the *pilegesh*, who was the "other" - who, outside the dependence continuum, constituted danger.

---

1 See, e.g., Moses I. Finley, "A Peculiar Institution?" *Times Literary Supplement,* July 2, 1976, 821.

1.1 THE *AMAH* AND THE *SHIFḤAH*: BREEDER, DRUDGE, CONCUBINE OR WIFE?

The terms אמה *amah* and שפחה *shifḥah*, found throughout the biblical text (as well as extra-biblical and post-biblical Hebrew texts), are conventionally taken to denote a female slave, bondswoman or the like.[2] With respect to pentateuchal usage, neither term is found in Numbers; *shifḥah* is well represented in Gen., and comparatively rare (one instance each) in Exod., Lev. and Deut; *amah*, conversely, is more widely found in the latter books, and is the term most commonly found in "legal" provisions. The three patriarchal "surrogate wives" in the Pentateuch (Hagar, Bilhah and Zilpah) are called by both terms;[3] of particular note is the fact that these women are also called *ishah*, wife.[4] In certain instances, both pentateuchal and non-pentateuchal, the terms *amah* or *shifḥah* are paired with the term *eved*.[5] In many of the non-pentateuchal instances, both terms are used in a self-effacing way, as terms of "courtesy", by women addressing God, or addressing men of apparently

---

2 E.J. Revell, *The Designation of the Individual. Expressive Usage in Biblical Narrative.* Contributions to Biblical Exegesis and Theology 14 (Kampen: Kok Pharos, 1996) 34, among others, notes that the term נערה can refer to someone who might be a debt-slave (as in 2Kings 5:2, 4); as he acknowledges, however, this term is not used biblically to indicate a precise legal status or relationship. For the purposes of this study, I concentrate on *shifḥah* and *amah* as being the primary terms in biblical and post-biblical texts for female slaves.

3 For Hagar, see e.g. Gen. 16:1 and 21:10, 12; and for Bilhah, see e.g. Gen. 29:29 and 30:3. Zilpah alone is never called an *amah*. Both she and Bilhah together, however, are called *shefaḥot* and *amahot*; see e.g. Gen. 31:33 and 32:23.

4 For Hagar, see Gen. 16:3; for Bilhah, Gen. 30:4; for Zilpah, Gen. 30:9.

5 The *amah* and the *eved* are paired in various pentateuchal laws: Exod. 20:10 and Deut. 5:14, the inclusion within the Decalogue Sabbath requirement; Exod. 20:14 and Deut. 5:18, inclusion within the Decalogue prohibition on coveting; Exod. 21:20, 26-7, regarding assaults; Exod. 21:32, regarding an attack by a goring ox; Lev. 25:6, partaking of Sabbatical year provisions; Lev. 25:44, regarding the taking of non-Israelites as slaves; Deut. 12:12, 18 and 16:11, 14, regarding inclusion in certain religious festivals; and the anomalous Deut. 15:17, regarding manumission (this provision will be discussed in chapter five). The *shifḥah* and the *eved* are paired in the Pentateuch primarily in lists of patriarchal property: Gen. 12:16, 20:14, 24:35, 30:43, 32:6, as well as the divine threat of enslavement in Deut. 26:68. Outside the Pentateuch it is *shifḥah* that is more often paired with *eved* (1Sam. 8:16, 2Kings 5:26; Isa. 14:2, 24:2; Jer. 34:9, 10, 11, 16; Joel 3:2; Ps. 123:2; Esth. 7:4; Eccl. 2:7; 2Chr. 28:10). The terms *amah* and *eved* are paired in Job 31:13, Ezra 2:65 and Neḥ. 7:67.

higher rank or status.[6] These uses suggest an attempt to create a mock servile relationship between the speaker and addressee, much as one sees in other languages (consider, for instance, the English "at your service," or the use of "slave" to indicate someone in thrall or dependence). There is a similar use of the male slave term *eved*.

Finally, there are various rules that suggest that a sexual use was assumed for both the *shifḥah* and the *amah:* 1) Exod. 21:7-11, concerning a father who sells his daughter as an *amah*; the pericope specifically provides that she is not to "go out as the *avadim* do" (v. 7), but must be redeemed only if she is "not assigned"[7] to someone, including her master's son; 2) the apparently contradictory Deut. 15:17, providing for the automatic release of an *amah* after six years; 3) Lev. 19:20-22, concerning an apparently adulterous *shifḥah*. We may also note the case of Exod. 21:4-5, which refers to an *ishah* who is mated to an *eved* in his master's household; it is not clear, however, whether such woman/wife is an *amah* or *shifḥah*.[8]

All but the Deut. passage, it may be seen, presume that these women will be involved in sexual relationships, and further, that these relationships will be regulated.

The existence of both terms raises two sets of issues:

(a) Are the terms *amah* and *shifḥah* simply the female counterpart(s) of

---

6 Hannah, for instance, refers to herself as אמתך before God and to the priest Eli (1Sam. 1:11, 16), and again as שפחתך to the priest Eli (1Sam. 1:18); Ruth calls herself both שפחתך and אמתך when addressing her prosperous kinsman Boaz, in Ruth 2:13, 3:9. This self-effacing use is more common with *amah*, and most prevalent in the books of Samuel and Kings. Other instances of the self-effacing use of these terms occur with respect to Avigail (1Sam. 25:24, 25, 28, 31, 41 for *amah*, and 1Sam. 24:27, 41 for *shifḥah*); Saul's necromancer (1Sam. 28: 21, 22 for *shifḥah*); the woman of Tekoah (2Sam. 14:15, 16 for *amah*, and 2Sam. 14:7, 12, 15, 17, 19 for *shifḥah*); the woman with Yoav (2Sam. 20:17 for *amah*); Batsheva (1Kings 1: 13, 17 for *amah*); the two *nashim zonot* addressing Solomon (1Kings 3:20 for *amah*); the widow to Elisha (2Kings 4:2, 16 for *shifḥah*). Non-self-effacement instances in these sources are: for *amah* - 2Sam. 6:20, 22; Judges 19:19; Job 19:15, 31:13; Naḥum 2:8; Ezra 2:65; Neḥ. 7:67, and for *shifḥah* - 1Sam. 8:16; 2Kings 5:26; Isa. 14:2, 24:2; Jer. 34:9, 10, 11, 16; Joel 3:2; Ps. 123:2; Prov. 30:23; Esth. 7:4; Eccl. 2:7; 2Chr. 28:10.

7 The meaning of the MT לא יעדה (Exod. 21:8) and the effect of its *qere* variant לו יעדה will be discussed further in chapter three.

8 This issue will be discussed further in chapter three.

the *eved* (עבד), the primary term taken to refer to a male slave in biblical and post-biblical texts, given that they do not appear to share a common etymology with the latter (or with each other)? There has been a gradual recognition in slave studies that the situation of female slaves must not automatically be assumed to correspond to that of male slaves. Female slaves, in other words, may be treated (legally, socially and politically) more like "females" than like "slaves,"[9] and this difference may result from the fact that their primary (if not exclusive) role is sexual. This is not to ignore that male slaves were also put to sexual use;[10] the issue with female slaves, however, is whether their primary use was sexual, and particularly whether they were used to "breed" more slaves.[11] This issue in turn raises further questions. Is it inevitable that female slaves will be put to sexual use? Meillassoux's classic study of certain African societies, for instance, proposed circumstances in which it was not economically feasible to have female slaves breed."[12] Does sexual use, however, inevitably mean breeding of new slaves, or does it more generally take the form of "concubinage" to the master or other "free" male in the household?[13]

---

9 Contra, e.g., Flesher, *Oxen, Women or Citizens?* 17 n. 17, who states with respect to slave rules in the Mishnah: "The Mishnah treats the female slave like a male slave, with the added attribute of sexual use." As will be argued throughout this paper, however, it is that sexual use that in fact results in non-symmetrical treatment of male and female slaves in rabbinic law. The sexual use, in other words, is significant. *Yam shel Shelomo* Kiddushin ch. 1, *siman* 22 *d.h.* 22 also discusses whether a Hebrew slave would be obligated to have sexual relations with a Canaanite slave woman given to him by his master during his tenure and concludes that he can be given such a wife even against his will and even if it constitutes "night work".

10 One might, for instance, treat the situation of Joseph and Potifar's wife as an example of the sexual coercion of a male slave (see contra Theodore Weinberger, "And Joseph Slept with Potiphar's Wife': A Re-Reading," *Literature and Theology* 11 (1997) 145-151, esp. 148-9, who argues that Joseph is actually being criticized for failing to engage in a legitimate act of sexual "subversion" against Potifar the slave-owner).

11 See, e.g., Marcia Wright, *Strategies of Slaves & Women. Life-Stories from East/Central Africa (*New York: Lilian Barber Press, 1993) 2, who suggests that in general female slaves are more easily absorbed into their new community as, among other roles, concubines and mothers.

12 Meillassoux, *Anthropologie de l'esclavage* 301-2. The "breeding" of slaves will be discussed further in chapter 2.

13 Scholars such as B. Cohen, *Jewish and Roman Law* 329 and Raphael Patai, *Sex and Family in the Bible and the Middle East* (New York: Doubleday, 1959) 42, have suggested that this

(b) The existence of two words for female slaves makes it relevant to ask whether the two terms are actually synonymous. As will be discussed below, they are generally treated as such in the various biblical Targumim.[14] Certain scholarly opinions, in contrast, suggest the terms reflect actual differences, particularly in legal status or in function, and that the *amah* might have been higher in "rank" than the *shifḥah*.

A review of the biblical evidence suggests, on the one hand, that a sexual role for the women was assumed. On the other hand, there is little indication that their fate would have inevitably have been either concubinage or the breeding of a new generation of slaves.

To substantiate these observations, I shall summarize the biblical instances of *shifḥah* and *amah*, review prior opinions on the meaning of these terms as well as early translations, and comment on certain epigraphic evidence of the use of *amah* and the way this evidence relates to the biblical terms. I shall examine in detail the key biblical texts relating to female slaves and concubines.

In general, we have two major characteristics that are supposedly indicative of female slaves: sexual use and dependence. But is there significance to the fact that there are two terms for female slaves? In particular, is this an indication of a difference in rank? Is the *amah* a type of secondary wife or concubine, as opposed to the *shifḥah*, who was simply sexually abused as *hefqer* or ownerless property? Or are both terms indicative of a quasi-wife status, maintained with the same rules against adultery and incest as are found biblically with respect to wives? Or, again, does the Bible seem to prohibit marriage, and particularly slave-free intermarriage, for female slaves?

I shall argue, first, that the two terms as used *biblically* are synonyms. The most likely reason, in my opinion, for the presence of two terms is that each has a different ethnic origin, and there is some, admittedly scanty, evidence for this. Sexual use of these women is assumed, though

---

type of concubinage was the inevitable fate of the female slave.

14 This type of overlap in meaning is not an unexpected phenomenon. As a modern example, one may note that Canadian English recognizes, as terms for child-minders, not only "nursemaid" and "nanny", but also (coincidentally) "*amah*", a term used in the Far East and ultimately derived from the Portuguese *ama*, "nurse" (*CED, s.v.* "*amah*").

based on the regulations in Exod. 21 and Lev. 19, to be discussed more fully in the following chapters, it cannot be assumed that the primary function of either was as a concubine or breeder or mistress to a male master. Nor is there evidence of any prohibition on marriage for slave women; on the contrary, I shall argue that both etymology and context have as their point the assimilation of these women within a family or kinship structure.

1.1.1 The Terms are Biblical Synonyms Indicating a Servile Status

This conclusion is based on essentially negative evidence: the complete absence of any discernable differences in their pattern of use.

1) There have been various contextual studies proposing a difference in meaning according to the use or status of the woman in question. Jepsen concluded that though there was some interchange in the use of the two terms, there were still basic differences between them: though both types of women were "unfree", the *shifḥah* was "unbehrührte," and would usually serve a woman, while the *amah* was either a "Nebenfrau" to the master or an "unfree" wife to a male slave. This distinction carried through to the use of the words as terms of courtesy: the use of *shifḥah* suggested a greater degree of subservience, while the *amah* was a woman seeking protection.[15] Riesener accepted the idea that there was an essential distinction in meaning between the two terms; she also made the reasonable point, however, that they need not be mutually exclusive, pointing in particular to their simultaneous use with the same person (e.g. Hagar, Bilhah and Zilpah, as noted above), to the fact that a *shifḥah* could serve a man (e.g. Gen. 29:24 and 29, in which Zilpah and Bilhah are referred to as שפחתו of Lavan), and to various instances contradicting the "unbehrührte" nature of the *shifḥah*, notably Lev. 19:20. Rather than a legal difference, Riesener suggested the terms emphasized different aspects of slavery: the use of *shifḥah* emphasized the slave as a possession (as in lists of one's patrimony, such as Gen. 12:16), while the use of *amah* emphasized

15 A. Jepsen, "Amah and Schiphchah," *VT* 8 (1958) 293-297, esp. 293, 295.

the sexual role of the female slave.[16] Yet this proposed distinction also fails to take account of the sexual nature of the offence regarding the *shifḥah neḥerefet* of Lev. 19:20; the significance of this passage is highlighted by the fact that the term *shifḥah* here is a type of *hapax*, since it is *amah* that is used in the other pentetuechal laws involving female slaves.

Finally, Mandelkern (*s.v.* אמה)[17] suggested that the *amah* must have had a higher status than the *shifḥah*, since Hagar is only called by this term once she becomes the "wife" of Abraham.[18] This pattern, however, does not hold true of the similar situations of Bilhah and Zilphah. Zilpah is never called an *amah* when mentioned alone.[19] Bilhah is called Rachel's *amah* before she is presented to Jacob (Gen. 30:3). Both are also called the *shefaḥot* of Jacob (Gen. 32:23), even after their mating with him.

2) As noted earlier in this chapter, in many of the non-pentateuchal instances, both terms are used self-effacingly or as terms of "courtesy," by women addressing God, or addressing men of apparently higher rank or status.

3) Source-Critical analysis suggests some distinctions of use in the Pentateuch, but nothing that points to a pattern. *Shifḥah* is used more often than *amah* in J and P sources, while *amah* is used more often than *shifḥah* in E and D sources.[20] As Jepson noted, however, the fact

---

16 Ingrid Riesener, "Der Stamm עבד im Alten Testament," *BZAW* 149 (Berlin: Walter de Gruyter, 1978) 78, 83.

17 [=Mandelkern] שלמה מאנדעלקערן, קונקורדנציא לתנ"ך. ירושלים: שוקן, 1955.

18 A similar distinction has been postulated among Ugaritic terms by L.M. Muntingh, "The Social and Legal Status of a Free Ugaritic Female," *JNES* 26 (1967) 102-13, esp. 103. It is also interesting to note that under Islamic law the *amah* would have been of higher rank than the *surriyya,* "concubine"; though both were slaves, the former was married, perhaps to another slave, and thus off limits to her master. As a wife, she would have at least a right to demand sexual fulfillment from her husband. See Donna Lee Bowen, "Muslim Juridical Opinions Concerning the Status of Women as Demonstrated by the Case of 'AZL [*coitus interruptus*]," *JNES* 40 (1981) 326.

19 She is called both an *amah* and *shifḥah* when mentioned with Bilhah; see supra note 8.

20 This point was suggested to me in a personal communication with Dr. Tzemaḥ Yoreh. The number of instances for each is summarized in the following table:

that both terms are used in all sources makes it difficult to assess the significance of these numerical statistics;[21] this overlap in fact supports his conclusion that the two terms came to be seen as synonyms.

The question of whether the “courtesy” nuance represents a development in these terms is addressed by Leshem, who makes the interesting observation that these self-effacement uses of the terms are found primarily in the books of Samuel and Kings. From this fact he concluded that the rise of the monarchy brought about an increasing emphasis on status distinctions, and thus resulted in the wider use of these “slave” terms.[22] Against this, however, one may argue that the redaction chronology of these books is not necessarily coincident with the early monarchy,[23] and the use of the terms may reflect the cultural attitudes of a later editor. Further, as Leshem himself notes, the male term *eved* is already used in “pre-monarchy” references as a term of subservience[24] - as, for instance, in reference to Moses as the *eved* of God (e.g. Num. 12:7-8; Deut. 34:5) or Jacob’s calling himself the *eved* of Esau (Gen. 32:5).

	amah	*shifḥah*
E	**14** (Gen. 20:17; 21:10, 12, 13; 31:33*; Exod. 2:5; 20:10, 14; 21:7, 20, 26, 27; 21:32; 23:12).	**2** (Gen. 20:14; 30:18)
J	**2** (Gen. 30:3; 31:33)	**19** (Gen. 12:16; 16:1, 2, 5, 6, 8; 24:35; 30:4, 7, 9, 10, 12, 43; 32:6, 23; 33:1, 2, 6; Exod. 11:5)
P	**2** (Lev. 25:6, 44)	**7** (Gen. 16:3; 25:12; 29:24, 29; 35:25, 26; Lev. 19:20)
D	**7** (Deut. 5:14, 18; 12:12, 18; 15:17; 16:11, 14)	**1** (Deut. 28:68)

* Gen. 31:33 is not divided between J and E

21 Jepsen, “*Amah* and Schiphchah” 296-7; Jepsen thus argued against the use of these terms as a criterion for distinguishing between the different sources.

22 Yosi Leshem, ”אמה ושפחה בסיפורי המלוכה שבמקרא,“ אסופת זיכרון לשושנה בהט, מ. בר אשר, עורך (ירושלים: האקדמיה ללשון העברית, תשנ“ד) 48-49. [="Amah and Shifḥah"]

23 See, e.g., P. Kyle McCarter, Jr., *I Samuel.* The Anchor Bible 8 (Garden City: Doubleday & Co., 1980) 22, who suggests a redaction date for the books of Samuel around the time of the destruction of the northern kingdom; and Mordechai Cogan and Hayim Tadmor, *2Kings,* The Anchor Bible 11 (Garden City: Doubleday & Co., 1988) 4, who suggest that the Kings chronologies may have been composed in the 7th century, then partially revised after the destruction of the Temple.

24 Leshem, “Amah and Shifḥah” 49.

4) Early biblical translations generally treat the two terms as synonymous.

The Jewish Targumim, with one exception regarding Bilhah and Zilpah that will be discussed in chapter seven, appear to make no distinction between the two terms, translating both as אמהא or אמתא.[25] The Peshitta (Gen. and Exod.) also uses forms of אמתא throughout. The Samaritan Targumim show considerable variation, though not with any discernible pattern. The S_j uses primarily forms of שמשה,[26] though this alternates with forms of אמתא. The S_a uses סולה or אסולה most frequently, but also other forms such as שמשה and אמאתא.[27]

The Septuagint [=LXX] is consistent in its translation in using either *παιδίσκη* or *δούλη* for both *amah* and *shifḥah,* with three notable exceptions: the *amah* of Exod. 21:7 and the *shifḥah* of Lev. 19:20 are both translated as *οἰκέτιν* or *οἰκέτις* , as is the *shifḥah* who is heir to her mistress in Prov. 30:23, while the *amah* of Exod. 21:26-7 is translated as *θεραπαίνης*. Whether any of these terms necessarily imply "slaves" is unclear, as it seems they could describe both slaves and

---

25 Marcus Jastrow, *Dictionary of the Targumim, Talmud Babli, Yerushalmi and Midrashic Literature.* New York:Pardes Publishing House, Inc., 1950, *s.v.* אמהא, אמתא, אמהתא considers them equivalent.

26 Michael Sokoloff, *A Dictionary of Jewish Palestinian Aramaic.* Ramat-Gan: Bar Ilan University Press, 1992, *s.v.* שמש has a masculine form שמש "attendant" or "servant," but notes that the verb שמש also has a sexual sense.

27 See Abraham Tal, התרגום השומרוני לתורה. 3 כרכים. אוניברסיטת תל אביב, 1988 [=Samaritan Targum]. The terms סולה and אסולה do not appear in the common dictionaries. Perhaps there is a connection with "goad" or "switch" (Gustaf Dalman, *Aramaisch-neuhebraisches Handworterbuch zu Targum, Talmud und Midrasch.* Hildesheim: Georg Olms erlagsbuchhandlung, 1967, *s.v.* סול), suggesting a whipped drudge, or with"fine flour" (Sokoloff, *s.v.* סולת) or possibly "rubbish" (Dalman, *s.v.* ס[ו]לתא), suggesting the tasks associated with such women. We may also note that in Babylonian Jewish Aramaic סול can mean "wooden pick" (Jastrow, *s.v.* סול); perhaps there is a connection with the slave whose ear is bored, as the following talmudic passage (*yQidd.* 1:2 59d) suggests:

אין לי אלא במרצע מניין אפילו בסול אפילו בקוץ אפילו בזכוכית תלמוד לומר ורצע

> I know only [that a permanent slave's ear is to be bored] with a borer; how do I know it is also with a splinter, a thorn, a piece of glass? It is thus stated: "and he shall bore [the 'and' implying inclusivity]."

Tal, *A Dictionary of Samaritan Aramaic.* Leiden, Boston and Cologne: E.J. Brill, 2000, *s.v.* סולה simply defines the word as maidservant without attempting a derivation.

non-slaves.[28] In analyzing the masculine term *οἰκέτης*, Spicq[29] notes a range of associations; it is used for *eved* in the LXX, apparently thus suggesting a "slave," but it is also used for people who do not seem "servile," and is often a synonym of *ὑπηρέτης*, the meanings of which include "assistant" and "aide-de-camp"[30] (Liddell/Scott). Gibbs and Feldman discuss the use of *οἰκέτης* in the later books of the LXX, Josephus and contemporary papyri, concluding that in all these sources this and other "slave" terms were increasingly regarded as synonyms; [31] they view this absence of systematization as simply a lack of interest in distinguishing "half-statuses," an attitude characteristic of Greek scholars generally.[32]

5) Traditional commentators suggested that the two terms connote differences in ethnicity, *amah* referring to the "Hebrew" slave, and *shifḥah* to the Canaanite. Against this conclusion we may note, first, that the term "Canaanite" in reference to *shifḥah* or *amah* is purely post-biblical;[33] further, there are instances of the term *shifḥah ivriah*,

---

28 See, e.g., Iza Biezunska-Malowist, *L'esclavage dans l'Égypte Gréco-Romaine*. Part 1: *Periode ptolémaïque*. Translated by J. Wolf and J. Kasinska (Wroclaw, 1974) 14-16, who analyzes occurrences of *παῖς* in Egyptian papyri; while she agrees with earlier scholars that the term can refer to a slave, rather than to a type of worker permanently attached to an estate, she notes that this assessment is not unequivocal, and must be assessed case by case. She cites (p. 17) Amusin's study of slave terms in the LXX, in which he seems to have accepted *παῖς*, *οἰκέτης*, *θεράπων* and their feminine equivalents as referring to slaves. Amusin's argument, however, may be circular, in that it assumes the meaning of the Greek terms from the biblical Hebrew terms they are translating. John Gibbs and Louis Feldman, "Josephus' Vocabulary for Slavery," *JQR* 76 (1986) 281-310, discussing the various "slave terms" used by Josephus, note *παιδίσκη* is used as both "young woman of marriageable age" and "slave girl' (p. 295); the male terms *θεράπων* and *οἰκέτης* often connote a person in a trusted or non-submissive position (pp. 293-294). The authors conclude that Josephus, like earlier Greek writers, did not use these words as precise technical terms (p. 297).

29 C. Spicq, "Le vocabulaire de l'esclavage dans le nouveau testament," *Revue Biblique* 85 (1978) 218-9.

30 H. G.Liddell and R. Scott, *A Greek-English Lexicon*. 9th edition with revised supplement. Oxford: Clarendon Press, 1996.

31 Gibbs and Feldman, "Josephus'" 290, 294, 295. They also note that the differing patterns of use of "slave" terms throughout the LXX raises the possibility of separate authorships (p. 300).

32 Gibbs and Feldman, "Josephus'" 292, 301.

33 As Flesher has noted (Flesher, *Oxen, Women or Citizens?* 203), six of the some 129

both biblically and post-biblically.[34] One might also question in this case why there is no similar division in terms for male slaves.

In summary: The evidence is consistent with the probability that the terms *amah* and *shifḥah* were a) considered synonyms, and that differences in use among the various pentateuchal books may be accounted for by editorial preference; b) were considered terms of servility.

1.1.2 North-East Semitic Versus North-West Semitic?

At least one scholar has attempted to relate the terms *shifḥah* and *amah* to apparent cognates in other Semitic languages. Morgenstern suggested a relationship between *amah* and אם, "mother," proposing that the clan of the *amah*-wife was called אום; he then proposed a derivation of *shifḥah* from a pre-biblical root שפח "to pour,"[35] noting an Arabic cognate, suggesting that this would indicate a woman into whom semen was "poured", and whose clan was called a משפחה.[36] His assessment of the meaning of *amah* and *shifḥah* took place within the context of his thesis that the biblical text reveals signs of a historical change from *beena* (matrilocal, matriarchat)-style marriage, in which the husband stays with the wife's clan, to *ba'al* (virilocal)-style marriage, in which the wife leaves with the husband. He thus concluded that both terms originally indicated a wife in a *beena* marriage. The later development of these words into slave terms was in his view a parallel of the change from *beena* to *ba'al* marriage, itself conditioned by increased access to foreign captive women and a consequent increase in the institutions of slavery and clientage.[37] The changeover involved in tracing one's lineage through one's father rather than through one's mother would, as Morgenstern notes, explain many of the differences in genealogy often noted between Genesis and Chronicles.[38] His conclusions

mishnaic sections relating to slaves refer to this distinction.

34 e.g. Jer. 34: 9; *mB.Metz.* 1:5.

35 One must note that the verb "to pour" in biblical and post-biblical Hebrew is spelled שפך.

36 Julian Morgenstern, "*Beena* Marriage (Matriarchat) in Ancient Israel and its Historical Implications," *ZAW* 47 (=n.s. 6) (1929) 99-101, 101-2.

37 Morgenstern, "*Beena* Marriage," 103.

38 Morgenstern, "*Beena* Marriage," 103ff.

were accepted by Bal, in forming her argument that the violence toward women reflected in the book of Judges was the result of this shift from what she calls patrilocal marriage to virilocal marriage, and the consequent tensions between father and husband.[39]

Morgenstern's observations do seem to suggest the quasi-kinship nature of both terms. Nonetheless, I believe his conclusions should be viewed with caution. Morgenstern offers other evidence in support of an original matrilocal clan organization: Jacob, for instance, stays with the clan of his wives; members of David's clan are referred to by the mothers' names; in non-P texts women "give birth" to children (-ילדה, ילדה ל), whereas in the later P texts it is men who "sire" them (the *Hifil* הוליד is used exclusively). While this evidence may hint at different types of social organization, it cannot conclusively support a linear, chronological change from matrilocal to virilocal organization, particularly as Morgenstern's theory seems to be predicated on a Bachofen-type assumption of an historical "advancement" from matriachal to patriarchal societies.[40]

Further, the etymological evidence that Morgenstern offers is not without difficulties. The term *amah* seems to be cognate with terms in other Semitic languages, including Akkadian *amtum* and Jewish Aramaic אמתא, אמהא, אמהתא.[41] Logically then, before one can argue for a connection between the Hebrew terms אמה, אם and אום, one would also be required to show that this slave woman/mother/clan relationship holds true in related languages.

With respect to the term *shifḥah*, certain of the dictionaries, like Morgenstern, have also suggested a connection between *shifḥah* and משפחה. Even-Shoshan (*s.v.* שפחה)[42] has noted a similar type of relationship between the Latin *famula*, "maid servant", and *familia*, "family." There is no agreement, however, as to the root of either of these Hebrew terms.

---

39 I shall discuss Bal's conclusions later on in chapter two.

40 Julian Morgenstern, "Additional Notes on *Beena* Marriage in Ancient Israel." *ZAW* 49 (=n.s. 8) (1931) 53. Blok, "Sexual Asymmentry" 29-31, has documented this tendency in 19th-20th century scholarship to find a "suppressed level of matriarchal culture" in ancient societies (p. 30), especially when scholars came across facts that appeared to contradict their assumption of a "norm" of male dominance.

41 There are also west Semitic cognates noted by J. Hoftijzer and K. Jongeling, *Dictionary of the North-West Semitic Inscriptions*. 2 parts. Leiden: E.J. Brill, 1995, *s.v.* אמה II.

42 אברהם אבן-שושן, המלון העברי המרכז. ירושלים: קרית ספר, תשמ"ח. [=Even-Shoshan]

Morgenstern's idea of "pouring" would seem to be more closely related to the biblical term שפך than to his proposed root שפח.[43] Another suggested derivation is the biblical ספח-שפח "to join," perhaps implying someone who is joined to the family; here too, however, there is no agreement as to the meaning of this root.[44]

The root *ŠPḤ* is also attested in other Semitic sources, specifically in Phoenician/Punic inscriptions. Some scholars argue for the meaning "clan, family" (Hoftijzer and Jongeling, *s.v.* *špḥ*$_1$), though other opinions are cited giving the meaning "servant" or "slave," particularly with respect to *Corpus Inscriptionum Semiticarum* [=CIS] i 165. This document is described as a tariff of payments for sacrifices at the Temple of Baal, probably deriving from Carthage and dating to the 4th century BCE.[45] After setting out the priestly tariff for various kinds of sacrifices, and exempting from payment those who are "poor in cattle or birds", lines 16-17 set out a further group of people (or sacrifices) who are to pay according to some fixed schedule; these lines are transliterated as follows:[46]

כל מזרח וכל שפח וכל מרזח אלם וכל אדמם אש יזבח [ ]
האדמם המת משאת על זבח כמדת שת בכתב[ת]

Cooke takes *ŠPḤ* here as related to Hebrew משפחה, and suggests the meaning "family"; Donner/Rollig similarly suggest a comparison with biblical Hebrew זבח משפחה, as in 1Sam. 20:6, 29.[47] Van den Branden,

---

43 There appears to be an Akkadian cognate in *sapāḫu* "to spill," though W. von Soden, *Akkadisches Handwörterbuch*. 3 vols. Wiesbaden: Otto Harrassowitz, 1965 [=*AWH*] relates this to a south Semitic root *ŠPḤ*.

44 Mandelkern assigns the meaning *adiungere* ("to connect") to the biblical ספח-שפח. There again appears to be an Akkadian cognate in *sapāḫu*, but with the opposite meaning of "to scatter" or "to disperse" particularly with respect to a household (*AHW* and Martha Roth, (current editor in charge) *The Assyrian Dictionary of the Oriental Institute of the University of Chicago*. Chicago: University of Chicago Press, 1956-2006 [=*CAD*]), based on which one might interpret the Hebrew *shifḥah* as referring to someone separated from her family. Adding to the confusion, Kohut (ed.) in , Vindobona, 1926 ,הערוך השלם [=Arukh] derives *shifḥah* from a root *shafaḥ* (translated simply as *unterjochen knechten)*, which it deems related to biblical ספחת "leprosy," A. Kohut (ed.), הערוך השלם Vindobona, 1926 *s.v* משפחה..

45 See Herbert Donner and Wolfgang Rollig, *Kanaanäische und aramäische Inschriften* (Wiesbaden Harrassowitz, 1962-1964) 2:84.

46 Donner and Rollig, *Kanaanäische und aramäische Inschriften.*

47 G.A. Cooke, *A Text-book of North-Semitic Inscriptions* (Oxford: Clarendon Press, 1903)

on the other hand, relates ŠPḤ to Hebrew *shifḥah*, assuming the latter to mean "*esclave qui répand l'eau sur les mains du maître*," and translates the provision as referring to various types of temple functionaries:

> *Tout allumeur et tout laveur at tout serviteur du banquet sacré, bref, tous les hommes (de cette categorie) qui offrirent un sacrifice...*[48]

Lidzbarski similarly gives the meaning "*Diener*."[49]

This evidence gives a slight hint that *amah* is more closely associated with East-Semitic sources such as Akkadian and Jewish Aramaic, and *shifḥah* with West-Semitic sources, such as Phoenician and Punic. In the former case, *amah*'s cognates suggest quasi-kinship terminology, while the *shifḥah*'s possible cognates may be more associated with the idea of a stranger or outsider taken within the family.[50] In biblical usage, as argued above, the terms became synonymous; it is interesting to consider, however, the kinship or quasi-kinship roles suggested by their cognate term.

1.1.2.A The amah as a Secondary Wife

We may note that the word *amah* has been found on a limited number of material remains, both pre- and post-exilic. Despite the assumption that *amah* refers to a slave, the context of these finds leads to the conclusion that the *amah* in each case was not a woman of low standing. The following summarizes the finds, based on scholarly articles:

121; Donner and Rollig, *Kanaanäische* 2:86. An attempt to get the sense of this word by comparison to the other terms is difficult, as these too are unclear. Both these works suggest מזרח may be related to Hebrew אזרח, perhaps implying "natives," or "a class of freemen," or "clan." For מרזח both note biblical Hebrew instances of this term (Jer. 16:5, Amos 6:7), which seem to indicate a type of celebration or "wake" (Cooke, *Text-book* 121-2; Donner and Rollig, *Kanaanäische* 186). מרזח is also attested in rabbinic Hebrew; חיים קסובסקי, אוצר לשון התלמוד (ירושלים: משרד החינוך והתרבות של ממשלת ישראל, 1954-1982) [=Kosovsky, *Concordance to Talmud*], *s.v.* רזח takes it as a combination of מרר and זחה (מרר / זח/זחה/זוח), and meaning similarly הרמת קול בין לבכי ובין לשמחה.

48 A. van den Branden, "Notes phéniciennes," *Bulletin du Musée de Beyrouth* 13 (1956) 94, 95.

49 M. Lidzbarski, *Handbuch der nordsemitischen Epigraphik nebst ausgewählten Inschriften.* Weimar: Felber 1898, 381, *s.v.* שפח.

50 See n. 65 of this chapter.

i) A Hebrew inscription associated with a tomb found in Siloam, identified as pre-exilic (approximately 700 B.C.E.), and reconstructed as follows:[51]

1. זאת [קברת...]יהו אשר על הבית אין פה כסף וזהב
2. [כי] אם עצמתו ועצמת אמתה אתה ארור האדם אשר
3. יפתח את זאת

1. This is [the grave of ...]yahu who was over[seer] of the house. Here there is no gold and silver,
2. [but] his bones and the bones of his *amah*[52] with him. Cursed is the person
3. who opens this.

ii) A seal from Amman, date pre-exilic, possibly 7th century B.C.E., with an Ammonite inscription:[53]

לעליה אמת חננאל

[belonging] to Aliyah, the *amah* of Ḥananel

iii) A 7th century seal with an Ammonite inscription transliterated as follows:[54]

'nmat *amah* dblbs

iv) A seal from the Jerusalem region, dated to the Persian province of Judah approximately 6th century B.C.E., with a Hebrew inscription, reconstructed as follows:[55]

---

51 Naḥman Avigad, "The Epitaph of a Royal Steward from Siloam Village." *IEJ* 3 (1953) 143, 150. The reconstruction and transliteration are those of Avigad.

52 Avigad ("Epitaph," 142-143) identifies אמתה אתה as an older form of possessive, using ה instead of ו; as a biblical instance of this construction he cites אהלה in Gen. 9:21.

53 Naḥhman Avigad, "A Seal of a Slave Wife," *Palestine Exploration Quarterly* (1946) 130; Walter Aufrecht, *A Corpus of Ammonite Inscriptions,* Ancient Near Eastern Texts and Studies 4 (Lewiston: Edwin Mellen Press, 1989) 87. Transliteration and translation are those of Avigad.

54 Adolf Reifenberg, *Ancient Hebrew Seals.* London: East and West Library. MCML (1950) #36; Naḥman Avigad, *Bullae and Seals from a Post-Exilic Judean Archive* Qedem 4. Transl. R. Grafman (Jerusalem: Hebrew University, 1976) 11, 19. The transliteration is that of Avigad.

55 Avigad, *Bullae and Seals* 11, 13, 17, 19 (English section); Ephraim Stern, *Material Culture*

לשלומית
אמת אלנ-
תן פח[וא]

[belonging to] Shelomit
amah of Elna-
tan gov[ernor]

The presumed meaning of *amah* as "slave woman" causes a certain scholarly dilemma. Aufrecht[56] notes the scholarly puzzlement at a "slave" being associated with a seal or tomb inscription, with some scholars suggesting[57] that *amah* in these cases refers to a royal title or an official functionary. Avigad, in his earlier articles discussing the Siloam description and the Aliyah seal, had maintained that the *amah* in each case must have been a "slave-wife"; he related this *amah* to the woman referred to in Exod. 21:7 given to an *eved* by his master. He assumed that she was not "legally" married, but possessing sufficient status to be buried with her "master," or to possess her own seal; alternatively, this might have been a widow, originally a slave, who, following the parallel of Code of Hammurapi [=CH] 171, became a freedwoman after her husband's death.[58] The Persian era seal, in contrast, caused him some doubt.

Though he still maintained the possible meaning of "concubine," that is, a slave woman with higher status by virtue of her relationship with her master, he also conceded that Albright's meaning of "functionary" could be appropriate.[59]

---

of the Land of the Bible in the Persian Period 538-332 BC (Warminster: Aris & Phillips, 1982) 200, 207, figure 329. The reconstruction and transliteration are those of Avigad.

56 Aufrecht, *Ammonite Inscriptions* 87-88.

57 See, e.g., Stern, *Material Culture* 200. Stern notes the prior opinion of Cross that Persian custom prescribed that only officials holding high rank possessed inscribed seals. He also refers to a seal of עשניהו עבד המלך (Ashnayahu *eved* of the king,) found at Tel Qasile, which he dates to the 4th century B.C.E. (p. 207). He cites the opinion of B. Mazar that the title עבד המלך was common in the First Temple period in Israel and Judah, and continued into the Persian period; the "king" in this case is taken to be the king of Persia. Cf. the opinion of Leshem, n. 22, who connects the self-deprecating use of *amah* with the rise of the monarchy.

58 Avigad, "Seal of a Slave Wife" 130-1; Avigad, "Epitaph of a Royal Steward" 145-6.

59 Avigad, *Bullae and Seals* 12-13. In support of the meaning of "concubine," Avigad cites the terse discussion in *yKet.* 5:2 29d of the legal status of the *pilegesh*, as indicating the potentially high standing of such a woman. The precise meaning of this passage, is however,

Avigad in his arguments notes an opinion (expressed by Y. Yadin) that the *amah* could be a "legal wife". This was supported by a Neo-Assyrian document in the name of Zaqûtum, consort of Sennacherib and mother of Esarhaddon; in it she describes herself with the sign GÉME.[60] This sign was read by certain scholars[61] as *amtu* (or the NA equivalent *antu*). This apparent association of an Akkadian slave term, cognate with the Hebrew *amah,* with a royal consort led Yadin to suppose that the Hebrew *amah* could also refer to someone of "wifely" rank.[62] Later opinion, however, reads the sign GÉME here as SAL.KUR; it is to be read as equivalent to SAL.É.GAL, and is to be Akkadianized as *ša ekalli* rather than *amtu.*[63] As such, it is understood as "the wife of a king" or "a woman of the highest rank."[64] Yet SAL.KUR is also associated with slaves; it has been read as "woman of the mountain", and, as such, an indication of the source of many slaves as "foreigners".[65] Again, this opinion seems circular, positing the alternate reading due to the apparent incompatibility between a king's consort and the presumed meaning of *amtu* as "slave." It would seem, therefore, that it is not necessary to interpret *amtu* as indicating a slave in this case.

I propose that from the context of these instances we may accept these women were sexual partners; perhaps we may call them quasi-wives.

---

a matter of issue; this will be discussed later on in this chapter.

60 Assyrian and Babylonian Letters [=ABL] XII 1239, line 2, titled by Leroy Waterman, *Royal Correspondence of the Assyrian Empire* (Ann Arbor: University of Michigan Press, 1930) [=*RCAE*] 1239, as "Oath of Fealty to Ashurbanipal." Line 1 has GÉME *ša Sin-aḫḫe-eriba*; GÉME is repeated in line 10.

61 For example, Waterman, *RCAE* 1239 and 327; Hildegard Lewy, "Nitokris Naqi'a," *JNES* 11 (1952) 282.

62 Yadin's opinion is noted by Avigad, "Epitaph of a Royal Steward" 146, n. 21.

63 See, e.g., *AHW, s.v. ekallu(m),* B2, and the opinion of H. Tadmor, cited by Avigad in *Bullae and Seals* 12-13, n. 20.

64 *CAD s.v. ekallu*, in *ša ekalli.*

65 See, e.g., Guillaume Cardascia, "Le statut de l'etranger dans la Mesopotamie ancienne," *Recueils de la Société Jean Bodin* 9 (1958) 106. Certain scholars have argued, based in particular on LH 280-281, that a distinction was made for "inland" slaves that protected them from being sold "abroad" (see, e.g., Koschaker, *Rechtsvergleichende* 106; contra Driver and Miles, *The Babylonian Laws* 1:224). Bernard J. Siegel, "Slavery During the Third Dynasty of Ur," *American Anthropologist* ns. 49, No. 1 pt. 2 (1947) 42-43 argues that a similar protection existed during the Ur III period. We may also note that *mGitt.* 4:6 provides that a slave sold outside the land of Israel ceases to be a slave.

1.1.3 Conclusion: On the Slave-Wife Continuum

The evidence above points to a presumption that female slaves and wives existed along the same continuum:

a) *shifḥah* and *amah* were used biblically as synonyms, their difference probably reflecting differences in ethnic origin;

b) these female slaves were dependants (whose dependence could be mimicked in the use of slave terms for non-slaves);

- the same woman could be both wife and slave; and there is material evidence of a wife-like status for some *amahot*;

c) consistent with the overarching notion of hierarchy as the ideal, the Bible displays great concern to place these women in some kind of family or kinship structure; conversely, there is no hint that marriage was prohibited to these women, or that their primary use was to be exploited as concubines or breeders.

Point (c) in particular will be brought out more fully in the next two chapters, specifically on the issues of the matrilineal principle and the slave as property. In the meantime, this exercise in philology will focus on two other sets of terms that shed light on the hierarchical structure that is envisioned biblically.

1.1.4 Conclusion

We may conclude that while the *amah* and *shifḥah* were dependants - this would account for the self-effacing use, and their use in lists with the term *eved* - their sexual use was carefully regulated. The biblical evidence suggests that the terms *shifḥah* and *amah*, if not completely synonymous, at least implied no difference in legal rank; yet the epigraphic evidence of *amah* does suggest the term was used, in pre- and post-exilic Israel, to describe someone of high social status. Further, we note that "wife" terminology, אשה, is applied to women also described as *shifḥah* and *amah*. Do these facts suggest that the biblical *amah* was a "concubine" or some other "close-to-wife" status? In chapter three we shall examine the provisions of Exod. 21:2-11, the most extensive pentateuchal regulation concerning the *amah*. We shall focus in particular on the supposed connection of v. 4 of this pericope with the matrilineal inheritance of slavery, and the effect of vv. 7-11, which seem to suggest that the *amah* was fated to be a "concubine" to the master.

1.2 ARE THERE BIBLICAL TERMS FOR SECOND GENERATION SLAVES?

Our next study of biblical terms should question whether there are definite biblical terms denoting second-generation slaves. Specifically, do the biblical phrases *ben amah*, *ben bayit* and *yelid bayit* suggest the existence of a specific status applied to second generation slaves, and thus the existence of a "hereditary" slave class? This possibility seems strengthened by the fact that in some cases the terms seem to be used in parallel with the male slave term *eved*. Further examination of the terms in their various contexts, however, suggests instead that they imply some inferior attribute or characteristic rather than a specific status, and in some cases might be applied to non-slaves.

1.2.1 ben amah

The question with respect to the *ben amah*, as Fensham notes, is whether *ben* in this case means literally "the son of", so that the term simply means "son of an *amah*" with no further implications as to status, or whether it implies "a member of the group of," and thus partaking of the social or legal position of the *amah*.[66] If it is the latter case, one might argue that the term implies the existence of a slave status inherited through the mother, and, in fact, three of the six biblical instances of *ben amah* appear to use this term as a synonym for the male slave term *eved*. Yet the various nuances of meaning connected with all the biblical occurrences, as well as the disappearance of this term (except in biblical references) in post-biblical sources, argue against its being incontrovertible evidence of a hereditary status. Furthermore, several instances point to the *amah* in this phrase as describing a type of secondary wife, rather than a slave.

66 F. Charles Fensham, "The Son of a Handmaid in Northwest Semitic," *VT* 19 (1969) 315.

1.2.1.A *Ishmael*

Three of the biblical instances of this term refer to specific individuals, thus offering the possibility of assessing their status contextually. Two describe Ishmael (the son of Hagar, the *amah/shifḥah* of Sarah and the *ishah* of Abraham), and specifically his standing in relation to his "half-brother" Isaac:

- Gen. 21:10 (E stratum), in which Sarah insists that Ishmael, "the son of that *amah*," not inherit with her own son Isaac.

- Gen. 21:13 (E stratum), the promise to Abraham that this *son of an amah* Ishmael, as his descendant, will, like Isaac, also lead a nation.

I would argue that there is nothing within the biblical context to indicate that Ishmael was addressed as or treated as an *eved*. There is evidently an issue, at least in the view of the wife Sarah, with respect to Ishmael's position *vis-à-vis* her biological son Isaac. The terminology in Gen. chapter 21 emphasizes this issue: vv. 9-10 highlight Sarah's view of Hagar and her son as rivals and outsiders: "the son of Hagar the Mitzrit, whom she had born to Abraham...", "cast out this *amah* and her son", while v. 11, which describes Abraham's view, calls Ishmael "his son". Underlying this rivalry may have been questions of the right to inherit the father's property, or position, yet there is nothing in the biblical narratives regarding Ishmael that suggests chattel slavery or other legal subordination to Isaac or Sarah.

The treatment of Ishmael in earlier post-biblical sources confirms that in these texts he was not associated with the term *eved*;[67] the concern is rather to emphasize his inferior standing in various respects in relation to Isaac, or to justify his harsh treatment at the hands of the matriarch Sarah.

Commenting on Gen. 25:9, which describes Isaac and Ishmael burying their father, *Gen. Rabbah* (Rom) at 62:3 states that the order of the names in this verse is deliberate:

---

67 The Targumim and Septuagint [=LXX] translate all the biblical instances of *ben amah* literally (בר אמתא, ‘o *υιος παιδισκης*), and thus offer no hint as to its meaning.

בן אמה חולק כבוד לבן הגבירה

The *ben amah* [Ishmael] defers to the son of the main wife [Isaac].

The midrash at 47:5 on Gen. 17:21 uses an *a fortiori* argument, to suggest that Isaac was the only one to benefit from the covenant:

רבי יוחנן בשם רבי יהושע בר חנינא בן הגבירה למד מבן האמה
הנה ברכתי אותו כבר שמעתי אותו זה יצחק וחפרתי אותו זה יצחק והרבתי אותו זה יצחק
ולישמעאל כבר שמעתי אותו ע"י מלאך רבי אבא בר כהנא בשם רבי בירי כאן בן האמה
למד מבן הגבירה הנה ברכתי אותו זה ישמעאל והפרתי אותו זה ישמעאל והרבתי אותו זה
ישמעאל ק"ו וזאת בריתי אקים את יצחק

R. Yoḥanan in the name of R. Joshua b. Ḥaninah: The son of the main wife learned [his status] from the *ben amah*: "I have blessed him" - this is Isaac; "I will make him fruitful" - this is Isaac; "I will make him multiply"- this is Isaac; while I have already informed Ishmael through an angel. R. Abba bar Kahana in the name of R. Biryai: the *ben amah* learned [his status] from the son of the main wife: "I will bless him" - this is Ishmael; "I will make him fruitful"- this is Ishmael; "I will make him multiply" -this is Ishmael; *a fortiori* "I will establish My covenant with Isaac [Gen. 17:21]."

Yet the same midrash, addressing the wording in Gen. 17:20, also confirms the promise to Abraham that Ishmael will receive a leader status equal to that of Isaac:

ולישמעאל שמעתיך הנה ברכתי אתו והפריתי אתו והרביתי אתו במאד מאד
שנים עשר נשיאם יוליד ונתתיו לגוי גדול

With respect to [your concerns for] Ishmael, I have heard you. I have blessed him, and will make him fruitful and cause him to multiply exceedingly; he will sire twelve princes, and I will make him into a great nation.

Concern thus seems to be to render Ishmael as inferior (because he is addressed only by an angel), but not servile, to Isaac as the preferred heir (because of the covenant).

The later biblical commentator Naḥmanides meticulously examined the subtle differences in terminology used in Gen. with respect to Isaac and Ishmael. The significance of these distinctions, in his opinion, lies in their different relationships to, and recognition by, their father Abraham. He notes, for instance, that in Gen. 25:19 Abraham's relationship to Isaac is described with אברהם הוליד את יצחק "Abraham sired Isaac";[68] this stands in contrast to Ishmael, described in 25:12 as ישמעאל בן אברהם אשר ילדה הגר המצרית שפחת שרה לאברהם... "Ishmael the son of Abraham whom Hagar the Egyptian, Sarah's *shifḥah*, bore to Abraham." This contrast, which lies in the reference to the siring by the father in the case of Isaac, emphasizes the difference in Abraham's relationships to his two descendants. Naḥmanides further notes (commentary to Gen. 30:5) the interesting point that though the sons of Bilhah and Zilpah are technically, like Ishmael, sons of *amahot* they are never described as such. This difference in his view again depended on the father's acknowledgment:[69]

> ותלד [בלהה] ליעקב בן: הזכיר בכל השפחות ליעקב להגיד כי הוא חפץ ומודה בהם ואיננו נקרא לו בן האמה רק בן ליעקב כבני הגבירות המתיחסים אליו...
>
> *And [Bilhah] gave birth to a son to Jacob*: [The particular wording *a son to Jacob*] is mentioned with respect to all Jacob's *shefaḥot*, to indicate that he wanted and acknowledged [these sons], and we do not refer to [such a son] as *ben ha-amah* but as a son to Jacob, like the sons of the main wives who were [automatically] his relations.[70]

What Naḥmanides' nuanced reading of the Genesis narratives again suggests is that the legal and financial situation of an "unacknowledged" *ben amah* was precarious, but not that of a slave.

---

68 [There was also significant concern about Abraham's paternity of Isaac given that Sarah had just been released by Avimelekh and the pregnancy is announced. Targum Yonatan [= TY] (Gen. 21:2) and other midrashim (e.g. Bereishit Rabbah (Theodor-Albeck) 52:1-2) emphasize Isaac's likeness to Abraham as proof of his paternity. The biblical text itself reemphasizes Abraham's paternity a number of times. TM.]

69 As will be noted below, Naḥmanides' emphasis on acknowledgment by the father happens to mirror the situation of a *mār amtim* in the Hammurapi laws.

70 This idea of legal precariousness and perhaps social inferiority with respect to the four sons of Bilhah and Zilpah is suggested also in Chap. 24 of the apocryphal document entitled "Joseph and Aseneth" in *The Old Testament Pseudepigrapha,* 1985, pp. 177-247, edited by J.H. Charlesworth. New York: Doubleday (trans. C. Burchard); perhaps reading between the lines of Gen. 37:2, it ascribes to the four sons feelings of envy, and has Pharaoh's son later inciting them to hatred of Joseph by claiming that the latter intended to have them disinherited as being only the "children of maidservants" (v. 9).

(Interestingly, Naḥmanides echoes here an argument found in the Laws of Hammurapi [=LH]. The semantic equivalent of *ben amah*, the *mār amtim*, is found rarely in Akkadian.[71] Significantly however, it is mentioned in LH 170-171, which speaks of the fate of children of an *awīlum* who have been borne to him by an *amtum*. In one instance they are referred to as *mārū amtim*, the literal equivalent of Hebrew בני אמה "sons of an *amah*." If acknowledged by the father,[72] they share the father's estate equally with children of the first-ranking wife (*mārū ḫīrtim*); if not, they are released from any claim of slavery (*wardūtum*) at the father's death. The children's existence also appears to affect the status of the mother in ss. 146-7: an *amtum* who has borne children to an *awīlum* may not be sold by a prior-ranking *nadītum* (a temple dedicatee who, if married, brought in other women to bear children for her husband). The legal effect of such provisions is to negate any possibility of "hereditary" slave status, at least for children of an *amtum* who were sired by the master.)

1.2.1.B *Avimelekh*

The third biblical instance of *ben amah*, in Judges 9:18, refers to Avimelekh, who is described as the son of Gideon by the latter's *pilegesh* (Judges 8:31) - again, there is the suggestion that this phrase applies to sons of secondary of inferior wives. Here Avimelekh's "half-brother" Yotam - again there is an issue of fraternal hierarchy - castigates the people of Shekhem for assisting Avimelekh in the slaughter of Gideon's other sons, and then appointing this בן אמתו as king. Again, the status of Avimelekh is nowhere explicitly stated or implied to be that of an *eved*; at most, the half-brother Yotam questions his right to kingship, perhaps by imputing to him an

71 There is also the phrase *mār amat ekalli*, found in Neo-Assyrian [=NA] documents. Radner considers this expression as the palace equivalent of a "houseborn slave", and it will be discussed below with reference to the *yelid bayit*.
We may also note the documents (primarily temple ration lists) from the Ur III period and earlier, that I. Gelb has called GÉME.DUMU texts (see, e.g. I.J. Gelb, "The Arua Institution." *RA* 66 1972] 1). In his opinion, however, the women referred to in these lists were not primarily slave women (and their children), but marginalized persons (including the elderly, female prisoners and *ex voto* women and children "donated" by families who could not support them), collected and maintained by the temple (ibid. 3, 9, 12).

72 Cf. the commentary of Naḥmanides, above at n. 3.

inferior and treacherous "stock," as suggested in his use of the parable of the thorn (Judges 9:15-20):

> ויאמר האטד אל העצים אם באמת משחים אתי למלך עליכם באו חסו בצלי ואם אין תצא אש מן האטד ותאכל את ארזי הלבנון...
> ואם באמת ובתמים עשיתם עם ירבעל ועם ביתו היום שמחו באבימלך וישמח גם הוא בכם. ואם אין תצא אש מאבימלך ותאכל את בעלי שכם

> The thorn said to the trees: If you are truly anointing me as king over you, come and have refuge in my shade; but if you are not, a fire will issue from the thorn and consume the cedars of Lebanon...
> [Similarly] If today you have acted truthfully and honestly with Yeruba'al and his house, rejoice in Avimelekh, and let him also rejoice in you. But if not, a fire will issue from Avimelekh and consume the Shekhemites...[73]

Morgenstern analyzed the Avimelekh story as a clear example of *beena* marriage, suggested in part by the fact that Avimelekh remained with his mother, and claimed the kingship perhaps because his mother's clan were natives of Shekhem (Judges 9:2), and the crown had previously been offered to his father Gideon.[74] His designation by Yotam as a *ben amah* may thus indicate a pejorative use, a reflection of Avimelekh's status as a usurper.

---

73 Thorn parables are found elsewhere in Near Eastern literature; see, e.g. 2Kings 14:9, and the Aḥiqar document (trans. J.M. Lindenberger, "Ahiqar," in *The Old Testament Pseudepigrapha,* ed. J.H. Charlesworth [New York: Doubleday, 1985] 2:479-507, at 506 ll. 165-166), both of which seem to associate the thorn with the idea of a rebuke against those accepting improper authority. The author known as Pseudo-Philo also made this connection explicit in his comment on Yotam's parable in Judges 9: "And now the bramblebush will be for you in this hour like Abimelech, who killed his brothers unjustly and wishes to rule among you. If Abimelech be worthy of them whom he wishes to rule for himself, let him be like the bramblebush that was made to rebuke the foolish among the people" (trans. D. J. Harrington, "Pseudo-Philo," in ibid. 2:297-377, esp. 350-351).

74 J. Morgenstern, "*Beena* Marriage" 93, 109 n. 4. As discussed earlier in this chapter (1.1.2), Morgenstern proposed that *amah* was the usual term to designate a woman in a *beena* marriage (ibid. 101-102); he also argued in Julian Morgenstern, "Additional Notes on *Beena* Marriage in Ancient Israel," *ZAW* 49 (=n.s. 8) (1931) 57-58, that the Judges editor called Avimelekh the son of a *pilegesh* because his readers, living in a time when *beena* marriage had been supplanted by the *ba'al* form, would not have understood the word *amah*. As I will argue later, *pilegesh* has a specific meaning not equivalent to *amah*.

1.2.1.C As Parallel to *eved* in Psalms and Sabbath Law

The three remaining biblical instances of *ben amah*, as noted, appear to treat the term as a parallel to *eved*. In two instances the parallel is explicit:

- Psalm 86, a plea by one who calls himself עבדך (v. 3), and then goes on to describe himself as a *ben amah* (v. 16): תנה עזך לעבדך והושיעה לבן אמתך "Give your strength to your *eved*, and save the son of your *amah*".

- Psalm 116:16, in which the supplicant describes himself as: אני עבדך בן אמתך. "I am your *eved*, the son of your *amah*..."

Fensham has summarized the scholarly treatment of the term *ben amah* in the two psalms,[75] noting that the phrase is either taken as indicating a "houseborn slave" or read as if the second noun were *emet*, not *amah*, as *ben amittekha*, "the son of your fidelity."[76] Fensham rejects, I believe correctly, both suppositions: a definite parallel between *eved* and *amah* (not *emet*) seems intended, but this is merely figurative, an expression of humility.[77] A similar difference in viewpoint may be seen among the traditional commentators to these Psalms.[78] Rashi and Metzudat David both equate the *ben amah* in Psalm 86:16 with a *yelid bayit*, "a houseborn person," and assumed this indicated a slave with a greater connection with, and thus greater feelings of humility toward, the master:

בן האמה משפיל את עצמו לפני אדוניו יותר ממקנת כסף
שבן האמה יליד בית הוא וגדל בחיק אדוניו

---

75 Fensham, "Son of a Handmaid" 320-321.

76 The latter is the position of M. Dahood, who suggests this phrase echoes the idea of faithfulness expressed in v. 11 of Psalm 86 (אהלך באמתך) and v. 10 of Psalm 116 (האמנתי). He suggests also a parallel with the Akkadian *arad kittišu*, "his true servant", found in the El-Amarna letters, as a type of address form used by a vassal to one's suzerain: in Mitchell Dahood, *Psalms II, 51-100.* Anchor Bible (Garden City: Doubleday, 1968) 296; Mitchell Dahood, *Psalms III, 101-150.* Anchor Bible (Garden City: Doubleday, 1981) 150. Dahood suggests on literary grounds that Ps. 116 is earlier than post-exilic (ibid. 145).

77 Fensham, "Son of a Handmaid" 320.

78 Each position also affects modern translations. Most of the English translations (e.g. KJV, JPS, Schocken) use the literal "son of a handmaid/slave girl" for the translation of the biblical *ben amah*; the Jerusalem Bible, which similarly translates "son of a slave girl" in the other four instances of *ben amah*, uses "son of a pious woman" for Pss. 86:16 and 116:16.

> The son of an *amah* supplicates more to his master than one bought with money, because the *ben amah* is a *yelid bayit*, and grew up in his master's household.

Radak (Psalm 86:16), on the other hand, assumed simply a figurative use of *ben amah* as indicating deference to the Deity, suggesting that one's attitudes in this regard are more closely influenced by the example set by one's mother:

> טבע האם נקשר בבן יותר מטבע האב...אני עבדך משני פנים
> שהרגלתי עצמי בעבודתך ועוד כי היה בטבעי ג"כ כי אמי היה* אמתך
>
> *likely an error for היתה
>
> The mother's nature is more closely connected to the son than the father's nature... "I am your servant" has two facets: I have become accustomed to serve You, and also it was in my nature because my mother was Your *amah*.

The sixth instance of *ben amah* occurs in Exod. 23:12 (E stratum), in which the Sabbath is explicitly extended to all "members" of the household: למען ינוח שורך וחמרך וינפש בן אמתך והגר "...so that your ox and your donkey may rest, and your *ben amah* and the stranger may be refreshed."[79] It is this occurrence of *ben amah*, in Fensham's opinion, that definitely refers to a slave, given its apparent parallel with the Sabbath observance provision in the two versions of the Decalogue, in which the terms *eved* and *amah* are used: Exod. 20:10 states אתה ובנך ובתך עבדך ואמתך ובהמתך וגרך "you and your son and your daughter and your slave (*eved*) and your maid servant (*amah*) and your cattle and your stranger," while the version in Deut. 5:14 states אתה ובנך ובתך ועבדך ואמתך ושורך וחמרך וכל בהמתך וגרך "you and your son and your daughter and your slave (*eved*) and your maid servant (*amah*) and your ox and your ass and all your cattle and your stranger." The Samaritan Pentateuch does in fact make this parallel explicit, as its Exod. 23:12b matches more closely the decalogue wording and order: למען ינוח עבדך ואמתך כמוך וכל בהמתך והגר "in order that your slave (*eved*) and your maid servant (*amah*) shall rest like you and all your cattle and the stranger."[80]

---

79 It is of interest to note that the verb וינפש is also used in Exod. 31:17 to describe God's ceasing work on the Sabbath.

80 The Samaritan Targumim correspond with the literal עבדך ואמתך (Sj) or שמשך ואמתך

Given, however, both the change in wording and the change in order in MT Exod. 23:12, it is not clear that the בן אמתך here is intended as a deliberate parallel to the עבדך of the Decalogue verses. As the phrase is used pentateuchally only by E, it may be interpreted with reference to its uses in Gen., as indicating in this case too simply a dependant family member, whether descended of the main wife or not.

The *Mekhilta deR. Ishmael, Dibaḥodesh,* on Exod. 20:10 (Lauterbach) also noted, but could not easily explain, the change in wording in Exod. 23:12. An assumption was made that the Decalogue verses referred to circumcised *avadim*, while Exod. 23 referred to uncircumcised *avadim:*

> עבדך ואמתך - אלו בני ברית. אתה אומר אלו בני ברית או אינו אלא עבד ערל.
> כשהוא אומר וינפש בן אמתך והגר הרי עבד ערל אמור, הא מה ת"ל ועבדך
> ואמתך אלו בני ברית.

> *Your eved and amah* [Exod. 20:10] - these are members of the covenant. You say these are members of the covenant, but perhaps this means an uncircumcised *eved*. When it says *so that the son of your amah... and the stranger may be refreshed* [Exod. 23:12], this is the uncircumcised *eved*, thus when Scripture says *your eved and amah,* these are members of the covenant.[81]

Further in the work, however, this attempted harmonization among the three Sabbath provisions leads to difficulty. It is noted that R. Eliezar actually prohibited the ownership of an uncircumcised *eved*; the Mekhilta (*Pisḥa*) then attempts, anonymously, to reconcile this prohibition with its comments on Exod. 23:12, restricting the latter to a somewhat farfetched case:

> אם כן מה תלמוד לומר וינפש בן אמתך והגר אלא הרי שלקחו רבו ערב שבת
> עם חשיכה ולא הספיק למולו עד שהחשיך, לכך נאמר וינפש בן אמתך

> [Given the prohibition against owning uncircumcised *avadim*, and the *Mekhilta's* assumption that Exod. 23:12 refers to uncircumcised *avadim*] What does Scripture mean by *so that the son of your amah and the stranger may be refreshed [in that verse]*? If the master bought [a male slave] on Sabbath eve and it was getting dark and the master was not able to circumcise him

(Sa).

81 This passage goes on with a parallel distinction in the use of the term *ger*: in Exod. 20:10 it means *ger tzedeq*, a convert, while in Exod. 23:12 it refers to a *ger toshav*.

before it got dark, it is for this [particular case] that it says *so that the son of your amah... may rest.*[82]

This tradition of interpreting the *ben amah* in Exod. 23:12 as referring to an issue of circumcision is also found in some of the Targumim, but not consistently. Pseudo-Jonathan for Exod. 23:12 translates בר אמתך ערל (the uncircumcised son of your *amah*), thus following the first quote in the *Mekhilta*. Neofiti,[83] however, has ברא דאמתך יהודייתה (the son of your Jewish *amah)*, a position which would contradict not only the *Mekhilta* but also the rule in *mQidd.* 1:2 that a Hebrew *amah* is to be released upon reaching puberty (i.e. before she can give birth). One may argue, therefore, that it is only through somewhat convoluted analysis that the *ben amah* of Exod. 23:12 is made equivalent to the *eved* of the Decalogue verses.

1.2.1.D Conclusion

We may argue that neither Ishmael nor Avimelekh is slave-like, though they are perhaps socially and legally in a precarious position, especially with respect to their "half-brothers." The other biblical instances of this term might be referring to slaves, but are not unequivocally indicative of an inherited slave status. If we take the biblical *ben amah* as the functional equivalent of the *mār amtim* in the LH, this would imply that the second generation (at least if they are also children of the master) does not remain enslaved.

1.2.2 yelid bayit - Houseborn Slave?

Though the literal meaning of this term (discussed further below) seems to be "child of the house", the term is often taken by traditional and modern translators to mean specifically a "houseborn *slave*."[84] The use of a specific

82 R. Eliezer's prohibition against ownership of uncircumcised slaves was not held unanimously, as illustrated in the following baraita in *bYev.* 48b:

ת"ר: מקיימין עבדים שאינם מלין דברי רבי ישמעאל רבי עקיבא אומר אין מקיימין...

Our sages taught: We retain slaves who are not circumcised: these are the words of R. Yishmael. R. Akiva says: We do not retain [uncircumcised slaves].

83 A.D.Macho, *Neophyti 1, Targum Palestinense ms. de la Biblioteca Vaticana,* Madrid: Consejo Superior de Investigaciones Científicas, 6 vol. 1968-79 [=Neofiti].

84 See, for instance, the JPS translation to Gen. 17:12, 23, 27 and Jer. 2:14, and the Schocken

term to refer to slaves born in the master's house is also noted in other legal systems. Wiedemann, for instance, notes that "houseborn slaves" were prized among the Greeks and Romans; such *οικογενεις* or *vernae* were, he suggests, more likely to be loyal and closer to "real" members of the family.[85] Further, the practice of referring generally to slaves, or even employees, as "children" is also widespread;[86] this terminology suggests a pejorative appellation, though it has been suggested that kin-based societies might deliberately create fictive kinship terms for slaves, to give them the appearance of being incorporated into the master's family.[87] It may also be argued that "houseborn" slave carries the connotation of "native-born," as opposed to "foreign"; there are frequent attestations in Near Eastern legal sources of a partiality toward "native" slaves, particularly evident in prohibitions or penalties with respect to the sale of such slaves outside their lands.[88]

Despite such precedents, however, I shall argue that the phrase *yelid bayit* in both biblical and post-biblical use is simply a general term for a household member, which may include, but is not restricted to, individuals who are also slaves. This argument is based first on an examination of the biblical contexts surrounding this term; second, on an assessment of the anomalous features of both the biblical term and the Akkadian *wilid bītim*; and third, on post-biblical use. This evidence suggests that the term is in the nature of a trope, connoting in some cases a loyal or trusted individual,

---

translation to Gen. 14:14.

85 Thomas Wiedemann, *Greek and Roman Slavery* (London: Croom Helm, 1981) 7, 112, 185.

86 We may note the use of Greek *παις* for a male slave, or the use of the pejorative "boy" for an adult male slave in the United States. S.D. Goitein, *A Mediterranean Society* (Berkeley: University of California Press, 1967) 1:93, notes that "employees" in the Geniza documents were referred to as "boys", whether they were free persons or slaves, even if such persons were "long past the stage of apprenticeship." In modern business practice adult female employees are still often referred to as "girls".

87 See, e.g., Orlando Patterson, *Slavery and Social Death: A Comparative Study* (Cambridge: Harvard University Press, 1982) 62-63; Igor Kopytoff and Suzanne Miers, "African 'Slavery' as an Institution of Marginality," in *Slavery in Africa. Historical and Anthropological Perspectives,* Eds. S. Miers and I. Kopytoff (Madison: University of Wisconsin Press, 1977) 23. The latter note that slavery and kinship relationships may both be redefined in terms of each other.

88 See the opinions cited in note 60 of this chapter, section 1.1.2.

rather than specifying a particular hereditary status.

Most significant with respect to the association of the *yelid bayit* with slavery is Jer. 2:14, in which the prophet refers to Israel's decline:

העבד ישראל האם יליד בית הוא מדוע היה לבז

Is Israel an *eved*? Is he a *yelid bayit*? Why has he become prey?

The parallelism here certainly suggests that *yelid bayit* is synonymous with the male slave term *eved*, and this verse generally suggests a reference to someone of subservient status. This is in fact the interpretation of Jer. 2:4 given in Midrash *Pesiqta Rabbati* (*parshah* 27, 3), which contrasts the position of a son with that of a purchased *eved*:

שמעו דבר ה' בית יעקב לאמר וכל משפחות בית ישראל...כשאתה עושה רצונו אביך ואתה בנו ואם לאו על כרחך שלא בטובתך קונך ואתה עבדו שנאמר העבד ישראל אם יליד בית הוא

Hear the word of the Lord, House of Jacob, and all the families of the House of Israel [Jer. 2: 4]...when you do as He desires He [is] your father and you are His son; if not, [you are] His purchase, against your will and not for your benefit, and you are His *eved*, as it says [ibid. v. 14]: *Is Israel an eved, a yelid bayit....*

Despite the strong parallelism in the verse from Jeremiah, the association with slavery is not explicit or even suggested in the remaining six occurrences of *yelid bayit*, which are all pentateuchal:

Gen. 14:14 (possibly E stratum) refers to the mustering of Abraham's household to free Lot:

וירק את חניכיו ילידי ביתו שמנה עשר ושלש מאות

...he mustered his retainers, his *yelidei bayit*, numbering 318...

The meaning of the word חניכיו, which seems to be used here as a parallel to *yelidei bayit*, is admittedly unclear.[89] Yet the number 318 is large for

89 Thomas Lambdin, "Egyptian Loan Words in the Old Testament," *JAOS* 73 (1953) 150 suggests the term has an early Egyptian cognate, and translates "armed retainers." Jubilees 13:25 (at least the English translation by Wintermute based on the Ethiopic) refers to

slaves, and we may posit that the verse is referring to all those with a blood relationship (real or even putative) to Abraham's household.[90]

There are five instances of the term in sections attributed to the P stratum. Gen. 17, regarding all the males in Abraham's house who were to be circumcised, contains four of these:

כל זכר לדרתיכם יליד בית ומקנת כסף מכל בן נכר אשר לא מזרעך הוא
המול ימול יליד ביתך ומקנת כספך

And throughout the generations, every male among you [shall be circumcised....] As for the *yelid bayit* and the one bought from an outsider who is not of your offspring, they must be circumcised, [both the] *yelid bayit* and one who has been bought by you (vv. 12-13)

ויקח אברהם את ישמעאל בנו ואת כל ילידי ביתו ואת כל מקנת כספו
כל זכר באנשי בית אברהם

Then Abraham took his son Ishmael, and all his *yelidei bayit* and all those he had bought, every male in Abraham's household... (v. 23)

וכל אנשי ביתו יליד בית ומקנת כסף מאת בני נכר

...and all his household, the *yelid bayit* and the one that was bought from an outsider... (v. 27)

Finally, Lev. 22:11 refers to the occupants of a priest's household who may eat קדש (that is, the priestly tithes):

וכהן כי יקנה נפש קנין כספו הוא יאכל בו ויליד ביתו

A priest who purchases someone - the one purchased may eat of them [the tithes], as well as his *yelid bayit*...

"servants," as does Josephus in *Ant.* 1:78 (*οικεταις*).

90 One tradition (cited below under *ben bayit*) mentions this difficulty and assumes the number refers only to Abraham's *ben bayit* Eliezer, as the letters of the name אליעזר add up under the rules of *gematria* to 318.

Most significant in these five instances is the fact that the term *yelid bayit* is paired with מקנת כסף or קנין כסף, that is, "one acquired with silver." One could argue that these pairs are intended as parallels, both referring to slaves, and suggesting the two methods, acquisition and birth, by which such slaves might be attached to a household, and emphasizing that both groups are to be treated equally with respect to these aspects of the cult. Yet it is not unequivocally clear that "one acquired for silver," i.e. purchased, necessarily refers to a slave. Certainly there are biblical instances in which slavery seems to be associated with subjection to purchase and sale: Lev. 25:42 provides, with respect to Hebrews, לא ימכרו ממכרת עבד "they shall not be sold in the [manner of] selling an *eved*"; there are also prohibitions against "resale" of the minor girl sold by her father as an *amah* (Exod. 21:8) and of the captive woman (Deut. 21:14).[91]

Yet as Kopytoff and Miers note, property-like transactions (whether sales, pawns, or other forms) are not necessarily restricted to, or characteristic of, slaves alone.[92] In the biblical text there are references to the pawning of children, and the acquisition of wives.[93] We may note, for example, the

---

91 I exclude the reference to כי כספו הוא in Exod. 21:21; this issue will be discussed further below.

92 Kopytoff and Miers, "African Slavery" 7, 11-12, note that, particularly in societies in which "rights-in-persons" form an integral part of kinship and marriage systems, such rights (for instance, in a wife, or her children) may be acquired through property-like transactions involving transfers of material goods.

93 Such examples also abound in Mesopotamian legal sources. See, e.g. the discussion of Siegel "Third Dynasty of Ur" 12-23 with respect to the sale of children in the Ur III period; LH ss. 114-116 with respect to the taking of a household member as a *nipûtum* ("distraint"), and ss. 117-119 with respect to the surrender of both family members and slaves to a creditor *ana kaspim* or *ana kiššātim* (sale or distraint); MAL A44, C+G2, 3 and 7 with respect to a non-slave used as a *šapartum* (pledge); and the discussion of M. Dandamaev, *Slavery in Babylonia, From Nabopolassar to Alexander the Great (626-331 BC),* Transl. Victoria Powell, Ed. Marvin Powell (DeKalb: Northern Illinois University Press, 1984) 157-180, with respect to the pledging of free persons in the NB period. The precise details of these human surety transactions are matters of debate, especially with respect to whether a family member could be permanently enslaved by such a transaction. A summary of many of these issues may be found in Chirichigno's discussion of the LH and MAL provisions, Chirichigno, *Debt Slavery* 61-85. It should also be noted that the precise functions of "distraints", "pledges" and other types of surety are not necessarily equivalent in different legal systems; a useful overview of the issues involved may be found in John H. Wigmore, "I. The Pledge-Idea; A Study in Comparative Legal Ideas," *Harvard Law Review* 10 (1897) 321-350.

phrasing in Gen. 31:15 of the complaint by Rachel and Leah against their father: הלוא נכריות נחשבנו לו כי מכרנו; "Were we not considered strangers to him, as he has sold us [to Jacob]." We may further note the specific wording of Exod. 12:43-5, which sets out who is allowed to eat of the Passover sacrifice:

> ...כל בן נכר לא יאכל בו. וכל עבד איש מקנת כסף ומלתה אתו אז יאכל בו
> תושב ושכיר לא יאכל בו.

> ...No stranger shall eat of it. Any *eved* of a man, acquired by silver - if he has circumcised him he may then eat of it. A sojourner and a hired worker may not eat of it.

The fact that *eved ish* needs to be specified here in addition to *miqnat kesef* suggests that the two are not synonymous.

I exclude here Exod. 21:21, regarding the *eved* who dies several days after a beating by his master; the master is exempted from the punishment that would be due if the *eved* died immediately, with the phrase כי כספו הוא. This would seem at first glance to be directly equating the *eved* with money, suggesting that the loss of this "money" is punishment enough. This interpretation would require כספו to be taken as a metaphor for "property" or "chattel," whereas the general biblical use of כסף seems to be in the literal meaning of "money" or "silver." I thus agree with Westbrook that the הוא in this phrase does not refer to the *eved*, but rather to the penalty assessed to the master,[94] and may be interpreted as "it is a matter of his [the master's] silver" - that is, as in v. 19 in connection with a non-slave, the perpetrator (here the master) must pay the relevant costs of the victim.[95]

94 Westbrook, *Biblical and Cuneiform Law* 100. We may note that Gen. 42:27, וירא את כספו והנה הוא , also contains the word הוא in the sense of "it is" in reference to כסף.

95 Rashi to Exod. 21:21 seems to be suggesting something similar: אף על פי ששהה מעת לעת קודם שמת חייב ("even though he lingers for a [specific] time before he dies, he [the master] is liable"). I agree, however, with Chirichigno, *Debt Slavery* 176, 179, that this verse, like 21:19, refers to a victim who recovers; contra Westbrook, *Biblical and Cuneiform Law* 100, who argues that the slave has died, and the master's "money" is a forfeiture of his debt. It is interesting to note on the latter point that Chirichigno and Westbrook have different views as to whether Exod. 21:20-21 refer to "debt slaves" or "chattel slaves." Chirichigno (ibid.) argues that the verses refer to chattel slaves. Westbrook (ibid.) argues that the verses concern debt slaves, and are to be seen as parallel to LH 116. The latter provides for

One may conclude that the term *yelid bayit* has less to do with the difference between a born slave and a bought slave and more to do with the distinction between an insider and an outsider and their relative degrees of assimilation into the household. The latter idea is explicitly suggested in Gen. 17, in which the מקנת כסף is described as מכל בן נכר אשר לא מזרעך הוא (v. 12), and as מאת בני נכר (v. 27). The same association between the sold person and the stranger is also suggested in several of the other passages noted above: Gen. 31:15 (Were we not considered strangers to him); Exod. 12:44 (while v. 43 prohibits any בן נכר from eating the Passover sacrifice, v. 44 seems to specifically exempt the stranger acquired as an *eved*, if he is circumcised); and Exod. 21:8 regarding the girl sold as an *amah* by her father, who may not be sold "outside": לעם נכרי לא ימשל למכרה. Gen. 14:14, in contrast, suggests that the *yelidei bayit* for Abraham were likely persons particularly loyal to his household, whether slaves or otherwise.

1.2.2.A The Form and Meaning of *yelid* and the Akkadian *wilid bītim*

The form *yelid* is unusual in biblical Hebrew. Mandelkern (*s.v.* יליד) treats it as the construct of a hypothetical noun *yalid*, meaning "child" or "offspring" (similar to the absolute and construct forms for נשיא and נתיב). The remaining instances of *yelid* not connected with *bayit* seem to refer to people who are natives of particular geographical areas.[96] One could argue that *yelid* is a participle form of the verb ילד so that the phrase does mean literally "houseborn"; yet the biblical passive participle form is ילוד.[97] One might thus posit that the form is an Aramaism, a form of the *Pe'al* passive participle; such a form, ילידא, is in fact used by Onkelos to translate יליד (as well as the feminine noun מולדת in Lev. 18:9, part of the incest provisions).

---

monetary compensation to be paid to a debtor who has provided a slave as a debt pledge, if the creditor has killed the pledge by striking or abuse. The biblical verses in his view also refer to a case of debt slavery, a Hebrew debtor in straitened circumstances having sold or pledged a family member or slave to his creditor, who has killed the pledge. I shall not debate this point here, but I do not think the asymmetry in the talionic remedies in Exod. necessarily points to a difference between debt and chattel slavery.

96 Num. 13:22, 28 and Josh. 15:14, referring to ילידי הענק; 2Sam. 21:16, 18 with בילידי הרפה; and similarly 1Chr. 20:4 with מילידי הרפאים.

97 See, e.g., 1Kings 3:26, 27; Job 14:1, 15:14, 25:4; 1Chr. 14:4 (in plural).

It must also be asked whether the biblical phrase bears any relationship to the Akkadian phrase *wilid bītim*. The word *wilid*, the construct of the noun *(w)ildu(m)*, "offspring, progeny" is found in most dialects;[98] the specific phrase *wilid bītim*, however, is attested according to the dictionaries only in Old Babylonian sources. If there is a semantic relationship between the Old Babylonian and biblical terms, an interesting question of influence is thus raised, as the Old Babylonian sources would predate the conventional redaction period for the P stratum, to which most of the pentateuchal instances of *yelid bayit* are attributed, by at least 1000 years.

Many of the OB occurrences of *wilid bītim* do happen to be applied to individuals otherwise identified as slaves; the dictionaries, as well as Mendelsohn,[99] thus accept the meaning of "houseborn slave." Nonetheless, it may be argued that the term is in the nature of a trope, rather than a description, as the same singular masculine form is used also with respect to females, and with respect to more than one person; further, there is the apparently anomalous (i.e. non-OB) use of the spelling *i-i-lid* in at least two cases. The following examples illustrate this range of use:

1) Cunieform Texts [=CT] VIII 28ᵇ = *Urkunden des Altbabylonischen Zivil- und Prozessrechts* [=UAZP] #288 (Sippar, Sumula-ilum) appears to be an inheritance dispute; lines 8-9 list among the disputed persons and items belonging to the "defendant" a male slave described as a *wilid bītim*, who is contrasted with a purchased slave:

   1 *wardum* PN1 *wilid bītīša* 1 *amtum* PN2 *ša ina ramānīša*
   PN3 *išāmuši*
   one male slave PN1, a *wilid* of her house, one female
   slave PN2, whom PN3 [the defendant] purchased for herself

   (The distinction appears to have been of no significance regarding the outcome of the claim against the defendant, which was rejected).

2) In *Vorderasiatische Schriftdenkmäler* [=VAS] 16 4:25 (a letter cited in

98 *CAD*, *s.v. ildu*; *AHW*, *s.v. wildum*.
99 Mendelsohn, *Slavery in the Ancient Near East* 57.

CAD, s.v. "*ildu*") the term is used to refer to a female slave. The context also suggests the idea of the *wilid bītim* possessing a specific training or skill:

aššum amtum ša tašpuram šumma wilid bītim u išparat šāmši
As to the female slave of whom you wrote me, if she is a *wilid bītim* and a weaver, buy her

3) In *Textes Cunéiforms du Louvre* [=CTL] 1 29 = *Vorderasiatische Bibliothek* [=VAB] 6 143 (Samsu-iluna), a letter appears to refer to two individuals as *ilid bītim* (lines 13-15):

PN1 *u* PN2 *ilid bītim ardūya ša ilki illakū*
PN1 and PN2, *ilid bitim*, are my slaves who perform my *ilku* service.

4) A "pedigree" statement was noted by J.J. Finkelstein in several slave sale documents of the late Old Babylonian period.[100] Certain slaves are described in these documents as *wilid bītim ša Bābilim* (the *wīlid bītim* of Babylon); in contrast, slaves in other of these sales are described simply as Subarians of various cities. In Finkelstein's opinion, the terms refer to two contrasting classes of slaves, foreigners and houseborn of Babylon (though the latter would have been ultimately of foreign descent).

5) Kraus came to a similar opinion regarding the use of the term *wilid bītim*in a provision of the Edict of Ammiṣaduqa (1646-1626 BCE). The provision is found in a section of the Edict that releases certain debt slaves, and contrasts the situation of the *wilid bītim* with other people who have been placed as pledges. Should a citizen of certain named cities have had a debt foreclosed against him, and so placed himself, his wife or his children into servitude as a pledge against the debt, they are now released as a result of the Edict. If, however, certain slaves of these cities were placed as pledges, their release is not

100 J.J. Finkelstein, "Ammiṣaduqa's Edict and the Babylonian Law Codes," *JCS* 15 (1961) 99.

effected; these slaves are described (section 19') as [*šumma*] GÉME. ARAD *ui-li-*[*i*]*d* É [*ša*] *mār Numḫia mār Emut-balum*... which Kraus took as referring to three separate groups, including "houseborn slaves," belonging to free persons of certain cities: "*Wenn eine Sklavin (oder) ein Sklave (oder) ein im Hause geborener (Sklave) eines freien Mannes von Numhia, eines freien Mannes von Emut-balum...*"[101] He argued that the essential characteristic of such houseborn slaves was that they were permanent; unlike those acquired by capture, sale or pledge, who might become free without any act of the owner (by ransom, redemption or proof of citizenship status). That is, with a houseborn slave, the owner ran no risk of loss.[102]

6) There is at least one instance, however, in which there is no explicit connection between *wilid bītim* and slavery. TCL 133 = UAZP #82 (Dilbat, 11 *Samsu-iluna*) is a slave sale contract in which a female slave is purchased (line 3) *ana wilid bītim ša Dilbat* (for the *wilid bītim* of Dilbat). The context suggests that perhaps the male, like the female, is also a slave, yet there is no indication (such as the determinative IR or SAG) that this individual is a slave. Based on this contract Schorr argued that *wilid bītim* was probably an official title, like *mār bītim* and *mār ekallim*.[103]

The instances above suggest the term is used most often with respect to slaves. It is arguable, however, that the term itself does not specifically connote a second generation slave, but is being used to give a "pedigree", to a slave or other dependant of a household, whose ancestry may not be known or considered relevant. One might hypothesize at this stage, given the apparent use of *wilid bītim* as a trope, the similarity to the biblical *yelid bayit*, and the possible Aramaic form of the latter, that both the Akkadian and Hebrew terms are borrowed.[104]

---

101 F.R. Kraus, *Ein Edikt des Königs Ammi-Ṣaduqa von Babylon* (Leiden: E.J. Brill, 1958) 41.

102 Kraus, *Ein Edikt des Königs* 173-174.

103 M. Schorr, *Urkunden des Altbabylonischen Zivil- und Prozessrechts* (Leipzig: J.C. Hinrichs'sche Buchhandlung, 1913) 127.

104 A further study might be undertaken to assess whether the term in OB documents is used in connection with West-Semitic names.

1.2.2.B Other Akkadian Equivalents

The phrase in the Old Babylonian texts reviewed always has *(w)ilid* spelled syllabically, while *bītim* may be syllabic or in the form É. Certain scholars argue that semantic equivalents to *wilid bītim* may be found in other dialects, sometimes spelled logographically. This is more tenuous, however, as it is not clear that these suggested terms actually refer to slaves.

umzarḫu/unzarḫu

This term is found in OB texts from Mari as well as later texts, including Neo-Assyrian [=NA] and Neo-Babylonian [=NB]. Radner argues (following K. Deller[105]) that when used in reference to slaves the term means "*im Haushalt geborener Sklave*," and is to be contrasted with the *ša šīme*, "*gekaufter Sklave*."[106] The NA texts she cites in support, however, are equivocal; they do not clearly refer to slaves, as the following examples indicate:

1) Assyrian Documents and Deeds [=ADD] 1041 = Kouyunjik Collections of the British Museum [=K] 958 = State Archives of Assyria [=SAA] XI 29
   This is identified in SAA XI as a "List of Audience Gifts and a Memorandum." Lines 6'-9' read:

   ina pān unzarḫī ša kalzani
   ša 3 MU.AN.NA.MEŠ
   sinnutu
   lā šaknu

   Concerning the 3 year old *unzarḫī* of the *kalzu*, the *sinnutu* is not established.
   While SAA XI takes *unzarḫī* as "domestic slaves", the *CAD* (*s.v. sinnutu*) takes it as "freedmen." Adding to the difficulty in this case are the precise meanings of *kalzu* and *sinnutu*. The former term is taken

105 K. Deller, "Assyrisch um/nzarḫu und Hebraisch 'azraḥ," *ZA* 74 (1984) 235-9, discusses the use of the Akkadian term as a loanword in Hebrew, in the form of אזרח.

106 Karen Radner, *Die neuassyrischen Privatrechtsurkunden als Quelle für Mensch and Umwelt* SAAS VI. (Helsinki: The Neo-Assyrian Text Corpus Project, 1997) 205.

as an area around or connected with the palace (SAA XI and *CAD, s.v. kalzu*); the *CAD* notes, however, that the word might be read *ribzu.* The latter term is taken by SAA XI as "brand marked," while the *CAD* tentatively assigns the meaning "assessed."

2) CT 53 21 = K 1097 + King's Excavations Collection at British Museum [= Ki] 1902-5, 10, 13 = SAA X 316
This is identified by SAA X as a letter from the physician Urad-Nanaya to Essarhaddon. Lines 7-14 relate a speech of the king regarding the loyalty of certain servants (LU*ARAD.MEŠ-*šu*). Lines 14-18 provide:

...dabābu
ša Ṣābī[šu] šarri bēlī
idubub unz[arḫī ḫard]ūte [gap]
ammar ṭēnšu hassūni
ina tirik libbi mētū

the king my lord made a speech about [his] men, and the [ale]rt *unz[arḫī]* ...as many as are remembering their orders are dying of a throbbing heart

In addition to the gap, the context is completely unclear.

mār amat ekalli = DUMU.GÉME.É.GAL (NA)

Radner considers this expression in NA documents as the palace equivalent of a houseborn slave; she suggests, however, that it could also refer to a high-ranking member of the court, given instances in which such persons own property.[107] One of the texts cited apposes such persons with "bought people," but it is not clear that either term refers to slaves; it may simply appose paid (outside) workers to those who are members of the court household:

1) Assyrian and Babylonian Letters (Harper) [=ABL] 99 (SAA I, 99)
This document is identified by SAA I as a letter to Sargon concerning

[107] Radner, *Die neuassyrischen* 206-207. In addition, such persons according to the texts cited act as witnesses, and one is a debtor.

the manpower available for repairs to the Ekallate. Lines 10'-16' read:

mārē šīme (DUMU.MEŠ ŠÁM.MEŠ-e) *iqabbūnišunu*
ulâ zakkûte ša rab ekalli annurig
lē'u ša amēlūti[108] *šāmūti*
ša mārē amat ekalli (DUMU.MEŠ GÉME É.GAL) *asaṭṭar ina pān šarri*
bēlīya usebbila 370 *šunu Ṣābe*
90 *Ṣābe šarri šunu* 90 *ša kutal*
190 *dullu ša šarri lêpušū*

[Are they] sons of bought persons, as they call them,
or exempt persons of the palace manager?
I am now inscribing a writing board with the bought personnel
[and] the "sons of the palace maidservant," and to the king
my lord I am sending it. They are 370 men.
90 are king's men, 90 are reserves,
let 190 do the king's work.

The context, according to Garelli, concerns the number of people available to Tab-Ṣil-Ešarra to perform work on the palace in Ekallate; the question seems to concern the status of some as exempt (*zakkûte*); he considers the DUMU.MEŠ ŠAM.MEŠ-e to refer not to slaves but to hired workers.[109] One might argue with respect to the DUMU.MEŠ GÉME É.GAL that this means simply those permanently attached to the palace, with GÉME meaning simply "woman".

1.2.2.C Post-Biblical Occurrences

The term *yelid bayit* does not appear in either Mishnah or Tosefta, despite the former work's clear establishment of hereditary slavery. One might have expected such a reference, for instance, in *mQidd.* 1:3, to specify the method by which a *yelid bayit* acquires his freedom. There are sporadic occurrences of the term in the Talmudim and aggadic works; these, however, give no consistent association of the term with slaves, and in fact show some controversy over the precise meaning of *yelid*.

108 SAA I reads DUMU.MEŠ, but the sign appears to be LÚ*.MEŠ.

109 Paul Garelli, "Problèmes de stratification sociale dans l'empire assyrien," *RAI* 18 (1972) 76.

Certain of the talmudic instances are primarily in the nature of quotes from Lev. 22:11 used to support rulings as to who is eligible to partake of priestly *terumah*, and here the phrase is clearly not restricted to slaves. *yYev.* 7:4 8b gives an interpretation of *yelid bayit* that seems to takes *yelid* as emphasizing the idea of an actual birth:

ומה טעמון דרבנין הם יאכלו והם יאכילו הראוי לוכל מאכיל ושאינו ראוי לוכל אינו מאכיל התיבון הרי ממזר הרי אינו ראוי לאכול ומאכיל שנייא היא דכתיב יליד בית מעתה הילוד מאכיל ושאינו ילוד אינו מאכיל

...What is the reason of the sages? *They* [the bought person and the *yelid bayit* of Lev. 22:11] *shall eat* [*terumah*]; *they shall eat* - one who is fit to eat [*terumah*] can render [his mother] capable of eating [*terumah*]; one who is not fit to eat [*terumah*] cannot render [another] capable... as it is written *yelid bayit* - thus one who is born [*yalud*] causes another to be capable of eating [*termuah*] and one who is not born does not render [another] capable of eating.

The effect of this passage is to interpret the *yelid bayit* of Lev. 22:11 as referring to someone actually born; such a person can also render his mother fit to eat *terumah*. One who is a fetus at the relevant time is not, in contrast, a *yelid bayit*, and thus cannot render its mother eligible to eat *terumah*. An example of the latter situation is given in *yYev.* 9:5 10b. This passage comments on the related *mYev.* 9:5, which debars various women from eating the priestly *terumah*; among such women is the *bat yisrael* married to and left pregnant by a priest, who then dies. The Gemara explains why such a case does not fit within Lev. 22:11:

מכהן ליליד בית אין כאן יליד בית...

(According to the wording proposed by Qorban HaEdah): [Pregnant] by a priest - [Lev. 22:11 includes] *a yelid bayit* - there is no *yelid bayit* in this case [i.e. since the fetus does not qualify to eat *terumah*, neither does its mother].

Sifra *Emor parshah* 5:4-5 (Weiss, 97b) questions why Lev. 22:11 needs to refer to both the *yelid bayit* and the *qinyan kesef* (acquired), appearing to assume, on the basis of an *a minore ad majorem* argument, that the *yelid* would be more closely related to the household, at least in cultic matters, than a *miqnat kesef*. It then questions whether the analogy should be based instead on the presumed monetary value of each; it concludes, however, that both are entitled to partake of *terumah* whether they have a monetary worth or not. In this case it is not clear whether either term refers specifically to a slave:

יליד בית מה תלמוד לומר אם הקנוי קנין כסף אוכל ויליד בית לא יאכל.
אילו כן היית אומר מה קנין כסף שיש בו כסף אף יליד בית שיש בו כסף
ומנין שאע"פ שאין שוה כלום תלמוד לומר ויליד בית מכל מקום.
עדין אני אומר יליד בית בין שיש בו כסף בין שאין בו כסף אוכל.
אבל קנין כסף אם יש בו כסף אוכל, אם אין בו כסף לא יאכל.
תלמוד לומר קנין כספו ויליד ביתו מה יליד ביתו
אף על פי שאינו שוה כלום אף קנין כספו שאינו שוה כלום.

> *yelid bayit* [Lev. 22:11] - why is this stated? If the one who is purchased – a *qinyan kesef* - partakes, would a *yelid bayit* not partake? But in that case you might have said just as a *qinyan kesef* has a monetary [value] so [it must also be] a *yelid bayit* who has a monetary [value]. How [would we justify a *yelid bayit*] worth nothing? Thus it says "*veyelid bayit*" - of any kind. I could still say that a *yelid bayit*, whether with or without money [value] partakes; a *qinyan kesef*, though, if he has money [value] partakes, but if has no money [value] he does not partake. Thus it says [both] *qinyan kaspo veyelid beito* - as [it includes] a *yelid bayit* worth nothing, so [it includes] a *qinyan kesef* worth nothing.[110]

The following discussion in *bShabb.* 135b does refer specifically to the child of a female slave. The passage discusses the necessity of circumcising a male convert or a male slave, and the particular interaction of this rule with the terminology in Gen. chap. 17; the question is posed as to when the child of one's female slave would be considered a *miqnat kesef* or a *yelid bayit*:

הא בהא תליא כתנאי יש יליד בית שנימול לאחד ויש יליד בית שנימול לשמנה
יש מקנת כסף שנימול לאחד ויש מקנת כסף שנימול לשמנה

110 The question of how there can be a *miqnat kesef* with no monetary value is discussed in *bGitt.* 42b-43a. The question arises within a general discussion of whether a slave with a tenuous connection to a priest's household (such as one whose value is contingent on the compensation the master might receive if the slave is gored by an ox, or a *miqnat kesef* without value) may eat *terumah*.

יש מקנת כסף שנימול לא' ויש מקנת כסף שנימול לשמנה, כיצד?
לקח שפחה מעוברת ואח"כ ילדה זהו מקנת כסף הנימול לשמונה
לקח שפחה וולדה עמה זו היא מקנת כסף שנימול לאחד
ויש יליד בית שנימול לשמנה כיצד?
לקח שפחה ונתעברה אצלו וילדה זהו יליד בית הנימול לשמנה
רב חמא אומר ילדה ואח"כ הטבילה זהו יליד בית הנימול לאחד
הטבילה ואחר כך ילדה זהו יליד בית הנימול לשמנה

This is dependent on a dispute between Tannaim. There is a *yelid bayit* who is circumcised on the first [day], and a *yelid bayit* who is circumcised on the eighth [day]; there is a purchased person who is circumcised on the first [day], and a purchased person who is circumcised on the eighth [day]. There is a purchased person who is circumcised on the first [day], and a purchased person who is circumcised on the eighth [day]: How [does this arise]? If one bought a pregnant *shifḥah* and she then gave birth, [the child] is a purchased person who is circumcised on the eighth day. If one bought a *shifḥah* and her [newborn] infant, [the child] is a purchased person who is circumcised on the first day. There is a *yelid bayit* who is circumcised on the eighth [day]: How [does this case arise]? If one bought a *shifḥah* and she became pregnant in his [house] and gave birth, this is a *yelid bayit* who is circumcised on the eighth day. Rav Ḥama says: If she gave birth and then had a ritual bath, this is a *yelid bayit* who is circumcised on the first day. If she had a ritual bath and then gave birth this is a *yelid bayit* who is circumcised on the eighth day.

Based on this passage, the tannaitic criterion for a slave who is a *yelid bayit* appears to be the place where the child was conceived. Thus no case is put forth for a *yelid bayit* circumcised on the first day. Any child conceived elsewhere, though born in the master's house, is still a purchased person. Rav Ḥama appears to address this lacuna by offering a further refinement, if not contradiction: a *yelid bayit* is someone born in the house, but his circumcision status depends on whether his mother was converted before she gave birth. If so, the child is an Israelite, and the usual eight-day rule applies. If not, the child is a foreigner, and must be converted immediately. There are, however, conflicting principles evidenced with respect to such cases. *Eccl. Rabbah* 7:3-4, part of a series of traditions about the sage Yaaqov of Kfar Gevuryah, seems to contradict *bShabb.* 135b:

הורה יעקב איש כפר גבוריא בצור על בנה של נכרית שהוא נימול בשבת.

> שמע רבי חגי שלח ואייתינה. א"ל מן הן הוריתה. א"ל מן הן דכתיב ויתילדו על משפחותם וכתיב יליד בית ומקנת כסף. אמר ארבעיניה דילקי. א"ל ובר נש דאמר מילתא דאורייתא ילקי. אמר לא הורית טבאות. א"ל מן הן...דאמר לא תתחתן בם. למה כי יסיר את בנך, בנך הבא מישראלית קרוי בנך ואין בנך הבא מן הגויה ומן השפחה קרוי בנך אלא בנה.
>
> Yaaqov of Kfar Gevurayah taught at Tyre regarding the son of a gentile woman, that he could be circumcised on the Sabbath. R. Ḥaggai heard [this] and sent for him to come. He said to him: Based on what did you teach [this]? He replied: From that which is written [Num. 1:18]: *they gave the pedigrees of their families* and it is written [Gen. 17:12] *a yelid bayit and one purchased with money*. [R. Ḥaggai] replied: Lie him down to be flogged. [Yaaqov] replied: Is a person who stated the substance of the Torah to be flogged? [R. Ḥaggai] said: You have not taught properly. [Yaaqov] replied: From what [should this be deduced]? [R. Ḥaggai replied]... As it says: *Do not marry them* [Deut. 7:3]. Why? *Because they will lead your son astray* [Deut. 7:4] - your son by an Israelite woman is called *your son*, your son by a gentile or slave woman is not called *your son*, but her son.

1.2.2.D Conclusion

The term *yelid bayit*, like the term *miqnat/qinyan kesef*, does not necessarily refer to slaves. It seems to particularly emphasize the aspect of houseborn, but for reasons other than to distinguish slaves from non-slaves. This is especially evident in the presumed earliest (E stratum)[111] occurrence of this term in Gen. 14:14. If there is a relationship between the biblical *yelid bayit* and the OB *wilid bītim*, one might posit a common Aramaic influence. Post-biblical sources confirm that *yelid bayit* could be used to describe non-slaves.

1.2.3 ben bayit

Though usually translated straightforwardly as "son of the house," this term is of interest because of its occasional translation as "houseborn slave." From the relevant biblical citations, however, it is not absolutely clear that it refers to slaves, as opposed to simply a general household member, or

111 See Tzemah Yoreh's website: www.biblecriticism.com and his book, *The First Book of God*, Berlin: Walter De Gruyter, 2010.

perhaps even a household administrator.

In Gen. 15:3 (J stratum), which states: והנה בן ביתי יורש אותי[112] - "my *ben bayit* will inherit [from] me," the term *ben bayit* apparently describes Abraham's potential heir Eliezer - "apparently" because he is not named in this verse, only in the immediately preceding one, though by tradition he is also the object of this verse. The Fragment Targum, for instance, has for the בן ביתי of Gen. 15:3 ואלי[עזר] בר בי[תי] Eliezer's status is, however, unclear, as he is described in the preceding v. 2 (possibly E) only with the exceedingly unclear ובן משק ביתי הוא דמשק אליעזר (and the one in charge of my household is Dameshek Eliezer). Mandelkern (*s.v.* משק) translates *mesheq* as *possessio* "possession", apparently suggesting that *ben mesheq* implies an "owned" person or chattel. Both the LXX and *Jubilees*, however, seem to have assumed that *mesheq* in v. 2 was a slave's name: the LXX at Gen. 15:2 has *ὁ δὲ υἱὸς μασεκ τῆς οἰκογενοῦς μου οὗτος δαμασκὸς ελιεζερ* (the son of Masek my home-born female slave, this Eliezer of Damascus), and follows through by translating the *ben bayit* of v. 3 as *οικογενης* ("house born" - Liddel and Scott), while Jubilees (14:2) has "And the son of Maseq the son of my handmaid is Eliezer of Damascus."[113] *Gen. Rabbah* (Rom) 44:11 equates the *ben mesheq* of Gen. 15:2 with a *ben bayit*,[114] and with the *yelidei bayit* of Gen. 14:14, through the person of Eliezer, though never explicitly calling him a slave:

> ר"ל בשם בר קפרא אמר בן משק ביתי בר ביתי הוא אליעזר שעל ידו רדפתי מלכים עד
> דמשק ואליעזר היה שמו שנא' וירק את חניכיו ילידי ביתו שי"ח
> מנין אליעזר הוי יח וג' מאות

> R. Lazar said in the name of Bar Qapara: *ben mesheq of my house* [Gen. 15:2] - he is a *ben bayit* of my house, Eliezer, with whose aid I chased kings to Damascus. And Eliezer was his name, as it says, *And he armed his retainers, his yelidei bayit* [318 of his house - Gen. 14:14]. Where do we get 318? [By

---

112 The Samaritan Pentateuch in this verse has the imperfect יירש instead of the participle form.

113 O.S. Wintermute, "Jubilees," in *The Old Testament Pseudepigrapha,* Ed. J.H. Charlesworth. (New York: Doubleday, 1985) 84 n. 14a.The translator suggests here that the author of Jubilees followed the LXX in this respect. H. Fox suggests that the *bayit* in this verse may have been understood as "woman," one of its post-biblical meanings.

114 The Peshitta translation similarly translates the *ben mesheq* in v. 2: ואליעזר דרמוסקיא בר ביתי ("Eliezer the Damascene my *ben bayit*").

gematria, the numerical equivalent of the letters of Eliezer] אליעזר is 318.

The term *ben bayit* is also found in Eccl. 2:7, where it is paired with purchased slaves: קניתי עבדים ושפחות ובני בית היה לי (I bought male and female slaves, and I acquired *benei bayit*...). Though the parallelism may suggest that the *benei bayit* are houseborn (as opposed to purchased) slaves, there is nothing else in the context to suggest a particular reference to slaves. The use of the accompanying verb היה in singular, though the phrase is in plural, further suggests the phrase is a collective noun, and may thus imply a general term for "household."

One further relevant citation may be the בני בית הרכבים (men of the house of the Rekhabites) in Jer. 35:5. Keukens suggests that these were homeborn slaves of the house of Rekhab.[115]

Most of the targumim for Gen. 15:3 translate *ben bayit* with the literal בר ביתי, giving no hint as to the precise meaning. This term בר ביתא, however, also appears in the Imperial Aramaic used at Elephantine. Several of the documents from the Ananiah archive (for instance, Porten B3.11) contain a witness signature of נחום בר ביתא.[116] What is unusual about this witness is the lack of a father's name. In contrast, other witnesses are described as PN1 *bar* PN2, or with an adjective of nationality. This may indicate that the בר ביתא here was a slave (though evidently capable of acting as a witness); but it may also have been sufficient to identify him as belonging to the house.

Targum Pseudo-Jonathan proves more enlightening in this case. In Genesis 15:3 the phrase is translated as בר פרנסת ביתי, implying someone dependent on the support of the household.[117] This phrase seems related to the Hebrew בן משק ביתי; in fact, Onkelos translates the בן משק ביתי in Gen. 15:2-3 as בר פרנסא. This term suggests someone dependent on the household, though not necessarily a slave. The Targum for Eccl. 2:7, in contrast, suggests the *benei bayit* were some sort of household administrators

115 K. Keukens, "*Die rekabitischen Haussklaven in Jeremia* 35," *Biblische Zeitschrift* n.f. 27 (1983) 230.

116 The *CAD* (*s.v.* "*bītu in mār bīti*") similarly cites a source (BE 91: 20) in which the Akkadian *mār bīti* describes a witness.

117 Sokoloff (*s.v.* פרנסה) and Dalman (*s.v.* פרנוסא) give as the meaning of פרנסה "support" or "maintenance." Dalman suggests a comparison with Greek *πϱονοος* "careful, prudent" (Liddell and Scott).

(גזברין), distinguished from the *eved* and *amah*, who contributed to the support of the household:

קניתי עבדין ואמהן מבניהון דחם ושאר עממיא ונכראין וגזברין
דממנן על מזונא דביתי הוו לפרנסא יתי...

I acquired male and female slaves from the children of Ḥam and other nations and foreigners, and [I had] stewards in charge of the food of my house for my support...

1.2.3.A Akkadian *mār bīti*

This phrase is the semantic equivalent of בן בית. The *AHW* (*s.v. marū* #10) takes *māru* in such phrases as *mār ālim* and *mār bītim* as generally *Angehöriger von*. It identifies *mār bīti* from OB sources on, and in an LB source, as referring specifically to a *Haussklave*. Dandamaev similarly suggested that the term in NB-LB sources was likely to refer to a "houseborn" slave.[118] The *CAD* (*s.v. bītu in mār bīti*), in contrast, identifies *mār bīti* as an LB term meaning "administrator within a household" (or, when referring to a deity, as the first-born son of a temple's god); at least one source (BE 9 14:6) is cited in which the same person is referred to as both a son (DUMU) to PN2 and a *mār bīti* (LÚ.DUMU.É) to PN3, making it unlikely that such person was a slave.[119] Dandamaev's conclusion is based primarily on the fact that most of the LB *mār bīti* sources, which are from the Murašu archives, seem to describe not "family members" but rather individuals who were used, like those identified as slaves, as agents in the family business. Yet he too acknowledges that the term might also include free persons, noting that there is nothing else in the sources indicating that this term is used as a synonym for other slave terms, or that these people were sold, branded

118 Dandamaev, *Slavery in Babylonia* 100-1. Mendelsohn, *Slavery in the Ancient Near East* 57 was also of the opinion that the phrase referred to a houseborn slave.

119 S. Kaufman, *The Akkadian Influences on Aramaic* (Chicago: University of Chicago Press, 1974) 70, similarly argues that the meaning in LB is "administrator, steward." He argues that both the Akkadian and Aramaic forms are calques (i.e. loan-translations) from Iranian, but that the בר ביתא found at Elephantine may be of a completely different origin. This logic is unclear, unless he is making an assumption that the Elephantine instance must refer to a slave; nor is it clear why the biblical references to בן בית need be loanwords.

or pledged, as one might expect of slaves. That is, there may be individuals “belonging to” a household who are neither family members nor slaves.

1.2.3.B Post-Biblical Sources

The majority of instances emphasize the *ben bayit* as one in a position of trust, and thus as someone who can be relied upon as an agent or representative. This is particularly clear from the mishnaic citations. In *mTer.* 3:4, the *ben bayit* is mentioned as one who can act as another’s agent with respect to the separation of *terumah*:

...הרשה את בן ביתו או את עבדו או את שפחתו לתרום תרומתו תרומה.

...One who authorizes his *ben bayit*, his *eved*, or his *shifḥah* to separate *terumah* - it is valid *terumah*.

We may note here that the term is specifically distinguished from slaves; it is also distinguished from the term פועלים in the following mishnah, perhaps implying that the *ben bayit* (like slaves) would have more than a temporary economic connection with the household. *MShevu’ot* 7:8 includes a *ben bayit* along with others who have control over another’s property, and who can be required to take an oath (with regard to this property) without a specific claim being made against them:

ואלו נשבעים שלא בטענה השתפין והאריסין והאפוטרופין והאשה הנושאת והנתונה בתוך הבית ובן הבית

These can be made to take an oath without a claim: partners, tenants, guardians, the wife who engages in business within the household, and the *ben habayit.*

Again, nothing in the section particularly indicates a slave. The commentator Penei Moshe (at *yShevu’ot* 7:8 38a *s.v. uven habayit*) took the term *ben habayit* here as literally the son of the house who has control over his father’s estate, as yet undivided, on behalf of the other beneficiaries; the Bavli, on the other hand, assumed it was a household member who engaged in business (*bShevu’ot* 48b):

תנא בן הבית שאמרו לא שנכנס ויוצא ברגליו אלא מכניס לו פועלין ומוציא לו פועלין

מכניס לו פירות ומוציא לו פירות ומאי שנא הני משום דמורו בה התירא

It was taught: the *ben bayit* spoken of is not one who walks in and out on his own legs [i.e. himself, as an employee], but who hires workers and makes use of income [from the assets]. Why is this one different? Because they rule [for themselves] permission in it [i.e. the assets, and are thus in a position of responsibility].

This idea of trust and accountability is again emphasized in *mTa'an.* 3:8: Ḥoni ha-Me'agel describes himself as like a *ben bayit* of God, who as such is asked by the populace to pray for rain:

על כל צרה שלא תבא על הצבור מתריעין עליה חוץ מרב גשמים.
מעשה שאמרו לו לחוני המעגל: התפלל שירדו גשמים... התפלל ולא ירדו גשמים.
מה עשה? עג עוגה ועמד בתוכה ואמר לפניו: רבונו של עולם בניך שמו פניהם עלי שאני
כבן בית לפניך. נשבע אני בשמך הגדול שאיני זז מכאן עד שתרחם על בניך.
התחילו גשמים מנטפין... עד שיצאו ישראל מירושלים להר הבית מפני הגשמים...

One prescribes a fast to stave off any trouble that may befall the community, except too much rain. It happened that [the people once] said to Ḥoni ha-Me'agel: Pray for rain to fall.... He prayed, but no rain fell. What did he do? He drew a circle and stood in it, and said before Him: Lord of the Universe, your people turned to me, as I am like your *ben bayit*. I swear in your great name that I will not move from here until you have mercy on your children. Rain began to fall ... until [after further pleas by Ḥoni to increase the amount of rain] the Israelites had to withdraw from Jerusalem to the Temple Mount because of the rain...

In aggadic literature, the *ben bayit* features in a number of parables of the *mashal-lemelekh* type. Ziegler assumed the term *ben bayit* meant *Freigelassener*, based on his premise that these "king-parables" may be explained by comparison with the law and customs of the Roman Empire. He explained the following midrash in *Exod. Rabbah* (Rom) 43:6, for instance, by noting that it was these freedmen who tended to be the money lenders in the Roman empire:[120]

120 Ignaz Ziegler, *Die Konigsgleichnisse des Midrasch beleuchtet durch die römanische Kaiserzeit.* (Breslau: Schlesische verlage-Anstalt, 1903) 247-248.

ד"א ויחל משה. מהו למה ה' יחרה אפך בעמך. ר' יהודה ור' נחמיה.
ר' יהודה אומר למה"ד למלך שהיה לו בן בית והשליטו על כל מה שהיה לו.
הלך אותו בן בית והלוה לבני אדם ע"י ערבים.
הלוה לזה נ' זהובים ולזה ק' ולזה מאתים ברחו הלווים.
אחר זמן שמע המלך ורע לו. א"ל השלטתיך על שלי אלא לאבדן.
א"ל בן בית אני הלויתי ובאחריותי הם לשלם אני מעמידך על הכל.
הרי פלוני ערב יש בידו ק' זהובים וביד פלוני נ'.
כך אמר משה להקב"ה למה אתה כועס לא בשביל תורתך באחריותי היא
שאני וחבירי נקיים אותה אהרן ובניו יקיימוה יהושע וכלב יקיימוה
יאיר ומכיר יקיימוה הצדיקים יקיימוה ואני אקיימנה. הוי למה ה' יחרה אפך.

Another matter: *And Moses implored* [the Lord - Exod. 32:11, after being made aware of the incident of the golden calf]. Why [did Moses then ask:] *Why, God, does your wrath burn concerning your people* [i.e. was the answer not obvious]. R. Judah and R. Neḥemiah [gave opinions]. R. Judah says: To what is this similar? To a king who had a *ben bayit* and appointed him over all his property. This *ben bayit* went and made loans to people through guarantors; he loaned this one 50 gold pieces and this one 100 and this one 200. The borrowers absconded. After a time the king heard, and was displeased; he said to him "I have appointed you over my property, only to lose it!" The *ben bayit* said to him: "I made the loans, and it is my responsibility to pay them back; I will stand you for all of them. This guarantor has in hand 100 gold pieces, and this one 50." Similarly Moses said to God: "Why are you angry? Not for your Torah - it is my responsibility, since I and my colleagues will uphold it: Aaron and his sons will uphold it, Joshua and Kalev will uphold it, Makhir and Ya'ir will uphold it, the righteous will uphold it, and I will uphold it." Thus [the question]: *Why, God, does your wrath burn...*

Ziegler noted also that a diminution of the wine ration was used as a mild punishment for slaves, suggesting a background for the following midrash (*VaYiqra Rabbah* (Margoliot) 12:1), part of an extended discussions on the pitfalls of wine-drinking:[121]

דרש ר' ישמעאל לא מתו שני בני אהרן אלא על ידי שנכנסו שתויי יין.
ר' פנחס בשם ר' לוי על הדא דר' ישמעאל למלך שמינ' לו בן בית נאמן
ושומרו עומד על פתח החנות התיז את ראשו בשתיקה ומינה לו בן בית אחר.
ואין אנו יודע' מפני מה הרג את הראשון אלא ממה שהמלך מצוה את השני

[121] Ziegler, *Die Konigsgleichnisse*, 240. Similar forms of this midrash are found in *VaYiqra Rab.* (Margoliot, p. 255) 12:5; *Lev. Rabbah* (ed. Rom) 12:1; and *Esther Rabbah* (ed. Rom) 5:1.

ואומר לו אל תיכנס לחנות אנו יודע שמתוך כן הרג את הראשון.

> R. Ishmael interpreted: The two sons of Aaron died only because they entered [the Holy of Holies] after having drunk wine. R. Pinḥas in the name of R. Levi [compares] this [opinion] of R. Ishmael to a king who had appointed a loyal *ben bayit*, and observed him in the entrance to the market. Without saying a word, he cut off his head, and appointed another *ben bayit*. We know why he killed the first one only from what he commanded the second; as he said to him, 'Do not enter the market,' we know that this is why he killed the first one.

We may also note a midrash (*yBer.* 9:1 13a, repeated in *Exod. Rabbah* 15:18, *Midrash Tehilim* 4:3) in which the head of a *ben bayit*'s household is called a *patron*; this may suggest the *ben bayit* was a type of client, confirming Ziegler's idea of a freedman.

Yet a dominant feature of this and other parables is their use to explain the relationship between the Deity and a biblical figure in terms of the interaction of a king with a *ben bayit*. Moses is prominent in these parables,[122] but they also include Aaron,[123] Aaron and Miriam,[124] David,[125] and even

---

122 Other parables in which Moses is compared to a king's *ben bayit* are *Exod. Rabbah* 35:6, *Num. Rabbah* 4:1, 21:15, *Midrash Tehilim* 1891 מדרש תהילים, וילנא 2:13, B.Mandelbaum, פסיקתא דרב כהנא, 2 כרכים, ניו יורק: בית המדרש לרבנים באמריקה, 1987. [=Pesiqta deRav Kahana] 1:3.

123 See , e.g. *Sifrei to Numbers* (Horovitz, 134-135) *pisqa* 117:

לכל קדשי בני ישראל, כרת הכתוב ברית עם אהרן על כל קדשי הקדשים
לגזור דין ולכרות להם ברית לפי שבא קרח כנגד אהרן וערער על הכהונה
משל למה הדבר דומה למלך בשר ודם שהיה לו בן בית
ונתן לו שדה אחת במתנה ולא כתב ולא חתם ולא העלה לו בערכיים
בא אחר וערער כנגדו על השדה אמר לו המלך כל מי שירצה
יבוא ויערער כנגדך על השדה בוא ואני כותב ואני חותם ואני מעלה לך בערכיים

> *For all the hallowed things of Israel* [Num. 18:8] - Scripture established a[n explicit] covenant with Aaron with respect to all hallowed things, to make a rule and establish a covenant. This is because Koraḥ came and claimed the priesthood from Aaron. To what is this similar? To a human king who had a *ben bayit* and gave him a field as a gift, but did not write and seal [a deed] or record it for him in the recorder's office. Someone came and claimed the field from him. The king said to him: Let anyone who wants come and claim the field from you; I shall write and seal [a deed] and record it for you...

124 Aaron and Miriam (as opposed to Moses the אוהב): *Sifrei Zuta* (Horovitz, 75) on Num. 12:5).

125 David: *Midrash Tehilim*, 24:2

Adam.[126] Given both the importance of these biblical personages and the impression of trust, responsibility and closeness suggested in these parables, likely the intended parallel here is to someone who is not a mere slave or client, but more of a trusted retainer. This is also the sense in which *ben bayit* is understood by certain later commentators such as Rashi. In *bSan.* 31b, for instance, Rashi comments on an address to one Uqva, expressed in the following terms: לדזיו ליה כבר בתיה (to him whose splendour is like that of *bar bityah*). According to Rashi *s.v.* (בר בתיה) ,לדזיו ליה כבר בתיה is Moses. He gives two reasons for this interpretation, the second of which is relevant to the issue of the *ben bayit*:

> כמשה, שהוא בן בתיה למי שמקרין עור פניו, כמשה שגידלתו בתיה בת פרעה.
> לשון אחר כבר ביתיה, כמשה, שהוא בן בית, דכתיב בכל ביתי נאמן הוא,
> לדזיו ליה, על שם שהיה חכם וכתיב חכמת אדם תאיר פניו...

> Like Moses, as he was the "son of Bityah" to the one whose face is lit up, Moses our Rabbi, who was raised by Bityah, the daughter of Pharaoh [Bityah is mentioned as a daughter of the Pharaoh in 1Chr. 4:18; according to tradition, this is the woman who raised Moses]. Another reading: *Like his ben bayit [kebar beitei]*, like Moses, as he was a *ben bayit*, as it is written: *He [Moses] is trusted in all My house* [Num. 12:7]; *to one whose splendour*, as he [Moses] was wise, and it is written: *A person's wisdom lights up his face* [Eccl. 8:1].

Certain other parables describing more ordinary personages appear to emphasize the *ben bayit* as putative kin. Ḥovav, for instance, who was the son of Moses' father-in-law and a member of the household, is described as a *ben bayit* in *Sifrei Numbers* (Horovitz) *pisqa* 78. *YSan.* 10:2 28d (regarding the curse of Balaam) describes the manner in which women shopkeepers would lure unsuspecting Israelites into idolatry; the use of the term here implies someone initially a stranger, though not a slave, who is then integrated into the household:

> מה עשו בנו להן קנקלין מבית הישימון עד הר השלג והושיבו שם נשים
> מוכרות מיני כיסנין הושיבו את הזקינה מבחוץ ואת הנערה מבפנים
> והיו ישראל אוכלין ושותין והיה אחד מהן יוצא לטייל בשוק ולוקח לו חפץ מן

126 Adam: *Pesiqta deRav Kahana* (Mandelbaum) 12:1, 26:3.

חנווני והיתה הזקנה מוכרת לו את החפץ בשוייו והנערה אומרת לו בא וטול לך בפחות כך ביום הראשון וכן ביום השני וכן ביום השלישי והיתה אומרת לו מיכן והילך אתה כבן בית היכנס ובור לך...

What did they do? They built enclosures from the house of the desert[127] to the mountain of snow, and placed women there to sell types of sweetmeats. They put the older woman outside, and the young woman inside. And Israelites would eat and drink, and one of them would go for a walk in the market and buy an item from the shopkeeper. The old woman would sell him the item at its value, but the young woman would say to him: Come and take it for less; and so on, the first day, second day and third day. And she would say to him: From now on you are like a *ben bayit*; come in and choose for yourself...

1.2.3.C Conclusion

We see the same pattern with respect to *ben bayit* as has been observed with the *ben amah* and *yelid bayit:* i) the biblical text is capable of supporting several meanings, among them "houseborn," or an actual son, or a household dependant, as well as other sorts of household relationships; ii) the term has vague associations with slaves, but seems to be used with non-slaves as well. If there is an association of the term with the Akkadian *mār bīti*, there is a suggestion that such person could have been a functionary of some rank within the household; this sense is also suggested by the Targum for Ecclesiastes.

127 Mandelkern gives for the biblical ישׁ[י]מן (as in Num. 21:20) *vastatio, desertum.*

CHAPTER 2

THE *PILEGESH*: STATUS OR TOPOS?

The term *pilegesh*, found in biblical and postbiblical Hebrew פלגש/פילגש, is generally taken as the equivalent of the English word "concubine".[1] Yet the idea of concubinage itself (like the idea of slavery) is quite vague,[2] and this lack of precision is exacerbated in the attempt to compare concubinage terms in different languages and periods.[3]

Further, it is often assumed that concubinage was in some way connected with female slaves. As Ellinson notes, for instance, postbiblical sources often assumed that the *pilegesh* was a *shifḥah* who had been sexually coerced by her master;[4] certain modern scholars also propose that a concubine would have started out as a slave, or that concubinage was in fact the inevitable disposition of all female slaves.[5]

In fact, the term appears sporadically in the Bible, in some instances associated with named individuals.[6] In the Pentateuch the term appears

---

1 This is so even in the earliest translations: we find such terms as פלקתא and לחנתא in the Targumim, παλλακή in the LXX, and *concubina* in the Vulgate (e.g., for Gen. 35:22).

2 "Concubine" is generally not used as a precise legal term in English, but can describe a variety of relationships, both temporary and permanent, monogamous or otherwise. On a social level, "concubine" may connote semi-respectability or licentiousness, depending on perspective.

3 I shall argue in chap. 7 that לחנתא, like its apparent Akkadian cognate *laḫḫi/anatu*, suggests a subordinate rather than a concubine.

4 Elyaqim Ellinson, *Nissuin Not in Accordance with the Law of Moses and Israel* [in Hebrew] (Tel Aviv: Dvir, 1975), 53. Ellison cites as one notable example the מעשה בוסתנאי in the *Iggeret Rav Sherirah Gaon*, in which an antecedent of a particular gaonic dynasty was accused of having married his slave woman.

5 See, e.g., B. Cohen, *Jewish and Roman Law,* 329; Patai, *Sex and Family*, 42; and Flesher, *Oxen, Women or Citizens?* 17 n. 17. This opinion will be discussed more fully below.

6 The named *pilagshim* are: Re'umah, the *pilegesh* of Naḥor (Gen. 22: 24); Bilhah, the slave-wife of Jacob (Gen. 35:22); Timnah, the *pilegesh* of Elifaz (Gen. 36:12); Ritzpah, the *pilegesh* of Saul (2Sam. 3:7 and 21:11); Qeturah, the *pilegesh* of Abraham (1Chr. 1:32,

only in the foundation narratives in Genesis and not in any of the legal portions. The term has only one direct association with slaves, and we may thus deem this association incidental: Bilhah, the slave-wife of Jacob, is termed a *pilegesh* in Gen. 35:22.[7] Unlike the terms *shifḥah* and *amah*, the term *pilegesh* is never associated with the male slave term *eved*. If it appears in lists at all, it is associated with wives (for instance, those of David in 2Sam. 5:13; of Solomon in 1Kings 11:3; and of the court in Cant. 6:8). The bizarre story of the *pilegesh* of Givah in Judges 19-21 uses kinship terminology otherwise associated with a marital-type situation: the woman is referred to as an *ishah pilegesh* (19:1, 28), the Levite as *ishah* ("her husband"; 19:3), and her father as the Levite's *ḥoten* ("father-in-law"; 19:4).[8] Further, Qeturah is described in Gen. 25:1 as the *ishah* of Abraham, while in 1Chr. 1:32 she is described as his *pilegesh*.[9]

Most significant, in my opinion, is that certain *pilagshim* are very noticeably associated with sexual assaults: the assault on Bilhah by Reuven (Gen. 35:22); the rape and dismemberment of the *pilegesh* of Givah (Judg. 19-21[10]); the alleged assault on Saul's *pilegesh* by Avner (2Sam. 3:7); the assault on David's *pilagshim* by his son Avshalom (2Sam. 16:21-2). There is the further curious point that the *pilagshim* in Ezek. 23:20, also associated with profligate sexual behavior, appear to be males.

The term all but disappears in the pre-gaonic legal canon, with two exceptions that will be discussed below. It does appear sporadically in

---

though in Gen. 25:1 she is called his *ishah*); Eifah and Ma'akhah, the *pilagshim* of Caleb (1Chr. 2:46, 48). There is only one direct instance in which *pilagshim* are associated in any way with slave terminology: Bilhah is called a *pilegesh* only in Gen. 35:22 and is otherwise described as an *amah*, *shifḥah*, or *ishah*. There is also an indirect association: Avimelekh, who is stated to be the son of Gideon's (unnamed) *pilegesh*, is in one instance called a *ben amah* (Judg. 9:18). The significance of these instances is discussed further in this chapter.

7 As mentioned above, there is one indirect association in Judg. 9:18, in which Avimelekh is called a *ben amah*.

8 Josephus in fact "upgraded" this woman to a wife (τών γονέων (his wife)); see *Ant.* 5:142 (trans. H. St. J. Thackeray; 9 vols.; London: Heinemann, 1926-1965).

9 A midrash associated with Rav (*Gen. Rab.* 61:4 and elsewhere) identifies Qeturah as Hagar.

10 As noted in Harris, R. L. et al., eds., *Theological Wordbook of the Old Testament* [=*TWOT*] (2 vols.; Chicago: Moody, 1981) *s.v.* "concubine," one-third of the biblical occurrences of *pilegesh* are in this Judges narrative.

aggadic material, but apparently describes a (female) consort of low social status, rather than a specific legal status,[11] as can be seen in the following midrash in Lev. Rabbah *parsha* 1:13:

> מה בין נביאי ישראל לנביאי עכו"ם...ורבנן אמרי למלך שהיה לו אשה ופלגש כשהוא הולך אצל אשתו הוא הולך בפרהסיא וכשהוא הולך אצל פלגשו הולך במטמוניות

> What is the difference between the prophets of Israel and the prophets of the other nations?... The Sages say: [it is like] a king who had an *ishah* and a *pilegesh* [in some versions a *shifḥah*]; when he goes out with his wife he does so in public view, but when he goes out with his *pilegesh* he does so discreetly.

Undoubtedly, the *pilegesh* was associated with sexual behavior, and undoubtedly a sexual use was one of the functions of a female slave, though not an inevitable function. Even if we describe this as "concubinage," however, I do not think the term "concubine" should be used as the translation for *pilegesh*. I will argue that a better translation is "consort," to avoid the sole association with females that is implicit in the modern term "concubine" and thus include the male *pilagshim* in Ezek. 23:20. Further, I argue that *pilegesh* is used in the Bible as part of a literary motif rather than as an indication of a particular status, and that there is no necessary association of the *pilegesh* with slavery. The *pilegesh* is outside the family; his or her sexuality is not licit in the normative sense and leads to disinheritance or death. It is the *pilegesh*, not the slave, who is the true "other."[12]

2.1 ON THE WIFE-SLAVE CONTINUUM?

As noted above, there is concern evidenced by both ancient and modern scholars to rank biblical females in comparison to a "legitimate" wife.[13] For

11 Several of these are discussed by Ellison, *Nissuin*, 47-49.

12 The pilegesh may have had some legal advantages in later periods as a contract can allow a mutual exit strategy. What became normative in later rabbinic law was the unilateral acquisition of the woman by the man accompanied by her inability to initiate divorce. [TM]

13 Modern Israeli law continues to use the term *pilegesh* with the specific legal meaning

the *pilegesh*, this is seen already in two apparently contradictory passages in the two Talmudim, which suggest a sort of unprotected wife. The first text is *yKetub.* 5:2 29d:

אי זו היא אשה ואי זו היא פילגש
רבי מאיר אומר אשה יש לה כתובה פילגש אין לה כתובה
רבי יהודה אומר אחת זו ואחת זו יש לה כתובה
אשה יש לה כתובה ותנאי כתובה פילגש יש לה כתובה ואין לה תנאי כתובה

What is a wife and what is a *pilegesh*? R. Meir says: a wife has a *ketubbah* [marriage contract], and a *pilegesh* does not have a *ketubbah.*
R. Yehudah says: each one has a *ketubbah;* a wife has [both] a [written] *ketubbah* and [negotiated] conditions, and a *pilegesh* has a [written] *ketubbah* and no [negotiated] conditions.

The second text is *bSan.* 21a:

מאי נשים ומאי פילגשים
אמר רב יהודה אמר רב נשים בכתובה ובקדושין פלגשים בלא כתובה
ובלא קדושין

What are wives and what are *pilagshim*? Rav Yehudah said in the name of Rav: wives have a *ketubbah* and *qiddushin*; *pilagshim* have neither a *ketubbah* nor *qiddushin.*

The Yerushalmi has been interpreted to mean[14] that the *pilegesh*, like the wife, has *qiddushin*, though possibly not a *ketubbah*, contrary to the

of "reputed wife" (A. L. Grivsky, "Concubinage in Israel" [in Hebrew] [Molad, 1959], 666-70), a woman in a long-term relationship who has not undergone the formalities of marriage. Such a woman may benefit from certain legal rights accorded to wives in "formal" marriages, such as pension rights (Pinḥas Shifman, "Marriage and Cohabitation in Israeli Law," *Israel Law Review* 16 [1981]: 456). Socially, however, she may be considered inferior (Daniel Friedmann, "The Unmarried Wife in Israeli Law," *Israel Yearbook on Human Rights* 2 [1972]: 298).

14 Rashi to Gen. 25:6, for instance, has נשים בכתובה פלגשים בלא כתובה (wives have a *ketubbah*, *pilagshim* do not have a *ketubbah*); this is taken as an indication that he understood the distinction between them to relate only to the *ketubbah* and thus assumed that both had *qiddushin* (see, e.g., Ellinson, *Nissuin*, 3).

opinion in the Bavli. Ellinson has argued that while the passages are likely not contradictory, at least with respect to the idea that a *pilegesh* has no *qiddushin*,[15] there is still no evidence in rabbinic law of any fixed halakhah with respect to the legal status of the *pilegesh*.[16] We must also remember that the terms *qiddushin*, *ketubbah,* and *tena'ei ketubbah* do not appear in the Bible; these passages seem to be an attempt to impose later law on a term with which the Rabbis had no familiarity in "real life."

The view of a *pilegesh* as a quasi-wife is also found among modern scholars. *TWOT* has for "concubine": "a true wife, though of secondary rank."[17] Grivsky assumes that the term *pilegesh* has always referred to a woman in a זיווג חפשי, a "free couple," arguing that ancient law made much less distinction than modern law between the legal rights of "wifehood" and those of less formal relationships; the distinction, he suggests, was primarily social.[18] Morgenstern[19] fit the *pilegesh* within his theory of marriage

---

15 Ellinson, *Nissuin*, 6. In Ellison's opinion, the Yerushalmi passage is discussing only the impact of the *ketubbah*, with no assumptions regarding *qiddushin*, and a *ketubbah* alone is not constitutive of marriage. As he notes, the assessment is complicated by the fact that there are alternate readings for each of the talmudic passages. MS Leiden for *yKetub.* 5:2 29d, for instance, has:

ר"מ אומר אשה יש לה כתובה
*[פילגש אין לה כתובה]
ר"י אומר אחת זו ואחת זו אין **לה כתובה...

* entire bracketed phrase added in margin by scribe possibly as a result of a homeotoleuton.
**אין erased and יש added in margin with a note by the scribe, נ"ל "It seems to me."
Ellinson argues (ibid., 6) that R. Yehudah's opinion in MS Leiden can be interpreted as meaning that a *ketubbah* is not constitutive; if it is present, the *pilegesh* gets whatever is explicitly set out, while the wife gets rights implied by law whether there is a contract or not. Several Bavli MSS for *bSan.* 21a have פלגשים בלא כתובה וקדושין, and an issue arises as to whether the word בלא governs both elements of the phrase or only the first. Ellinson (ibid., 2) agrees with the assessment of Naḥmanides on Gen. 25:6 (*contra* Abarbanel on Gen. 17 *s.v.* ושרי אשת אברהם and Rashi on Gen (25:6) that it does govern both elements, and the passage is thus stating that a *pilegesh* has neither *qiddushin* nor *ketubbah.*

16 Ellinson, *Nissuin*, 96.

17 R. Laird Harris *et al.*, eds., *Theological Wordbook of the Old Testament* (database updated 2006).

18 Grivsky, "Concubinage in Israel," 666, 667. Grivsky notes that in the Roman case, the distinction was used to indicate that the female in a "marriage" was a person of lower rank than her husband.

19 See Morgenstern, "Additional Notes," 56-57.

development by arguing that the *pilegesh* was a woman in an incipient *ba'al* marriage — that is, unlike the woman in the *beena* marriage, who stayed with her father's group, the *pilegesh*, likely acquired as a war captive or by an exchange of some kind, remained with the husband. Morgenstern argued that this type of incipient *ba'al* marriage likely always existed alongside the *beena* marriage type, until it gradually became the prevailing mode. He supports this proposition by noting, first, that the likelihood that *pilegesh* is a non-Semitic word may indicate that it was originally applied to foreign captives, and second, that this meaning (a foreign wife who stays with the husband) would fit the biblical instances of this term recording "ancient" traditions — the Genesis texts and Judges 19.[20] After *ba'al* marriage became prevalent, the term *pilegesh,* in Morgenstern's opinion, "could acquire only one meaning, 'concubine,' since from the first it designated a wife of an inferior type and standing."[21]

One may, however, argue against these (generally non-contextual) studies, particularly that of Morgenstern, that they are circular, starting with the premise that *pilegesh* must refer to a female and must refer to a type of relationship inferior to marriage.[22]

A second view places the *pilegesh* closer to the female slave and makes the specific assumption that a *pilegesh* would have started out as a slave in her master's household. We have noted Ellinson's observation that a blurring of the distinction between the *pilegesh* and the slave woman is already noticeable among early commentators, as can be seen in the following statement by the 12th century sage Avraham ben David (Rabad):[23]

---

20 Morgenstern, "*Beena* Marriage," 57-58, notes that Avimelekh's mother is called a *pilegesh* in Judg. 8:31, though this seems to be a *beena* marriage with Gideon. He explains this exception in a somewhat farfetched way, by arguing that she could not be called an *ishah*, since this referred to a woman in a *ba'al* marriage; but the readers of this text, though it belongs to an "older" tradition, would not have understood *amah* and *shifḥah* in their original connections to *beena* marriage. This seems unlikely, if for no other reason that Avimelekh is actually called a *ben amah* in Judg. 9:18.

21 Morgenstern, "*Beena* Marriage," 58.

22 Further cautions with respect to Morgenstern's argument were noted earlier in this chapter.

23 Ellinson, *Nissuin*, 54. We may note the similar opinion of Naḥmanides on Lev. 19:20:

...יאמר הכתוב שהיא שפחה נערה לאיש ידוע כי הפלגש אשר היא משרת את האיש וישכב
עמה תקרא נערה לו...

...ובעלי הלשון דורשין פילגש...פי שגל. לפעמים למשגל ולשמש את הבית.
הפילגש נחשבה למעשה לשפחה המשמשת את בעלה...לעתים לתענוגות ולעתים למלאכות.

[Rabad states:] 'The language experts explain *pilegesh* ... as *pi shagel* [*shagel* = intercourse],[24] at times to service and to serve the household.' The *pilegesh*...is [thus] perceived as a *shifḥah* who services her master...sometimes for pleasure and sometimes for labor.

More recent opinion also sees the *pilegesh* as a wife who is "tainted" in some way by slavery; this interaction of "slavery" with "wifehood," however, is not understood consistently. Ariel, basing himself on the traditional etymology of *pilegesh* as פלג אשה, "half wife," argues that such a woman was more than likely to have started life as a slave, given that a free woman would never have agreed to such a presumably reduced status, while a slave may have seen it as a step up, or was in any event coerced into such a relationship.[25] Patai suggests that such a woman would have retained her slave status and this is what would distinguish her from a "wife."[26] Neufeld saw no philological difference between *amah*, *shifḥah*, and *pilegesh*, though he argued that the *pilegesh* may have been associated with a greater laxity of morals (based, for instance, on the Bilhah-Reuven incident of Gen. 35:22, to be discussed further below), and was possibly more akin to a prostitute.[27] McComisky also treated the three terms as synonymous, but seems to have considered them all equivalent to "concubine," which he took to be in essence a "secondary wife."[28] Epstein, in contrast, designates concubinage

Scripture is saying that she is a *shifḥah* girl for a certain man. It is known that the *pilegesh* who serves a man and with whom he lies is called his 'girl' (*na'arah*)...

24 We may also note the association in the LXX of Aramiac שגלתה of Dan. 5:2, 3, 23 with the Greek παλλακαι, "concubines"; see further the discussion in chap. 7.

25 Yaqov Ariel, "The *Pilegesh* and her Halakhic Status in the Bible," Megadim 8 (1989): 58-59. The essence of *pilagshut* that differentiated it from "wifehood" was, in Ariel's opinion, that it started as a real *qinyan* (purchase); with wifehood, in contrast, the term *ba'al* signified not a monetary transaction but a legal relationship with superficial resemblances to a *qinyan*.

26 Patai, *Sex and Family*, 41-42.

27 E. Neufeld, *Ancient Hebrew Marriage Laws* (London: Longmans, Green, 1944), 121, 123.

28 Thomas McComiskey, "The Status of the Secondary Wife: Its Development in Ancient Near Eastern Law, A Study and Comprehensive Index" (Ph.D. dissertation, Brandeis

as a specific legal status higher than that of the "slave-wife." The biblical *pilegesh* reflects what he calls the "oriental" type of concubinage; she is part of a patriarchal, extended family structure in which the concubine is in essence a wife, with the same legal strictures regarding inheritance, adultery, and incest, but of lower rank than the chief wife. This type of extended family structure might also have included the freedwoman, captive wife, slave wife, and female slave, with associated legal statuses of descending rank, though not necessarily with discrete boundaries between these categories.[29] This type of concubinage, in his opinion, disappeared as family structure changed, with the rise of non-agriculture based economies and the increased centrality of the individual; he argues that the later sages were unfamiliar with the "oriental" (corporate) style of concubinage and that their understanding of *pilegesh* reflects the "occidental" type of concubinage.[30]

There are difficulties with each of these arguments. The biblical evidence explicitly associates *pilegesh* with a slave in only one instance, so that one must question both the necessity of associating the term with slavery and its synonymy with *amah* and *shifḥah*. Epstein's argument, on the other hand, seems to assume more of a legal distinction than is supported by the biblical text. While it is possible, or perhaps inevitable, that there were ranks of women within a complex household, this cannot be supported simply by assuming, first, that *pilegesh* means "female concubine," and second, that all women were to be legally ranked according to a single concept of "marriage." In summary, I do not think that there is compelling evidence to place the *pilegesh* anywhere on a wife-slave continuum.

2.2 FOREIGN LOANWORD?

Following on the idea that the *pilegesh* is not part of any status hierarchy, the most interesting scholarly opinion is etymological: the term may be a foreign loanword.

University, 1965), 1, 91.

29 Epstein, "The Institution of Concubinage," 154, 156. Raymond Westbrook, *Old Babylonian Marriage Law* (Horn: Ferdinand Berger, 1988), 111, also argues that there was a distinction between a "slave-wife" and a "slave-concubine" in Old Babylonian law.

30 Epstein, "The Institution of Concubinage" 156, 159.

There are traditions deriving *pilegesh* from a combination of Hebrew words, such as *palag, peleg*, and *ishah*, in effect meaning "half-wife" (Mandelkern, *s.v.* פלגש), or *pilug* and *shimush*, with the implication of a woman "used" by different men (*Midrash Sekhel Tov* to Gen. 35:22). As will be discussed in chapter 7, there is in fact evidence of half statuses in mishnaic and later law. Other scholars, however, suggest that these derivations are folk etymologies[31] and question whether the term is Hebrew, or even Semitic, in origin. A computer search of the biblical text confirms that the combination *lgš* (or *lqš*) is in fact rare in biblical Hebrew, the only other instance being the description of the prophet Naḥum as האלקשי (Naḥum 1:1). A further point against a Hebrew origin, suggested by Rabin, is the absence in biblical Hebrew of a noun with a similar pattern[32] (although we may note that there are *proper* nouns that seem to have the same form, particularly פלשת and תגלת).[33] But the conclusive point, in Rabin's view, arguing against a Semitic origin in general, is the lack of any phonetic-semantic parallels in other Semitic languages.[34] This suggests the possibility of a loanword, and the consequent speculation as to why the term was borrowed.

Scholars have proposed various other languages of origin, including Egyptian (Mandelkern, *s.v.* פלגש), Greek παλλακὴ, and Hittite, as well as the reverse possibility that the term entered Greek and Latin as a Phoenicio-Semitic loanword.[35] Rabin's own proposal[36] is that the term is composed of two Indo-European elements: the prefix *pi-*, "at, on, towards," and the root *legh-*, "to lie down," plus a suffix. The term is taken to mean "by-lier," a concept that Rabin notes is expressed in other

31 Regarding the former derivation, at least, this is the opinion of Even-Shoshan (*s.v.* פלגש).

32 C. Rabin, "The Origin of the Hebrew Word Pilegeš," *JJS* 25 (1974): 356.

33 The latter represents the biblical version of the Akkadian (Tukultī) *apil-ešarra*. This suggests a possibility, which I shall not explore further here, that *pilegesh* is derived from an Akkadian compound that includes the term *apil*, "heir of." The association with a male figure would certainly fit with the idea of male *pilagshim* in Ezekiel.

34 Rabin, "Origin," 356-57.

35 See, e.g., McComiskey, "Secondary Wife," 91 (Greek); John Pairman Brown, *Israel and Hellas* (ZAW Supp. 231; Berlin: De Gruyter, 1995), 70 (Hittite); Epstein, "Concubinage," 153 (Phoenicio-Semitic). A summary of earlier speculations on the origin of *pilegesh* is found in Rabin, "Origin," 353 nn. 2-6.

36 Rabin, "Origin," 358.

Indo-European languages, though with different terms. He suggests that the most likely Indo-European contact with Hebrew in this case would have been through the Philistines, though of course he can cite no extant parallels. While he acknowledges the difficulty posed by selecting linguistic elements from the "unlimited possibilities of the phonology of an unknown language," he supports his contention by noting that many of the biblical references to *pilagshim* in the Israelite period have to do with men from Judah and Benjamin, two areas in close contact with the Philistines.[37]

Levin supports this contention, adding a possible motive for the borrowing of this word: the prefix *(e)pi* suggests a non-endogamous woman, and the Philistines (=Pelasgians in Greek tradition) had a reputation (as attested in Herodotus) for "craving foreign women."[38] The attraction of this practice, particularly for men such as the Levite of Judges 19-20 who did not have a stable residence and might thus find it difficult to attract a wife, led to this type of "intermarriage" being incorporated within other cultures in contact with the Philistines, though subject to much censure.[39]

Again, there is the difficulty with the arguments of Rabin and Levin that they start with the assumption that *pilegesh* refers to a female concubine, and thus that one must look for its derivation in appropriate phonetic-semantic combinations suggesting this sort of relationship.[40] Against this association is the use of *pilegesh* in Ezek. 23:30 and its apparent reference to males. Another difficulty with Rabin's proposal, as he himself acknowledges, is the lack of an explicit "Philistine" connection for the Genesis narratives. Assuming that the "concubines" in these narratives are primarily slaves — specifically Hagar, Bilhah and Zilpah — he posits that later editors may have been reluctant to apply the term *pilegesh* to slave women. Their solution was thus to describe the women as both *amah* and *ishah*, to indicate their "in-betweenness" and lesser status.[41] Again, this

37 Rabin, "Origin," 360, 361.

38 Saul Levin, "Hebrew {pi(y)légeš}, Greek παλλακὴ, Latin *paelex:* The Origin of Intermarriage Among the Early Indo-Europeans and Semites," *General Linguistics* 23 (1983): 192, 194; Levin cites Herodotus, *Histories*, 6.137ff.

39 See Levin, "Hebrew," 193.

40 See, for example, Rabin, "Origin," 363.

41 Rabin, "Origin," 362-63.

argument is circular, as there is nothing to indicate that the term *pilegesh* in any of the Genesis narratives means "concubine." As we have noted, Bilhah is in fact the only slave woman who is actually called a *pilegesh*, in the unusual verse Gen. 35:22, which describes her rape or seduction by Jacob's son Reuven.[42] This argument also overlooks Judg. 19:1, in which the Levite's *pilegesh* is also called an *ishah*.

2.3 THE *PILEGESH* AS A LITERARY *TOPOS?*

Various scholars, more correctly in my opinion, focus on the biblical *pilegesh* as a key player in a particular kind of motif. Several of these scholars have posited a succession scenario. Brown, for instance, notes the similarity between some of the biblical *pilegesh* references and various incidents from Greek literature, in which the act of taking the father's concubine is primarily political. The *pilegesh* in his opinion is thus an "honorific" institution, with a key role in royal succession.[43] Other scholars have similarly suggested a succession motif underlying the various biblical instances in which males have or demand intercourse with a *pilegesh* of their father or military superior: Reuven's rape/seduction of Bilhah, disqualifying him from first-born status (Gen. 35:22, 49:3-4); Ish Boshet's accusation against Avner regarding Saul's *pilegesh* Ritzpah, leading to Avner's defection to David (2Sam. 3:7); Avshalom's public sex with David's *pilagshim* (2Sam. 16:21-22), leading to Avshalom's disqualification from kingship; and Adoniahu's request to Solomon (through Batsheva) for Avishag, his father's consort, which leads to his death (1Kings 2:22). Solomon understood this request as an explicit threat to his kingship:

---

42 Rabin, "Origin," 362, also argues that Gen. 25:6, which refers to the sons of Abraham's *pilagshim*, would include under the plural *pilagshim* both Qeturah, who is actually called a *pilegesh* in 1Chr. 1:31 (and a wife in Gen. 25:1), and Hagar, who is never explicitly called a *pilegesh*. As noted above (n. 130), there is a midrashic suggestion that Qeturah actually was Hagar, returned after Sarah's death, yet this is not at all clear in the biblical text. Further, the verse refers to the sons of the *pilagshim* being given gifts, yet Hagar's son Ishmael had already left.

43 Brown, *Israel and Hellas,* 68-70. Brown raises the further issue, which will not be examined here, of whether this particular motif has been borrowed. He suggests that the term was Hittite or Luvian in origin, was borrowed by the Philistines, and was borrowed from the Philistines by both Israel and Greece (ibid., 70).

> [The king replied to his mother:] Why request Avishag the Shunamite for Adoniah? Request the kingship for him! For he is my older brother...

The purpose of these actions, Patai suggests, is a claim on a superior's authority; in his opinion (based apparently on social anthropology assumptions) it was customary for a son, after his father's death, to marry all the father's wives and concubines with the exception of his own mother, "to demonstrate definitely the fact of succession." He suggests, based on the wording of Ezek. 22:10 ערות אב גלה בך (they have uncovered their father's nakedness in you [Jerusalem]), that the custom was still in practice in Ezekiel's time, though it was abhorred.[44] Ariel, assuming that the *pilegesh* would have ranked somewhere between a semi-queen and slave-property, argued that such a status fitted her for this kind of role in securing succession.[45]

This assumption that the *pilegesh* was a key player in a succession motif would not explain other instances of the term, such as that in Ezek. 23:20.[46] We may, however, consider the succession issue as simply one type of a more general class of aetiological motifs. Zakovitch and Shinan[47] note that "sex stories" in general are frequently used in the Bible to justify later events, particularly a loss of status. In addition to the *pilegesh* stories, they note, for instance, the incest of Lot's daughters (Gen. 19:30-8), which explains the scornful attitude toward Ammon and Moav; the slaughter of the men of Shekhem by Simon and Levi to avenge the rape/seduction of their sister (Gen. 34:25, 49:5-7), which disqualifies them from first-born status after Reuven; and Amnon's rape of his half-sister Tamar (2Sam. 13),

44 Patai, *Sex and Family*, 101, 103; see also Matitiahu Tsevat, "Marriage and Monarchical Legitimacy in Ugarit and Israel," *JSS* 3 (1958): 242. In support of his contention, Tsevat also notes that the Targum to 2Sam. 16:21 (regarding Avshalom) translates *niveshet* with *itgaryah,* "to provoke, challenge." See also the suggestion of Tirzah Meacham, "The Missing Daughter: Leviticus 18 and 20," *ZAW* 109 (1997): 254-59, at 258, who argues that the Leviticus incest rules are both an apologetic for the behavior of the patriarchs and a priestly polemic against the house of David and its profligate ways.

45 Ariel, "The *Pilegesh*," 64.

46 On a plain reading, the incident of the *pilegesh* of Givah (Judg. 19-21) would also seem to be unrelated to succession; I shall argue below, however, that there may be a succession issue implicit in this story.

47 Yair Zakovitch and Avigdor Shinan, *The Story of Reuven and Bilhah* [in Hebrew] (Mif'ale hameḥqar shel hamakhon lemada'e ha-yehadut; Jerusalem: Hebrew University, 1984), 1.

which leads to his disqualification from kingship. We may thus propose that the *pilegesh* is one player in a number of "non-wife" relationships used for such aetiological stories. What characterizes *pilagshim*, whether male or female, is that they are "non-licit" sexual partners; as such, they attract danger, which leads to chaos.[48] A more detailed examination of the use of *pilegesh* in certain passages will support the proposition that this term has a literary function rather than reflecting a specific status of concubine. We shall focus in particular on the apparent reference in Ezek. 23:20 to male *pilagshim* as well as the Bilhah-Reuven incident in Gen. 25:32 and the Judges 19-21 narrative.

2.4 BIBLICAL EXAMPLES OF THREE INSTANCES OF *PILEGESH* AS *TOPOS*

2.4.A The Male pilagshim of Ezekiel. 23:20

Ezekiel 23 concerns the unfaithfulness of Jerusalem and Samaria, represented metaphorically as the sexual licentiousness of the sisters Oholah and Oholibah with their "lovers," Egypt, Assyria, and Babylon. In verse 20, the *pilagshim* who are the object of Oholibah's attentions in Egypt are, on a plain reading of the text, males, whose profligate sexuality leads to the breaking of the proper relationship with God:

ותעגבה על פלגשיהם אשר בשר חמורים בשרם וזרמת סוסים זרמתם

> She lusted for their *pilagshim*, whose members were like those of asses and whose flow [of semen, according to Rashi] was like those of stallions.

Rabin suggests that this use of a female term to refer to males may be a later, pejorative development.[49] Yet it is just as reasonable to assume that it is the restriction of the term *pilegesh* to females which is the later development, much as the English term "concubine" has developed from

---

48 It is possible that narratives of such an offense or attempted offense with a wife — e.g., Pharaoh and Sarah, Joseph and Potifar's wife, David and Batsheva — have a different aetiological purpose.

49 Rabin, "Origin," 361.

a generic term for a "lover" to a term restricted to females.[50] It is in fact in postbiblical translations and commentaries that the term *pilegesh* is restricted to females, a restriction that causes particular difficulties for those commenting on the Ezekiel verse.

The LXX to Ezek. 23:20 seems to acknowledge the "maleness" of the *pilagshim* here but avoids the issue by translating the term as *Χαλδαίους*, "Chaldeans"; other interpretations simply reject the idea of male *pilagshim*. The Targum to Ezekiel has:

ואתרעיאת למהוי שמשא* להון דבסר חמרין בסריהון וצחנת סוסין צחנתהון
[שמוטא in some editions*]

She took pleasure in being a servant*[51] to them whose flesh was the flesh of donkeys, and whose flow of semen was the flow of horses
[*in some editions 'abandoned']

In an extended comment on this verse, Radak explains that it is appropriate to refer to female lewdness (a characteristic associated, of course, only with *pilagshim*, not wives) using male sexual terms:

ותעגבה על פלגשיהם - פירשו המפרשים פלגשים עבדיהם כי פלגשים במקום הזה אנשים ולא נשים ויורה על זה אשר בשר חמורים בשרם שהוא כנוי לאבר האיש... והנכון בעיני שהוא כמשמעו ופירוש על כמו עם וכמוהו ויבאו האנשים על הנשים והדומים לו אמר כל כך חשקה בהם עד שנדמתה להם כמו פלגשיהם לא נשותיהם ולענין זה נוטה דעת המתרג' שתרגם ואתרעיאת למהוי שמוטא להון בטי"ת בקצת נוסחאות פי' שמוטא להם ובקצת נוסחאות שמשא כמו שפחה אשר בשר חמורים בשרם - וטעמו על הפילגשים כי גם ערות הנקבה מכונה בלשון בשר...

And she lusted after their pilagshim: The commentators interpreted *their pilagshim* as 'their male slaves' because *pilagshim* in that place were men, not women; and this is shown by *whose flesh is like the flesh of donkeys,* which describes the male member... In my view the correct [interpretation] is the

50 In current usage according of *The New Shorter Oxford English Dictionary on Historical Principles* (Oxford: Clarendon, 1993), a "concubine" is a female: "one who cohabits with a man without being his wife," a "kept mistress," or, in polygamous societies, a "secondary wife." In Late Middle English, however, the term also referred to a woman's male lover (ibid.). Perhaps "consort" would be an appropriate term.

51 Here, too, there is a sexual connotation in the root *ŠMŠ*.

literal one. The interpretation of *al* is like *im*, such as 'the men came with the women' and similar. [The verse thus stated]: She lusted after them to such an extent that she seemed to them like their *pilagshim*, not their wives. The [Aramaic] translator took this view of the issue, translating ואתרעיאת למהוי שמוטא להון, with a *tet* in several versions, whose translation is 'she was abandoned to them,' and in several versions שמשא, like a female slave. *Their flesh is like the flesh of donkeys* — its usage is with respect to the *pilagshim*, because female genitalia are also described using terms like 'flesh'...

Other commentaries and translations twist the verse, so as to render the term *pilegesh* as an abstract noun meaning "concubinage."[52] Rashi, for instance, has:

ותעגבה על פלגשיהם: על פלגשות' להיות להם לפלגש

And she lusted after their pilagshim: after [their] concubinage, to be a *pilegesh* to them.

The Vulgate translates על פלגשיהם as *super concubito eorum* (after lying with them).

Yet the context here clearly suggests a female associated with several males. A halakhic midrash in fact confirms that there was a belief, at least among later sages, that the Egyptians engaged in such polyandrous practices. This midrash comments on the introduction to the incest provisions in Leviticus 18, which contains a general warning against following the practices of Egypt and Canaan (v. 3):

כמעשה ארץ מצרים...וכמעשה ארץ כנען...לא תעשו

You shall not copy the practices of the land of Egypt...or the land of Canaan...

The sages set out their understanding of the nature of these practices

52 Certain English translations are less reticent, using general terms for sexual partners such as "paramours" (KJV) or "profligates" (Jerusalem Bible). The Yiddish translation of Aaron Bergmann, *The Old Testament in Hebrew and Yiddish* (London: British and Foreign Bible Society, 1912), is quite direct, translating the word as קעבסמענער, "half husbands," apparently the male equivalent of the female קעבסוויב, "half wife" or "concubine."

(*Sifra Aharei Mot* 9:8, Weiss p. 85d[53]):

ומה היו עושים? האיש נושא לאיש, והאשה לאשה, האיש נושא
אשה ובתה, ואשה ניסת לשנים.

And what did they do? A man would marry a man, a woman [would marry] a woman, a man would marry a woman and her daughter, and a woman would marry two [men].

We may thus conclude that the *pilagshim* in this verse are male "consorts," and it is the (immoderate) association with them that leads to censure on the part of the prophet.

2.4.B Gen. 35:22: Bilhah as pilegesh

This verse is placed after a description of the travels of Jacob and his entourage south from Padan Aram. At Bethel (later part of the territory of Ephraim) Jacob is renamed "Israel"; the text then recounts the birth of Benjamin on the way to Efrat (Bethlehem in Judah, which is in a direct line south). Rachel dies after this birth, and it is then that one would expect a summary such as "the sons of Jacob were twelve." Instead, the Bible interrupts this summary with the record of an incident between Reuven and Jacob's "slave-wife" Bilhah. This passage is both disturbing in content and unusual in structure:

ויהי בשכן ישראל בארץ ההוא וילך ראובן וישכב את בלהה פילגש אביו וישמע ישראל
ויהו בני יעקב שנים עשר

And when Israel dwelt in that land, Reuven went and lay with Bilhah his father's *pilegesh* and Israel heard
[There is here a lacuna in the text, marked in some printed editions with a

53 W. Ward argues based on linguistic evidence that it is in fact unlikely that "concubinage" existed in Pharaonic (Old and Middle Kingdom) Egypt, suggesting that the existence of harems and concubinage would have been inconsistent with the monogamy and legal equality that were the rule at this time. William Ward, "Reflections on Some Egyptian Terms Presumed to Mean 'Harem, Harem-Woman, Concubine,'" *Berytus* 31 (1983): 68, 74.

פ, the Masoretic sign for *parashah petuḥah* indicating the end of a section.[54] There are also two different cantillation signs for the word ישראל: a *sof pasuq*, i.e., a full stop, associated with eastern MS traditions, and an *etnaḥta*, major pause/comma, associated with western MS traditions.[55] Both are disjunctive accents.[56]]
And the sons of Jacob were twelve.

The strange insertion at this point of the incident of Bilhah and Reuven, the physical lacuna in the text, and the apparent lack of reaction by Jacob suggest to some scholars that the text has been deliberately manipulated: material has been left out, or the abruptness of the text is meant to suggest that the rest of the story is to be found elsewhere.[57] I suggest that there is a further puzzle in the use of the words "his father's *pilegesh*" to describe Bilhah; the description seems, on the one hand, superfluous, and on the other hand contradictory, given that she has already been called his *ishah*. Further, the word is not used to describe Hagar or Zilpah, though their situations were similar.

The lacuna, called a *pisqa be-emtsa pasuq* [=*PBP*], is a section division occurring in the middle of a verse, which is presumed to be the result of exegetical activity, i.e., someone's subjective assessment that there is a change in the content of the text, requiring a break.[58] Source criticism in fact assigns the verse to two different strata: 22a is assigned to J and 22b to P. In the opinion of some scholars, however, this structure suggests the possibility that something has actually been dropped out of the text.[59] The possibility of variant readings of this verse is indicated by the LXX rendition, which attributes a reaction to Jacob with the words καὶ πονηρὸν

54 See, e.g., Emanuel Tov, *Textual Criticism of the Hebrew Bible* (Minneapolis: Fortress, 1992), 50-51, for a discussion of the origins of these text divisions.

55 Zakovitch and Shinan, *The Story of Revuen and Bilhah*, 23.

56 These signs indicate a separation from the following words, with the *sof pasuq* (*silluq*) being "stronger" than the *etnaḥta*. See, e.g., Tov, *Textual Criticism*, 69.

57 See, e.g., Shemaryahu Talmon, "'*Pisqah Be'emṣa Pasuq*' and 11QP5ᵃ," *Textus* 5 (1966): 18, who suggests that the lacuna in Gen. 35:22 points to 1Chr. 5:1.

58 Tov, *Textual Criticism*, 51, 54-55. According to Tov (ibid., 51), the practice found in the Masoretic group of texts of using spaces to indicate sections is also known from much earlier texts, including biblical texts found among the Dead Sea documents.

59 These arguments are summarized in Zakovitch and Shinan, *The Story of Reuven and Bilhah*, 23.

ἐφάνη ἐναντίον αὐτου, "and the thing appeared grievous before him."[60] Tov suggests that this addition is actually a Hebraism, a translation of the phrase וירע בעיניו (and it was evil in his eyes), similarly translated by the LXX in Gen. 38:10; it was thus in his view likely based on a variant text which had these additional words.[61]

The motive behind such variations is similarly speculated upon by scholars, and is generally assumed to be related to the aetiological function of the incident. As the text was presumably manipulated, one wonders whether the reference to Bilhah as a *pilegesh* was deliberately inserted in order to give this incident the form of an aetiological "set piece."

Certainly the episode of Bilhah and Reuven was already represented in the Bible as the cause of Reuben's disqualification from the status of firstborn. Genesis 49, for instance, records Jacob's blessings for his sons; verse 4, itself something of a circumlocution, provides for Reuven:

פחז כמים אל תותר כי עלית משכבי אביך אז חללת יצועי עלה

Boiling over like water — you will not surpass; you mounted your father's bed(s), and then you committed defilement — he mounted my couch.[62]

1Chronicles 5:1-3 gives the similarly convoluted statement:[63]

---

60 Translation of L. Brenton, *The Septuagint Version: Greek and English* (Grand Rapids, Mich.: Zondervan). We may note that Targum Yonatan also attributes a reaction to Jacob; see note 65.

61 Emanuel Tov, *The Text-Critical Use of the Septuagint in Biblical Research* (Jerusalem Biblical Studies 8; Jerusalem: Simor, 1997), 84.

62 The verse has a number of unusual features aside from its obscure meaning. Gesenius suggests that the absence of a verb in the first phrase is a feature of exclamatory speech. See E. Kautzsch, *Gesenius' Hebrew Grammar* (revised by A. E. Cowley; Oxford: Clarendon, 1970), section 147c. As G. Brooke, "4Q Commentary on Genesis A," in *Qumran Cave 4, XVII, Parabiblical Texts, Part 3* (*DJD* 22; Oxford: Clarendon, 1996), 204, has noted, a verb in 2 m.s. perf. is found in other texts. The Samaritan Pentateuch [=SP], for instance, based on the MS used by Abraham Tal, *The Samaritan Targum*, has פחזת (you were hasty) instead of the noun פחז; the LXX has ἐξυβρίσας (you were insolent). Other features noted are the use here, as in Ruth 2:14, of תותר instead of the expected תותיר (SP has תותיר), the use of the plural משכבי, and the abrupt transition from 2nd to 3rd person, suggested to be a feature of poetic speech (Gesenius, 53n, 124b, 144p).

63 The comments on Reuven appear to take the form of an aside inserted into the main text. Zakovitch and Shinan, *The Story of Reuven and Bilhah*, 14, suggest that vv. 1-3 are structured as a chiasmus.

ובני ראובן בכור ישראל כי הוא הבכור ובחללו יצועי אביו נתנה בכורתו
לבני יוסף בן ישראל ולא להתיחש לבכרה כי יהודה גבר באחיו ולנגיד ממנו
והבכרה ליוסף בני ראובן בכור ישראל חנוך ופלוא חצרון וכרמי

And the sons of Reuven, the firstborn of Israel — though he was the firstborn, in his defiling of the couches of his father his birthright was given to the sons of Joseph the son of Israel, so that he was not included in the birthright; though Judah prevailed over his brothers, and a leader [came] of him, the birthright was Joseph's — the sons of Reuven, the firstborn of Israel, were Ḥanokh and Palu, Ḥetzron and Karmi.

Zakovitch and Shinan point also to a possible relationship of the incident to Deut. 33:6, a part of Moses' blessings of the tribes, which states:

יחי ראובן ואל ימת ויהי מתיו מספר

Let Reuven live and not die, but his men shall be few.

They suggest that this verse was possibly aware of a version of Gen. 35:22 that referred to a curse upon Reuven condemning him to death and attempted here to blunt its effect;[64] a later editor actually removed the curse from 35:22, which accounts for its odd structure.

These circumlocutions and the sense that something has been left out of Gen. 35:22 suggest that the biblical editors already had difficulty with the precise nature of Reuven's sin, and consequently with the role of Bilhah. Did Reuven commit incest with his father's *wife*? Was the phrase פלגש אביו (his father's *pilegesh)*, inserted precisely to mitigate such an implication? Was it inserted because this story was seen as a well-known moral lesson in which the *pilegesh* plays an important role? There are two pieces of evidence that support the latter interpretation.

Qumran document 4Q252 reacts to the mention of a *pilegesh* in this verse. The document in general highlights certain Genesis narratives in order to clarify or re-present them.[65] Column iv of this document contains

64 Zakovitch and Shinan, *The Story of Reuven and Bilhah*, 14.

65 Robert Eisenman and Michael Wise, *The Dead Sea Scrolls Uncovered* (New York: Penguin Books, 1992), 77.

two references to *pilagshim*: it juxtaposes Timna (the *pilegesh* of Eliphaz, the son of Esau, in Gen. 36:12) and Bilhah (though, as we have noted, she is called the *pilegesh* of Reuven's father only in Gen. 35:22):[66]

> תמנע היתה פילגש לאליפז בן עשיו ותלד לו את עמלק הוא אשר הכ[ה] שאול [...] כאשר דבר למושה באחרית ה[י]מים תמחה את זכר עמלק מתחת השמים[...] ברכות יעקוב ראובן בכורי אתה ורישית אוני יתר שאת ויתר עוז פחזתה כמים אל תותר עליתה משכבי אביכה אז חללתה יצועיו עלה.[...]פשרו אשר הוכיחו אשר שכב עם בלהה פילגשו ו[א]מר בכו[רי...]ל[...]ראובן הוא ראשית ער[...]

> Timna was the *pilegesh* of Eliphaz, the son of Esau. And she bore him Amaleq, he whom Saul destroyed [...] as He spoke to Moses: *In the latter days you will wipe out the memory of Amaleq from under the heavens* [Deut. 25:19] [...] The blessings of Jacob: *Reuben, you are my firstborn and the first fruits of my strength, excelling in dignity and excelling in power. You were unstable as water; you shall no longer excel. You went up onto your father's bed. Then you defiled. He went up on his couches* [...] its interpretation is[67] that he reproved him in that he lay with Bilhah his *pilegesh*. And he [s]aid *[My] first[born.....]Reuven* he was the first[...]

I believe that this passage serves, among other possible functions,[68] as a polemic against *pilagshim*. Two *pilegesh* references from Genesis are linked to each other and to Jacob's blessing by means of two types of commentary: the use of other biblical references (in this case from Deuteronomy) to explain the verses in Genesis, and a *pesher*-type commentary explaining the meaning of 49:4b as a reproof.[69] Through these various juxtapositions, the text makes an explicit aetiological connection between a relationship with

66 The Hebrew is taken from Brooke, "4Q Commentary," 203-4.

67 According to the editor, this is a standard introductory formula in a *pesher* (204, note L. 5).

68 Compare, e.g., the suggestion by Eisenman and Wise, *The Dead Sea Scrolls Uncovered*, 83-85, that the document is ultimately a Messianic pronouncement with a collateral condemnation of fornication, and the contrary suggestion by Moshe Bernstein, "4Q252: From Re-Written Bible to Biblical Commentary," *JJS* 45 (1994): 124, to consider the document simply as a series of commentaries and to avoid seeking "artificial unifiers" in the text.

69 Bernstein, "4Q252," 19, questions the use of the *pesher* form here, on the assumption that this form is connected with "sectarian commentary"; he posits, based on this sample, that the use of the *pesher* form may be broader.

a *pilegesh* and later loss of status, or worse; it reinforces the idea that the result of dealing with such women is disaster — the destruction of one's descendants (Amaleq, supposedly the descendant of Esau, by Saul in 1Sam. 14:48; 15:3, 7) or the removal of the rights of the firstborn (from Reuven, in Gen. 49). Of further interest are the variants in the biblical *lemmata*, particularly the use of שכב עם (lay with) for the MT שכב (lay) in Gen. 35:22,[70] and פחזתה (you were unstable) for the MT פחז (he was unstable) in Gen. 49:4.[71] This might be further indication that the biblical verses in question were unstable.

A second piece of evidence is found in Targum Neofiti. In the edition of Diez Macho the words פילגש אביו (his father's *pilegesh*) are left untranslated in the primary MS,[72] which has:

> והוי כדי שרון ישראל בארעא ההיא ואזל ראובן וישכב ית בלהה ושמע ישראל והוון בנוי יעקב תרין עשר

The words פילגש אבוי have been added as an interlinear gloss.

Diez Macho and other scholars have suggested that this omission is in fact a reflection of the mishnaic prohibition in *mMeg.* 4:10; this restricts the public dissemination of the Bilhah-Reuven incident, among others:

> מעשה ראובן נקרא ולא מתרגם מעשה תמר מתרגם ונקרא מעשה עגל ראשון נקרא ומתרגם והשני נקרא ולא מתרגם ברכת כהנים מעשה דוד ואמנון לא נקראין ולא מתרגמין

> The incident of Reuven is read [in public] but not translated. The incident of Tamar [and Judah, in Gen. 38] is read and translated. The first incident of the calf [Exod. 32:1-20] is read and translated; the second [the continuation of the chapter in vv. 21-35] is read but not translated. The blessing of the

70 It is not clear whether different nuances are implied by את and עם. The Bible uses both, as well as various prepositions with שכב including אצל (as in Gen. 39:10). It is perhaps significant that three instances referring to a שכבת זרע also use the particle את (Lev. 15:18, 19:20, and Num. 5:13). Brown, *Israel and Hellas*, 68, suggests that the difference might be comparable to that in modern "vulgar" English between "lay" and "lie with."

71 As noted above (n. 58), both the SP and LXX have a verb in 2 m.s. perf.

72 This Targum uses לחנתה elsewhere in Genesis in the same manner as Onkelos for *pilegesh* and certain *amah/shifḥah* references to Bilhah and Zilpah; for Re'umah, however (Gen. 22:24), it uses פלקה.

priests [Num. 6:24-6] and the incident of David and Amnon [with respect to Tamar, according to the Gemara (*b. Meg.* 25ab), in 2Sam. 13:1] are not read and not translated.

The precise application of this rule is unclear, particularly whether the prohibition referred to the written Targumim. An expanded version of the ruling is found in *tMeg.* (Lieberman) 3:35, associated with R. Ḥaninah ben Gamliel, a second generation tanna:[73]

מעשה ראובן נקרא ולא מיתרגם ומעשה בר' חנינה בן גמליאל שהיה
קורא בכבול וילך ראובן וישכב את בלהה וגו' ויהיו בני יעקב שנים עשר, ואמ' למתרגם, אל
תתרגם אלא אחרון

The incident of Reuven is read but not translated. And it happened that R. Ḥaninah ben Gamliel, who used to read in Kabul[74]: ...*Reuven went and lay with Bilhah*, etc., *and the sons of Jacob were twelve*, told the translator: 'Translate only the last [part].'

What is included in the "etc.," however, is not clear from any of the MSS cited in the apparatus.[75] We may note also that the Aramaic Targumim do actually translate this verse, more or less literally (TY adds an interpretation that is found in *bShabb.* 55b, among other places.[76]) McNamara, however, claims that all the restricted texts in *mMeg.* are missing in Neofiti, and thus that this Targum is dependent on a tradition

73 In the opinion of P. S. Alexander, "The Rabbinic Lists of Forbidden Targumim," *JJS* 27 (1976): 180, R. Ḥaninah is the source of this ruling.

74 The first printed edition has בעכו.

75 MS ל is missing the words from את to עשר, but such shortening of verse quotations is common in rabbinic literature.

76 This talmudic reaction will be discussed below. The TY reads:

והוה כד שרא ישראל בארעא ההיא ואזל ראובן ובלבל ית מצעא דבלהה פילקתיה
דאבוי דהות מסדרא כל קבל מצעא דלאה אימיה ואיתחשיב עילוי כאילו שמיש עימה
ושמע ישראל ובאיש ליה ואמר ויי דילמא נפיק מיני פסולא...

And it was when Israel dwelt in that land, Reuven went and disarranged the bed of Bilhah, his father's concubine, which was arranged alongside the bed of his mother Leah; and it was attributed to him as if he had had intercourse with her. And Israel heard, and was ashamed, and said: 'Woe lest an unworthy person is descended from me...'

abiding by the mishnaic legislation.[77] Alexander too argues that the pattern of omissions in Targum Neofiti confirms a rabbinic interest in regulating the Targum in general, and that this Targum was directly edited or followed a variant that had been edited. Zakovitch and Shinan,[78] noting the mixture of Aramaic and Hebrew, especially the use of the word וישכב (he lay), suggest that in fact none of the "offending" part of the verse was translated at first; various hands later translated different words. This explanation might account for the mixture of languages, yet it would seem that none of the explanations is sufficient to explain why only the words פילגש אביו are missing, and how such an omission would be seen as fulfilling the requirements of *mMeg* 4:10. It is possible, on the one hand, that the redactor thought that simply omitting these words would avoid shedding light on the situation; on the other hand, it is also possible that there was a textual tradition used by the translator that did not have these words in the original Hebrew. Again, such a possibility suggests that the word *pilegesh* in the biblical text plays a specific role. I would argue, therefore, that there is support for the possibility that the term *pilegesh* was not original to the verse in all MT versions and was deliberately added to impart a stereotypical moral lesson.

It is interesting to note that much extrabiblical and postbiblical writing on this incident is concerned with dissociating Reuven from any suggestion of incest. To the extent that these discussions reflect on Bilhah's status, I shall discuss them further in chapter 7, as a further indication that Bilhah remained a biblical "insider" until relatively late.

2.4.C The ishah pilegesh of Judges 19

The last section of the book of Judges, ending with the civil war between Benjamin and the rest of the tribes (chs. 19-21), begins in chapter 19 with the bizarre story of the *ishah pilegesh*. Judges 19:1-3 describe her relationship with a certain Levite:

---

77 Martin McNamara, *The New Testament and the Palestinian Targum to the Pentateuch* (Rome: Pontifical Biblical Institute, 1966), 47.

78 Zakovitch and Shinan, *The Story of Reuven and Bilhah*, 15-16. They note (p. 16) that in the related verse Gen. 49:4 (Jacob's blessing of Reuven), the sin of Reuven is also left untranslated, and may have been thought to have been included in the prohibition in *mMeg*.

ויהי בימים ההם ומלך אין בישראל ויהי איש לוי גר בירכתי הר אפרים
ויקח לו אשה פילגש מבית לחם יהודה. ותזנה עליו פילגשו ותלך מאתו אל
בית אביה אל בית לחם יהודה ותהי שם ימים ארבעה חדשים. ויקם אישה וילך אחריה לדבר
על לבה להשיבו*
*qere = להשיבה

In those days, when there was no king in Israel, there was a Levite man living in the foothills of Mount Ephraim; he took an *ishah pilegesh* from Bethlehem [in] Judah. And his *pilegesh* ended her relationship with him[79] and went away from him to her father's house to Bethlehem [in] Judah and was there four whole months. And her husband arose and went after her to speak kindly to her and to bring her back [according to the *qere*]...

On their return journey, lodging in Givah with an Ephraimite, they are beset by a mob of Benjaminites, who demand that the Levite be sent out to them to be used sexually. The host sends out the Levite's *pilegesh* instead; she is repeatedly raped and is found lying by the door in the morning (Judg. 19:27-8):

ויקם אדניה בבקר ויפתח דלתות הבית ויצא ללכת לדרכו והנה האשה פילגשו נפלת פתח
הבית וידיה על הסף. ויאמר אליה קומי ונלכה ואין ענה...

And her lord rose up in the morning, and opened the doors of the house, and went out to go his way; and behold his *ishah pilegesh* was fallen down at the entrance of the house, and her hands were on the threshold. And he said to her, 'Get up and let us go.' But there was no answer...

The Levite cuts her body into twelve pieces and sends them throughout Israel, inviting vengeance on Givah. A civil war ensues in which the tribe of Benjamin is nearly destroyed. Having vowed not to give their daughters in marriage to any Benjaminites, the remaining tribes nonetheless arrange to provide the remnant with women taken forcibly from Yavesh Gilad, and thereafter invite the Benjaminites to replenish their supply of wives by setting upon the women at the yearly festival at Shiloh.

It is generally recognized that there is more to this narrative than simply

---

79 This is not the usual translation of ותזנה עליו which is usually taken to imply some type of harlotry or other sexual misbehavior. I shall explain my translation in more detail below.

the supposed "decadence" of later Hebrew literature.[80] There is evidence of a deliberate attempt to emphasize the macabre and dehumanizing aspects of the narrative, especially in chapter 19, through various devices, many of which have been discussed by scholars: the use of darkness as a portent of danger and as associated with the sexuality of "unusual" women;[81] the anonymity of the participants; the exaggerated, nightmare-like delay of the group's departure from Bethlehem and their consequent failure to reach shelter before dark;[82] and parody or mocking of other biblical events, through the use of similar themes or theme words: the young lad, pair of donkeys, and knife used by the Levite recalling the two young men, the donkey, and the knife accompanying Abraham on his way to sacrifice Isaac (Gen. 22:3, 10); the offer of a woman's sexual services in order to save a male guest from homosexual rape, as at Sodom (Gen. 19:8); Saul's cutting up of oxen into twelve pieces to rally the people, this time in defense of Yavesh Gilad (1Sam. 11:7).[83]

---

80 As noted by Robert Boling, *Judges* (Anchor Bible 6A; Garden City, New York: Doubleday, 1975), 278, citing earlier opinions of Wellhausen and Moore.

81 See, e.g., Weston Fields, "The Motif 'Night as Danger' Associated with Three Biblical Destruction Narratives," in *Sha'arei Talmon: Studies in the Bible, Qumran and the Ancient Near East Presented to Shemaryahu Talmon* (ed. M. Fishbane and E. Tov; Winona Lake, Ind.: Eisenbrauns, 1992), 22, 26 who notes a similar use of darkness with respect to the destruction of Sodom in Gen. 19 and the final plague in Exod. 12:29 ("And it came to pass at midnight"). He describes the association of night and irregular types of female sexuality as an "allo-motif" running throughout the Bible.

82 See. e.g., Yair Zakovitch, "The Literary Paradigm Three-Four in the Bible" [in Hebrew] (Ph.D. diss., Hebrew University, 1977), 334, 336, who suggests that the impression of a deliberate manipulation of time is created in the narrative by a variation of the "three-four" pattern that he argues is prevalent in the biblical text. The Levite's five-day stay at his father-in-law's has three distinct periods: the first three days; the fourth day, when by the usual three-four pattern one would expect the group to leave; and the fifth day, when the group actually leaves. The description of the fourth day is marked by a lengthening of phrases, and the fifth by a shortening of phrases and feeling of urgency; the effect is thus to create peaks and troughs of tension.

83 See, e.g. Jeremiah Unterman, "The Literary Influence of 'The Binding of Isaac' (Genesis 22) on 'The Outrage at Gibeah' (Judges 19)," *Hebrew Annual Review* 4 (1980): 161-66, esp. 162-63, on the parallels to the sacrifice of Isaac; Ken Stone, "Gender and Homosexuality in Judges 19: Subject-Honor, Object-Shame?" *JSOT* 67 (1995): 87-107, at 100, on the theme of homosexual rape as an act of asserting relative power relations and the rape of the Levite's concubine as a proxy for this act; Yairah Amit, "The Story of the *Pilegesh* in Givea in the Hidden Dispute Against the Kingship of Shaul (Judges 19-21)" [in Hebrew], *Bet Miqra* 37 (1991) on the use of place names and events reminiscent of Saul narratives

The number of such devices and allusions suggests that their inclusion is not coincidental and that they are meant to draw the reader's attention to non-explicit aspects of the story. As Stone has noted,[84] however, this very complexity leaves open the possibility for a variety of interpretations, at different levels of reading or with different socio-historical foci. Earlier commentators attempted to rationalize aspects of the story. Josephus and Pseudo-Philo, for instance, both attempt to justify the treatment of the *pilegesh*. Pseudo-Philo asserts not only that both the "concubine" and the Levite were dragged out by the mob, but that the woman was being punished because she "committed sin with Amalekites" (45:3).[85] Josephus specifically calls the woman *τῶν γονέων* (his wife), and states that she left the Levite because they quarreled; the Benjaminites demanded her and took her by force, and she was ashamed to show her face to her husband (*Ant.* 5:142). Certain rabbinic interpretations emphasized the story as a revelation of divine justice. According to a passage in *bSan.* 103b, the Israelites were overcome by the Benjaminites because they valued human honor (i.e, the Levite's) over divine honor:

> אמר להן הקב"ה הניחו לו שפתו מצויה לעוברי דרכים ועל דבר זה נענשו אנשי פ"בג אמר להן הקב"ה בכבודי לא מחיתם על כבודו של בשר ודם מחיתם

> The Lord Blessed-Be-He said to them: 'They left him [Micah, in Judg. 18] alone, as his bread was available to travelers; but on this matter the people of the *pilegesh* of Givah were punished.' The Lord Blessed-Be-He said to them: 'You did not protest on behalf of my honor, but you did protest about the honor of flesh and blood.'

Tanḥuma Vayeshev 2 similarly contrasts the Israelites' avenging of the human affront in Judges 19-21 with their failure to act against Micah's idol in the immediately preceding chapter of Judges:

> תדע לך כח החרם שהרי השבטים שקנאו על פלגש בגבעה ולא קנאו על פסל מיכה הרגו בהן בני בנימין פעם ראשונה ושניה ושלישית...

---

in 1Sam.

84 Stone, "Gender and Homosexuality," 88-89.

85 This translation is by Harrington, "Pseudo-Philo."

> Know the power of the ban: The tribes who were incensed regarding the *pilegesh* of Givah but not about Micah's idol had their people slain by Benjamin once, twice, three times...[86]

Certain scholars have interpreted the three chapters from a political perspective, either as reflecting in some degree actual events, or as promulgating some sort of political message.[87]

Other scholars prefer to see the elements of the narrative as the "materialization of a social reality of which they are a part and to which they respond."[88] Bal, in particular, emphasizes the role of the *pilegesh* within the larger social reality apparently represented in the book of Judges; the coherence of this book, in her view, lies not in a particular political chronology but in the systematic violence against women portrayed throughout the text.[89] This perspective helps to focus on what from our point of view are the essential questions in chapter 19: Why a *pilegesh*, and what point do her rape and murder serve in the story? We may posit that it is her precariousness that makes her appropriate as a victim, again highlighting the use of the idea of the *pilegesh* as a player in a set piece.

We may note first that the focus on the woman and her "unusualness" is highlighted by the use of inconsistent kinship terminology. In Judg. 19:27 the Levite is referred to as the woman's *adon*, "lord," a term which might suggest a master-slave relationship. Yet up to this point he has been called simply her *ish*, "man" or "husband" (e.g., 19:3, 20:4); the relationship

---

86 Pseudo-Philo also proposes a linkage of the Micah and Givah texts: the Israelites were punished because they overlooked the sin of Micah's idol while allowing themselves to be provoked about the fate of the concubine (45:6, 46:7).

87 See, as a representative sample, Jan Fokkelman, "Structural Remarks on Judges 9 and 19," in *Sha'arei Talmon*, 43, who argues that the chapters are a pro-monarchy polemic, with the phrase "there was no king in Israel" framing the narrative in its first and last verses (19:1 and 21:25) in order to underline the social chaos that results from the absence of a king; Amit, "The Story of the *Pilegesh* in Giveah," 118, who sees the narrative as pro-Davidic, serving to emphasize the ineffectiveness of the Benjaminite Saul, who is from Yavesh Gilad (1Sam. 10:26), as compared to David, of the family of Boaz, who is related to Naomi's husband from Bet Leḥem (Ruth 4:22); and Boling, *Judges*, 278, who sees the narrative as a postexilic exhortation to return to a united Israel and give up the antiquated notion of a loosely organized tribal confederation.

88 See Mieke Bal, *Death and Dissymmetry: The Politics of Coherence in the Book of Judges* (Chicago: University of Chicago Press, 1988), 6.

89 Bal, *Death and Dissymmetry*, 5.

between the Levite and the woman's father is expressed with *ḥoten*/*ḥatan*, "in-law" (e.g., 19:4, 5, 7, 9). The woman herself is referred to in various ways: with respect to the Levite, as an *ishah pilegesh* (a term unique to chapter 19, vv. 1, 27, and perhaps a contradiction in terms, if we take it as "consort-wife"), as simply *pilegesh*, or as simply *ishah*; with respect to her father, as *na'arah*; and by the host as an *amah* (19:19). The unusual relationship is heightened by the use of the ambiguous verb זנה *ZNH* in verse 2, sometimes translated here with reference to harlotry (e.g., KJV: "played the whore"), or as denoting faithlessness, particularly sexual. Rashi, for instance, has:

> זנתה מביתו אל החוץ כל לשון זנות אינו אלא לשון יוצאת נפקת ברא יוצאת מבעלה לאהוב את אחרים
>
> She went out from his house to the outside; the language of *zenut* is simply 'one who goes out,' [i.e.,] a prostitute — she goes out from her husband to be a lover to others.

The Targum to Judges has ובסרת עלוהי , "she slighted him" (Jastrow).

Bal has challenged, correctly I believe,[90] the conventional meanings assigned to *pilegesh* as "concubine" and *zonah* as associated with harlotry. She interprets this chapter, among other narratives in Judges, as reflecting the tensions arising from the change between patrilocal marriage, in which the wife remains with her father, her natural "owner," and virilocal marriage, in which the wife goes with her husband, a culturally-assigned owner.[91] Bal accepts the interpretation of *pilegesh* as a woman in the *beena*-type, patrilocal marriage described by Morgenstern (1929, 1931); the *pilegesh* in Judges 19 had challenged the virilocal system by leaving her husband (the implication of the term *ZNH* here)[92] to return to her father, and had to

90 In my article, "A Re-embracement of Judges 19: Challenging Public-Private Boundaries," in *Vixens Disturbing Vineyards: Embarrassment and Embracement of Scriptures, Festschrift in Honor of Harry Fox leVeit Yoreh* (ed. Tzemah Yoreh *et al.*; Boston: Academic Studies Press), 53-64, I argue again that "consort" is a better translation of *pilegesh* and that ותזנה עליו should be translated here as "she went away in anger."

91 Bal, *Death and Dissymmetry*, 5, 89.

92 On the question of the etymology of the biblical root *ZNH*, see, e.g., L. Koehler and W. Baumgartner, *The Hebrew and Aramaic Lexicon of the Old Testament* (Leiden: Brill, 1995), *s.v.* זנה I and זנה II. The first root is connected both with the idea of harlotry

be eliminated.[93] The "faithlessness" exhibited by the *pilegesh* would thus be interpreted differently by father and husband.[94]

While I do not wish to contest in detail Bal's proposition, I think that her definition of *pilegesh* is too narrow; as Exum, among others, has noted, the idea of a *beena*-wife would not fit all biblical uses of *pilegesh*.[95] I do, however, agree that the vagueness of the terminology is deliberate, and that, as she notes, the story is structured around the tension between "inside" and "outside" the house.[96] I suggest that Judges 19-21 again associates the *pilegesh*, the woman outside "normal" boundaries, with an aetiological challenge to authority (whether or not this passage represents an actual event). In this case there is an attempt by representatives of the youngest brother Benjamin (through the men of Givah) to challenge the authority of the older brother Judah, now the "legal" firstborn, through the medium of the *pilegesh* of Bethlehem, a representative of Judah. Judah's priority, we may note, is emphasized both at the beginning and at the end of this book, and the language is similar: Judah is nominated by God as first to the attack at the conquest (Judg. 1:1-2 and similarly nominated during the civil war (Judg. 20:18).

There is a further intra-biblical allusion to another "unusual" woman that reinforces the idea that the use of the *pilegesh* is an intentional literary device. Judges 19:27, quoted above, describes the action of the woman's husband (now called her "lord") after her night of terror: ויפתח דלתות הבית (and he opened [*vayiftaḥ*] the doors of the house); these words specifically recall the vow of Yiftaḥ in Judg. 11:31 that ultimately leads to the sacrifice

and the idea of apostasy. The authors connect the second root with Akkadian *zenû*, "to hate," a term found in Mesopotamian "divorce" clauses (see, e.g., CT 6 26a, ll. 9-12, as translated by Westbrook, *Old Babylonian Marriage Law*, 117). They also note, however, that the meaning "to be apostate" associated with the first root may be an extension of the meaning "to hate." One might posit that the biblical language of *zenut* implies in general an idea of moving apart from the Deity or a person, whether the motive is faithlessness, hatred, or adultery. It thus need not imply the specific sin of harlotry.

93 Bal, *Death and Dissymmetry*, 85, 92-93.

94 Bal, *Death and Dissymmetry*, 88. Bal notes the definitions of *zonah* given by Koehler and Baumgartner as including a husband who does not live with his wife's tribe. In the 1995 edition of this work, however *zonah* is defined simply as "a woman occasionally or professionally committing fornication, prostitute, harlot."

95 J. Cheryl Exum, *Fragmented Women* (Valley Forge, Pa.: Trinity, 1993), 177 n. 13.

96 Bal, *Death and Dissymmetry*, 90.

of his daughter:

והיה היוצא אשר יצא מדלתי ביתי לקראתי בשובי בשלום מבני עמון
והיה לה' והעליתיהו עולה

...whatever comes out from the doors of my house to meet me upon my safe return from the Ammonites will be God's, and I will sacrifice it as an *'olah*.

The threshold is significant in both stories. Exum suggests that the *pilegesh* text is a castigation regarding of the dangers to an autonomous woman,[97] one who has violated the boundaries between the domestic and the public spheres by leaving her husband. As Bal notes: "The boundary between inside and outside gives rise to 'an almost obscene conflation of private and public. It brings with it all the solitude of absolute privacy with none of its safety...'"[98] Possibly the involuntary and coerced "prostitution" of the *pilegesh* serves as an ironic contrast to her autonomy and results in her being permanently excluded from the household, permanently on the threshold.[99] The "proper" order is restored by allowing the taking of unmarried women.

We may also argue that there are a number of allusions to the incident of Bilhah and Reuven and the Genesis text in which it is set: the unusual

---

97 Exum, *Fragmented Women*, 179.

98 Bal, *Death and Dissymmetry*, 195, quoting Elaine Scarry, *The Body in Pain: The Making and Unmaking of the World* (New York: Oxford University Press, 1985), 53. Interestingly, it is this violation of public-private spheres that caught the attention of a later sage, as recorded in the following statement in *bGitt.* 6b:

אמר רב חסדא לעולם אל יטיל אדם אימה יתירה בתוך ביתו שהרי פילגש בגבעה
הטיל עליה בעלה אימה יתירה והפילה כמה רבבות מישראל

Rav Ḥisda said: A man should not throw excessive terror into his household, given [the story of] the *pilegesh* in Gibeah – her husband terrorized her excessively, and it [or she] caused the downfall of tens of thousands of Israelites.

I discuss this opinion further in "A Re-embracement of Judges 19: Challenging Public-Private Boundaries."

99 This association between thresholds and ambiguous status is powerfully suggested Margaret Atwood, *The Handmaid's Tale* (Toronto: McClelland & Stewart, 1985), a novel that depicts a dystopia in which young women are forced to bear children to a male elite whose wives are barren. The "handmaid" of the title describes her entry into an elite household in this way (ibid. 13): "On our first days we are permitted front doors, but after that we're supposed to use the back. Things haven't settled down, it's too soon, everyone is unsure about our exact status. After a while, it will be either all front doors or all back."

(non-)reactions of both Jacob and the Levite to the violence committed against the women; the emphasis on the twelve sons of Jacob in Genesis and the twelve dismembered body parts in Judges; and the juxtaposition of Judah (Rachel dies near Bethlehem; the *pilegesh* originates in Bethlehem), Joseph, the first of Rachel's sons (the Levite and his host are Ephraimites) and Benjamin, the second of Rachel's sons (the murderers are Benjaminites). This pattern of intra-biblical parallels, like the others noted by scholars, suggests the deliberate use of a motif.

2.5 CONCLUSION

We may conclude that the *pilegesh,* the "consort," is a convenient figure in biblical aetiologies: illicit sexual behaviour with the *pilegesh* may lead to disaster, yet the term is sufficiently vague to allow the patriarchs to associate with them with no diminution of patriarchal stature. The use of the term *pilegesh* in Gen. 35:22 may thus have been an intentional insertion — to suggest the danger associated with the *pilegesh* (in this case, Reuven's loss of firstborn status), but also to "soften" the suggestion that Reuven committed incest with his father's wife (a concern quite evident in postbiblical sources). Similarly, Qeturah's description as a *pilegesh* in Chronicles, though she is called an *ishah* in Genesis, may have been intended to "soften" Abraham's relationship with her and thus enhance Sarah's preeminence as Abraham's only "wife." Our results also indicate that the biblical *pilegesh* was also not conclusively associated with slavery.

CHAPTER 3

THE *AMAH* OF EXODUS 21:2-11

As a source of information concerning slaves, the Pentateuch provides a number of conflicting laws that have served as the subject of much speculation concerning the historical development both of the pentateuchal text and of Israelite society. There is a notable disagreement in particular between the manumission rules of Exod. 21:2-11 and those of Deut. 15:12-18 concerning the *amah*; the former pericope seems to emphasize her sexual function, suggesting that her role was that of either permanent breeder or concubine, while the latter pericope contains no such emphasis and in fact limits her term of service to six years. I suggest that the Exodus pericope is concerned with the question of competing control over a female and her children, a question that is also reflected in a number of Mesopotamian sources, but in no way suggests the automatic operation of a matrilineal inheritance of slavery or that the inevitable fate of the *amah* was concubinage. To support this suggestion, it is necessary to first assess this pericope in relation to certain of the conflicting manumission rules. We may then examine some of the structural and textual problems associated with this pericope and attempt to understand its function through a comparison with Mesopotamian parallels.

3.1 EXODUS 21:2-11 AND ITS RELATION TO OTHER MANUMISSION RULES[1]

Exodus 21:2-11 is one of a number of different pentateuchal rules on the subject of manumission of slaves. Each of the three pentateuchal "codes" in fact contains sections dealing with manumission. I will set out the texts

1 Chapter five contains discussions of some of the postbiblical reactions to these rules.

and translations in some detail here, so as to highlight some of the textual and philological problems:

1) Exodus 21:2-11 (E stratum) gives two apparently different rules with respect to the Hebrew *eved* and the *amah*. Verses 2-6 deal first with the male, limiting his term of service to six years unless he becomes attached to the household as an *eved olam*, called in later law the *nirtza* (i.e., one whose ear is pierced). The following pericope (vv. 7-11), however, specifies that the female sold by her father as an *amah* does not go out as "as the *avadim* do," but must be assigned or redeemed:

2. כי תקנה עבד עברי שש שנים יעבד ובשבעת יצא לחפשי חנם.

3. אם בגפו יבא בגפו יצא אם בעל אשה הוא ויצאה אשתו עמו.

4. אם אדניו יתן לו אשה וילדה לו בנים או בנות האשה וילדיה תהיה לאדניה (*) והוא יצא בגפו.

5. ואם אמר יאמר העבד אהבתי את אדני את אשתי ואת בני לא אצא חפשי.

6. והגישו אדניו אל האלהים והגישו אל הדלת או אל המזוזה ורצע אדניו את אזנו במרצע ועבדו לעלם.

7. וכי ימכר איש את בתו לאמה לא תצא כצאת העבדים.

8. אם רעה בעיני אדניה אשר לא יעדה (*) והפדה לעם נכרי לא ימשל למכרה בבגדו בה.

9. ואם לבנו ייעדנה (*) כמשפט הבנות יעשה לה.

10. אם אחרת יקח לו שארה כסותה וענתה (*) לא יגרע.

11. ואם שלש אלה לא יעשה לה ויצאה חנם אין כסף.

Variants marked by (*)
Line 4: the Samaritan Pentateuch has לאדניו instead of לאדניה
Line 8: the *qere* is לו יעדה instead of לא יעדה
:the Samaritan Pentateuch has העידה instead of יעדה
Line 9: the Samaritan Pentateuch has יעידנה instead of ייעדנה
Line 10: the Samaritan Pentateuch has וענותה instead of וענתה

Translation

(2) If you purchase a Hebrew *eved*, he shall work for six years, and in the seventh year he shall go out free with no obligation.

(3) If he came in by himself, he shall leave by himself; if he has a wife, his wife shall go out with him.

(4) If his master gave him a wife and she bore him sons or daughters, the woman and her children shall belong to her master, and he shall go out by himself.

(5) If the *eved* shall say: 'I love my master, my wife and my children, I shall not go out free,'

(6) his master shall bring him near the god,[2] near the door or the post, and shall pierce his ear with a piercer, and he shall serve him forever.

(7) If a man sells his daughter as an *amah*, she shall not go out as the male slaves go out.

(8) If she is bad in the eyes of her master who has not assigned her [read: who has assigned her to him], she shall be redeemed; he is not allowed to sell her to a foreign nation, in trifling with her.

(9) And if he has assigned her to his son, he shall treat her according to the law of daughters.

(10) If he takes another, he shall not diminish her food, clothing, and sexual relations.

(11) If he does not do these three things for her, she shall go out with no obligation; there is no money.

2) Following a discussion of murder and the talionic rule, Exod. 21:26-27 specifies that an *eved* or *amah* must be released in the case of destruction of an eye or tooth:

26. וכי יכה איש את עין עבדו או את עין אמתו ושחתה לחפשי ישלחנו תחת עינו.

---

2 The traditional interpretation of אל האלהים is "before the judges"; Onkelos, for instance, translates לקדם דיניא.

27. ואם שן עבדו או שן אמתו יפיל לחפשי ישלחנו תחת שנו.

Translation

26. If a man strikes the eye of his *eved* or the eye of his *amah* and puts it out, he shall send him free for his eye.

27. And if he knocks out the tooth of his *eved* or the tooth of his *amah*, he shall send him free for his tooth.

3) The deuteronomic code, in contrast to Exodus 21, specifies a six-year limit of servitude for both Hebrew males and females. It also seems to add the possibility for the female to become an *eved olam*: Deuteronomy 15:12-18:

12. כי ימכר לך אחיך העברי או העבריה ועבדך שש שנים ובשנה השביעת תשלחנו חפשי מעמך.

13. וכי תשלחנו חפשי מעמך לא תשלחנו ריקם.

14. העניק תעניק לו מצאנך ומגרנך ומיקבך אשר ברכך ה' אלהיך תתן לו.

15. וזכרת כי עבד היית בארץ מצרים ויפדך ה' אלהיך על כן אנכי מצוך את הדבר הזה היום.

16. והיה כי יאמר אליך לא אצא מעמך כי אהבך ואת ביתך כי טוב לו עמך.

17. ולקחת את המרצע ונתתה באזנו ובדלת והיה לך עבד עולם ואף לאמתך תעשה כן.

18. לא יקשה בעינך בשלחך אתו חפשי מעמך כי משנה שכר שכיר עבדך שש שנים וברכך ה' אלהיך בכל אשר תעשה.

Translation

(12) If your fellow Israelite, or female Israelite, is sold to you, he shall work for you six years, and in the seventh year you shall send him free from you.

(13) And when you send him free from you, you shall not send him empty-handed.

(14) You shall certainly furnish him from your flock, your threshing-floor and your winepress — from that with which the Lord your God has blessed you, you shall give him.

(15) And you shall remember that you were an *eved* in the land of Egypt, and the Lord your God redeemed you; because of this I command this matter to you today.

(16) And if he says to you: 'I will not leave you because I love you and your house,' because he fares well with you,

(17) you shall take the piercer and put it through his ear and the door, and he shall be a permanent *eved* to you; and you shall do this even to your *amah*.

(18) It shall not seem hard in your eyes when you send him free from you, because he has doubled the value of a hired worker, having worked for you six years, and the Lord your God will bless you in all that you do.

4) Leviticus 25:39-46 (P stratum) provides yet another method of calculation of the slave's term, in which the maximum term lasts until the Jubilee and any redemption paid is to be calculated with reference to this year. It also makes explicit that such a limited term applies only to those called *aḥ* (brother) (or at least to males):

39. וכי ימוך אחיך עמך ונמכר לך לא תעבד בו עבדת עבד.

40. כשכיר כתושב יהיה עמך עד שנת היבל יעבד עמך.

41. ויצא מעמך הוא ובניו עמו ושב אל משפחתו ואל אחזת אבתיו ישוב.

42. כי עבדי הם אשר הוצאתי אתם מארץ מצרים לא ימכרו ממכרת עבד.

43. לא תרדה בו בפרך ויראת מאלהיך.

44. ועבדך ואמתך (*) אשר יהיו לך מאת הגוים אשר סביבתיכם מהם תקנו (*) עבד ואמה.

45. וגם מבני התושבים הגרים עמכם מהם תקנו וממשפחתם אשר עמכם אשר הולידו (*) בארצכם והיו לכם לאחזה.

46. והתנחלתם אתם לבניכם אחריכם לרשת אחזה לעלם בהם תעבדו (*) ובאחיכם בני ישראל איש באחיו לא תרדה בו בפרך.

Samaritan Pentateuch Variants

Line 44: ועבדיך ואמתיך in the plural instead of ועבדך ואמתך, and תקנהו in

the singular with a pronominal suffix instead of תקנו in the plural.
Line 45: הולדו instead of הולידו which could either be a shortened spelling or a change in verb pattern.
Line 46: תעבידו instead of תעבדו which changes the verb pattern to a *Hifil.*

Translation

(39) If your brother becomes poor among you and has been sold to you, do not work him with the work of an *eved*.

(40) He shall be like a hired worker, like a *toshav*,[3] with you; he shall work with you until the year of the Jubilee.

(41) And he shall go out, he and his children with him, and he shall return to his family, and he shall return to his ancestral holding.

(42) Because they are My *avadim*, whom I took out from the land of Egypt; they shall not be sold in the manner of an *eved*.

(43) Do not lord it over[4] him; and you shall fear your God.

---

3 The meaning of this term will be discussed in chapter five.

4 The term *perekh* (lord it over), is often associated with physical harshness, especially to describe the lot of the Hebrew slaves in Egypt, as in Exod. 1:13, 14. Rashi at Exod. 1:13, for instance, explains it as עבודה קשה, המפרכת את הגוף ומשברתו (hard work that crushes the body and breaks it). In rabbinic literature, however, it has a more general psychological nuance, as seen in the following interpretation of the phrase in Sifra *BeHar parshah* 6:2-3 (Weiss, p. 109d):

1. לא תרדה בו בפרך: שלא תאמר בו:'החם את הכוס הזה' - והוא אינו צריך
2. 'הצנן לי את הכוס' - והוא אינו צריך,
3. 'עדור תחת הגפן עד שאבוא'.
4. שמא תאמר:'לצורך עצמי אני עושה',
5. והרי הדבר מסור ללב, שנא' 'ויראת מאלהיך' וגו'
6. הא כל דבר שהוא מסור ללב נאמר בו 'ויראת מאלהיך'

(1) *Do not rule over him with perekh*: Do not say to him, 'Heat up this cup' when it is not necessary, (2)'Cool off this cup' when it is not necessary, (3) 'Hoe this vine until I return.' (4) Lest you say 'I really do need this [done],' (5) the matter is assigned to your conscience, as it is said, *You shall fear your God,* etc. (6) Behold it is stated about anything which is assigned to [your] conscience: *You shall fear your God.*

(44) And your *eved* and your *amah* that you shall have — from the nations that surround you — from them you shall purchase *eved* and *amah*.

(45) And also from the children of the *toshavim* who reside with you — from them you shall buy, and from their families who are with them whom they sired in your land; and they will be a holding to you.

(46) And you shall bequeath them to your sons after you, as an inherited holding; you may[5] work them forever, but with your brothers, the Israelites, you shall not lord it over each other.

Finally, Lev. 25:47-55 reiterates the requirement to redeem an *aḥ* sold to a *toshav* or stranger, and provides for the method of calculating a yearly rate, like that of a שכיר (hired person), based on the number of years to the Jubilee.

3.1.1 THE SIGNIFICANCE OF THE DIFFERENT *AMAH* RULES

Our interest in the biblical meaning of *amah* leads us in particular to the difference in treatment between males and females in Exod. 21:2-11 and the absence of this difference in Deut. 15:12-18. It seems to me that these pericopes have a major, if not primary, focus on the *amah*, as opposed to the male *eved*. Most significantly, Exod. 21:4 is used in midrash halakhah as the basis of the matrilineal principle for both slaves and gentiles (*Mekhilta de R. Ishmael*, as noted in the Introduction).

In addition to various textual problems associated with these passages,[6] there are also several apparent conflicts in substance. Is the Deuteronomy provision a reinterpretation of Exod. 2:4-11?[7] Scholarly assessment of the competing manumission rules in general, and the different treatments of

---

The essence of *perekh*, according to this passage, is the assigning of useless or imprecise work, simply for the sake of exerting one's sense of control.

5 This phrase was the subject of a tannaitic debate as to whether it implied an obligation or merely permission.

6 Many of these passages and the scholarly opinions surrounding them have been summarized by Chirichigno in *Debt-Slavery*.

7 For an analysis of Deuteronomy as containing reinterpreted layers, see Bernard Levinson, *Deuteronomy and the Hermeneutics of Legal Innovation* (New York: Oxford University Press, 1997), 3ff.

the *amah* in particular, offer no consistent approach or explanation. The interpretation of these rules has resolved itself into two basic trends. Certain scholars argue that these manumission provisions reflect a chronological development. It must be noted, however, that the stages of the chronology that each scholar proposes are dependent on the developmental model chosen. Some posit the relative lateness of the Leviticus provisions. Noth, for instance, relying on source-critical theory, accepts that the Leviticus Holiness Code (17:1-26:46) is to be dated to the transition between the pre – and postexilic cult.[8] Kleiman argues specifically for the lateness of the slave provisions in Leviticus, using an economic model. He suggests that the redemption provisions of Lev. 25:47-50, in which the "income stream" is shortened based on the time remaining until the Jubilee year, reflect a more advanced economic system in which "opportunity cost" had to include a time variable; the redemption of the *amah* (פדיון) in Exod. 21:9, in contrast, looks more like a fixed sum, which approximates opportunity cost in a more stagnant, and thus possibly less developed, economy.[9] Weinfeld argues for the lateness of the D stratum based on its more "humanistic" social philosophy; he in fact relies in part on the slave provisions of Deuteronomy 15 in support of this view, suggesting that these provisions represent a progressive amelioration in the treatment of the slave.[10] Schenker argues similarly that the manumission provisions of Deuteronomy 15 actually replaced those of Exodus 21, at least with respect to the female. In his view, Exod. 21:7-11 was designed to protect the male slave who desired to remain permanently with a mate given to him by the master by preventing

8 Martin Noth, *Leviticus, A Commentary* (Old Testament Library; Philadelphia: Westminster, 1965), 128. Noth acknowledges that some of the material of which the Holiness Code is composed may be "quite old." Cf. Karl Elliger, *Leviticus* (Handbuch zum Alten Testament Erste Reihe 4; Herausgegeben von O. Eissfeldt; Tübingen: Mohr, 1966), 16, who also sees the Holiness Code as an insert into the basic priestly writing.

9 Ephraim Kleiman, "Opportunity Cost, Human Capital, and Some Related Economic Concepts in Talmudic Literature," *History of Political Economy* 19 (1987): 264, 277.

10 Weinfeld, *Deuteronomy and the Deuteronomic School*, 282-83. Weinfeld also suggests (ibid., 233) that the change in Deut. 15:17 regarding the method of creating an *eved olam* presupposes the existence of cult centralization; while Exod. 21:6 speaks of bringing the slave before God at one's own door, this idea is eliminated in Deut. because the latter presumes the existence of an exclusive sanctuary in Jerusalem. Martin Noth, *Exodus: A Commentary* (Old Testament Library; London: SCM Press, 1962), 173-75, also argues that the deuteronomic provision is a more "progressive" stage in the development of the law.

the master from selling her; Deut. 15:12 provided a simpler solution by allowing the female to go out after seven years like the male.[11] Finally, the recent analysis of Van Seters offers the controversial view that Exodus is actually the later work. He too relies in part on the slave provisions in support of his view, arguing, among other points, that the reference to "buying" a Hebrew slave in Exod. 21:2 implies the purchase of someone who was already a slave, as opposed to a debt-slave, and thus points to an era in which there was already commercial traffic in Hebrew slaves.[12]

A second trend of interpretation aims at reconciling at least some of the competing provisions (rather than regarding them as evidence of development) by arguing that each one reflects a different type of slavery, or at least a different facet of slavery. Here again, however, there is no consistent approach. Chirichigno[13] has most recently made an extremely detailed study of the biblical manumission rules in which he posits that these rules were all part of a comprehensive social welfare scheme designed to restrict the permanent enslavement of Israelites and their dependants for debt, as well as the permanent alienation of patrimonial land. He further suggests that these rules could all have been operative in a very early period. Chirichigno, like Mendelsohn, argues that Exod. 21:2-6 and Deuteronomy 15 both deal with a Hebrew "debt-slave," that is, one who has been taken into slavery upon failure to pay a debt; Lev. 25:44, on the other hand, deals

11 Adrian Schenker, "Affranchissement d'une esclave selon Ex 21,7-11," *Biblica* 69 (1988): 555. Schenker suggests that it was at this point that the *ketiv* לא in Exod. 21:8 was amended to the *qere* לו. This issue will be discussed further below. Another scholar who accepts that Deut. was intended to provide a more liberal treatment for the *amah* is G. Vermes, *Postbiblical Jewish Studies* (Leiden: Brill, 1975), 69-70.

12 John Van Seters, "The Law of the Hebrew Slave," 540, 545. He also argues (ibid., 541) that the piercing ritual for the permanent slave in Deut. 15:16, which refers simply to a door, is a private ceremony, while Exod. 21:6, with its reference to האלהים (the god), reflects a later, more public ceremony. This view contradicts conventional source-critical theory, which regards the Covenant Code as early and sees in the simplified procedure of Deut. 15:16 a move from private to centralized cult rituals. For a critique of Van Seters' general views on the lateness of Exod. with regard to cult provisions, see Heger, "The Law of the Hebrew Slave," *ZAW* 108 (1999): 138-41.

13 Chirichigno, *Debt-Slavery*; see, e.g., his summary on p. 346.

with a Hebrew who has sold himself into slavery.[14] Cardellini[15] explains the differences between Exodus and Deuteronomy as theological, rather than differences in the substance of manumission.

Given that a diachronic view of the manumission rules is very much dependent on the model chosen, I do not see any compelling reason to view Exodus and Deuteronomy as conflicting with respect to the Hebrew female. I argue that the Exodus pericope is addressing a particular type of problem, the question of competing rights to the same woman (and her children), whether between a master and a husband or a master and a father.

I propose that from a functional viewpoint Exod. 21:2-11 must be read as a unified scheme referring to various types of family situations involving the *eved* and the *amah*:

1. A male bought as an *eved* is released after six years, with no further obligation.

2. A wife who goes in with the *eved* is also released after six years; a wife given to an *eved* by the master, along with her children, is not. In the latter case, the *eved* can choose to remain with her.

3. A female sold to a third party by her father as an *amah* is subject to various conditions:
   a) if she is not "assigned" to anyone, she must be redeemed by her father, and cannot be resold by the third party;
   b) if she is assigned to the master's son, she receives "the law of daughters";
   c) she cannot be "constructively" sold to another by denying her her maintenance; if she is denied these rights, she is released, with no further obligation.

---

14 Chirichigno, *Debt-Slavery*, 184-85, 351-52; Mendelsohn, *Slavery in the Ancient Near East*, 85, 89. Chirichigno in fact bases his opinion on the assumption (Chirichigno, *Debt-Slavery*, 183-84) that the expression עבד עברי must mean "debt-slave," though he offers no etymological or comparative grounds for this view.

15 Innocenzo Cardellini, *Die biblischen "Sklaven" — Gesetze im Lichte des keilschriftlichen Sklavenrechts*. (Bonner Biblische Beiträge 55; Bonn: Peter Hanstein, 1981), 342.

In effect, there are at least four "categories" of women referred to in this section:

(i) a woman who goes into slavery with her husband, and is released with him;

(ii) a woman of unspecified status given to an *eved* by his master; she remains with the master, but the *eved* can choose to stay with her;

(iii) a woman (presumably a young woman) sold by her father as an *amah*, assigned to the master's son; she must not be relegated in that case to a state of impoverishment;

(iv) a woman sold as an *amah* who is not assigned; she must be allowed to be redeemed rather than being resold by the master.

Underlying these verses, in my opinion, are questions regarding competing rights to women, with the overarching ethical concern of providing stability to family relationships. Concerning the rights of an *eved* versus those of his master, the text answers the question, "Who has rights to the *eved's* wife?" A wife brought in by the *eved* follows him (v. 3); a wife given to him by the master follows the master, as do her children, but the *eved* has the option of choosing to remain with her in exchange for the rather overwhelming trade-off of permanent servitude (vv. 4-6). Concerning the rights of a father who sells his daughter and those of the buyer, who apparently buys her with the intention that she be "assigned," the text answers the question, "Who has rights to the daughter?" If she is not assigned, she must be redeemed by the father, and the buyer forfeits all rights to her, including the right to resell her. If she is assigned to the buyer's son, the "law of daughters" applies; this vague expression may imply, among other restrictions, that the buyer himself has no sexual rights to her.[16] Once she has been assigned, she cannot be "constructively" removed in exchange for a replacement; if she is denied her appropriate rights, she must in effect be divorced, without her father having to redeem her.

16 Cf. the incest rules regarding daughters-in-law in Lev. 18:15.

A different situation may be addressed in Deuteronomy 15; the *amah* in this case may be an adult who has sold herself, or the text may refer to the wife whom an *eved* brings with him when goes into servitude; according to the Deuteronomy rules, this *amah*, too, is to be provided with maintenance upon departure. With respect to the extension of permanent servitude to the female, Deuteronomy may address a lacuna in the Exodus pericope, namely, the case of an *eved* who has brought in his own wife but wants to stay permanently, a situation that does not seem to be covered in Exod. 21:3. Such an interpretation would then explain the absence in the Deuteronomy pericope of the words "I love my wife" as a motive for the *eved olam* remaining with the master.

In support of this interpretation of Exod. 21:2-11, I shall look at various textual issues in this pericope that support the argument that it can be read as a unified whole. I shall then compare both Exod. 21:4 and 7-11 to functional equivalents from various Mesopotamian sources in which questions of control over women and children are also reflected.

3.2 AN ANALYSIS OF EXOD. 21:2-11

3.2.1 Is the Passage to be Read as a Unity?

As noted above, the conventional interpretation of this pericope sees verses 2-6 and 7-11 as addressing separate situations; certain scholars maintain that the two pericopes may in fact derive from different eras.[17] Verses 2-6 seem a straightforward limitation of the term of a Hebrew *eved* to six years. Verses 7-11 are taken as referring to a situation in which a girl (likely a minor, though this is not explicit in the text) is sold by her father to a third party to be mated — whether to him or his son or some other male. The section then prohibits the buyer from selling her if he is displeased with her or attempting to "constructively" divorce her by withholding her "wifely" rights. This interpretation is based on certain assumptions regarding various terms used in this section. In particular, the meaning of the term יעד in verse 8 and the question of whether the *ketiv* לא or the *qere* לו in this verse is the original reading are crucial to an understanding

[17] See, e.g., Noth, *Exodus*, 177; Cardellini, *"Sklaven,"* 342.

of the referents of the passage — i.e., what is to be done with the *amah* and with whom. The term יעד often translated "assigned," is interpreted by many scholars as indicating a specific type of relationship between a master and an *amah* (as opposed to, for instance, the ארש of Deut. 22:23 for the betrothal of a "free" woman, or the חרף of Lev. 19:20 for the "betrothal" of a slave woman). It is also assumed by many scholars[18] that the *qere*, אשר לו יעדה (who has assigned her to him), is the original reading, indicating that it is the master to whom the girl was "assigned" and suggesting that his deceiving of her (בגד בה) consists of finding her displeasing and wanting to sell her.

Other scholars posit a connection between the two pericopes based on literary analysis but view the two passages as symmetrical opposites. Zakovitch,[19] for instance, views the two parts of Exod. 21:2-11 as examples of the "three-four" pattern that he identifies throughout the Bible. In this case, the pattern is revealed in the structure of the two pericopes. Each pericope consists of a main law and four sub-laws.[20] The first three sub-laws in each case follow the main law, while the fourth sub-law differs. For the *eved*, the main rule (v. 2) is that he goes out after six years חנם, "with no obligation"; the situations in verses 3-4 accord with this rule, while the *eved olam* in verses 5-6 is an exception. Similarly, the main rule for the *amah* (v. 7) is that she does not go out like the *eved*; the cases in verses 8-10 follow this rule, while in the case in verse 11 she goes out חנם. Thus the three-four pattern of the sub-rules emphasizes the exception in the fourth case:

> בעוד ששלושת סעיפי המשנה הראשונים עולים בקנה אחד עם החוק העיקרי (העבד "יצא לחפשי חנם" והאמה "לא תצא כצאת העבדים"), סעיף המשנה הרביעי חריג ואף יוצא דופן מן החוק העיקרי: העבד אומר: "לא אצא לחפשי" והוא עובד את אדוניו עבודות עולם, ואילו האמה תצא "חנם אין כסף".

While the three first parts of the pericope fit with the essential law (the *eved*

18 As summarized by Chirichigno, *Debt-Slavery*, 247 n. 2.

19 Zakovitch, "Literary Paradigm," 450.

20 He also notes Cassuto's comment that the 5+5 pattern is a deliberate reference to the 10 laws of the decalogue ("Literary Paradigm," 450 n. 41).

> 'goes out with no obligation' and the *amah* 'shall not go out like the *avadim*'), the fourth part of the pericope is irregular and even exceptional with respect to the essential law: the *eved* says: 'I will not go out to freedom' and he serves his master forever, while the *amah* 'goes out free without money.'

Zakovitch also suggests, based on this interpretation, that the two pericopes together form a chiastic structure: the main case for the *eved* corresponds to the exception for the *amah* and vice versa.[21]

Jackson also suggests a chiastic structure, but comprising the larger unit of Exod. 21:2-27.[22] He does view 2-6 and 7-11 as related but argues that this occurs through a type of positional analogy: the two pericopes contrast the male "debt-slave," who can be used for breeding without changing his status, with a female, who must have permanent status within the family (as an *amah*) before being used for breeding. In his view, this analogy emphasizes the difference between superficially similar cases in the two pericopes and thus highlights the case that is omitted: that of the female "debt-slave," as she may not be used for temporary breeding.[23]

It must be noted, however, as argued by Meillassoux, that the question of whether female slaves are used for "breeding," and the corollary question of whether "breeding" was a major source of slaves in any given period, are matters of debate, involving a complex underpinning of economics and ideology. Meillassoux posited circumstances in which it would more economical to have all slaves engage in production of goods that could be exchanged for more slaves.[24] A connection between any part of Exod. 21:2-11 and the "breeding" of slaves should therefore not be automatically assumed.

Schenker also argues that verses 7-11, which deal with the (Hebrew) female sold by her father, are symmetrically opposite to verses 2-6, which deal with the Hebrew male: his term is limited, subject to one exception

21 Zakovitch, "Literary Paradigm," 452.

22 Jackson, "Analogy in Legal Science," 159.

23 Jackson, "Analogy in Legal Science," 162-63.

24 Meillassoux, *Anthropologie de l'esclavage*, 292-93. Meillassoux argued (ibid., 302) that the greater the trend toward this kind of production, the greater the *déféminisation* of female slaves (and the lower the price differential between female and male slaves):

> *S'il n'y a pas de préférence a priori sur l'un ou l'autre sexe, c'est que les esclaves sont recherchés comme agents asexués de travail et que la qualité procréatrice des femmes n'entre pas en compte pour leur valeur.*

for permanent servitude; her term is permanent, subject to various types of redemption. Schenker prefers לא (the *ketiv*) in verse 8 as the original reading, and suggests that לו (the *qere*) was introduced as a result of the deuteronomic revisions to slave law:

(1) Verse 8 was designed to prevent the master from selling a female slave "assigned" to the *eved olam* of verses 5-6. Its purpose was to protect this permanent *eved* from losing his mate; that is, the "marital" bond is given precedence over the master's rights over slaves.[25] Schenker deduces this purpose from the wording of verse 8: it says explicitly that the master may allow her redemption or give her to a son if he has not assigned her, thus by implication he may not do so if he has assigned her. (One may question, however, why this would not simply be stated directly if this were the main intent.)

(2) Schenker offers two arguments against the *qere* being the original reading in verse 8:

   a) The situation implied by the *qere* — that is, a female slave mated to her master — would in his opinion apply to only a small proportion of female slaves; that is, most female slaves were *not* destined to be concubines.[26] The word יעד (assigned) need not imply a permanent relationship, and thus the *qere* could apply to any female.

   b) This situation would in his opinion also demand that רעה (bad), be interpreted in a sexual sense, and in his opinion it does not carry this meaning. Comparing the use of this term in Gen. 28:8 (Isaac's reaction to Canaanite women as potential mates for his son Esau), Schenker suggests a meaning of "unsuitable for marriage"; the term *amah* in this pericope would thus specifically suggest someone sold to be given in marriage.

---

25 Schenker, "Affranchissement," 550.

26 Schenker, "Affranchissement," 551. Contra, among others, B. Cohen, *Jewish and Roman Law*, 329, and Patai, *Sex and Family*, 42, who argue that the fate of most female slaves was to become concubines to their masters or to other "free" men.

(3) As noted above, Schenker assumes that the difference between Exodus and Deuteronomy with respect to the treatment of the *amah* reflects a development in the law: the Deuteronomy provision, by allowing the female to become an *eved olam*, solved the problem of protecting the permanent slave. This would also explain why the choice to become an *eved olam* in Deuteronomy no longer includes the statement, "I love my wife." At this point, the Exodus provision was reread with the *qere* form, to deal with the specific situation of a master who wanted to divorce a slave he had married (parallel to the situation of the captive woman in Deut. 21:14, but in this case for a Hebrew woman).[27]

Chirichigno also assumes a relationship between the pericopes and (like Jackson) accepts the existence of a chiasmus in the larger passage consisting of verses 2-27.[28] Like both Jackson and Zakovitch, he sees verses 2-6 and verses 7-11 as deliberately emphasizing opposing situations: verses 2-6, in his opinion, contemplate the sale of a (male) dependent by a debtor (not the sale of the debtor himself), parallel to LH 117, and like that section aim at restricting the permanent enslavement of such dependants;[29] verses 7-11, in contrast, contemplate the type of transaction found elsewhere in the ancient Near East in which a female is adopted to be given in marriage and is not to be released unless this agreement is breached.[30] Chirichigno suggests further that in this case *amah* is not to be given the same meaning here as in other biblical passages, where it denotes a chattel slave.[31]

I, too, agree that verses 2-6 and verses 7-11 are related. I do not agree, however, that they reflect opposite cases; rather, they are different permutations of issues of control. Such permutations find various functional parallels in Mesopotamian sources, several of which will be set out below.

---

27 Schenker, "Affranchissement," 555.

28 Chirichigno, *Debt-Slavery*, 196.

29 Chirichigno, *Debt-Slavery*, 222-23.

30 Chirichigno, *Debt-Slavery*, 246. The case of a female sold for non-sexual purposes is, in his opinion, covered in Deut. 15:12-18.

31 Chirichigno, *Debt-Slavery*, 251.

3.2.2 Akkadian Parallels

There are a number of cuneiform documents from various eras that have to do with transactions in female slaves. While a review of these documents is beyond the scope of this book, it may be noted that scholars agree that Mesopotamian evidence regarding the use of female slaves for "breeding," or of the inheritance of slavery in general, is equivocal.[32] What is apparent in many of these documents, however, is a concern with specifying who had rights to these women, and also to their children. A sample of document types from different eras, to be cited below, reveals a functional similarity to the issues in Exod. 21:2-11. This is not to suggest a particular continuity among these documents, nor is it possible to point to a particular legal system as the specific origin of or influence on the biblical verses. Nonetheless, as functional equivalents, these parallels assist in illuminating specific points about the biblical provisions.

We may note first the "fitting-out" contracts, whereby a girl is sold, often by her parents, to a third party who is to fit her out for marriage. In Nuzi sources these third-party arrangements are often found within the so-called "adoption" contracts. Cassin lists a number of such adoption contracts involving the giving of girls to a third party either (i) *ana martūti u kallūti* (for daughtership and daughter-in-lawship) or (ii) *ana aḫātūti* (for sistership),[33] all of which specify that the third party is to give the girl in

32 For the 3rd-2nd millennium BCE, for instance, Diakonoff seems to have assumed that slave children would have been fathered by the master or someone on his household (I. M. Diakonoff, "Socio-Economic Classes in Babylonia and the Babylonian Concept of Social Stratification," *RAI* 18 [1972]: 46; Diakonoff, "Slaves, Helots and Serfs," 71), while Gelb suggested that the deliberate breeding of slaves was unlikely (I. J. Gelb, "From Slavery to Freedom," 84-86.). Siegel's assessment of certain Ur III documents led him to conclude that slavery in that period was "inherited, sometimes for as much as three generations after generations" (Siegel, "Third Dynasty of Ur," 39); yet he also noted (ibid., 42) that the distinction between slave and free was not rigid, given the considerable documentary evidence of manumission as well as the absence of a strict class endogamy indicated by evidence of marriages between slaves and non-slaves. For the NB period, in *Slavery in Babylonia*, 656, Dandamaev concluded that slaves were more likely to have constituted a "hereditary estate" than a socioeconomic class; yet he also acknowledged that there is not enough evidence to determine any general rules regarding the status of offspring of slave-free marriages (ibid., 411).

33 "Sistership" has various manifestations in both biblical and cuneiform sources. As just one example, Westbrook, *Old Babylonian Marriage Law*, 106, has discussed the possible

marriage. Cassin has divided these contracts into two types, depending on whom the girl is to be married to: in those characterized as *in matrimonium servile*, which use wording (i), the girl is given as a wife to a slave; in those characterized as *in matrimonium conjugale*, which use both wording (i) and wording (ii), the girl is given to a non-slave.[34] The two types, however, also share characteristics: there are specified alternatives to marriage, including giving the girl as a wife "at the gate"; and many of both types contain a clause[35] prohibiting some third party from claiming the girl back from the buyer. Mendelsohn[36] saw in this specification of alternatives a parallel to Exod. 21:7-11 and thus interpreted the biblical provision limiting the right to sell the girl as specifically reacting to the Nuzi situation. Whether Nuzi sources lie behind the biblical provision cannot be determined simply on the basis of the parallel, but one may note the similar concern in both cases with the fate of the girl and the powers of the third party over her.

Westbrook has also considered the possibility that Exod. 21:7ff represents the matrimonial adoption situation.[37] He discusses three OB contracts that he regards as reflecting such a matrimonial adoption.[38] In each case a daughter is given to a third party in exchange for a *terḫatum* (brideprice) and the exchange is expressed as some variation of *ana*

meaning of "sistership" in OB marriage contracts that involve polygyny, suggesting that if the wives in such a case are described as "sisters," the children of each may share in the dowries of both mothers.

34 E. M. Cassin, *L'adoption 'a Nuzi* (Paris: Adrien Maisonneuve, 1938), 299ff. and 310ff. See, e.g., ibid., n. 433 (304-6), as an example of type (i), and Harvard Semitic Studies [=HSS] IX 145 (312-14) as an example of type (ii). In the latter case, an *amtu* is the third-party buyer and the purchased girl may to be given to her son, who does not seem to be a slave (as the contract specifically forbids her to give the girl in marriage to an *ardu*). Cassin (ibid., 314, note to line 5) suggests that *amtu* here does not mean "slave"; but an equally plausible explanation of the son's status is that the son of an *amtu* was not automatically considered an *ardu*.

35 This is usually a warranty with some form of the root *BQR/PQR*; this term will be discussed in chapter four.

36 Isaac Mendelsohn, "The Conditional Sale into Slavery of Free-Born Daughters in Nuzi and the Law of Ex. 21:7-11," *JAOS* 55 (1935): 190, and Mendelsohn, *Slavery in the Ancient Near East*, 12-13.

37 See Raymond Westbrook, *Property and the Family in Biblical Law* (JSOT Supplement Series 113; Sheffield: JSOT Press, 1991), 88 n. 2. He notes, however, that there is an issue as to whether this type of adoption can exist in a system in which levirate marriage takes place. This issue is beyond the scope of this work.

38 Westbrook, *Old Babylonian Marriage Law*, 39ff. The three documents cited are CT 47 40, Waterman 72, and CT 33 34.

martūtim u kallūtim (for daughtership and daughter-in-lawship); in one case it is explicitly stated that the third party is to fit the girl out and give her in marriage. Westbrook analyzes such documents as a hybrid of adoption and acquisition of a daughter-in-law; the adoption allows the buyer to give the girl to someone other than his son, as he would be required to do under a straight daughter-in-law acquisition (which he characterizes as a type of "inchoate" marriage, as in LH 155-56). If Westbrook's analysis is correct, these contracts again reveal a concern with limiting where the girl is to be placed.

Middle Assyrian Law [=MAL] A 43 is also relevant to the topic of control. While it deals with the case of a girl who has been betrothed rather than a girl sold as an *antu*, this passage illustrates concern with the respective rights of the father and the prospective father-in-law when the son to whom the girl was "assigned" (*uddu*, stated by Paul to be a cognate of Hebrew יעד[39]) has died or disappeared. The passage sets out in great detail who has the right to dispose of the girl:

> If... the son to whom he [the father-in-law] has assigned the wife has either died or disappeared, he may give her to whichever he pleases of the rest of his sons from the eldest to the youngest who is 10 years old. If the father is dead and the son to whom he assigned the wife is dead but the dead son has a son who is 10 years old, he shall marry her; but if the grandsons are less than 10 years old, the girl's father, if he pleases, shall give his daughter (to one of them) or, if he pleases, shall make a return (of the gifts) on equal terms...[40]

Second, we may note that there are various references in the cuneiform sources to the question of ownership of the offspring of a slave and a non-slave. Two of the law collections refer to the situation in which a male slave sires children; the outcomes are not consistent, suggesting that there is no

39 Shalom Paul, "Exod. 21:10: A Threefold Maintenance Clause," *JNES* 28 (1969): 48 n. 2. Paul neither agrees nor disagrees that Exod. 21:7-11 is a reflex of Nuzi contracts (ibid., 49), but does relate some of the biblical terminology to Akkadian terms. In addition to the relationship between יעד and *uddu*, he also suggests that בגד in Exod. 21:8 is an "interdialectal functional equivalent" of Akkadian *nabalkutu* "to break an agreement" (ibid., 48 n. 6).

40 Translation of Martha Roth, *Law Collections from Mesopotamia and Asia Minor* (Atlanta: Scholars Press, 1995), 169-70.

underlying principle that the child follows the mother.[41] LU [= Laws of Ur-Namma] 5 provides that if a male slave marries a "native" woman, one child goes into the service of the master; LH 175, in contrast, provides that if a *warad ekallim* or *warad muškēnim* marries a *mārat awīlim*, the master has no claim to the children. A further issue concerns the offspring of a slave woman and free man and the ranking between the children of a first wife and those of the slave woman. Both LL [=Laws of Lipit Ishhtar] 25-28 and LH 170-71 state that the children of the slave woman are not to be treated as slaves (in the latter case, the acknowledgement of these children by the father affects only their rights to his estate).

The concern with the status of the offspring of such "mixed" unions is also reflected in various contracts. In several of the Nuzi documents of the *in matrimonium servile* type[42] it is specified that the third party is to own any children of the marriage; in the first case the children are specifically described with the slave terms *amtu* and *ardu*. This express provision suggests that the matter was not automatic, and had to be specified. Similarly, Saarisalo cites one contract in which a mother buys a woman (who is not a slave) as a wife for a slave belonging to her son; here too the purchased woman's children are described as "in the category of slaves" (*ša ina libbi ardi u amti*) and are to belong to the son.[43] Westbrook notes, in contrast, an OB contract in which it is the children of a slave male and a free female who are to belong to the slave's master.[44]

We may note, finally, the type of contract in which a slave is freed, or a slave or non-slave adopted, on the express condition that he is to serve the master or adopter until the latter's death. Such contracts will be discussed more fully in chapter five (where it is proposed that, like the *eved olam* of Exodus 21 and Deuteronomy 15, they reflect a "half slave, half free" status). We may briefly note here several examples of Nuzi

41 See also Hittite Laws 31-33, as to how the children are to be divided when one or both partners are slaves.

42 N. 432 (Cassin, *L'adoption 'a Nuzi*, 302-4), n. 433 (ibid., 304-6).

43 NII, 120 (Aapeli Saarisalo, "New Kirkuk Documents Relating to Slaves" [*Studia Orientalia* 3; Helsinki: 1934], 25). The author assumes that the wife would become a slave once she married a slave, but this is nowhere explicit in the text (ibid., 62).

44 Westbrook, *Old Babylonian Marriage Law*, 67, citing CT 48 53.

contracts cited by Breneman[45] in which males are "adopted" (*ana marūti*, "for sonship"). Of interest is the fact that they are to be given a wife by the adopter; in several of these contracts both the adopted male and the wife are to serve (*PLḤ*) the adopter until the latter's death, and then the male may take his wife and children and go where he pleases.[46]

These sources, if they may be taken as a representative sample, indicate a concern with the disposition of women and their offspring in situations outside a "normal" marriage transaction conducted between the father of a woman and her prospective husband — cases, for instance, in which a female is provided for someone in service (as in Exod. 21:4-6), or in which a third party has contracted to give a girl in marriage (as in Exod. 21:7-11). It may thus be argued that this is the concern that underlies the examples in Exod. 21:2-11. Further, precise (and inconsistent) specifications in a variety of the cuneiform sources concerning the disposition of children in cases of "mixed" marriage suggest that there was no automatic assumption regarding the slave status of any offspring.

3.2.3 Specific Textual Issues in Exod. 21:7-11

3.2.3.A *Ketiv* (לא) Versus *qere* (לו) in Verse 8 and the Significance of *bQiddushin* 18ab

I posit that the *ketiv* לא is the original (and preferred) reading, as it is consistent with the issue addressed by the passage — that is, the question of who retains rights to the girl if she has not been assigned. Further, there seems to be talmudic evidence (*bQidd.* 18ab) that the *qere* versus *ketiv* issue was still being debated in the postbiblical period, which suggests that one cannot argue decisively that the *qere* was the original reading.

It is to be noted, as Chirichigno[47] suggests, that the majority opinion among scholars prefers the *qere*. Zakovitch, for instance, prefers the reading לו יעדה (assigned her to him), from both a stylistic and logical point of view:

---

45 J. Mervin Breneman, "Nuzi Marriage Tablets" (Ph.D. dissertation, Brandeis University, 1971), 215ff. He cites, for instance, HSS XIX 37, 40, 45, 39, 49, HSS V 57, Joint Expedition at Nuzi [=JEN] 572.

46 One example is HSS XIX 45.

47 Chirichigno, *Debt-Slavery*, 247-48.

(i) this reading would parallel the wording לבנו ייעדנה (assigned her to his son), in verse 9; (ii) the *ketiv* לא יעדה (if he does not assign her), creates a logical difficulty: it implies that she must be redeemed if not assigned, but in that case, why would her relatives not simply argue that the condition in verse 11 applies (that is, she is being denied her maintenance rights), and claim her back without payment (אין כסף)?[48] Chirichigno[49] notes, however, that there is also a logical problem created by the *qere* (though he does accept the *qere*): if verse 8 allows the master to rid himself of the woman he has assigned to himself (לו), why does verse 11, in contrast, seem to uphold her rights? Schenker, as noted above, posits a development from the *ketiv* to the *qere* as part of the deuteronomic revision in Deuteronomy 15.[50] Breuer[51] also argues for the *qere*: accepting that יעוד means "assignment" (זימון), he suggests that it is impossible to speak of such an assignment without designating to whom the girl is assigned. In his view, the later sages who accepted the *ketiv* were interpreting יעוד in its postbiblical sense as synonymous with *qiddushin*. Against this view, however, one might argue that it is possible to "assign" someone without specifying an object. Further, there are other reasons that the Sages might have preferred the *ketiv*, as will be argued below.

Bavli Qidd. 18a supports the idea, first, that Exod. 21:7-11 was seen by the Sages as involving an issue of control, and second, that the *ketiv/qere* debate had still not been resolved in the postbiblical period. The passage is part of a discussion regarding the manumission rules applicable to Hebrew females:[52]

> הא קתני אינה נמכרת ונשנת ומני ר"ש היא דתניא מוכר אדם את בתו לאישות ושונה לשפחות ושונה לאישות אחר שפחות אבל לא לשפחות אחר אישות רש"א כשם שאין אדם מוכר את בתו לשפחות אחר אישות כך אין אדם מוכר את בתו לשפחות אחר שפחות ובפלוגתא דהני תנאי דתניא בבגדו בה כיון שפירש טליתו עליה שוב אין רשאי למוכרה דברי ר"ע ר"א אומר בבגדו בה כיון שבגד בה שוב אין רשאי למוכרה במאי קמיפלגי ר"א סבר יש אם למסורת ור"ע סבר יש אם למקרא ור"ש סבר יש אם למקרא ולמסורת.

48 Zakovitch, "Literary Paradigm," 451, 452.

49 Chirichigno, *Debt-Slavery*, 248.

50 Schenker also suggests that לא is the *lectio difficilior* (Schenker, "Affranchissement," 552).

51 Mordechai Breuer, "*Amah Ivriah* and *Shifḥah Neḥerefet*" [in Hebrew], Megadim 16 (1992), 21.

52 This passage will be discussed in more detail in chapter five.

> Was it not taught [in a baraita]: She can not be sold and sold again. Whose [opinion] is this [that a girl may not be sold into slavery more than once]? That of R. Shimon, as it is taught [in a baraita]: A man may sell his daughter into wifehood more than once, into slavery more than once, into wifehood after slavery, but not into slavery after wifehood. R. Shimon said: Just as a man may not sell his daughter into slavery after wifehood, he may not sell his daughter into slavery after slavery. The dispute of these tannaim is like another dispute of tannaim, as it is taught [in a baraita]: *bevigdo bah* [Exod. 21:8] — once he has spread his *talit* over her he may not sell her — these are the words of R. Akiva. R. Eliezer says: *bevigdo bah* — because he trifled with her, he may not sell her again. On what do they dispute? R. Eliezer held that there is validity to the *masorah*, and R. Akiva held that there is validity to the accepted pronunciation (*miqra*), and R. Shimon held there is validity to both.

The first part of the section discusses a tannaitic debate as to whether a father can sell his daughter into "slavery" (*shifḥut*) more than once. The essence of the debate between the anonymous view and that of R. Shimon seems to be an issue of when the father loses his right of control over the girl, at least with respect to selling her into slavery: only after he has given her into marriage, or after once selling her into slavery.

The talmudic editor then relates this dispute to another tannaitic debate, this one between R. Akiva and R. Eliezer, apparently regarding the meaning of בגד in Exod. 21:8. R. Akiva is said to have taken בבגדו as associated with בֶּגֶד (clothing): once the master has spread his talit over the girl (presumably to be taken in a sexual sense), the father loses his rights to resell the girl, as he would after a marriage. R. Eliezer understands בגד in its usual sense of deceit:[53] since the girl has been deceived once with respect to a *shifḥut* transaction, she cannot be sold into *shifḥut* again. The two disputes are summed up as a matter of *masoret* versus *miqra* (terminology that will be explained below): R. Akiva prefers the *miqra* (here associated with the reading בֶּגֶד), R. Eliezer prefers the *masoret* (בגד in its usual sense), and R. Shimon accepts both.

53 Chirichigno, *Debt-Slavery*, 249-50, summarizes the contextual studies that have been made of this biblical term. Like Chirichigno, I accept that in Exod. 21:8 it refers to the breach of an agreement rather than the breaking of a relationship, in keeping with my interpretation of the pericope as a whole.

I propose, however, that it is more logical to read this second debate as involving the issue of לא versus לו in Exod. 21:8 — that is, the *miqra / masoret* issue relates to this term, and not to the term בגד.[54] In other words, if בגד equals פרישת טלית (spreading the *tallit*), this would imply that the girl has become the master's sexual partner in some way, in which case the *qere* לו is the preferred reading. However, if בגד equals בגידה (deceit), this would imply that the master has not performed his part of the bargain, in which case the *ketiv* is the preferred reading. This separate argument then became associated with the first debate with respect to the issue of control.

This argument is based on two points:

1) In the maxims יש אם למסרת (there is validity to the *masoret)*, and יש אם למקרא (there is validity to the *miqra)*, *masoret* is taken to refer to the consonantal text, while *miqra* refers to the vocalization of the text as handed down by tradition. It may be argued that בֶּגֶד (clothing), the reading attributed to R. Akiva, fits neither of these criteria. The maxim would, however, be quite appropriate to the בֶּגֶד/בגידה argument if it referred to an underlying association with the *qere/ketiv* distinction לו/לא.

2) There is some textual instability with respect to this second debate, which suggests that this argument may have been amended over time. We may note first that the argument appears in both the *Mekhilta de R. Yishmael*, *Neziqin*, *parshah* 3 (Horovitz) and the Yerushalmi (*yQidd.* 1:2 59c), but with different (or anonymous) attributions:

Mekhilta de R. Yishmael: מכילתא דרבי ישמעאל משפטים - מסכתא דנזיקין פרשה ג

בבגדו בה. מאחר שבגד בה, נהג בה מנהג בזיון ולא נהג בה כמשפט הבנות, אף הוא אינו רשאי לקיימה, דברי ר' יונתן בן אבטלמוס; ואין בגידה אלא שקירה, שנאמר [מלאכי ב י] בגדה יהודה ואומר [ירמיה ה יא] כי בגוד בגדו בי בית ישראל; רבי ישמעאל אומר, באדון הכתוב מדבר אשר לקחה על מנת לייעד ולא ייעד, אף הוא אינו רשאי לקיימה; רבי עקיבא אומר, בבגדו בה, מאחר שפרש בגדו עליה.

54 I am not aware of much research concerning the relationship of the talmudic terms *miqra* and *masoret* with what eventually became the Masoretic *qere* versus *ketiv*; in this case, however, I think the issues are related. See Harry Fox, "There is a Source to the Verse" [in Hebrew], Sinai 116 (1995), 131-35.

bevigdo bah: Since he trifled with her and treated her with contempt and did not treat her according to the law of daughters, he is not allowed to keep her — these are the words of R. Yonatan ben Astolmos. *Begidah* is simply the language of deceit, as it said [Mal. 2:11]: *Judah has dealt treacherously*, and it says [Jer. 5:11]: *[Judah and Israel] have indeed dealt treacherously with me,* etc. R. Ishmael says: Scripture speaks of the master, who took her on condition that he assign [her] and did not; he may not keep her. R. Akiva says: *bevigdo bah* — since he spread his *beged* over her.

yQidd. 1:2 59c:

תני ר' שמעון בר יוחי כשם שאינו מוכרה לשפחות אחר אשות אף לא שפחות אחר שפחות מה טעמא דרשב"י בבגדו בה פעם אחת הוא בוגד בה ואינו בוגד בה פעם שניה מה מקיימין רבנן טעמא דר' שמעון בר יוחי בבגדו בה מכיון שפירש טליתו עליה עוד אין לאביה בה רשות

R. Shimon bar Yoḥai taught: Just as one does not sell [his daughter] into slavery after wifehood, [one does not sell her into] slavery after slavery. What is the reason of R. Shimon bar Yoḥai? *bevigdo bah* — he trifles with her once, but does not trifle with her a second time. How do the Sages interpret [*bevigdo bah* according to] the reason of R. Shimon bar Yoḥai? Since he spread his *talit* over her, her father no longer has authority over her.

Second, we may note that Rashi at *bQidd.* 18a *s.v.* ובפלוגתא דהני תנאי states:

בדברי ר"ע גרסינן כיון שפירש טליתו עליה

We read in the words of R. Akiva: Because he has spread his *talit* over her.

This is, in fact, exactly what the printed text now reads. MS Munich 95, MS Oxford Opp. 248 (367)[55] and MS Vatican 110-11 also support the reading as it stands in the current printed text, as do the Venice Edition and an early Spanish version.[56] Rashi's statement, however, suggests that

55 Oxford Opp. 248 (367) changes the gender of the expression, אב למקרא and אב למסורת, according to the Talmud Text Databank of the Saul Lieberman Institute of Talmudic Research of JTS.

56 *B.Bekh.* 34a also associates R. Eliezer with *bagad* and *masoret*, exactly as in the extant version of *bQidd.* 18a:

he had a text in which the attributions were reversed: *beged* was associated with R. Eliezer and *miqra*, while *bagad* was associated with R. Akiva and *masoret*. The existence of such an alternative version is supported by two factors. First, the *Yalqut Shimoni* (*remez* 320 on Exod. 21) in fact contains a direct quote of such an alternative version:

> תניא מוכר אדם את בתו לאישות ושונה לשפחות ושונה לאישות אחר שפחות אבל לא
> לשפחות אחר אישות ור' שמעון אומר כשם שאין אדם מוכר את בתו לשפחות אחר אישות
> כך אין אדם מוכר את בתו לשפחות אחר שפחות ובפלוגתא דהני תנאי דתניא בבגדו בה כיון
> שפירס טליתו עליה שוב אין רשאי למכרה דברי ר"א רע"א כיון שבגד בה שוב אין רשאי
> למכרה ר"א סבר יש אם למקרא ור"ע סבר יש אם למסורת ור"ש סבר יש אם למקרא ולמסורת

> It was taught: A man may sell his daughter into wifehood more than once, into slavery more than once, into wifehood after slavery, but not into slavery after wifehood. R. Shimon said: Just as a man may not sell his daughter into slavery after wifehood, he may not sell his daughter into slavery after slavery. And in the dispute of these tannaim [it is like another dispute of tannaim], as it was taught: *bevigdo bah*: [Once] he has spread his *talit* over her he may not sell her again — these are the words of R. Eliezer. R. Akiva says: Because he trifled with her, he may not sell her again. [On what do they dispute?] R. Eliezer says there is validity to *miqra*, R. Akiva held there is validity to *masoret*, and R. Shimon held there is validity to both. [emphasis added]

Further, while later commentators either agreed or disagreed with Rashi's proposal, they did not express surprise at the fact that changes were proposed. Rashba, for instance, states (*Ḥidushim*, *bQidd.* 18b, *s.v.* דתניא):

> דתניא בבגדו בה כיון שפרס טליתו עליה שוב אינו רשאי למוכרה דברי ר"ע
> ר' אליעזר אומר כיון שבגד בה שוב אינו רשאי למוכרה. כך גריס רש"י ז"ל
> ור"ת ז"ל גריס איפכא כיון שפרס טליתו עליה כו' דברי ר' אליעזר ר"ע אומר כיון שבגד בה

> [As] it was taught: *bevigdo bah* — Once he has spread his *talit* over her he may

---

דר' אליעזר סבר יש אם למקרא רמינהי בבגדו בה כיון שפירש טליתו עליה שוב אינו רשאי
למוכרה דברי ר"ע ר"א אומר כיון שבגד בה שוב אינו רשאי למוכרה.

That R. Eliezer holds that there is validity to *miqra*. [And a baraita] is opposed to this: *bevigda bah*: once he has spread his *tallit* over her he is not allowed to sell her — [these are] the words of R. Akiva. R. Eliezer says: Once he has trifled with her he may not sell her again.

not sell her again — these are the words of R. Akiva. R. Eliezer says: Because he trifled with her, he may not sell her again. This is how Rashi *z"l* reads it. And R. Tam *z"l* reads it the opposite: Once he has spread his *talit* over her, etc. — the words of R. Eliezer; R. Akiva says: Because he trifled with her.

This seems to imply that both versions were familiar to these *rishonim.*

This alternate version may be the *lectio difficilior*, as it reverses the usual principles associated with the respective sages. This difficulty was noted, for instance, by Rashi (that is, *masoret* was usually associated with R. Eliezer, and *miqra* with R. Akiva, just as Rashi has proposed for *bQidd.* 18b *s.v.* כיון שפירס טליתו עליה):

דעל כרחך מיבעי ליה לאוקמי יש אם למקרא כר"ע כדאמרינן בסנהדרין בפ"ק
ויש אם למסורת כר"א כדדייקי' בבכורות...

Of necessity it has to be interpreted that 'there is validity to the *miqra*' is according to R. Akiva, as we say in the first chapter of tractate *Sanhedrin*, and 'there is validity in the *masoret*' is according to R. Eliezer, as we determine in tractate *Bekhorot*...

As Rashba notes, the alternate version would place R. Eliezer ahead of R. Akiva, which would be appropriate, דר' אליעזר רביה דר"ע הוה (as R. Eliezer was the teacher of R. Akiva). It would also, however, associate R. Eliezer with the majority opinion that there is no slavery after wifehood; Rashi suggests (*bQidd.* 19a, *s.v.* דאמר לשפחות) that this would be inappropriate, משום דשמותי הוא (because he is a Shammaite).[57]

J. N. Epstein[58] also considered the alternate version as the original, citing additional references, and summarizing:

...וכך כתוב בכל הנוסחאות שלא עבר עליהן קולמוסן של מגיהי ספרים

...it is written in this way in all the versions which have not had editorial revisions.

57 The implication is, perhaps, that being a Shammaite he would not have preferred the reading that seems more lenient, according to the common assumption that Shammaites took the stricter view of halakhah.

58 J. N. Epstein, *Introductions to Amoraic Literature* [in Hebrew] (Jerusalem : Magnes, 1962), 99 n. 11.

In his opinion, this is an example of a *sugya muḥlefet*, in which the opinions are reversed, and as such may be considered part of the pre-edited original source of the talmudic text.

Finally, and most significantly, it appears that there was disagreement as to the workings of the particular analogy with בֶּגֶד/בגידה. The commentators were forced to propose somewhat far-fetched explanations. Rashi (*bQidd.* 18b, *s.v.* למסורת), for instance, suggested that the explanation for the analogy was the absence of כתיב מלא (*plene* spelling):

בבגדו בה כתיב ולא בביגדו אין הברת חירק בלא יו"ד

It is written *bivgado* [with his garment] and not *bevigdo* [in his trifling] — there is no *ḥiriq* in a syllable without a *yod*.

A different reason was suggested in *Tosafot HaRosh* (at *bQidd.* 18b):

וקצת קשה לי היכי דדייקינן שהמסורת הוא לשון בגידה מדלא כתיב בביגדו ביו"ד, אדרבה נידוק שהוא לשון בגד מדלא כתיב בבוגדו בוא"ו... המסורת היא לשון בגידה, דאי לשון פרישת טלית היה לו לכתוב 'בבגדו עליה'

It is a bit difficult for me how we analyze that the *masoret* is a language of trifling on the basis that it is not written *bevigdo* with a *yod*, or even more so that it is the language of clothing, since it is not written *bevogedo* with a *vav*... the *masoret* is the language of trifling, since if it were the language of 'spreading a *talit*,' it should have written in his spreading over her (*aleha*).

It is plausible, therefore, to argue that the original argument as represented in the baraita in *bQidd.* 18ab had to do not with בגד but with the *qere/ketiv* distinction in Exod. 21:8. Over the course of time, this argument became associated with a בגד debate and with a *masoret/miqra* debate attributed to R. Akiva and R. Eliezer, necessitating various adjustments to the passage to make the arguments appear consistent. Given such a possibility, therefore, it cannot be conclusively argued that the *qere* לו was the original reading in verse 8.

3.2.3.B "If He Takes Another" (אם אחרת יקח לו) in Verse 10

I argue that לו in this verse refers to the buyer's son in verse 9, as opposed to the buyer himself. That is, the *amah* has been given to the son, and the son has then taken another wife. The verb יקח (takes), may refer either to the son himself taking a wife, or to his father procuring for him another woman; the essence of the problem is that the first girl sold as an *amah* has her rights withdrawn in consequence and must then be allowed to go out. This interpretation would resolve the inconsistency, noted above, that arises in the passage if it is assumed that it is the buyer who is taking another woman for himself and consequently mistreating the *amah*: rather than be forced to redeem his daughter according to the situation in verse 8 (however that is interpreted), the father of the *amah* might simply wait to argue that she has been denied the rights specified in verse 10, and she would then, according to v. 11, simply "go out" (ויצאה).

We may further argue that verse 10 is to be read as a continuation of verse 9, rather than as the start of a new point, by noting that the verse begins with אם (if), without a conjunctive *vav*. In contrast, the three major "remedies" provided in this section all begin with conjunctive *vav*: והפדה (she shall be redeemed), in verse 8; ואם לבנו ייעדנה (if he assigns her to his son), in verse 9; ואם שלש אלה (and if these three things), in verse 11. Such a continuation suggests that the term כמשפט הבנות (according to the law of the daughters), in verse 9 — the precise meaning of which is unclear[59] — might in fact be referring to this type of problem: the withdrawal of maintenance rights.[60] Finally, it may be argued that this interpretation is consistent with *realia*: a girl forced upon the son by a father anxious to maintain this valuable reproductive asset in his household would be vulnerable to abuse.

3.2.3.C "These Three Things" (שלש אלה) in Verse 11

As a consequence, I argue that this phrase refers to the three rights specified in verse 10, rather than the three alternatives in the entire passage

59 In the opinion of John W. Wevers, *Notes on the Greek Text of Exodus* (SBL Septuagint and Cognate Studies Series 30; Atlanta: Scholars Press, 1990), 327, the "law" in this phrase is referring to the rules stated in vv. 7-8.

60 While I do not wish to speculate in detail on the precise meaning of this term, it could also refer to prohibitions against incest of the type found in Lev. We may note also provisions in various Mesopotamian law collections concerning the sexual use by a father of a woman who has been designated for his son. See, for example, LH 155-56.

(redemption, assignment to the son, provision of maintenance rights).[61] As argued above, the third remedy is actually the one in verse 11, with provision of maintenance rights being part of verse 9. The meaning of these three rights, particularly the last one,[62] is not clear, but this does not affect the argument; from the context, they seem to refer to standard marital obligations.

3.3 CONCLUSION

It has been argued in this chapter that the cases addressed by Exod. 21:2-11 find functional equivalents in cuneiform sources and concern competing rights of ownership of women and children in "non-standard" types of marriage situations, especially between slave and non-slave. Two points have been proposed in particular: 1) There was no commonly held assumption that the child of a slave woman would become a slave; rather, the status of the offspring of either a male or female slave, if relevant, needed to be expressly specified. The concern of Exod. 21:4, therefore, is not to express the matrilineal inheritance of slave status, but, on the contrary, to specify the fate of the offspring of a male slave who has not brought his own wife into service. 2) Exod. 21:7-11 suggest that an *amah*, at least one sold by her father, was a female placed in a dependent position and, if otherwise "unassigned," given as a wife. The pericope may be compared to the "fitting-out" contracts that are found in cuneiform sources; the concern of the pericope is thus to provide for the disposition of the girl if she is not assigned in marriage. It cannot, therefore, be used as evidence that the inevitable fate of the *amah* was to be a concubine to her master.

---

61 Contra Chirichigno, *Debt-Slavery*, 253. For a summary of the different tannaitic opinions regarding this phrase, see David Henshke, "On the Nature of the Relationship of Targum Pseudo-Jonathan to Midreshe Halakha" [in Hebrew], *Tarbits* 68:2 (1999) 187-210, at 191-97.

62 ענתה is usually taken to refer to a right to sexual intercourse. Targum Onkelos, for instance, translates it as עונתה and TY has מעייל לה (both terms suggesting "marital duty" according to Jastrow), while the LXX has *ὁμιλίαν* ("intercourse," "companionship"). Paul, in contrast, argues that the term refers to an oil ration (Paul, "Exod. 21:10," 52). He notes that the triad barley, clothing, and oil is found in maintenance clauses in cuneiform documents from various eras, as well as in Hos. 2:7 and Eccl. 9:7-8. He does not, however, explain the etymology of the Hebrew term.

CHAPTER 4

THE *SHIFḤAH NEḤEREFET* OF LEVITICUS 19:20-22

4.1 TREASON AND TRESPASS

A crucial biblical passage pertaining to the issue of a female slave's marital status is the difficult law in Lev. 19:20-22, which describes an apparent sexual offense committed with a slave woman:

ואיש כי ישכב את אשה שכבת זרע והוא שפחה נחרפת לאיש והפדה לא נפדתה
או חפשה לא נתן לה בקרת תהיה לא יומתו כי לא חפשה.
והביא את אשמו לה' פתח אהל מועד איל אשם.
וכפר עליו הכהן באיל האשם לפני ה' על חטאתו אשר חטא ונסלח לו מחטאתו אשר חטא.

[The underlined section in the Samaritan Pentateuch reads, בקרת תהיה לו לא יומת]. The Samaritan text has included both the *qere* and the *ketiv* possibly testifying to the early existence of both readings. This directs the *biqqoret* and the avoided death sentence only to the man .

If a man has carnal relations with a woman who is a slave [*shifḥah*] and *has been designated* [*neḥerefet*] for another man, but has not been redeemed or given her freedom, there shall be an *indemnity* [*biqqoret*]*;* they shall not, however, be put to death, since she has not been freed. But he must bring to the entrance of the Tent of Meeting, as his guilt offering [*asham*] to the Lord, a ram of guilt offering. With the ram of guilt offering the priest shall make expiation for him before the Lord for the sin that he committed, and the sin that he committed will be forgiven him. (JPS translation; emphasis added).

Because of its mention of a double death penalty, this passage on its surface suggests a comparison to the married woman who commits adultery (Deut. 22:22 — אשה בעלת בעל), or perhaps the case of a man who has intercourse with a betrothed virgin within a city[1] (Deut. 22:23 — נער[ה] בתולה מארשה לאיש). Unlike the participants in these other offenses, however, the woman and the male offender in this case escape the death penalty, apparently because the woman is a slave. The slave woman is, it seems, not to be considered as partaking of the type of marital relationship with first the *ish* that would render a "free" woman (and the male perpetrator) liable for death for adultery.

Is this passage a confirmation of the mishnaic rule that marriage with slaves is impossible? At first glance it would appear to be strong support for this concept, stronger in fact than Exod. 21:4, which as we have seen is used as the traditional midrashic support for this element of the matrilineal principle.

The precise implications of the passage, however, remain difficult to pinpoint, for a number of reasons:

a) There is no universal agreement on the meaning of the various *hapax*es in verse 20, particularly *neḥerefet* and *biqqoret.*[2] The JPS *Tanakh* translation quoted above, for instance, uses "designated," one of the traditional interpretations of *neḥerefet.*[3] Another trend of interpretation, however, considers *neḥerefet* to mean "betrothed," based on a rabbinic understanding of Lev. 19:20 as referring to a woman half slave and half free, and betrothed, perhaps, to another slave.[4] The JPS translation of *biqqoret* as "indemnity" is based on recent scholarly opinion that this term is cognate with the Akkadian root *BQR/PQR*, which has been related to the idea of a property claim;[5] variations of this term are

---

1 Thus deemed to be consensual, as otherwise she could have cried for help.

2 As B. Schwartz notes ("A Literary Study of the Slave-Girl Pericope — Leviticus 19:20-22," in *Studies in Bible* [Scripta Hierosolymitana 31; ed. S. Japhet; Jerusalem: Magnes, 1986], 244, 247), the phrase חופש נתן is a *hapax*, the usual term for manumission (as in Exod. 21:26-7) being לחפש שלח. Further, the use of *shifḥah* within the "legal" sections of the Pentateuch is also a *hapax*, the usual term being *amah*.

3 Onkelos, for instance, has אמה אחידא לגבר (an *amah* joined to a man); the LXX has *οἰκέτις διαπεφυλαγμένη ἀνθρώπῳ* (a slave kept for a man).

4 This half slave/half free/betrothed idea, attributed to R. Akiva, is found with substantial variation in *mKer.* 2:5, *tKer.* 1:18, *Sifra Qedoshim pereq* 5:2-4, *yQidd.* 1:1 59a, and *bKer.* 11a. The variants will be discussed in greater detail in chap. 6.

5 See, e.g., E. A. Speiser, "Leviticus and the Critics," in *Yehezkel Kaufmann Jubilee Volume* (ed. M. Haran; Jerusalem: Magnes, 1960), 29-45, at 35-36, based primarily on the work of San Nicolo on OB sources. These opinions will be discussed further below.

found in "warranty" provisions in cuneiform sale documents, including slave sales. This interpretation stands in contrast to the traditional understanding of *biqqoret* as either "investigation" or "lashes."

b) The meaning and implications of the Samaritan Pentateuch variant are unclear though the verb is in the singular.

c) There are various structural oddities associated with the passage, including its casuistic form (unique in Lev. 19)[6] and the jarring (at least to the modern eye) placement of this text in the middle of a group of agricultural regulations — restrictions on agricultural mixtures (כלאים in v. 19) and on collecting the fruit of young trees (ערלה in vv. 23-25).

I shall argue that the passage is, like Exod. 21:4-11 and Deut. 15:12-18, concerned with the question of who has control over the slave woman and thus over any potential progeny. I propose that *neḥerefet* means "to be trifled with," in this case, judging from the context, sexually. The implication here is that sexual intercourse with the first *ish* should have constituted a marital-like bond between him and the *shifḥah.* Due, however, to the dubious nature of the intercourse — engaged in by the man with no intention of creating a permanent relationship, given the woman's unfree status and therefore her inability to protect herself – no such bond is created. I take *neḥerefet* to be similar to *be'ulah*, the term used in Deut. 22:22, but with a nuance of humiliation, as in unwanted sex. The term *be'ulah* is thus avoided here precisely because this woman is not to be considered a *be'ulat ba'al*, a woman with a husband. Consequently, there is no question of adultery, and neither the female slave nor the second *ish* is liable for death.

As a consequence, therefore, this case is taken out of the realm of sexual crime and treated as a "trespass" in the general sense of an interference with a right. As a result, there is to be a claim, which I take as the meaning of *biqqoret,* by the first *ish,* and the second *ish* is to bring an *asham,* the usual sacrifice for a trespass. That is, by having carnal relations with another's man's slave who has already been used sexually, the second *ish* has challenged the first *ish*'s right to her, whatever that right may be. The first

6 For a summary of the various structural issues, see, e.g., Karl Elliger, *Leviticus,* 249.

ish is therefore entitled to a claim against him, though whether this is for compensation or another remedy is unspecified, and the second *ish* must bring an *asham* sacrifice, consistent with other cases of biblical trespass.

Lev. 19:20 can then be translated:

> If a man has carnal relations with a woman who is a slave and has [already] been trifled with [sexually] by a man, but has not been redeemed or given her freedom, it shall be a claim of trespass; they shall not, however, be put to death, since she has not been freed.

When interpreted in this way, it can be argued that the verse has to some extent a functional similarity to the case described in Laws of Eshnunna [=LE] section 31, one of a series of laws in that collection (ss. 25-35) dealing with the establishment of rights over women and/or progeny.[7] That section reads:

> *šumma awīlum amat awīlim ittaqab* 1/3 *mana kaspam*
> *išaqqal u amtum ša bēlīšama*
>
> If a man has deflowered[8] the slave woman of [another] man, he
> shall weigh out 1/3 manna of silver, but the slave woman is her master's.

Though this case deals with a woman who is a virgin and the question of what damages are to be paid for her loss of virginity, it does establish, like Lev. 19:20, that one does not acquire someone's else's female slave by intercourse, though compensation is required.

What is the connection between the woman's unfree status and the absence of adultery? This is not, I propose, an indication of a biblical

7 The various sections cover the following: section 25 — bride given to someone else; 26 — abduction of bride; 27-28 — marriage without consent of woman's parents; 29 — second marriage of someone whose husband was abducted; 30 — second marriage of someone whose husband repudiated his city; 32 — price to be paid for child given for caregiving before it can be taken away; 33 — master's right to slave's child given away; 34 — master's right to child of slave woman of the palace; 35 — one who adopts a child a slave woman of the palace gives another slave.

8 The *AHW* gives for *naqābu* in the G stem: *durchbohren, deflorieren,* implying that the slave here was a virgin. This verb seems to be cognate with the Hebrew נקב "bore" or "perforate" and possibly with נקבה "female."

prohibition on slave-free marriage. Rather, as suggested in the introduction, this is a result of the overarching dependence hierarchy in the Bible. In marriage, as in the relationship between God and Israel, a breach of such trust by the "lesser" party is treason. To restore the proper balance, both the wife and the adulterer must be killed.[9] (Similarly, Israel's treason against God invites punishment both for Israel and for the object of her idolatry.) The slave woman, being coerced, is incapable of such treason. (At some point, it is to be noted, the penalty for adultery was commuted, perhaps as the basis of the husband-wife relationship began to be seen as something founded in property law rather than a question of trust.)

What precisely is the nature of the "crime" committed by the second *ish* in Lev. 19:20? As will be shown below, much has been written on the meaning of *biqqoret* and whether it is a type of remedy (such as an indemnity) or a claim for a breach of some specific type of property. One modern trend of thought takes it as implying the Roman idea of an *actio in rem.* I believe this question is significant: as will be argued below, it has implications regarding the development of property rights within a legal system. I shall argue that *biqqoret* means a claim with regard to any breach of one's rightful due, however that right arises; and the crime it covers may be more properly called a trespass in its broadest sense. As such, *biqqoret* represents a less sophisticated concept than a claim for a specific property right. In the case of Lev. 19:20, I argue that the right in question is a vaguely proprietary right resembling ownership.

In support of these interpretations, I shall propose that the apparently odd format and placement of this pericope support an emphasis on the issue of mixed ownership. I shall then analyze in depth the two *hapax*es *neḥerefet* and *biqqoret,* including an assessment of Akkadian cognates and of postbiblical usage. Though I am arguing some functional equivalence with LE, I do not suggest any early borrowing from Eshnunna. In fact, there are indications that the passage is a late biblical text, as will be argued further below.

9 Finkelstein has made this argument with respect to the goring ox of Exod. 21; the ox, having killed a human, has upset the hierarchy and thus must be put to death to restore the hierarchy. Would the slave woman who murdered her master also be put to death, much like the *petit*-treason idea in English common law?

4.2 THE ISSUE: MIXED OWNERSHIP

Scholars such as Noth and Elliger, focusing on the *asham* requirement in the pericope, deem the Lev. 19:20-22 passage to be a secondary insertion in the Holiness Code.[10] Noth bases his conclusion on the fact that no particular animal is required for the *asham* sacrifice in this passage, suggesting that *asham* here means simply "compensation." Noting the similarity to Lev. 5:15, where the penalty for an unintentional trespass of a sacred object (מעילה) is the monetary value of a ram as opposed to the animal itself, Noth argues that the Leviticus 19 passage also reflects a later simplification and secularization of cultic requirements.[11] Elliger also suggests a literary dependence of verse 21 on Lev. 5:6 and 15. Our verse 20, he argues, was conceived as a continuation of verse 21, rather than being a self-standing legal rule, and this is shown by its structure: the casuistic formulation in 20a and the fact that the legal consequence in 20b is formulated in the negative.[12]

Whether or not the passage is a secondary insertion, we may note that Deuteronomy 22 contains a similar juxtaposition of the laws of seed mixtures (vineyard with another crop together), animals of different species working together, and mixtures of wool and linen woven together (vv. 9-11) with sexual offenses (vv. 14ff.), including the adultery and rape passages noted above. These associations suggest that the concern underlying both the Leviticus and Deuteronomy sections is the mixture of seed. This may account for the emphasis on seed in the phrase שכבת זרע (literally: a lying of seed) in verse 20 (used, with respect to sexual offenses, only two other times, both with respect to adultery: Lev. 18:20, and Num. 5:13).

Why, then, not include our passage in Deuteronomy 22? I would argue that this is again to emphasize its difference from the case of adultery. First, it is not unusual to find slaves treated as agricultural assets: in the biblical text slaves are listed with cattle (and in some cases with sons and daughters)

10 B. Schwartz, "A Literary Study" 244 argues that it is the *asham* command of vv. 21-22a that must be the central concern of the periscope, as it is syntactically the main clause, and constitutes half of the fifty-two words of the periscope.

11 Noth, *Leviticus*, 143, 146-47.

12 Elliger, *Leviticus*, 249.

as part of the patrimony of a pastoralist or farmer,[13] and this vaguely proprietary association is found in other ancient legal systems as well.[14] This sort of connection is hinted at in *Num. Rab.* 10:1, which attempts to harmonize the disparate ideas in Leviticus 19 by positing an agricultural setting and drawing a moral conclusion from the word *asham*:

> וכי תבאו אל הארץ ונטעתם כל עץ מאכל וערלתם ערלתו את פריו מה כתוב לפניה ואיש כי ישכב וכי מה ענין זה לזה אלא אדם שהוא הולך ומתחבר בחברו בנטיעותיו ומתוך שהוא נכנס ויוצא בתוך ביתו הוא נחשד על שפחתו וכשם שאדם פורש את עצמו מן פרות ערלה כך יהיו המקלקלים בשפחות פורשים מן הכשרים ליום הדין שאמר ר' יודן בשם ר' לוי אלו שהם נוהגים התר בשפחות בעולם הזה עתידים להתלות בקדקדי ראשיהם לעתיד לבוא שנאמר אך אלהים ימחץ ראש איביו קדקד שער מתהלך באשמיו

> *When you enter the land and plant any tree for food, you shall regard its fruit as forbidden* [Lev. 19:23]. What is written before this? *A man who has carnal relations* [Lev. 19:20ff]. What does one issue have to do with the other? [It refers to] one who goes and teams up with his friend [to help him with his] planting, and as a result of entering and leaving his house is suspected [of having a relationship] with [his friend's] *shifḥah.* As a man separates himself from forbidden fruit, so those who sin with *shefaḥot* are separated from the righteous on the Day of Judgment, as R. Yudan said in the name of R. Levi:

---

13 Gen. 24:35, for instance, has the following descriptions of Abraham: וה' ברך את אדני מאד ויגדל ויתן לו צאן ובקר וכסף וזהב ועבדים ושפחות וגמלים וחמורים (And the Lord has blessed my master greatly and he has become great and He has given to him flocks and cattle and silver and gold and slaves and maidservants and camels and asses). Similar lists are found in Gen. 12:16 and 20:14 with respect to Abraham, and 30:43 with respect to Jacob. Job is similarly described (1:3):

> ויהי מקנהו שבעת אלפי צאן ושלשת אלפי גמלים וחמש מאות צמד בקר וחמש מאות אתנות ועבדה רבה מאד...

> And his property was seven thousand sheep, and three thousand camels, and five hundred yoke of oxen and five hundred she-asses, and a very great slave-force...

14 As one example, one may note the recommendation of Xenophon that slaves may benefit from the same kind of training given to animals (*Xenophon's Socratic Discourse: An Interpretation of the Oeconomicus* [trans. C. Lord; commentary by Leo Strauss; Ithaca: Cornell University Press, 1970], 56, XIII: 6), as well as the need to prevent slaves, like animals, from producing offspring without the master's knowledge (ibid., 41, IX:5). We may also briefly note here the fact that Mesopotamian *BQR/PQR* warranties are found in particular in sale documents involving land, fixtures, slaves, and cattle. This association, which will be discussed further below, also recalls the Roman concept of *res mancipi*, applicable to slaves, real estate, and animals.

> Those who behave in a loose manner with *shefaḥot* in this world will be suspended by the top of their heads in the time to come, as it is said: *God will smash the heads of His enemies, the hairy crown of him who walks about in his guilt* [*asham* — Ps. 68:22].

Certain scholars have posited that the preoccupation with mixtures, especially in the P stratum, is connected with a matrilineal idea. M. Weber, for instance, argued that this preoccupation with mixtures reflects the priestly struggle against mixed marriages detailed in Ezra and Neḥemiah, while S. Cohen argues that these laws of prohibited mixtures provided an ideological context for the later development of the matrilineal principle by postbiblical sages.[15]

It is my contention, however, that the specific emphasis of Lev. 19:20-22 goes beyond simply a desire to avoid mixtures of seed. It is the ownership of any progeny that might result from such mixture with which this section is concerned. This question arises (as it does in the case of adultery and the similar case in LE 31), because there are two apparent "owners" of the *shifḥah*. This concern would also explain the *asham* requirement, as the case is treated as one of trespass rather than as adultery. If the phrase *biqqoret tihyeh* is taken to mean "it will be a claim" (as I shall argue below), the structure of verse 20 can be characterized as a tripartite diagnosis pattern, found elsewhere in the P stratum. As Yaron[16] explains, this pattern consists of: a) a protasis in casuistic form, describing the situation ("if X..."); b) a diagnostic phrase, characterizing the situation ("she is guilty," or, as in this case, "it will be a claim"); c) an apodosis, giving the consequences (here, "he will bring an *asham*"). Perhaps not coincidentally, another example of this pattern may be found in the *asham* provision of Num. 5:6-7, which specifies the action to be taken in the case of trespass. Like Lev. 19:20, this section also begins with the איש כי (if X...) formula:

דבר אל בני ישראל

---

15 Max Weber, *Ancient Judaism* (trans. H. Gerth and D. Martindale; New York: Free Press, 1952), 350; S. Cohen, *The Beginnings of Jewishness*, 300. For a summary of other scholarly opinions on the biblical preoccupation with mixtures, see S. Cohen, *The Beginnings of Jewishness*, 301.

16 Reuven Yaron, *Introduction to the Law of the Aramaic Papyri* (Oxford: Clarendon, 1961), 110-11.

1) איש או אשה כי יעשו מכל חטאת האדם למעל מעל בה'

2) ואשמה הנפש ההוא

3) והתודו את חטאתם אשר עשו והשיב את אשמו בראשו
וחמישתו יסף עליו ונתן לאשר אשם לו

Speak to the Israelites:

[a] When a man or a woman commits any sin toward a fellow man, thus breaking faith with the Lord,

[b] that person will be guilty;[17]

[c] they [JPS = he] shall confess the wrong that they have [JPS = he has] done; he shall make restitution in the principal amount, and add one-fifth to it, giving it to him whom he has wronged.

The situation in Lev. 19:20 can thus be characterized as a claim of trespass by the first *ish as* against the second, who has challenged his right to the slave, the appropriate consequence being (as in Num. 5:6-7) an *asham.*

4.3 THE RELATIONSHIP: THE MEANING OF *NEḤEREFET LA-ISH*

4.3.1 Prior Opinions

Though the form *neḥerefet* is considered a *hapax,* the root *ḤRP* does exist in the Bible. Most dictionaries identify at least two homonyms: *ḤRP II*, meaning "to spend the winter," and *ḤRP I* (with its associated noun *ḥerpah*) connected in both the *Qal* and the *Pi'el* with the idea of slandering, insulting, and abasing. Even-Shoshan is definite in assigning *neḥerefet* to an unspecified third root; Mandelkern (*s.v.* חרפ I) suggests a connection between *neḥerefet* (as well as certain other instances of *ḤRP I*)

17 The JPS translation has "and that person realizes his guilt." The verb אשמה, according to Mandelkern, is a 3rd f.s. perfect; together with the *vav inverso,* I think it may be translated as above.

and an Arabic root meaning "to sell," proposing for *neḥerefet* the meaning משתפת (partnered). Ben-Ḥayim similarly looks to a Semitic cognate, suggesting a connection with the Ge'ez *PḤR* (despite the inversion of letters), meaning a prenuptial covenant or promise. He notes that this root is also used for the Ge'ez translation of the biblical ארש (betrothed).[18]

It must be acknowledged, however, that these scholarly assessments have been influenced by the traditional ideas of *neḥerefet* as "betrothed" or "assigned," and that these ideas in turn are derived solely from the presumed analogy with Deut. 22:22 or 23. The assumption is that the slave woman must be in some sort of relationship with a male (given the apparent parallel to the Deuteronomy provisions[19]), but her slave status prevents her from being "fully" married (a position supported in later law by *mQidd.* 3:12); hence a description for this lesser relationship had to be found.

The idea that *neḥerefet* means "assigned," found in some of the Targumim and the LXX, may have been suggested by a comparison with the *pidyon* and *ḥofesh* terminology in Exod. 21:7-11 and an assumption that the slave woman אשר לא יעדה (who was not assigned) in that passage must be the slave woman referred to in Lev. 19:20.[20] The origin of the "betrothal" idea[21] is less clear, although there is a tradition discussed in *bQidd.* 6a that seems to associate the idea with a Judean custom:

> איבעיא להו חרופתי מהו ת"ש דתניא האומר חרופתי מקודשת שכן ביהודה
> קורין לארוסה חרופה ויהודה הויא רובא דעלמא ה"ק האומר חרופתי מקודשת
> שנאמר והיא שפחה נחרפת לאיש ועוד ביהודה קורין לארוסה חרופה ועוד לקרא
>
> אלא ה"ק האומר חרופה ביהודה מקודשת שכן ביהודה קורין לארוסה חרופה

---

[18] Ze'ev Ben-Ḥayim, "And She is a *Shifḥa Neḥerefet* to Man (Leviticus 19:20)" [in Hebrew], *Leshonenu* 7 (1935): 364.

[19] In Shmuel Loewenstamm, "*Biqqoret Tiḥyeh*" [in Hebrew], *Shenaton* 4 (1980):94, Loewenstamm argues:

> והרי אין טעם להבדיל אלא בין מקרים דומים בלבד, משמע שגם כאן נמצא יחס של אישות.
>
> There is no reason to distinguish except between similar situations, meaning that here also is a relationship of marriage.

[20] This is Ibn Ezra's view on Lev. 19:20. Against this idea must be noted the fact that neither the Targumim nor the LXX use the same word to translate *neḥerefet* in Lev. 19:20 and *ye'adah* in Exod. 21:8, apparently seeing no connection between them.

[21] As reflected in the rabbinic sources listed in n. 4 above.

> It was asked [of the sages]: [Regarding the specific wording by which a man may indicate to a woman that she is betrothed to him,] What about ['You are] my *ḥarufah?* Come and hear, as it was taught [in a baraita]: If one says ['You are] my *ḥarufah,'* she is betrothed, because in Judah they call a betrothed woman a *ḥarufah.* And is Judah the majority of the world? [No, therefore] this is the way it should be stated: If one says ['You are] my *ḥarufah,'* she is betrothed, as it is stated [in Lev. 19:20]: *And she is a slave woman neḥerefet to a man*, and also, in Judah they call a betrothed woman a *ḥarufah.* And [do we need the confirmation of Judean custom] in addition to a biblical statement? [No;] rather this is the way it should be stated: If one says *in Judah* ['You are] my *ḥarufah,'* she is betrothed, because in Judah they call a betrothed woman a *ḥarufah.* [emphasis added]

It is not clear, however, whether this custom was the origin of the betrothal idea or a later development. The betrothal idea may also underlie the Samaritan Pentateuch variant בקרת תהיה לו לא יומת (there shall be a *biqqoret* for him; he shall not be put to death). The emphasis on "*he* shall not be put to death," rather than the MT's "they shall not be put to death," suggests a parallel with Deut. 22:25-27, non-consensual intercourse with the betrothed virgin, where only the male is liable for death. Targums Onkelos and Yonatan for Lev. 19:20 may be interpreted as being familiar with both the "betrothed" and "assigned" traditions. TO has: והיא אמא אחידא לגבר (and she is a maidservant assigned to a man). TY has: אמתא וחרתא מתארסא לגבר (a maidservant and freed woman betrothed to a man).

The "betrothal" idea had a following among later commentators,[22] although no explanation is given as to why *neḥerefet* would have been preferred to the biblical ארש. Certain modern scholars attempt to address this issue by suggesting that the term *neḥerefet* is reserved for the special

22 Maimonides, *Hil. Issurei Biyah* 3:13 has שפחה חרופה האמורה בתורה היא שחציה שפחה וחציה בת חורין ומקדשת לעבד עברי (The *shifḥah neḥerefet* mentioned in the Torah is she who is half-slave and half-free betrothed to a Hebrew slave). He explains the nature of this relationship at *Hil. Ishut* 4:16: המקדש אשה שחציה שפחה וחציה בת חורין אינה מקודשת קידושין גמורין עד שתשתחרר (One who betroths a woman who is half slave and half free: she is not betrothed in full betrothal until she shall be freed). Rashi on Lev. 19:20 equates the "assigned" and "betrothed" traditions: מיועדת ומיוחדת לאיש...ובשפחה כנענית חציה שפחה וחציה בת חורין המאורסת לעבד עברי (who is designated [*meyu'edet*] and betrothed [*meyuḥedet*] to a man... [refers] to a Canaanite slave woman who is half free betrothed to a Hebrew slave). The KJV translation at Lev. 19:20 simply has "betrothed."

condition of a slave betrothed to someone other than her owner,[23] or for a type of inchoate betrothal where the transfer of the slave to her new "purchaser" is not yet complete.[24] Other scholars simply accept one or the other (or both) of the traditional meanings.[25]

R. Westbrook, in contrast, sought a resolution to this issue by going outside the traditional meanings, and argued that the term is a *Nifal* of ערב, taking the latter in its sense of "to pledge."[26] He thus proposes that this is a case of a wife (taking *ishah* here as "wife" rather than "woman") who has been pledged to a creditor by her husband to pay off a debt. While in the creditor's household, she has been sexually abused by him (reading MT *le-ish* as *la-ish,* i.e, *that* man). Her husband may then claim her back (Westbrook's translation of *biqqoret,* as will be explained below) without paying off the rest of his debt, though without this being a case of adultery. His translation would thus be, "If a man has sexual intercourse with a married woman, she being a slave pledged to the man..." There is some support for the meaning "pledged" in the Targumim: Neofiti translates שפחה נחרפת לאיש as אמתא משעבדה לגבר (a maidservant pledged to a man), and לשעבד can be equivalent to להשכן (to pledge) (Jastrow, *s.v.* ,עבד *Shafel*), while MS A of the Samaritan Targum has סולה מרהנה לגבר, with רהן again

23 Schwartz, "A Literary Study," 246.

24 Neufeld, *Ancient Hebrew Marriage Laws*, 165; Noth, *Leviticus*, 142-43. Neufeld argued (perhaps influenced by the rabbinic characterization of Lev. 19:20 as involving a woman half slave, half free) that Lev. 19:20 is "qualified" adultery, involving a *shifḥah* who has been sold for marriage or concubinage but for whom the full purchase price has not been paid; thus the purchaser has not yet fully redeemed her and the seller has not yet set her free.

25 Ben-Ḥayim, "*Shifḥah Neḥerefet*," 365, followed by Loewenstamm, "*Biqqoret Tihyeh*," 94, argued in favor of "designated" or at least that "betrothed" should not be taken in its later technical legal sense as an element of marriage. Other scholars simply accept "betrothal" (see, e.g., Elliger, *Leviticus*, 249; Gordon Hugenberger, *Marriage as a Covenant: A Study of Biblical Law and Ethics Governing Marriage Developed from the Perspective of Malachi.* [VT Supp. 52; Leiden: Brill, 1994], 287-88), or equate "betrothal" with "designated" (see, e.g., Even-Shoshan, *s.v.* חרף; and Milgrom, "The Betrothed Slave-Girl, Lev. 19 20-22," *ZAW* 89 [1977]: 43-50, at 43 n. 1).

26 Westbrook, *Biblical and Cuneiform Law*, 106. Westbrook explains the derivation of *neḥerefet* from *arav* by arguing for the "known" interchange of *ayin* with *ḥet* and *bet* with *peh.* He further supports his argument by suggesting a functional similarity between Lev. 19:20 and the category of pledge cases found elsewhere in the Near Eastern Codes (for instance, LH sections 115-19), which include situations in which the pledged person is injured or killed while in the creditor's control. Westbrook's arguments will be further examined below.

meaning "to pledge" (Jastrow, *s.v.* רהן, *Hifil*). Yet the proposed interchange from נערב to נחרף is unclear. In the rare use of the passive idea of "to be pledged (or made surety)" (as in Gen. 43:9), a construction with the *Qal* form is used.[27] Further, there is no suggestion that *shifḥah* here refers specifically to a debt-slave.[28]

While I do not agree with Westbrook's proposed explanation, I do agree that the resolution of this *hapax* is to be found outside the traditional meanings, and specifically within the range of meanings already associated with the biblical *ḤRP I*. A brief review of the biblical occurrences of this root follows.

4.3.2 The Semantic Range of the Biblical ḤRP I

An inductive/contextual survey of this term throughout the Bible reveals a general idea of dishonoring someone by failing to give them their due or expected status, in both *Qal* and *Pi'el*, and regardless of the relative dating of the various sources in which it occurs. Based on the parallelism in Proverbs 14:31, the presumed opposite of לחרף is לכבד, "to honor":

עשק דל חרף עשהו, ומכבדו חנן אביון

> He who withholds what is due to the poor *affronts* [*ḤRP*] his Maker, he who shows pity for the needy *honors* Him. [JPS translation, emphasis added]

Terms complementing this verb include לגדף, קלון, דראון and most significantly לגדל על, suggesting that through someone else's aggrandizement one's own status is diminished (Zeph. 2:10; Ps. 55:13; Job 19:5). This sense would fit with many, if not all, of the occurrences of *ḤRP I*, notably Isaiah's accusation against Sennaḥerib concerning his insult to the Deity – את מי חרפת וגדפת (Whom have you *blasphemed* and reviled...) (2Kings 19:22, Isa. 37:23, emphasis added), though the word is not always or necessarily

---

27 Gen. 43:9 has: אנכי אערבנו (I [Judah] will be surety for him [Benjamin]).

28 Mendelsohn, *Slavery in the Ancient Near East*, 55 similarly assumed that Lev. 19:20 referred to a betrothed woman who had been pledged as a debt slave and that the right to sexually use a female slave was commonly assumed in the ancient Near East, but gave no explanation for his derivations.

used with someone of high status. In several instances the reduction in status implied by this word is a matter requiring payback: from Naval, for refusing food to David's troops (1Sam. 25:39); from Ephraim, for looking to Egypt and Assyria instead of seeking divine aid (Hos. 12:15). The idea of an affront to one's status as a matter requiring compensation is found elsewhere in the ancient Near East.[29]

Looking now to the noun *ḥerpah* as a lowering of status, it is significant that a woman's *ḥerpah* is often connected to uncontrolled or unproductive sexuality. The metaphorical description of Babylon as a female slave (one of the few explicit connections of *ḤRP* with slavery) associates the slave's *ḥerpah* with her nakedness (Isa. 47:3). Other instances of a woman's *ḥerpah* include 2Sam. 13:13, where the term is associated with a non-virgin in a state of non-marriage (the raped woman, Tamar, who cannot look to her half-brother the rapist for marriage); Isa. 54:4, where it is associated with a widow; Isa. 4:1, where it is associated with a single woman; and Gen. 30:23, where it is associated with childlessness.

Rachel's statement in the latter verse after the birth of Joseph — אסף ה' את חרפתי (God has taken away my *ḥerpah*) — does not convey an idea of "reproach" (the KJV translation, following the LXX[30]) or "shame," but suggests that she had been replaced in Jacob's esteem by her sister and the two slave women, since they had given birth to sons.[31]

Though the principal meaning of biblical *Nifal* is considered to be

---

29 The Akkadian law collections mention in particular the offense of slapping another's cheek as a matter requiring compensation (LE 42, LH 202-5); in LH the penalty varies according to the degree of inequality of status between the offender and the victim. The offense of cheek-slapping is also mentioned in the Hebrew Bible and New Testament [=NT]. In Lam. 3:30 it is specifically associated with *ḥerpah*:

יתן למכהו לחי ישבע בחרפה

> [With respect to the advantage of bearing insult while maintaining one's faith:]
> Let him offer his cheek to the smiter; let him be surfeited with mockery.

30 The LXX uses the form of *ὄνειδος*, "blame" or "reproach" (Liddell and Scott).

31 Perhaps a similar connection with improper male sexuality is reflected in the association of *ḤRP I* with the state of being uncircumcised. Thus the Israelites' uncircumcised state in Egypt is described as *ḥerpah* (Josh. 5:9); Goliath, accused repeatedly of dishonoring Israel (with variations of *ḤRP I*: 1Sam. 17:10, 26, 36, 45), is called by David הערל הפלשתי הזה (that uncircumcised Philistine – vv. 26, 36); the giving of Dina to the uncircumcised Shekhem is called *ḥerpah* by her brothers (Gen. 34:14); the word of God is described as *ḥerpah* to those with "uncircumcised ears" Jer. 6:10).

reflexive, the *binyan* can also serve as the passive for both *Qal* and *Pi'el*.[32] It is interesting to note that in postbiblical Hebrew only the *Qal* passive participle form *ḥarufah* is apparent, often used as a substantive (in only one instance, *bQidd.* 6a, with respect to betrothal terminology, is it associated with anyone other than the slave woman of Lev. 19).[33] Of particular interest in this respect is the biblical word *yeḥeraf* in Job 27:6:

בצדקתי החזקתי ולא ארפה לא ירחף לבבי מימי

A recent article by Joösten suggests that *yeḥeraf* here is a *Qal* middle (or stative) form, rather than a *Qal* active imperfect, given the *qametz* as the second vowel rather than the expected *ḥolem*.[34] The verse would thus carry a more passive meaning, which we propose to translate:

> I held fast to my righteousness, and will not let go; my heart will not be dishonored /moved from its place all my life.

This sense appears to be confirmed by the Targum to Job. Stec's critical edition gives the following as the primary variant for 27:6, using the the verb חסד;[35] according to Jastrow this verb is to be taken in a passive sense as "to be put to shame":[36]

בזכותי תקיפית לא אשבקנה
לא יחסד לבביי מן יומיי

---

32 Paul Joüon, *A Grammar of Biblical Hebrew* (2 vols.; trans. and rev. by T. Muraoka; Subsidia Biblica 14/I, II; Rome: Pontificio Instituto Biblico, 1996), 1:150-51.

33 See, e.g., *mZev.* 5:5; *tKer.* 1:16, 19; 4:5; Sifra *Qedoshim pereq* 5:10 (Weiss 89d); Sifra *Dibura DeḤovah pereq* 21:7 (Weiss 27c); *yQidd.* 1:1 59a; *yYev.* 6:1 7b; *yNaz.* 8:1 57a; *bShabb.* 72a, *bYev.* 55ab, *bGitt.* 43a, *bZevah.* 48a, 54b, *bKer.* 11a, 12b, 25b. M. Moreshet, *Lexicon of the New Verbs in Middle Hebrew* [in Hebrew] (Ramat Gan: Tel Aviv University, 1981) does not indicate *ḤRP I* in his list of new tannaitic verbs, suggesting that *ḥarufah* is not a new form.

34 Jan Joösten, "The Function of the Semitic D Stem: Biblical Hebrew Materials for a Comparative-Historical Approach," *Orientalia* 67 (1998): 202-31, at 212.

35 Other MSS, identified by D. Stec, *The Text of the Targum of Job: An Introduction and Critical Edition* (Studies in the History and Culture of the Ancient Near East 14; Leiden: Brill, 1998), as belonging to a Spanish/North African family, have יהרהר (Jastrow: "to entertain impure thoughts").

36 The verb חסד is used, for instance, in the Targum to Pss 40:15 and 71:24, to translate MT חפר (to be ashamed).

I held firmly to my merit, I will not let go,
My heart will never be put to shame.

Joösten goes on to suggest that *Qal* middle forms may have been replaced by other stems, particularly the *Nifal* in Hebrew; that is, though the *Nifal* is defined as primarily a reflexive form, it could also express a meaning closer to a *Qal* middle.[37] The *Nifal neḥerefet* of Lev. 19:20 could then be related to the *yeḥeraf* of Job, in the sense of "dishonored," depending, of course, on the relative date of this passage.[38] It is of interest to note that the later commentator Maimonides did in fact connect the *neḥerefet* of Leviticus with the *yeḥeraf* of Job; he related both terms, however, to an Arabic cognate meaning "to turn away," and was constrained to interpret Lev. 19:20 accordingly:

> And in the same way this meaning [of לב as indicating a deficiency of opinion] is to be found in the dictum *My heart shall not turn away so long as I live*, the meaning of which is: my opinion shall not turn away from, and shall not let go of, this matter. For the beginning of this passage reads: *My righteousness I hold fast and will not let it go; My heart shall not turn away so long as I live.* In my opinion, it is with reference to this meaning of *yeḥeraf* that the expression *shiphḥah neḥerefet le-ish* is to be explained, [the term *neḥerefet*] being akin to an Arabic word, namely *munḥarifa*ʾ [turned away] — that is, one who turns from being possessed as a slave to being possessed as a wife.[39]

4.3.3 A Possible Akkadian Cognate

Levine has raised the possibility that the biblical *neḥerefet* is related to the Akkadian verb, *ḫarāpu*. This verb is translated as *fruh werden,* "to be early" (*AHW s.v. ḫarāpu* I, *CAD s.v. ḫarāpu* A); Levine makes the

---

37 Joösten, "Semitic D Stem," 228.

38 The dating of Job is a matter of issue; Pope, for instance, argues that while the final redaction might be dated to the 3rd century B.C.E., the Dialogue portion may have antecedents going back to the 7th century (Marvin H. Pope, *Job* [Anchor Bible 15; Garden City: Doubleday, 1965], xxxvi-xxxvii).

39 Maimonides, *The Guide of the Perplexed* (trans. S. Pines), Part I, chapter 39, 88. The translator, Pines (ibid., 88 nn. 13, 16, 18), though accepting that the Arabic *inḥarafa* (meaning "to turn away," "to deviate") was cognate with the *yeḥeraf* of Job, nonetheless preferred the traditional "shall not reproach" for the translation of this verse.

connection with the biblical term by translating *neḥerefet* as "assigned in advance" and positing that it is therefore outside the usual meaning of biblical *ḤRP* as "to blaspheme" or "to slander."[40] I think it is possible to accept that the Hebrew and Akkadian terms are cognate without the necessity of accepting either of Levine's propositions. In the following instances, taken from Neo-Assyrian [=NA] and Late Babylonian [=LB] sources, one may argue that the sense of the Akkadian *ḫarāpu* I is not simply to be early, or first, but to act in another's place, and by extension to take (or attempt to take) precedence over someone:

a) Assyrian and Babylonian Letters [= ABL] 3 (K 492; SAA 10, 191); NA, 672-669 B.C.), a letter from Adadšumu-uṣur to Essarhaddon regarding the testing of a medicinal drug for the prince:

 11. *qallāti ammûte*
 12. *niḫarrup*
 13. *nišaqqi*

 Let us make these slaves go first [i.e., in place of the prince] and give them to drink...

b) ABL 1164 (British Museum – Signature Budge) [=BU] 89-4-26,6; *Rituels Accadiens* p. 113); Seleucid era letter found at Uruk regarding the *akitu* festival of Ishtar of Arbella; the statue of the deity is being returned to Arbella from Melkia, and a question is addressed to the king as to the appropriate protocol:

 2. *Ištar ultu Melkia*
 3. *taḫarrupu pān šarri terrab*
 4. *idati šarru errab*
 5. *ulâ šarru errab*
 6. *idati Ištar terrab*

 Should Ishtar go first out of Melkia, enter before the king, and the king at her side, or should the king enter with Ishtar at his side

40 Baruch Levine, *Leviticus* (JPS Torah Commentary; Philadelphia: Jewish Publication Society, 1989), 130.

3) ABL 311 (K 630, SAA 5, 199); NA, letter to Sargon II from Šarru-emuranni, quoting the king's accusation of a breach of protocol:

5. *mā attā taḫarrupu*
6. *tunammeše mā ina pān bēl pāḫāti*
7. *ša Arrapḫa lā tadgul*

...you are precipitate, you set out; you did not wait upon the governor of Arrapḫa [i.e., he should have gone first, and you have usurped his position]

We may thus posit that this nuance of the Akkadian term is quite similar to the biblical *ḤRP I* (including the term *neḥerefet)* in the sense of usurping or denying someone's status.[41]

4.3.4 Proposed Meaning of neḥerefet la-ish

I maintain that Lev. 19:20, rather than referring to a woman connected with a man in some legally recognized relationship such assignment, betrothal, or marriage, in fact refers to the opposite: a woman humbled sexually by a man and thus degraded as not being in any legally reputable relationship. The question is: Does this type of relationship carry with it the same prohibitions against incest as the other relationships do? It is interesting to note that there is some precedent in the rabbinic sources specifically connecting *neḥerefet* to sexuality. One may note, first, the explanation given by Aquilas for *neḥerefet* in *yQidd.* 1:1 59a:[42]

דאמר ר' יוסי בשם ר' יוחנן תרגם עקילס הגר לפני רבי עקיבה והיא שפחה נחרפת לאיש בכתושה לפני איש כמה דאת אמר ותשטח עליו הרפות אמר ר' חייה בשם ר' יוחנן כן פירשה ר' לעזר בי רבי שמעון לפני חכמים והיא שפחה נחרפת לאיש בכתושה לפני איש כמה דתימר בתוך הריפות בעלי

41 Levine himself (ibid.) argues for this sense in a biblical instance, Judg. 5:18, translating חרף נפשו למות there as "his soul precipitously exposed itself to death."

42 Saul Lieberman, *Greek in Jewish Palestine* (New York: JTSA, 1965), 19, suggests that this is one of only two occasions when Aquilas does not translate into Greek. This perhaps indicates that the meaning was unclear even to Aquilas, and he thus tried to use a Hebrew metaphor rather than a precise Greek equivalent.

As R. Yose said in the name of R. Yoḥanan: Aquilas the proselyte translated before R. Akiva: *And she is a shifḥah neḥerefet...* — ground before a man, as you say: *...and scattered groats [i.e., grains] on top of it...* [2Sam. 17:19, with respect to the woman who disguised the well]. R. Ḥiyya said in the name of R. Yoḥanan: R. Lazar of the house of R. Shimon explained before the sages: *And she is a shifḥah neḥerefet to a man* — ground before a man, as you say: [*Though you pound the fool in a mortar*] *with a pestle along with the grain...* [Prov. 27:22].

The word כתושה "crushing" or "pounding" (Jastrow), seems to be a euphemism here for sexual intercourse, with the later sages attempting to explain this derivation of Aquilas in a somewhat forced manner by associating *neḥerefet* with *harifot*, "small grains" (i.e., material that has been ground with a pestle). A similar derivation is found in *bKer.* 11a:

א"ר יצחק לעולם אינו חייב אלא על שפחה בעולה בלבד שנאמר והיא שפחה נחרפת לאיש ומאי משמע דהאי נחרפת לישנא דשנויי הוא דכתיב ותשטח עליו הריפות...

R. Isaac said: He is never liable except for a *shifḥah* with whom he has had intercourse, as it is said: *and she is a shifḥah neḥerefet le-ish.* What is the meaning of this *neḥerefet?* It is language [implying] a change [in condition], as it is written [2Sam. 17:19]: *...and scattered groats on top of it.*

Both Naḥmanides and Ibn Ezra also looked to other instances of *ḤRP* for elucidation, each detecting in Lev. 19:20 a sexually vague sort of status for the woman. Ibn Ezra associated *neḥerefet* directly with the noun *ḥerpah.* He stated that this woman is definitely the Hebrew slave of Exod. 21:7, assigned to a master or his son, and her *ḥerpah* consisted in the fact that her status was in limbo; true betrothal would not take place until she was freed or redeemed:

ומלה נחרפת...לפי דעתי שהמלה מגזרת חרפה בעבור היותה שפחה והיא בתולה ברשות אחר ואינה מאורשה

[Concerning] *neḥerefet...* in my opinion the word is derived from *ḥerpah,* on account of her being a slave: she is a virgin in the control of another but not betrothed.

Naḥmanides conversely assumed this was a serving woman in a free relationship with her master. He derived *neḥerefet* from *ḥoref* (winter), arguing:

...והנראה אלי כי הוא מלשון כאשר הייתי בימי חרפי בימי נעורי וכן לא יחרף לבבי מימי שלא יהיה לי לב נער ויקראו ימי הנעורים ימי חורף כי החרף בראשית השנים...
יאמר הכתוב שהיא שפחה נערה לאיש ידוע כי הפלגש אשר היא משרת את האיש וישכב עמה תקרא נערה לו כי גם כל משרת האדם יקרא נערו ומורגל בלשון חכמים לאמר על השוכבת עם האיש משמשת עמו...מנסיפדה בלע"ז וכן בלשון חכמים דקרו לה רביתא דפלניא והענין שאינה אשתו לגמרי אבל נתן לה קדושין והיא לו לנערה משמשת

It seems to me that this is from the language in *When I was in the days of my ḥoref* [Job 29:4] — the days of my boyhood; also *My heart will never yeḥeraf* [Job 27:6] — that I will not have the heart of a boy. And they call boyhood the days of *ḥoref* [winter], because winter is at year's beginning... Scripture is saying that she is a *shifḥah,* a man's 'girl' (*na'arah*). It is known that the *pilegesh* who serves a man and whom he lies with is called his 'girl,' just as a male who serves a man is called his 'boy.' And it is usual in the language of the Sages to describe a woman who lies with a man as 'servicing' him... *mancipada* in the vernacular,[43] and also in the language of the sages, who called her 'the girl of so-and-so.' The key is that she is not fully his wife, though he has given her *qiddushin* and she is a girl who 'services' him.

Ben Ḥayim, though noting the talmudic precedents, rejected any association of *neḥerefet* with the language of *be'ilah*, apparently because he objected to the attempts of modern commentators to derive this association from an Arabic cognate meaning "to pick" or "to pluck."[44] Considering this association too vague, he also suggested that the preposition in the phrase *le-ish* would be inappropriate with the idea of *niv'elet.* One may argue

43 The meaning of this word is unclear. One may note, however, the word *mançeba* in medieval Spanish, meaning "female servant," "concubine," "young girl," indicating a blending of various concepts: R.S. Boggs *et al.*, *Tentative Dictionary of Medieval Spanish* (2 vols.; Chapel Hill, N.C., 1946), *s.v. mançeba.*

44 Ben-Ḥayim, "*Shifḥah Neḥerefet*," 363, 364. One may note, however, a similar association of intercourse with the idea of "plucking" in *Gen. Rab.* 45:2. Commenting on the reference to Hagar in Gen. 16:1 as the *shifḥah* of Sarai, the Midrash states:

שפחת מלוג היתה והיה חייב במזונותיה ולא היה רשאי למכרה בעון קומי ריש לקיש מהו דתנא עבדי מלוג אמר להון כמה דתימא מלוג מלוג

She was a *shifḥah* who was [part of the wife's property in which the husband had] a usufruct (*melog*); [the husband] was obliged to maintain her but could not sell her. They asked before Resh Laqish: What was taught [about] *melog* slaves? He said to them: What is plucked is plucked [from the root מלג, 'to pluck'; that is, the husband had a right to 'use' such slaves, including sexually, but was not obligated for such use].

against this, however, that the biblical range of *ḤRP* does directly suggest a sexually inappropriate status, without the need to find the support of a cognate; the preposition *le* – would then carry the meaning of "before" — i.e., "humiliated" or "humbled" before a man.[45]

4.4 THE OUTCOME: THE PHRASE *BIQQORET TIHYEH*

The precise nature of the remedy for a vaguely proprietary crime is also of interest in connection with the more general question of the development of "true" property rights in a legal system. Essential to such rights is the ability to transfer the property completely out of one person's control and into another's; essential to that idea is a transferee's ability to claim his or her right to the property against the entire world. Specifically, the transferee may trace the property beyond the immediate transferor so as to ensure there will be no trouble from previous owners. And key to that ability is the development of a certain type of warranty, in which the transferor warrants to the transferee that there will be no claim against the property by some third party (such as a previous owner); if such a claim is made, the transferor warrants it will in some way guarantee the transferor's right against the world at large — for instance, by ensuring that the claimant will come to court to argue his or her right against the new transferee. It is this kind of warranty that many scholars claim to lie behind the *PQR/BQR* warranties, and, by extension, the word *biqqoret.*

There is, however, a remedy of compensation for injury as between two people, X and Y, where one has injured the other. The injury need not necessarily be a claim against property; it may be a physical injury, or an interference with someone's status relationship (for instance, X claims that Y's slave is not really his slave), or a trespass on property in the modern sense (X interferes with Y's use of his property without actually claiming the property is his). The claim here is relevant only between X and Y.
It is this kind of warranty that is assumed to lie behind the *PQR/BQR* warranties in Akkadian slave sales.

45 It may also be noted that *l* - can be taken as indicating agency with a passive form, translated as "by." See, e.g., Gesenius 121f, though it is argued in Joüon/Muraoka, *A Grammar of Biblical Hebrew*, 2:483-84, that this use of *l* – is probably infrequent.

4.4.1 Prior Opinions

There are two main trends of interpretation of this phrase, as Loewenstamm notes, among the traditional translations and commentaries. One tradition accepts a straightforward connection with biblical Hebrew *levaqqer* in the general sense of "to look into," "to examine" (Mandelkern: *diligenter inspicere, animum advertere*), and translates *biqqoret* as "inquiry." Thus the LXX has ἐπισκοπὴ ἔσται αὐτοῖς (there shall be an inspection to them[46]), an idea reflected in certain modern translations.[47] A second tradition, prevalent among the Aramaic Targumim[48] and tannaitic opinion, associated *biqqoret* with an idea of punishment; yet within this tradition there is no consistency as to who is to be punished or how. Targum Neofiti suggests that both the man and woman were punished, with מרדו אנון חייבין (they are subject to chastisement[49]). Tannaitic opinion, in contrast, specified that the woman alone was to be flogged:

ומה בין השפחה לבין כל העריות ...כל העריות אחד האיש ואחד האשה שוין במכות ובקרבן ובשפחה לא השוה את האיש לאשה במכות ולא את האשה לאיש בקרבן

What is the difference between the *shifḥah* [of Lev. 19:20] and all the other sexual sins [such as incest]? ...In the case of the other sexual sins the man and the woman are equal with respect to flogging and sacrifice, but in the case of the *shifḥah* the man is not treated equally to the woman with respect to flogging, and the woman is not treated equally to the man with respect to the sacrifice. (*mKer.* 2:4)[50]

Pseudo-Jonathan covers both trends with פישפוש יהוי בדינא למלקי היא מחייבא (there shall be an inquiry in law; she is subject to lashes). The Vulgate

---

46 Certain manuscripts have αὐτῶν (of them") or αὐτῇ (of her); a later version has ὄνειδος ἔσται αυτῷ (there shall be blame to him), which the editor suggests is comparable to the Samaritan Targum version(s) at Lev. 19:20.

47 The older JPS translation, for instance, has "inquisition."

48 The term בקורתא used by Onkelos appears to be a *hapax* in that Targum, and thus its meaning is unclear. The Samaritan Targum MS A translates the term as בגנו, possibly equivalent to ערוה; this concept is central to the discussion of this verse in *Sifra Qedoshim,* to be discussed in chapter six.

49 Jastrow *s.v.* מרדו, מרדותא.

50 This Mishnah reflects one version of a unit that also appears in *tKer.* and *Sifra Qedoshim* with substantial variations, and these will be analyzed in more detail in chapter six.

assumed flogging, but for both: *vapulabunt ambo* (they shall be flogged together). The punishment of the female slave was widely accepted among later commentators and translations.[51] As Loewenstamm notes, however,[52] the linguistic association of *biqqoret* with the idea of punishment is extremely difficult, though there were attempts to explain the association by a play on words; several such (not particularly convincing) attempts are summarized in *Midrash Leqaḥ Tov* to Lev. 19:20 (ed. Rom):

> בקרת תהיה מלמד שהיא לוקה יכול אף הוא ילקה ת"ל תהיה. היא לוקה והוא אינו לוקה. ד"א בקרת תהיה (ב' קראי) [בקראי] תהא דתנו רבנן במסכת מכות גדול שבדיינין קורא והשני מכה והשלישי אומר הכהו. מאי קורא אם לא תשמור לעשות את כל דברי התורה הזאת וגו'. אמרי לה בקורת ברצועות של בקר כדתנן ורצועה של עגל בידו כפולה אחת לשתים ושתים לארבעה ושתי רצועות עולות ויורדות בה

> *biqqoret tihyeh*: This [phrase] teaches that she is whipped. Perhaps he should also be whipped? The text has *she shall* [the verb in 3 f.s.]; [thus] she is whipped, and he is not. Another matter: [Read the phrase *biqoret tihyeh* as] 'It shall be with reading,' as it was taught in Tractate *Makkot* [with respect to the procedure for whipping]: 'The highest ranking judge reads out, the second does the whipping, and the third says: 'He has hit him.' What does he read? *If you do not take care to keep all the matters of this Torah,* etc.' [Deut. 28:58; additional verses are set out in *mMak.* 3:14]. Some say *biqqoret* [means] with straps of cow[hide] [i.e., apparently deriving *biqqoret* from *baqar* (cattle)], as it was taught in a Mishnah [*mMak.* 3:12, regarding the whip to be used]: 'And a strap of calf[skin] is in his hand, folded into two and then into four, and two straps run up and down it....'[53]

---

51 Rashi, for instance, at Lev. 19:20, *s.v.* בקרת תהיה, has היא לוקה ולא הוא (She is flogged and he is not). Maimonides specifies (*Hil. Issurei Biyah* 3:14):

> ביאת שפחה זו משנה מכל ביאות אסורות שבתורה, שהרי היא לוקה...והוא חיב קרבן אשם

> The intercourse of this slave woman differs from all other forbidden acts of intercourse in the Torah for she is flogged... and he is liable for a guilt offering.

The KJV to Lev. 19:20 translates "she shall be scourged."

52 Loewenstamm, "*Biqqoret Tihyeh*," 97.

53 Another possible derivation of the idea of punishment is suggested by Mandelkern's translation of *biqqoret* (among other meanings) as *animadversio.* This noun is translated generally as 'notice' but particularly 'unfavourable notice,' and by extension 'blame,' 'punishment' (*The Pocket Oxford Latin Dictionary*, Oxford: Oxford University Press, 1994). A similar extension of the idea of 'inspection' to a concept of 'punishment' may also have existed in biblical Hebrew. I shall argue, however, that *biqqoret* is more closely connected

A third possibility associates *biqqoret* with an issue of ownership. This idea seems to have first been raised by Naḥmanides, who related *biqqoret* to the idea of *hefqer/hevqer,* usually translated, "ownerless property." In his explanation of *biqqoret tihyeh*, Naḥmanides wrote:

ואני סבור שהיא מילה יחידית בכתוב אבל היא מורגלת בלשון ארמית ובדברי רבותינו מלשון הפקר... ופירוש הפסוק הזה שאמר בשפחה הזאת אע"פ שהיא נחרפת לאיש, לא תהיה לו לאשה כי בקרת תהיה לו, כלומר מופקרת תחשב אצלו...

> I think that though this is a unique word in Scripture, it is common in Aramaic and in the works of our sages, from the language of *hefqer* ... and the interpretation of this verse is that [Scripture] said about this slave woman that even though she is 'servicing' a man, she is not to be considered his wife, but a *biqqoret* for him — that is, she is deemed ownerless property with respect to him [and thus available to all, so there is no question of adultery].

In so relating *biqqoret* to an idea of property, Naḥmanides coincidentally anticipated a modern line of research which associates both *biqqoret* and the postbiblical *hefqer/hevqer* with the Akkadian root *BQR/PQR*. The latter root has among its meanings (*AHW s.v. baqāru*) *vindizieren,* in essence, to assert a claim in property. Various modern scholars, particularly E. A. Speiser, have accepted this association, based particularly on the work of M. San Nicolo.[54] Some of the modern biblical interpretations (such as the JPS version quoted at the beginning of the chapter) have followed Speiser's line of reasoning, translating *biqqoret* as "indemnity."[55]

There is no agreement, however, as to precisely what San Nicolo's research revealed and its applicability to the Hebrew *biqqoret,* and the various debates have become rather complex. As will be summarized in more detail below, Speiser's interpretation of San Nicolo has been rejected by such scholars as Loewenstamm and Westbrook, yet the question of the association of the Akkadian and Hebrew terms has not been resolved.

I shall argue that *biqqoret* in Lev. 19:20 does mean "claim" in the

---

to the idea of "claim," and it is equally possible that the idea of "inspection" or "inquiry" may itself be an extension of that concept.

54 Speiser, "Leviticus and the Critics," 35-36. For a summary of scholarly opinions on the Akkadian connection, see Loewenstamm, "*Biqqoret Tihyeh*," 94-95; Schwartz, "A Literary Study," 250 n. 36; and Westbrook, *Biblical and Cuneiform Law*, 102-3.

55 As noted by Westbrook, *Biblical and Cuneiform Law*, 105.

general sense of a challenge to someone else's ownership, whether or not in the form of a specifically legal demand. In support of this argument I posit the following: a) there are in fact several biblical instances of *BQR* meaning "claim"; b) the Hebrew *biqqoret* is cognate with Akkadian *BQR/PQR* forms, found particularly in warranty clauses;[56] and c) contrary to the assertion of Loewenstamm,[57] there is evidence in postbiblical Hebrew of the use of the root *BQR/PQR* as a legal term in the sense of "claim," particularly in the expressions *iggeret biqqoret* and *hefqer/hevqer*. These points will now be argued in more detail.

4.4.2 Biblical Instances of BQR as "Claim for Trespass"

Within the passage in question, it should first be noted that the meaning "claim" fits the requirement of an *asham* offering in Lev. 19:20 — that is, an offering brought to expiate a trespass, in this case a challenge to the ownership of another's slave woman.[58] This meaning also fits well within the diagnostic pattern of verse 20, as I have argued above.

Further, contrary to Schwartz's contention that there are no other biblical occurrences of forms of *BQR/PQR* for which a meaning of "claim"

56 These are provisions often found in sale contracts (or other transactions) involving land, fixtures and slaves, in which the seller agrees to protect the buyer (in various ways) should the sale be attacked. These will be discussed more fully below.

57 Loewenstamm, "*Biqqoret Tihyeh*," 96, n. 13.

58 For a summary of the nature of the *asham*, see, e.g., Jacob Milgrom, *Cult and Conscience: The Asham and the Priestly Doctrine of Repentance* (Studies in Judaism in Late Antiquity 18; Leiden: Brill, 1976), 125. One must note here Milgrom's proposition (ibid., 124-25) that there are two categories of *asham:* inadvertent trespass against sacred objects (the cases enumerated in Lev. 5:14-16 and 17-19) and trespass against the Lord's name through the making of a false oath (the cases enumerated in Lev. 5:20-26 and its variant in Num. 5:6-8). For the case of Lev. 19:20-22, he suggests that the oath that has been breached is the adultery prohibition of the Sinaitic covenant, to which every Israelite had sworn allegiance (Milgrom, "The Betrothed Slave-girl," 48-49). While it is beyond the scope of the study to investigate the detailed nature of the *asham,* I disagree with the opinion that the false oath is the single principle underlying the non-sacred trespass cases in Lev. 5:20-25/Num. 5:6-8; this latter proposition of Milgrom is in part based on reading the phrase ונשבע על שקר in Lev. 5:22 as applicable to all the cases of non-sacred trespass (Milgrom, *Cult and Conscience*, 100-101), which seems too broad a reading. Therefore I do not agree that a false oath needs to underlie the Lev. 19:20-22 passage in order to explain the *asham* requirement.

would be appropriate,[59] we may note several instances in which a claim idea does in fact suit the context. Mandelkern in his concordance cites eight other biblical occurrences of forms of *BQR*, all, it may be noted, in supposedly later works.[60] Ezekiel 34:11-12 contains in particular three attestations of the term that may be translated "claim":

כי כה אמר אדני ה': הנני אני ודרשתי את צאני ובקרתים. כבקרת רעה עדרו ביום היותו בתוך צאנו נפרשות, כן אבקר את צאני והצלתי אתהם מכל המקומות אשר נפצו שם ביום ענן וארפל.

Behold thus says the Lord God: I shall *demand* my sheep and *claim* them. Like the *claim* of a shepherd over his flock when he is among his scattered sheep,[61] so I will *claim* my sheep and I will rescue them from all the places to which they were dispersed on the day of cloud and dust [emphasis added].

The contextual fit provides a strong argument for the meaning "claim" in this case, particularly given that the following verse 13 starts with והוצאתים (And I will take them out); the passage describes, in other words, the actions of a shepherd in retrieving parts of his flock that have become intermingled with others. There are, in addition, two other suggestive points. In verse 11 the term ובקרתים can be seen as a complement to ודרשתי (I shall demand).[62] The term *DRŠ*, like*BQR*, can have the sense of visiting or investigating, but can also have a more "urgent" sense of demanding or requiring (Mandelkern, *s.v.* דרש: *poscere*[63]). The Targum

---

59 Schwartz, "A Literary Study," 250.

60 Lev. 13:36 and 27:33, 2Kings 16:15, Ezek. 34:11-12 (3x), Ps. 27:4, and Prov. 20:25.

61 In Moshe Greenberg, *Ezekiel 21-37* (Anchor Bible 22A; Garden City, N.Y.: Doubleday, 1997), 699-700, Greenberg considers this reading "strained" and suggests instead "when there are among his flock some [animals that have got] separated." This reading seems to be supported by the Targum to Ezekiel which has:

ביומא דהוי עניה ומפריש להון

On the day that there was one [among] his flock and separated from them.

One may argue, however, that the implication is the same in both readings: the flock, or part of it, has become dispersed, requiring the shepherd to go and physically retrieve the sheep.

62 Greenberg, *Ezekiel*, 699-700, suggests that the pair *drš-bqr* in this verse is a deliberate variation of the pair *drš-bqš* in verse 6.

63 This sense may be taken, for instance, in Gen. 42:22:

for Ezekiel in fact translates ודרשתי here as ואתבע, which can have the meaning "claim" (Jastrow, *s.v.* תבע). One may argue for a similar extension of meaning for *BQR*. The second point relates to the noun *biqqoret*, part of the long construct chain at the beginning of verse 12. This form is taken by Mandelkern as the construct form of a noun *biqqrah*, and like the *biqqoret* of Lev. 19:20 it is a biblical *hapax*.[64] One may posit that these nouns are synonyms, or at least related in meaning, both perhaps related to the *Pi'el* of *BQR*, similar to the pattern observed with the nouns *yabbashah* and *yabbeshet*, both of which mean "dry land."[65]

One may also note 2Kings 16:15, Aḥaz' instructions to Uriah regarding the altars of the First Temple. The first part of this verse is as follows:

> ויצוהו המלך אחז את אוריה הכהן לאמר על המזבח הגדול הקטר את עלת הבקר ואת מנחת הערב ואת עלת המלך ואת מנחתו ואת עלת כל עם הארץ ומנחתם ונסכיהם וכל דם זבח עליו תזרק...

> And King Aḥaz commanded the priest Uriah: On the great altar you shall offer the morning burnt offering, and the evening meal offering, and the king's burnt offering and his meal offering, with the burnt offerings of all the people of the land, their meal offerings, and their libations. And against it you shall dash the blood of all the burnt offerings and all the blood of the sacrifices...

The last clause of this verse then provides: ומזבח הנחשת יהיה לי לבקר, which the JPS translates as "And I will decide about the bronze altar," noting that the meaning of the Hebrew is unclear. Heger argues that the verse implies that while Aḥaz had formulated a new and elaborate sacrificial

---

ויען ראובן אתם לאמר הלוא אמרתי אליכם לאמר אל תחטאו בילד ולא שמעתם וגם דמו הנה נדרש

> And Reuven answered them saying: Did I not say to you saying, 'Do not sin against the child'? And you did not heed [them — the words], and behold, his blood is demanded.

64 Further, there are no instances of this noun (that I can detect) in tannaitic sources.

65 While Mandelkern does not specifically associate *yabbeshet* with *yabbashah* (or with any other verbal root), Gesenius does (Kautzsch, *Gesenius' Hebrew Grammar* section 84^{b} b), deriving both from the *Pi'el* of *YBŠ*. Joüon/Muraoka also give the two words as synonyms, including them within the group of nouns with doubled second consonants and two short vowels (Joüon, *A Grammar of Biblical Hebrew*, 1:252, s. 88a). The latter group, as they state, tend to have as feminine fours *qattalah* or *qattelet*. If *baqqarah* and *biqqoret* fall under this pattern, the vocalization of the latter would have to be explained.

ritual to go along with the new altar he had built which gave a greater role to the priests, he reserved the right to minister by himself at the older bronze altar.[66] The last clause in the verse may thus mean: "The bronze altar is mine to claim [i.e., it is still my right to worship there]."

4.4.3 BQR/PQR as "Claim" in Akkadian Sources

Scholarly discussion of the association of the Hebrew *biqqoret* with the Akkadian *BQR/PQR* centers around M. San Nicolo's research of the Akkadian forms in his 1922 work on the *Schlussklauseln* of OB contracts (i.e., the end sections, which are taken to be the operative sections). His research is understood to have concluded that the Akkadian terms connote the idea of the Roman *actio in rem* — that is, claim for the return of an item based on a particular type of "property right."[67] I shall argue that the use of this technical Roman term has been misleading, and that Akkadian *BQR/PQR* forms can be translated to simply mean "claim." Positing a more general sense for the Akkadian *BQR/PQR* not tied to a particular type of claim makes it easier to assert a connection with the biblical *biqqoret,* without having to devise (as R. Westbrook has done) a specific scenario appropriate to an *actio in rem* concept. A brief review both of the scholarly discussions and of various instances of *BQR/PQR* will illustrate this proposal.

4.4.3.A San Nicolo's Study of *BQR* in Old Babylonian Sources

The verb *baqāru* (*AHW s.v. baqāru*), is found throughout Babylonian as well as in OA sources. From MB onward, the form is mainly *paqāru*. There are two categories of meaning given for the G stem (with appropriate variations of meaning in Gt, S, D and N): a more general meaning of *anfechten,* "to dispute," and a more specific meaning of *vindizieren* – that is, to assert a claim of an item which is currently in the possession of another party, claiming that one's own right to the item is superior.[68] The second meaning

---

66 Paul Heger, *Three Biblical Altar Laws*, 272, n. 110.

67 For detailed explanations of these terms see below, n. 82.

68 This is something like the English law concept of *replevin*, a claim made by one whose chattels are wrongfully removed. There are related noun forms with corresponding meanings; however, no feminine forms are given. Thus, following the *AHW* definitions,

is associated particularly with the use of *BQR/PQR* in sale documents and similar transactions, usually involving land, buildings, fixtures, and large animals, as well as slaves; such documents, particularly from the OB, NB and LB periods, often contain a *BQR/PQR* warranty. In essence, these warranties provide that the buyer will be protected in some way if a *BQR/ PQR* claim arises in the slave or other "object." The term is also found in "process" documents, which record proceedings before judges.

Earlier discussions of *BQR/ PQR* forms in warranties sought to give much more narrow interpretations to these forms, often by analogy to modern legal remedies. Thus it was proposed that *BQR/PQR* in a warranty meant a redhibitory action by the *buyer*, who might seek to annul the sale and have his money returned on the grounds that there was some flaw in the sale or sold item.[69] Cassin's translation of *PQR* forms in Nuzi documents uses *revendication,*[70] which in its strict legal sense implies an action by an unpaid seller to reclaim possession of the sold goods until paid. These narrower meanings have been specifically rejected.[71] The *ana ittišu* lists, in contrast, appear to assign a very wide meaning to *baqāru*; it is given as the Akkadian equivalent of INIM.GÁ.GÁ, along with *ragāmu*, which has the very general sense of "claim."[72]

The specific meaning of *vindizieren* received a detailed analysis and support in San Nicolo's work, in which he surveyed the use of *BQR* both in OB documents and in the LH. He noted, first, that this material seems to include not only claims of (unpaid) vendors but also those of third parties (that is, persons other than the buyer and seller in a particular transaction).[73] Second, he suggested that *BQR* as a verb always has as direct

the claim itself, *der Vindikation,* is expressed by *baqrū* (MB and NB *paqrū*), as well as by the infinitive *paqāru* in NB. (The Nuzi form, according to the *AHW*, can also be *pirqu*, which is attributed to a metathesis). The claimant, *der Vindikant,* is expressed by a form derived from the participle, *baqirānum* (MB onward *paqirānu*, Nuzi also *pariqānu*), and also occasionally by the participle itself *pāqiru* (MB, Nuzi).

69 J. Oppert, "Une femme gardienne de son mari," *ZA* 3 (1888): 21.

70 See e.g., Cassin, *L'adoption 'a Nuzi*, 301.

71 See, e.g. Paul Koschaker, *Babylonsich-Assyrisches Burgschaftsrecht* (Leipzig: Teubner, 1911), 176 n. 8; Guillaume Cardascia, *Les archives des Murasu, une famille d'hommes d'affaires babyloniens a l'epoque perse* (Paris: Imprimerie Nationale, 1951), 147 n. 3.

72 Materials for the Sumerian Lexicon [= MSL], 1, 80, 18.

73 M. San Nicolo, *Die Schlussklauseln der altbabylonische Kauf— und Tauschvertrage* (Munich: Oskar Beck, 1922), 160.

object a particular item, such as a field or slave (as opposed, for instance, to the more general claim term *ragāmu*, which might apply also to a claim against a person).[74] Finally, he argued that all the surveyed occurrences of *BQR* are found together with some *dingliche* ("real") right of such vendor or third party — that is, a claim of some sort on the particular item that is the object of the transaction.[75] This right is often not named expressly in the document, but is to be deduced from the context. Such property rights would include, for instance, Cassin's idea of the right of an unpaid vendor to take back the goods conveyed and hold them until he received payment, as well as pre-emptive rights (*Naherechte*) on the part of a vendor's heirs (for instance, the right to contest a sale of items which would form part of their ultimate inheritance).

As examples of the types of "real" rights that might form the basis for a *BQR* claim, San Nicolo classified the various forms of *BQR* that are found in the LH, which may be summarized as follows:[76]

Section 279: a warranty applicable to the sale of slaves, providing that the seller is to "answer" for a *BQR* claim in the slave:

šumma awīlum wardam amtam išāmma baqrī irtaši nādinānšu baqrī ippal.

Section 118, the sale of a pledged slave by a creditor cannot be challenged (*ul ibbaqqar*); according to San Nicolo this assumes the right of a (perhaps unfairly) foreclosed debtor to assert his ownership right in the slave.

Section 150, a wife's bequest of her husband's estate where there is a written document cannot be challenged by her sons (*ul ibaqqarūši*); and

Section 179, a bequest by an *entum*, *nadītum*, or *zikrum* cannot be challenged by her brothers (*ul ibaqqarūši*). According to San Nicolo, these sections reflect underlying *Naherechte* on the part of the woman's sons or brothers, which would allow these heirs to contest the disposal

---

74 San Nicolo, *Die Schlussklauseln*, 174.

75 San Nicolo, *Die Schlussklauseln*, 156.

76 San Nicolo, *Die Schlussklauseln*, 156-57.

of her husband's or father's estate.

Section 185 (a child adopted by an *awilum*);

Section 187 (a child of a *girsiqûm, muzzaz ekallim* or *zikrum*); and

Section 188 (a child adopted by a *mār ummānim*), each with the prohibition *ul ibbaqqar*, assume the right of some third party, perhaps the natural parent, to claim the child.

Based on his review, San Nicolo concluded that, despite the *ana ittišu* listing, *BQR* had a different nuance than *RGM*, and was to be interpreted more narrowly, as:

> *...der Inanspruchnahme einer in fremder Gewere befindlichen Sache auf Grund eines behaupteten dinglichen Rechtes an derselben....Formell glaube ich die eigenliche Beteutung von baqâru noch enger fassen zu müssen, and zwar einfach als den für die Eigentumsverfolgung typischen Ausdruck, der dann als solcher neben das römische vindicare zu stellen ist.*[77]

Driver and Miles, in their study of the LH, came to a similar conclusion: "*baqārum* is the technical term for claiming property in an action, expressing what the Roman phrase *vindictam imponere* implies."[78]

4.4.3.B The Scholarly Debate on the Relationship of *biqqoret* to Akkadian *BQR/PQR*

As noted above, the JPS translation of *biqqoret* in Lev. 19:20 as "indemnity" is based on recent scholarly opinion that this term is cognate with the Akkadian root *BQR/PQR*. One of the first to suggest this association was E. A. Speiser,[79]

---

77 San Nicolo, *Die Schlussklauseln*, 164-65. *Vindicare* is in essence to assert a right in a thing; see further the definition of actions *in rem, infra* n. 82.

78 Driver and Miles, *The Babylonian Laws*, 1:97.

79 Speiser, "Leviticus and the Critics," 35-36. Saul Lieberman, *Tosefta KiFshutah* [in Hebrew] (New York: Bet Ha-Midrash Le-Rabbanim Be-Ameriqa, 1955-1988) 6:360 n. 5 and E. Y. Kutscher, "On the Terminology of Documents in the Talmud and Geonic Literature" [in Hebrew], in *Hebrew and Aramaic Studies* (Jerusalem: Press, 1977), 126, accepted Speiser's association, without, however, substantiating it. For a summary of scholarly opinions on

who in turn quoted the study by San Nicolo. Speiser argued that the Hebrew *biqqoret* implied an obligation to make good the economic loss caused by the impairment of the slave's value (on the assumption that she had been a virgin, and could therefore no longer command a full brideprice).[80]

Loewenstamm, however, argued against associating the Hebrew *biqqoret* with the Akkadian root. He suggested that Speiser had misinterpreted San Nicolo, and assumed that the latter was speaking of a remedy (in damages) against a particular person, rather than a claim in a particular object:

> דיונו המפורט של סן ניקולו כולו מוקדש לראיה שמינוח המשפט האכדי ייחד את המונחים baqru [בקרו] ו-baqāru [בקרו] ללא יוצא מן הכלל לאותן התביעות המכונות במשפט הרומי *actio in rem* (מילולית: תביעה אל החפץ) ואף פעם לא לסוג האחר המכונה שם *actio in personam* (מילולית: תביעה על בן אדם).
>
> San Nicolo's detailed discussion was entirely dedicated to showing that Akkadian legal terminology assigned the terms *baqrū* and *baqāru* without exception to those claims that were called in Roman law *actio in rem* (literally: a claim in an object) and never to the other type that was called *actio in personam* (literally: a claim against a person).[81]

Loewenstamm went on to explain the difference as being that an *actio in rem* means a claim that one's right in an object is good against the world at large, while an *actio in personam* is a claim for damages against a specific person.[82] He did not, however, discuss whether such an *actio in rem* idea would be an appropriate interpretation of Hebrew *biqqoret;* he simply argued that there was no question in the Leviticus pericope of anything to indemnify, and adopted the traditional interpretation of "investigation" for *biqqoret*.[83]

---

the Akkadian connection, see Loewenstamm, "*Biqqoret Tibyeh*," 94-95; Schwartz, "A Literary Study," 250 n. 36; and Westbrook, *Biblical and Cuneiform Law*, 102-3.

80 Speiser, "Leviticus and the Critics," 36.

81 Loewenstamm, "*Biqqoret Tibyeh*," 95.

82 As defined by Adolph Berger, *Encyclopedic Dictionary of Roman Law* (Transactions of the American Philosophical Society ns 43/2 [1953]), actions *in rem* in Roman law (also called *vindicationes)* were actions in which the plaintiff asserted a right (such as ownership, or a servitude) to a certain thing; they could be asserted against anyone who held the thing. In contrast, actions *in personam* were actions in which a plaintiff's claim was based on some obligation (contractual or delictual) owed to him by a specific person.

83 Loewenstamm, "*Biqqoret Tibyeh*," 97.

Milgrom and Schwartz, both noting Loewenstamm's argument, also rejected the meaning of "indemnity"; Schwartz further argued that "no known Hebrew use of פקר/בקר is even close to the suggested sense," and proposed the meaning "legal dichotomy," based on the idea of "split, divide" associated with the Hebrew root.[84] Several scholars have also extended this discussion of the Akkadian connection to postbiblical Hebrew and Aramiac forms of *BQR/PQR*.[85]

Westbrook agreed with this criticism of Speiser's translation, but still argued in favor of the Akkadian connection; he thus interpreted *biqqoret tihyeh* as "'there is an *actio in rem'* i.e. 'the owner of the property has the right to claim his property back.'"[86] In order to interpret Lev. 19:20 as encompassing a return of property, however, he was obliged to compare it to LH 117, arguing that it referred to a wife pledged as a debt-slave, and allowing the husband a claim for her return (without a claim for adultery) if she had been sexually violated by the creditor while in his house.[87]

One may posit that one of Loewenstamm's concerns (though he did not state this explicitly) was that by accepting an association between the Akkadian or Hebrew terms and the Roman *actio in rem* idea, one is also assuming that the legal systems in question were aware of the Roman type distinction between "property" and "persons." Further, one is then forced to posit that a slave would have been considered "property" (i.e., like a *res*) in such a system. Conversely, by accepting the specific association made by Loewenstamm and Westbrook between *BQR/PQR* and the Roman *actio in rem,* one is then forced to posit "return of property" scenarios that may not be consistent with the biblical text.

---

84 Milgrom, "The Betrothed Slave-girl," 43 n. 2; Schwartz, "A Literary Study," 250, 251. The dichotomy in the latter's opinion resulted from the fact that this was a capital case in which no death penalty could be exacted and an *asham* must be offered.

85 Speiser, "Leviticus and the Critics," 35-36; Lieberman, *Tosefta KiFeshutah,* 6:360 n. 5; and Kutscher, "Terminology of Documents," 126, all go so far as to suggest that all the postbiblical *BQR/PQR* forms are related to Akkadian. S. Kaufman, *Akkadian Influences on Aramaic*, 80, on the other hand, considers this postbiblical connection to Akkadian to be somewhat "forced"; in his opinion a better etymology, at least for the postbiblical form *hefqer/hevqer,* would be the Syriac and Mandaic *PQR*, meaning "to run wild."

86 Westbrook, *Biblical and Cuneiform Law*, 105. As noted above (re the meaning of *neḥerefet),* Westbrook takes Lev. 19:20 as similar to LH s. 117: a man has pledged his wife as a debt-slave; the wife has been sexually violated by the creditor while in his house; and now "an action lies for her return," but with no claim for adultery.

87 The difficulties with Westbrook's position have been noted above.

I think it is possible to answer the question at hand — whether there is an association in meaning between Hebrew *biqqoret* and Akkadian *BQR/PQR* — in the affirmative, without the necessity of taking a position on any of the larger issues in this dispute (including, for instance, whether the Roman *actio in rem* idea meant simply a remedy or implied the actual existence of an underlying "property right,"[88] whether any legal system in the ancient Near East had a concept of "property rights,"[89] and whether slaves would have been considered "property" in such systems[90]). Several examples of the use of *BQR/PQR*, in a sample of both OB and later Babylonian documents (including warranties and process documents) suggest that its meaning is not as narrow as San Nicolo proposed. The root may be taken as indicating a more general idea of "claim" — one not necessarily associated with the assertion of a specific "property right," but more generally denoting a dispute about someone's relationship with a person or item.

88 On this issue, see e.g. the discussion of H. Jolowicz, *Roman Foundations of Modern Law* (Oxford: Oxford University Press, 1957; repr. Westport, Conn.: Greenwood, 1978), 77-78.

89 For a brief idea of the range of opinion on this complex topic, we may note the view of Cardascia, "*Le concept babylonien,*" 25, who argued that Babylonian sources reflect only an undifferentiated concept of ownership, a direct relationship between person and object, without the type of constitutive elements that were recognized in the Roman system and without a clear differentiation between ownership of an item and possession of it; and the view of Koschaker, *Rechtsvergleichende Studien,* who argued that the LH consists of various layers, some layers reflecting more "primitive" ideas of ownership. Koschaker argued specifically that the slave warranty in s. 279 seems to presuppose that a claim might be raised in the slave by some third party without it being alleged that the vendor or buyer was a thief; this stands in contrast to LH ss. 9-13, where the mere presence of a third party claim seems to put the onus on buyer and seller to prove their contractual right to the item (p. 51). He also argued (p. 46) that while the warranty in s. 279 assumes that a third party could trace an item into the hands of the current possessor, LH 125, the case of goods stolen while on deposit, appears to assume that an owner who has parted with possession of an item, in this case the "depositor," must look for satisfaction only to the person to whom he has ceded possession, the "depositee," if the goods are stolen; he may not, therefore, follow the goods into the hands of the thief or the current possessor. In the latter situation he found a parallel to the concept of *Hand wahre Hand* in early Germanic law, by which someone who voluntarily gave up possession of an item without actually conveying it (such as in a deposit) retained only the right to claim it back from the depositee.

90 In the Mishnah, as one example, slaves seem at times to be classed with "movable" property, at times with "immovables," and at times with persons; see Introduction, n. 99 on this issue.

4.4.3.C "Non-Narrow" Uses of *BQR/PQR* in Process Documents and Warranties

a) We may note first an OB process document in which *BQR* is used in connection with a dispute in land:

In TD 232 (UAZP 265, Lagaš, Rim-Sin), S and A (apparently not the vendors) dispute an orchard (S *u* A *ibqurūma*). The outcome of the case is that the "plaintiffs" acknowledged the right of the "defendant," and agree not to *BQR* further:

[dayyānū] ubbirūšunukunūšim lā nitûru lā nibaqrukama

[The judges] took from them for you [the following affirmation]: We will not contest and not *BQR* you.

Thus in contrast to San Nicolo's suggestion that *BQR/PQR* verbs have as their direct object the item claimed, the person being "sued" seems to be treated as the direct object in this case, suggesting that the *BQR* form here means something like "we will not make a claim against you." This form also recalls the form *ul ibaqqarūši* in LH ss. 150 and 179; these again seem to imply that the woman herself in these sections is the object of the verb, rather than some specific property.

b) In CT II 39 (UAZP 262, Sippar, Sabium), S (apparently not the vendor) disputes with respect to the house of S2, and the dispute goes before the judges (S *ibqurma ana dayyānū illikūma*). The outcome is:

dayyānū dīnam ušahizūšunūti S *arnam imidūšuma kunukkam ša lā ragāmi ušēzibūšu ul itārma* S *ana bītim* S2 *ul iraggamu*

The judges caused a decision to be rendered for them; they imposed a fine on S, and caused a document to be made [by which] S will not contest or claim [against] S2 [with respect to] the house

No reason for the process is given in this case. It may be asked whether the issue was precisely that the possessor had been disturbed for no particular reason; in other words, the *BQR* implies simply an interference with someone's relationship with the object in question. In this regard, one may also note that an *arnum* (penalty) is imposed against the *baqirānu* (claimant). The imposition of a fine or penalty would seem to be a curious result if the *BQR* were merely a claim of ownership which had failed. It may be posited that the penalty reflects a punishment for an unwarranted disturbance. Further, one may note that *ragāmu* (claim) in the outcome clause seems to be used as a synonym for the term *baqāru* with which the process started.

As San Nicolo himself noted, the "property right" supposedly underlying the *BQR* may be difficult to ascertain or no longer recognizable.[91] Cases such as the above illustrate that the "claim" may in fact be quite general or remote, without necessarily implying ownership in a particular item or person by the claimant.

c) Certain cases in which a person seems to be the "object" of the *BQR* form suggest that the nature of the relationship is being disputed, rather than an ownership claim being asserted. This is seen, for instance, in an OB adoption document cited by Ellis,[92] in which A has been adopted by T. The document contains the following statement (as reconstructed by Ellis):

bāqir A T *ibaqqa[ru] mana kaspam išaqqal*

Ellis has translated this as "a claimant of A who claims against T [shall pay 1 mana of silver]," suggesting that A will be claimed by some third party, perhaps A's natural mother, though it is not clear from the context who is anticipated as the *baqirānu* (claimant). Veenhof,[93] however, suggests that the object of the *BQR* is A's status, not A herself, a dispute which might perhaps be raised by T's heirs. In other

91 San Nicolo, *Die Schlussklauseln*, 162.

92 Maria de J. Ellis, "An Old Babylonian Contract from Tel Harmel," *JCS* 27 (1975): 135 lines 20-2 (text), and 136 (translation).

93 K. R. Veenhof, "A Deed of Manumission and Adoption from the Later Old Assyrian Period," in *zikir šumim — Assyriological Studies Presented to F. R. Kraus on the Occasion of his Seventieth Birthday* (Leiden: Brill, 1982), 380 n. 60.

words, the essence of the *BQR* is a contestation of the relationship between the adopter and the person adopted, rather than a claim for the return of the person. With this concept in mind we may turn again to the phrase *ul ibbaqqar* in LH ss. 185, 187 and 188, and propose that these may be interpreted as "*it* [the adoption] shall not be disputed" rather than "*he* [the child] shall not be claimed."

d) One final doubt with respect to interpreting *BQR/PQR* too narrowly may be raised with respect to the operation of *BQR/PQR* clauses in slave sale warranties. A form of *BQR/PQR* appears in Babylonian slave sale documents (or other transactions in slaves, such as exchange or pledge) from the OB period onward. From the LB period, however, the range of contingencies warranted against expands considerably; further, the remedy specified seems to change. The following table represents a very brief summary of the key elements of these warranties found in documents from the OB and LB periods, in order to illustrate this transition:

OB[94]	*ana baqrīšu/ši* [i.e., of the Slave] [Vendor] *izzaz* or *itanappal* The Vendor will stand [or answer] for a *baqrum* in the Slave
LB[95] (Darius I)	*pūt lā siḫi lā paqirānu lā arad šarrūtu lā* *mār banûtu lā širkūtu lā bīt sisî lā bīt kussî* *lā bīt narkabti ša ina muḫḫi* [Slave] *illâ* [Vendor] *nāši* Vendor bears the responsibility that no rebelliousness, *PQR*-er, royal service, freedom, temple service, attendant service, cavalry

94 See, e.g., TD 133 (UAZP 82, 11 *Samsu-iluna*), VS VII 50 (UAZP 84, 7 *Ammi-ditana*), TD 156 (UAZP 85, 37 *Ammi-ditana*). The latter states as the remedy *kīma ṣimdat šarri izzazzū*, possibly a reference to the *baqrūm* warranty imposed in LH 279. The latter two documents also contain a warranty providing for a three-day examination and a one-month warranty against the appearance of epilepsy: *ūm* 3.KAM *teb'ītum warḫum* 1.KAM *benNum*. A *bennum* warranty is also mentioned in LH 278.

95 See, e.g., Aug. 65, Dar. 212, VS V 73, VS V 85, PSBA 6: 102, Dar. 537, VS V 126 (all from the time of Darius I).

service, throne service, chariotry service will arise in the Slave

or

pūt [contingency] *ša ina muḫḫi* [Slave] *illâ* [Vendor] *nāši*

and/or

ūmu ša paqāri ina muḫḫi [Slave] *ittabšū* [Vendor] [Slave] (*ina pan dayyānē*) *umarraqamma ana* [Buyer] *inamdin*

On the day that there will be a *paqāru* in the Slave, the Vendor will clear the Slave (before the judges) and give [him] to the buyer.

The reason for the expansion of contingencies has been debated by scholars. Krückmann and others have proposed that many of the added contingencies consist of new obligations and duties of a public legal nature, reflecting a more complex social organization.[96] Krückmann treated these contingencies as separate and grouped them into private claims (which included the *BQR/PQR* forms), public claims of state and temple, and latent defects in the slave. Despite Krückmann's analysis, however, it is not clear that all the terms are necessarily mutually exclusive. *BQR/PQR* in its various forms, for instance, may have been a generic term comprising any interference with the new owner's possession of the item; the additional terms may have been added simply for clarity. Yaron[97] has noted this tendency to redundancy in both ancient and modern documents.

An LB process document gives a hint of this generic use. Cyr 332 (Marx pp. 32-35,) concerns a slave "S." "A" appears to have been an original owner of this slave; while the document is broken, she appears to have sold him to "N" (Marx, for instance, reconstructs a transaction consisting of the

96 See, e.g. O. Krückmann, *Babylonische Rechts – und Verhaltungs-Urkunden aus der Zeit Alexanders und der Diadochen* (Leipzig: Hof-Buchdruckerei, 1931), 39; Herbert Petschow, *Die neubabylonischen Kaufformulare* (Leipzig: Theodor Weicher, 1939), 57.

97 Reuven Yaron, "On Defension Clauses of Some Oriental Deeds of Sale and Lease, From Mesopotamia and Egypt," *BiOr* 15 (1958): 18, a process he terms "fatty degeneration."

word *iddinu*[98]). After several further transactions, the slave was sold by the wife of "N" to "I," who seems to be one of the litigants in the process. His declaration (to the judge) is:

> ... A *aššat*...[ ]*da ana paqāru* S *ana muḫḫīya tallikuma riqqi*...*ana maḫarka allika itti* A

> ..."A," the wife of...has come before me "*PQR*"ing the slave [as] a temple officer... I have come before you with "A"

The process continues:

> ...A *ūbilma maḫaršunu ušzizzi* A *istassūma mimma ša riqqūtu u mār banûtu ša* S *lā tukallimu*...

> ...He brought "A" and set her before them. They (questioned?) "A," [but] she does not prove anything about the temple post or free status of "S."

"I," on the other hand, was able to show contracts for all the transactions in the slave starting from "A." The decision was therefore:

> 1 *mana* 50 *šiqil kaspam adi* [ ] *mana kaspam eli* A *iprusūma ana* I *iddinū*... *kūm ša* A *muquttû ša mār banûtu ša* S *ana* I *tamqutu*

> Against "A" they decided 1 *mana* 50 shekels together with [ ] of silver and gave it to "I"...because "A" had lodged a claim against "I" with respect to the free status of "S."

In other words, this was a process started by the *paqrū* of "A," yet there appears to be no personal ownership claim being made by "A." Rather, she is claiming that the slave either belongs to the temple or has been freed. As Marx noted,[99] it is completely unclear what interest "A" would have had in bringing this claim. Dandamaev[100] assumed that the amount levied against "A" by the judges was a fine for having brought a false suit, the

---

98 Victor Marx, "*Die Stellung der Frauen in Babylonien gemäss den Kontrakten aus der Zeit von Nebukadnezar bis Darius*," *Beitrage zur Assyriologie* 4 (1902): 32-33.

99 Marx, "*Die Stellung*" 34:25.

100 Dandamaev, *Slavery in Babylonia*, 194.

amount of the fine being equal to the last sale price of the slave, plus an addition. Kohler/Peiser,[101] on the other hand, argued that there was some sort of ownership right being claimed by "A": either a type of pre-emption privilege (*Zugrecht*) that could be exercised by the first vendor each time a new sale occurred, or the right to claim the services of a freed slave as some sort of patron. In this case, the amount paid by "A" was assumed to consist of the last sale price plus interest. Even assuming such a right, however, this would still not explain why "A" would be claiming the status of temple officer for the slave in question. Marx suggested that the process may have been a claim for a *mandattu* (payment), perhaps for arrears in rent owed while "S" was performing temple services; again, this would not explain why "A" would have been claiming free status for him. In summary, this appears to be a use of *BQR/PQR* outside a specific ownership claim.

4.4.3.D Conclusion

The above examples show that *BQR/PQR* is used in contexts that suggest it means a general "claim" or contest of someone's relationship with the person or item, without specifically implying a return of the item based on superior ownership. An *actio in rem* scenario can, in fact, be posited to explain some of the instances of Akkadian *BQR/PQR*, particularly in warranties; in other instances, however, it is difficult to pinpoint what, if any, "property right" is being asserted. Further, the *actio in rem* concept suggests the existence of a precise distinction between "persons" and "property," as existed in later Roman law. While it is true that forms of *BQR/PQR* are often associated with transfers of land, fixtures, slaves, and large animals--items that could be considered essential "property" in an agricultural society--I do not think that the Roman concept of "property" can be automatically applied to the Mesopotamian or biblical systems without much further investigation.[102]

---

101 J. Kohler and F. E. Peiser, *Aus dem Babylonischen Rechtstleben* (Leipzig: Eduard Pfeiffer, 1891), 2:46.

102 I suggest that one fruitful area for such an investigation might be a comparison between the pattern of use of *BQR/PQR* in connection with slaves, animals and immovables with the Roman concept of *res mancipi* (see Berger, *Encyclopedic Dictionary of Roman Law, s.v. res mancipi, mancipatio*).

4.4.4 BQR/PQR as "Claim" in Postbiblical Hebrew

There are numerous instances of the roots *BQR/PQR* in both postbiblical Hebrew and Aramaic. The Hebrew forms have such a wide range of meaning that scholars both ancient and modern have proposed at least two, and even three, different original roots, though there is no agreement as to what these were.[103] There are, however, at least two forms of this root in postbiblical Hebrew that in my opinion are connected to the idea of "claim":

1) The noun *biqqoret* is found three times in tannaitic law collections, in *tArakh.* 4:3 (one MS), and in *mKet.* 11:5 and *tKet.* 11:3 in connection with a document called an *iggeret biqqoret*. These sources deal with the issue of competing claims against land. One case involves land inherited by orphans from their father, which is also claimed by their father's widow in order to realize upon her *ketubbah*, or by a creditor of their father; another case involves land which was to be available to satisfy the ketubah obligation to a divorced woman, but which the husband had dedicated as sanctified property (*heqdesh*) before the divorce. From contextual analysis of these sources, as well as an examination of the

103 The *Arukh*, for instance, assumed that there was one root relating to the idea of quarrel and another to the idea of freedom:

	PQR 1	**PQR 2**	**BQR**
	derived from a Persian root	derived from the noun אפיקורוס	equal to *PQR* 2
QAL	*feindliche Absicht*	*zugellos*	*zugellos*
Hifil	*etwas freigeben*	*etwas freigeben*	

Among modern scholars, Moreshet, *Lexicon of New Verbs*, 114 and 289-90, suggested one root which relates to the idea of a place of pasturage and another related to the noun אפיקורוס. The entries in the Talmud Concordances (Ch. Kosovsky, *Otsar Lashon ha-Talmud*; M. Kosovsky, *Concordance of the Talmud Yerushalmi* [New York: JTSA, 1982]) suggest three trends of meaning, relating to the ideas of inspect, quarrel, and abandonment, and varying according to *binyan:*

	Bavli	**Yerushalmi**
QAL	*PQR* 1: deny, cast off the laws of the Torah	*BQR* 1: inspect, rebel, act insolently
Hifil	*PQR* 2: abandon, quit or take out take out of one's control	*BQR* 2: abandon, quit or of one's control

wording of the *iggeret biqqoret* in post-tannaitic formularies, one may conclude that *biqqoret* means "claim." The *iggeret biqqoret* is seen to be a document issued by a Beit Din when land was sold at its direction to meet the claims of a widow or creditor, and was intended to give the purchaser of the land the same protection as a deed of sale; the term *biqqoret* referred to the circumstances (i.e., a claim) which led to the sale. Very similar in effect and content was the *iggeret mazon,* issued when land was sold to provide a wife with maintenance, and again referring to the circumstances which led to the sale.

2) The tannaitic sources in general (Mishnah, Tosefta, halakhic midrash and the baraitot in the Talmudim) also contain numerous instances of the noun *hefqer/hevqer* and its related *Hifil* and *Hofal* verb forms.[104] These forms are generally interpreted as having to do with abandoned or ownerless property (see, e.g. Jastrow, *s.v.* בקר). I shall argue that a more precise translation of *hevqer/hefqer* is "claimable property." To render one's property "ownerless" is in effect to allow it to be claimed by someone else. This idea is particularly noticeable in the application of *hefqer/hevqer* to slave women, to suggest that they have been sexually available to all.

With respect to Aramaic instances of *BQR/ PQR*, we may briefly note here that certain of the Targumim use *BQR/PQR* in the sense of "to cast free" or "to be unbridled,"[105] concepts that might be argued to relate to the idea

104 Forms of *BQR* are generally found in the Mishnah, while in other sources forms of *PQR* predominate.

105 *Qal* forms of *BQR* and *PQR*, found rarely in tannaitic sources, are more frequent in various Jewish Aramaic sources, including the Targumim. A summary of the Targum uses follows:

a) Targum Pseudo Jonathan uses *PQR* in the general sense of "to let go free":

Verse	Context	MT	Targum
Exod. 22:4	cause [a field] to be eaten	יבער	יפקר
Exod. 23:11	let [the land...] lie fallow	ונטשתה	ותפקר פירהא
Deut. 25:5	[the levirate widow] shall not be married abroad unto one not of his kin	לא תהיה החוצה לאיש זר	לא תהוי אתת שכיבא הפקירא בשוקא לגבר חילונאי

b) *BQR/PQR* in Targum Neofiti similarly has the sense of "to cast off" or "let go free"; however, Kaufman and Sokoloff in their Neofiti concordance have also assumed an equivalence of *PQR* with *PKR*, "to demolish":

of "abandonment."[106]

4.4.4.A The *iggeret biqqoret*

a) Orphan's Property: *mKet.* 11:5 and *tKet.* 11:3

When orphans' property was subject to a claim by their father's widow or by one of their father's creditors, a specific procedure had to be followed in order that the property could be sold. The property was valued, and then advertised for a specific period of time, set out in *mArakh.* 6:1:[107]

שום היתומים שלשים יום ושום ההקדש ששים יום ומכריזין בבקר ובערב...

The valuation [period] for [the property of] orphans is thirty days, and the valuation [period] for consecrated property is sixty days, and one advertises in the morning and evening...

An issue that would naturally arise in such cases is whether the property had been properly valued, so that the orphans would realize the maximum amount possible after the claim against the property had been met. *MKet.* 11:2-4 discusses the case of a widow who has undertaken on

---

Verse	Context	MT	Targum
Exod. 22:4	cause [a field] to be eaten	יבער	יפקר
Exod. 23:24	utterly overthrow [idols]	הרס תהרסם	(מפכרא) תפגר
Exod. 32:2	break off [gold rings]	פרקו	פכרו
Lev. 26:30	I will cast your carcasses	ונתתי את פגריכם	ואפקר ית פגריכון

c) Targum Jonathan to the Prophets uses *BQR* in the sense of "unbridled":

Verse	Context	MT	Targum
Jud. 9:4	vain and light [fellows]	ריקים ופחזים	סריקין ובקרין
Jer. 23:32	by their lies and their wantonness [false prophets]	בשקריהם ובפחזותם	בשקריהון ובבקרותהון

106 As noted above at n. 85, Kaufman, *The Akkadian Influences on Aramaic*, 80, suggested that Hebrew *hefqer/hevqer* is related to Mandaic and Syriac *PQR,* meaning "to run wild."

107 When the Mishnah is quoted without an apparatus, it indicates that there are not significant variants in the Mishnah codices. If the codices generally agree on a reading which is not in the printed editions, the Mishnah will be quoted according to one of the codices.

her own to value and sell her husband's property, to support herself or realize on her *ketubbah*, and the question of whether her sale would be valid in the event of a misvaluation of the property. Mishnah 5 then discusses the case in which the valuation and sale are undertaken by a Beit Din and a misvaluation has occurred. The issue is made dependent on the presence of an *iggeret biqqoret.* The following sets out *mKet.* 11:5 according to the Mishnah codices and two MSS of *bKet.* 99b (Vatican Ebr. 113= ז and Vatican Ebr. 130 = ט) and several of its variants:

1. שום הדינין שפחת שתות או הותיר שתות מכרן בטל.
2. אמר רבן שמעון בן גמליאל אם כן מה כח בית דין יפה.
3. אבל אם עשו אגרת בקרת אפלו מכרו שוה מנה במאתים או שוה מאתים במנה מכרן קים.

Variants

1. שפחת] = קפלרט   שפחתו = ז   הותיר] = קפלט   שהותיר = ר   הוסיפו = ז
2. אמר רבן שמעון בן גמליאל] = קפלר   רבן שמעון בן גמליאל אומר] = זט
   אם כן] = קפר   מיכרן קיים] = לזט
3. אלא אם] = קל   ואם = פ   אבל אם] = רזט

The variants are not particularly significant. They denote efforts at clarification (line 1) and different formulations of phrases (line 3) as well as what seems to be some differences in the Babylonian formulation (line 2).

Translation

> [1] A valuation of the judges that is a sixth too small or a sixth too large [over "market"[108] value] – their sale is invalid.
>
> [2] R. Shimon ben Gamliel [RSB"G] said: the sale is valid, otherwise how is the power of the Beit Din superior?
>
> [3] But if they drew up an *iggeret biqqoret,* even if they sold [something] worth one *maneh* for 200, or worth 200 for one *maneh*, their sale is valid.

The precise meaning of *iggeret biqqoret* is not evident from the context. Its *effect*, however, may be understood as follows: unless an *iggeret biqqoret* is issued, any misvaluation by the judges greater than 1/6 of the actual value

108 I use "market value" here in the sense of what the item would fetch at a public auction, and do not imply the existence of any particular type of market economy.

would render a sale invalid; if an *iggeret* is issued, however, any claim (at least for misvaluation) is precluded, regardless of the amount of any error. The *iggeret,* in other words, was the buyer's protection, much like a deed, against the sale being challenged; without it, even though the property had been publicly advertised, it would still have been possible to overturn a sale. The contrasting opinion of RSB"G (clause 2 above) suggests that any transfer by a Beit Din would be valid, regardless of the amount of misvaluation.

This interpretation seems confirmed in the corresponding passage in *tKet.* 11:3 (Lieberman), which also defines the *iggeret biqqoret* in terms of its effect:

אי זו היא איגרת בקורת? שום היתומים שלשים יום, ושום הקדש ששים יום. מכרו שוה מנה במאתים, או שוה מאתים במנה, מכרו קיים. רבן שמעון בן גמליאל אומ: שום הדיינין שפחת שתות, או הותיר שתות, מכרן קיים.

היא שמכרה שוה מנה ודינר במנה, אפי אומרת אני אחזיר את הדינר ליורשין מכרה בטל. רבן שמעון בן גמליאל אומ לעולם מכרה קיים, ותחזיר את הדינר ליורשין, ובלבד שתשייר מקצת. לפיכך אם פחתה, או הותירה, אין לה אלא כשער שמכרה.

[1] What is an *iggeret biqqoret?* The valuation [period] for [the property of] orphans is thirty days, and the valuation [period] for consecrated property is sixty days. If they sold [something] worth a *maneh* for 200, or worth 200 for one *maneh*, his sale is valid. R. Shimon ben Gamliel says: A valuation of the judges that is under by one-sixth, or over by one-sixth, their sale is valid.

[2] She [a widow] who sold [something] worth a *maneh* plus a dinar for a *maneh*, even if she says 'I will return the dinar to the heirs,' her sale is invalid. R. Shimon ben Gamliel says: Her sale is always valid, and she returns the dinar to the heirs, as long as she leaves a portion. Thus if she estimated it under or over, she claims only the price at which she sold it.

The first clause summarizes the effects of *mArakh.* 6:1 and the last clause of *mKet.* 11:5: a court[109] advertises orphans' property for 30 days,

109 Lieberman notes (*Tosefta KiFeshutah,* 6:361) that the Erfurt MS has:

אף שום היתומים הדיינין...ונמחקה המלה "יתומים"

Also the evaluation of the orphans the judges... And the word "orphans" is erased.

and if an *iggeret* is given, the sale is valid regardless of any misvaluation. RSB"G's contrary opinion here suggests that without an *iggeret* the sale is still valid if the misvaluation is within certain limits. S. Lieberman confirms this interpretation:

...אם שמו הדיינין ומכרו בלי בקורת, וטעו בשתות, מכרן בטל. אבל אם עשו אגרת בקורת אפילו טעו הרבה מכרן קיים, ודברי רשב"ג הוא מאמר המוסגר. ולפ"ז היה אפשר לפרש שרשב"ג אינו חולק אלא על טעות בשתות, אבל ביותר משתות אף הוא מודה שמכרן בטל, כמפורש בתוספתא כאן.

> ...If the judges made a valuation and sold [the property] without a *biqqoret* and erred by a sixth, their sale was invalid. But if they executed an *iggeret biqqoret,* even if they erred by much their sale was valid, and the words of RSB"G are bracketed [i.e., between clauses 1 and 3 in *mKet.* 11:5]. According to this, it could be interpreted that RSB"G disputed [with the *tanna qamma*, the anonymous first opinion] only with respect to an error in the amount of a sixth; but if [the error] was more than a sixth, even he agrees that their sale was invalid, as explained in Tosefta here.

(Clause 2 then deals with a further dispute between the majority and RSB"G, reflected in *mKet.* 11:4, concerning the case of a widow who wants to realize her *ketubbah* by selling land belonging to the orphans.)

It should be noted here that there is a textual issue associated with *mKet.* 11:5: it is possible to read clause 3 of this mishnah as also belonging to RSB"G rather than to the *tanna qamma* — that is, it is RSB"G who is suggesting that the *iggeret biqqoret* issued by a Beit Din is what precludes any claims of misevaluation. This reading is suggested in particular by some of the Mishnah MSS, which, as noted above, show a great deal of variability in clauses 2-3a.[110] I believe that whether the opinion belongs to RSB"G or the *tanna qamma* makes no difference to the question of the meaning of *biqqoret*; according to either opinion, the effect of the *iggeret* would be to protect the purchaser in the event of a misvaluation. I shall simply note here that the traditional view[111] attributes clause 3 to the *tanna*

110 In particular, it is the readings in the MSS Kaufmann and Parma, which lacks the words מכרן קיים, that suggest that it is RSB"G who is associated with the *iggeret biqqoret*.

111 Modern scholars are not in agreement on this point. Lieberman, as indicated in the quote above, did not attribute clause 3 to RSB"G; David Halivni, "Commentaries on Mishnah

qamma, as Maimonides indicates in his commentary to this mishnah:

אגרת חקירה ודקדוק, והיא שהיתה שם שומה והכרזה וכותבין שהם הרבו להתישב ולדקדק כפי יכלתם, וגם זה דברי תנא קמא והלכה כמותו

[The *iggeret biqqoret* is] a letter of research and inspection, that there was a valuation and public announcement, and they write that they sat and checked much, to the best of their ability; this [part of the Mishnah] is also [attributed] to the *tanna qamma*, and the halakhah follows his opinion.[112]

Returning to the issue of the meaning of *biqqoret*, the above quote from Maimonides also indicates the main trend of traditional interpretation: the essence of the document was its confirmation that the property had been advertised. *Biqqoret*, in other words, was understood as "inspection," and the

---

and Baraita" [in Hebrew], *Tarbits* 29 (1959-1960):32-46, at 45, in contrast, did, based primarily on the evidence of MS Kaufmann:

וזה מניע אותי לפרש שמחלוקת רבן שמעון בן גמליאל וחכמים היא רק כשעשו איגרת ביקורת. וכך מתפרשת המשנה: תנא קמא סובר מכרן בטל אף אם האונאה לא היתה יותר משתות. על זה טוען רבן שמעון בן גמליאל: אם כן מה כוח בית דין (שעשה אגרת ביקורת) יפה? (ומהו הדין)? אלא אם עשו איגרת ביקורת אפילו מכרו שווה מנה...מכרן קיים... ומכאן נובע שאין מאמר מוסגר במשנה זו.

And this drives me to explain that the dispute between Raban Shimon ben Gamliel and the sages is only when they made an *iggeret biqqoret*. Thus the Mishnah is explained: the first *tanna* holds that their sale is canceled even if the difference was not more than one sixth. On this Rabban Shimon ben Gamliel claims: if that is so how is the power of the beit din (which made the *iggeret biqqoret*) greater? (And what is the law)? Rather if they made an *iggeret biqqoret* even if they sold what was worth a maneh... their sale... And from here flows the fact that there is no parenthetical remark in this Mishnah.

112 Kapaḥ, in his edition of Maimonides' Mishnah commentary, notes that other MSS of this commentary have different versions of this last phrase; the reading above, however, seems confirmed by Maimonides' opinion in *Hil. Malveh veLoveh*, 12:11:

ובית דין שהכריזו ובדקו יפה יפה ודקדקו בשומא אף על פי שטעו ומכרו שוה מנה במאתים או מאתים במנה הרי מכרם קים .אבל אם לא בדקו בשומא ולא כתבו אגרת בקרת...וטעו והותירו שתות או פחתו שתות מכרם בטל.

And the court which advertised and checked very carefully and examined the evaluation even though they erred and sold what was worth a maneh for 200 or 200 for a maneh – behold their sale stands. But if they did not check the evaluation and did not write an *iggeret biqqoret*... and they erred more than one sixth or less than one sixth – their sale is canceled.

document invited prospective buyers to inspect the property and confirm for themselves the valuation assigned by the Beit Din.[113] It seems that the earliest detailed association of the *iggeret biqqoret* with advertisement appears in amoraic and later layers of talmudim. In the Bavli, for instance, by accepting that the *iggeret biqqoret* refers to an advertisement, the sages were compelled to conclude that since the *iggeret* is mentioned only in clause 3 of the mishnah, clause 1 must refer to cases in which there was no *iggeret*, and thus no advertisement, and were thus constrained to explain why no advertisement was performed. Various proposals and customs are cited to suggest that, despite the wording in *mArakh.* 6:1, advertisement was in fact dependent on the type of property, the nature of the transaction, or the locality (*bKet.* 100b):

> הא מדסיפא בדאכרוז הוי רושא בדלא אכרוז...ולא קשיא כאן בדברים שמכריזין עליהן כאן בדברים שאין מכריזין עליהן ואלו הן דברים שאין מכריזין עליהן העבדים והמטלטלין והשטרות... ואיבעית אימא כאן בשעה שמכריזין כאן בשעה שאין מכריזין דאמרי נהרדעי לכרגא למזוני ולקבורה מזבנינן בלא אכרזתא ואב"א כאן במקום שמכריזין כאן במקום שאין מכריזין דאמר רב נחמן מעולם לא עשו אגרת בקורת בנהרדעא סבוא מינה משום דבקיאי בשומא א"ל רב יוסף בר מניומי לדידי מיפרשא לי מיניה דרב נחמן משום דקרו להו בני אכלי נכסי דאכרזתא

> Since in the last clause [it says that] an inspection [takes place], the first clause must [refer to cases] with no inspection... This is not a difficulty: the last clause [refers to] items that they announce, the first clause to items that they do not announce. *These are items that are not announced: slaves, movable property, and deeds...* And [alternatively] if you want, say the last clause refers to a time when they announce and the first clause to a time when they do not announce, as the Nehardeans say that for poll-tax, maintenance and burial [expenses] one sells without an announcement. And if you want, say the last clause refers to a place where they announce and the first clause to a place where they do not announce, as Rav Naḥman said: They never drew up an *iggeret biqqoret* in Nehardea. [People] understood from this that they were experts in valuation, [but] Rav Yosef ben Minyomi said to them: Rav Naḥman explained to me that it was because they called them consumers of publicly auctioned goods. [emphasis added]

---

113 Rashi at *bKet.* 99b, *s.v.* אגרת בקרת, also states:

> הכרזה ולשון בקורת שמבקרין אותה בני אדם ע"י הכרזה.
>
> A public announcement and an *iggeret biqqoret* which people examine/evaluate through the public announcement.

The underlined dictum is a summary of a longer discussion quoted in *yMeg.* 4:4 65b attributed to western amoraim of the third to fourth generations:[114]

תני עבדים והשטרות ומיטלטלין אין להם איגרת ביקורת מהו איגר' ביקורת ר' יודה בר פזי
אמר אכרזה עולה בר' ישמעאל אמר עבדים שלא יברחו שטרות ומיטלטלין שלא יגנבו

It was taught in a baraita: There is no *iggeret biqqoret* for male or female slaves or for movable property. What is an *iggeret biqqoret*? R. Yudah bar Pazi said: an announcement. Ulla bar R. Ishmael said: [One avoids giving any hint of a sale of] slaves, so that they will not [be tempted to] flee; [and one avoids announcing the value of] deeds and movables, so they will not be stolen.

Despite these Talmudic discussions, however, I suggest that *biqqoret* means "claim," and this may be seen more precisely by examining actual samples of this document.[115] Various forms of a document called *iggeret biqqoret* are found in the formularies of Rav Hai Gaon (10th century, Pumbedita) and Rav Yehudah b. Barzilai (12th century, Barcelona), and in the Sefer ha-Itur (12th century). There are in addition two other types of deed called *iggeret*: the *iggeret mazon* and the *iggeret mered*. Based on an analysis of these documents, I shall argue that the term *biqqoret* is a reflection of the circumstances under which this document was issued – that is, as the result of a "claim" by a widow or creditor against land belonging to orphans.

b) Document Samples from the Various Mediaeval Formularies

One must first address the question of whether these mediaeval documents can serve as useful evidence of the association of *biqqoret* with the idea of "claim," despite their later dates.

114 This passage appears with minor differences in *ySan.* 1:2 19b and in a shortened form in *yKet.* 11:6 34c quoted below::

מהו אגרת בקרת ר' יהודה בר פזי אמר אכרזה עולא בר ישמעאל אמר עבדים שלא יברחו
ושטרות ומטלטלין שלא יגנבו

115 Lieberman (*Tosefta KiFeshutah,* 6:360 n. 25), noting Speiser's definition of the biblical *biqqoret*, also argued that the original meaning of postbiblical *iggeret biqqoret* had to do with a claim or dispute, stating: וכוונת המלה "בקר" הוא לתבוע, לדרוש (the meaning of the word *baqar* is 'to claim, to demand').

The question of the relationship among the formularies, and the documents used as precedents, is open. Assaf suggests, however, that as documents had to be drafted by scribes, under the control of the Beit Din, their general structure (נוסחא) was likely fixed, though not necessarily the finer points (השופרא דשטרא).[116] He states further that though Rav Hai's is the oldest extant gaonic formulary, there was likely an earlier formulary belonging to Rav Saadya, and that it is possible Rav Yehudah b. Barzilai made use of material from the latter.[117] Halberstam similarly suggests that the compiler of the Itur was also familiar with at least some of the works of Rav Yehudah.[118] We may thus assume that there was some degree of continuity in the content of these documents, so that it is not beyond the realm of probability that the documents reflect much older concepts. This assumption is at least partly confirmed by the fact that, as will be shown, the general structure of the *iggeret* is consistent in all the samples.

The following sets out the operative passages of the *iggeret biqqoret* samples found in the formularies. I have marked the operative passages of each document as a-d in the translations:

Iggeret biqqoret: Formulary of Rav Hai Gaon (10th century Pumbedita):[119]

[א] אנן בידינא דחתימין לתתא כד הוינא במותב תלתא כחדא ועלו לקדמנא פלוני ופלוני בני פלוני מיתנא ואמרו בי [כי] בחיוהי דאבונא פלוני הוא מסיק [=הוה] ביה פלוני בן פלוני שטר חוב או מלוה... ובעה מננא לשלאמא ליה נשייה דאית ליה על אבונא ...ואנן לית אנחנא יכלין למיזבאן ההיא (על) ארעא אלא על ממריהן דדכירנא [צ"ל דבי דינא]...

[ב] - ואנן בידינא ידענא ואשתמודענא דארעא הדא די פלוני מיתנא היא ובדקנא ועיינא במילאייהון ואשכחנא דצריכי להתעסק בצורכייהו ואכרזנא על ההיא ארעא תלתין יומין

[ג] ...וזבן יתה בהון פלוני בן פלוני ושלים הלין זוזי דמי זיבונא דנא ויהבנון להו לפלוני

116 Simḥah Assaf, "Sefer HaShetarot of Rav Hai Gaon" [in Hebrew], *Musaf Hatarbits 1* (1930): 6.

117 Assaf, "Sefer HaShetarot," 7.

118 Shlomoh Halberstam, *The Book of Documents of the Rabbi and Patriarch Rabbenu Yehuda bar R. Barzilai of Barcelona* [in Hebrew] (new ed.; Jerusalem, 1967), 4.

119 Hebrew text from Assaf, "Sefer HaShetarot," 71-72; the amendments in square brackets are those of Assaf. Though Assaf notes (p. 67) that this sample is not found in either of the two main MSS of the formulary, but rather in another collection, he identifies it (p. 68) as unquestionably of gaonic origin.

דהו בעל החוב עד גמירא...
[ד] ...וכדו איסתלקא ידוהון [צ"ל ידהון] ורשותהון דהנהו יאתמי ורשותא [ד]כל דאתי מחמתיהון סילוק גמור מההיא ארעא ולית להון חולק ואחסנא בגוה ולא דין ולא דברים ואנו ב"ד מכרנו לפלוני זה מכירה זו מכירה גמורה חתוכה וחלוטה שרירא וקיימא דלא למיהדר מינה ודלא להשניא ולא נשתייר בה כלום ליתומים הנזכרים שום שיור בעולם... וכותב למן היום ולהכא לא יהא רשות ליתומים אלו ולא לשום אדם שיבא מארבע רוחות העולם לעורר על פלוני זה הקונה ולא על הבא מכחו מחמת מכירה זו או מחמת קרקע זה שקנה על פינו ומאמירנו וברשותינו אין ערעורו שוה כלום וכל מי שיבא עם כל כתב של לכל [של כל] לשון בן ובת ואח ואחר [צ"ל ואחות] קרוב ורחוק יורש ונוחל יהודי וארמאי דיקום ויהגה ויטעון ויערער על פלוני זה יהיו דבריו וטענותיו ושטרותיו הבל ואין בם מועיל וחשובין כחרש הנשבר שאין בו ממש ואנו ב"ד ראינו שמצוה על היתומים לפרוע חוב שעל אביהם ועל כן החזקנו כל זה במכירה זו ואנו ב"ד ידענו והכרנו שהקרקע שקנה פלוני מן פלוני בן פלוני הנפטר וכל אחריות דאתי הוא על היתומים...

Translation

(a) We the members of the Beit Din [whose names are] sealed below, in a session of three [judges] as one [state]: A and B the sons of C, deceased, came before us and said: [Since] our father's lifetime X son of X' holds a note of obligation (or loan) against him...and he has asked us to pay the burden that he has against our father... We are not able to sell this land [out of which we want to pay the debt] except according to the orders of the Beit Din...
(b) We the Beit Din found out and satisfied ourselves about this land that belonged to C the deceased, and we examined and investigated their affairs, and found the necessity to occupy ourselves in their needs. We advertised about this land thirty days...
(c) Z bought it for this amount and paid these *zuzei,* the amount of this purchase, and they gave them to X, the creditor, in full...
(d) And now the authority and right of these orphans and the right of anyone [claiming] on their behalf has completely ceased in this land, and they have neither portion nor inheritance in it, and no suit or process.[120]

---

120 The phrase לא דין ולא דברים, found in postbiblical Hebrew (see, e.g., the wording in *mKet.* 9:1: דין ודברים אין לי בנכסיך), is the semantic equivalent of the Akkadian *dēnu dabābu laššu* (there shall be no suit or litigation) and the Aramaic ולא דין ולא דבב. This form of the Akkadian phrase is found in particular in NA contracts, though various forms of *dēnu-dabābu* clauses are also found, according to the *AHW* and the *CAD*, in MA, Nuzi and NB documents. The phrase is often found in connection with an exclusion or renunciation of claims against the new owner of land or other items; see, e.g., Governor's Palace Archive [=GPA] 17 (Kalah, 8th century BCE), ll. 10ff, a sale of a field by one eunuch to another, which contains an exclusion of claims against the buyer of the land, starting

We the Beit Din have made this sale to this Z, a complete sale, irreversible and permanent, fit and established, not be reneged upon or changed; and there remains to the orphans mentioned no remnant [in the land] at all... And he writes: From this day on, neither these orphans nor anyone anywhere in the world have any right to make a claim against this Z the purchaser or anyone [claiming] through him, on account of this sale or on account of this land that he purchased according to our word, authorization, and right; the claim of such a person is worth nothing. Anyone who comes with any written document in any language, [whether] son, daughter, brother, sister, near or far, heir or inheritor, Hebrew or Aramean, who may stand and argue and claim and protest against this Z, his words, claims, and deeds shall be worthless; there shall be no effect to them, and they are considered like a broken potsherd with no substance. We the Beit Din considered that it was a commandment on the orphans to satisfy their father's debt; thus we have upheld this with this sale. We the Beit Din knew and recognized that this land that Z bought from the late A son of B and all the liability thereon is on the orphans.

Iggeret biqqoret: Sefer ha-Itur (12th century, Marseilles):[121]

[א] כתב בכך ובכך איך פלו' מזמין ליתמי דפלו' לדינא ואפיק שטר חוב וכתובה דהוה ליה על אבוהון וחזינא מדינא למגבי מנכסי דיתמי מדינא לרווחא דידהו ואפיכנן אזכותא דידהו

[ב] ואכריזנן על ארעא דהיא זיבורית דילהון תלתין יומין

[ג] ולבתר הכי אתא פלו' דנן ואוסיף עלנא דמי דההיא ארעא כך וכך וזבינּנא ליה אנחנא בי דינא לפלו' בן פלו' והוא דילי' ואשלים אילין זוזי לידנא ויהבינן להו לבעל חוב כמה

---

with the words *tuāru dēnu dabābu laššu aḫīšu lū mār aḫīšu lū mammanušu qurbu* (there shall be nor return, suit, or litigation [whether] by his [the seller's] brothers, nephews, or anyone related to him). The Aramaic phrase is found frequently in Elephantine contracts, with a similar idea of precluding any claim or process. See, e.g., Bezalel Porten and Ada Yardeni, *Contracts*, vol. 2 of *Textbook of Aramaic Documents from Egypt* (Jerusalem: Hebrew University, 1989), 2.2, ll. 12ff., a settlement of the boundaries of a parcel of land, in which the complainant then agrees not to bring any further claims:

12. ...לא אכהל אגרנך דין ודבב אנה ובר לי וברה

13. לי (אח ואחה לי קריב ורחיק) על ארקא זך...

> I shall not be able to institute against you suit or litigation — I or my son or my daughter (my brother or sister, near or far) on that land...

121 Hebrew text from ספר העיטור (תש"ל) (דפוס צילום ווארשא תרמ"ה), חלק ראשון, אות ב' בקורת ג ע"ב [*Sefer HaItur*]. The title of the document in this formulary is given as והיא הכרזה, indicating that the advertisement was thought to be the primary element.

דאיתחייבו יתמי מדינ'

[ד] ואשלימנ' הדא ארעא לפלו' דנן לי' ולירתוהי בתרוהי ומן יומא דנן ולעל' ולא ליהוי רשותא ליתמי לערעורי בההיא ארעא מידי ואחריות דהאי זבינא איתמי כחומר כל שטר זביני דנהיגין בישראל דלא כאסמכתא ודלא כטופסא דשטרי וכו'

(a) He wrote as follows: How X summoned the orphans of Y to law, and produced a note of obligation or *ketubbah* that he had against their father. We saw that by law [we must] collect from the property of the orphans for your satisfaction, and we looked after your right.

(b) We advertised land out of the poorest [level of the orphans' estate] for 30 days.

(c) After this Z came and paid us the value of this land to such and such an amount and we the Beit Din sold it to him, to Z son of Z', and it is his; he paid these *zuzei* into our hand, and we gave them to the creditor, according to what the orphans owed by law,

(d) And we gave over this land to Z, to him and to his heirs after him from this day onwards and the orphans shall have no right to claim anything on this land. And the responsibility of this sale is complete as the stringencies of any sale contract which is practiced in Israel – not like reliances and not like the formula of contracts.

Iggeret biqqoret: Formulary of Rav Yehudah b. Barzilai:[122]

[א] אלו בית דין החתומין למטה כך היה שיצא שטר חוב או משכונה או שטר כתובה או שטר בית דין שהיה לו לגבות כך וכך דינרין מנכסי פלוני שנפטר...וראינו מן הדין שהיה לנו לגבות מנכסי היתומים לאלתר ולא היה בנו כח להשהות אותן השטרות עד שיגדלו היתומים מפני ייפוי כח דינם...

[ב] חפשנו אחר עזבון הנפטר ומצינו שדה פלוני שהיא ראויה לימכר...ואכריזנא על ארעא דא תלתין יומין כדאמור רבנן...

[ג] אתא פלוני דנן על דמי ארעא כך וכך וזבנינא ליה אנחנא בי דינא להא ארעא לפלוני בר פלוני והיא דיליה ואשלים אילין זוזי דמיה זיבונא לידנא אנחנא בי דינא ויהיבנא לה לאיתתא או לבעל חוב כמא דאיתחייב יתמי מן דינא

122 Halberstam, *Book of Documents*, 16.

[ד] ומיומא דנן ולעלם לא ביתמי ולא בשום איניש בעלמא לתבוע ללוקח הזה בהאי ארעא מידי ואחריותא דהאי ארעא דזבינַנא לפלוני דנן יהא איתמי ושטר הכרזה זו ובקרות זו ומכירה זו חתוכה וחלוטה וכו'

Translation

(a) The [members] of the Beit Din [whose names are] sealed below [state] thus: A note of obligation, or a security, or a *ketubbah*, or a document of the Beit Din, has arisen [that allowed the holder] to collect so many *dinarin* from the property of X, who died... We saw that by law we were required to collect [the amount] from the orphans' property immediately; we did not have the power to delay [the implementation of] these deeds until the orphans became adults, as their legal position was stronger...

(b) We sought deposited merchandise[123] of the deceased and found a field suitable for sale... and we advertised about this land for thirty days, as was stated by our Sages...

(c) This Z came [and offered] on the value of the land such and such, and we the Beit Din sold this land to Z son of Z' and it is his. He paid these *zuzei*, the value of the sale, to us, the Beit Din, and we gave [it] to the woman, or the creditor, according to what the orphans owed by law.

(d) From this day and forever neither the orphans nor anyone else may make any claim whatever about this land against this purchaser. The liability of this land that we have sold to this Z shall be to the orphans. The deed of this advertisement, *baqrut*, and sale is final and irredeemable.

From an analysis of these sections we may argue that the samples display a consistent structure:

a) A statement of how the Beit Din came to be involved, as the result of claims against property belonging to orphans, either by their father's widow, wanting to realize upon her *ketubbah*, or by one of their father's creditors.

b) An affirmation that some land of the orphans was chosen by the Beit Din for sale and advertised for thirty days. In the formulary of Rav

123 Koehler and Baumgartner, *Hebrew and Aramaic Lexicon*, *s.v.* עיזבון.

Yehudah (section d above) it is reiterated that the advertisement and the *baqrut* are separate stages.

c) A confirmation that the property was purchased and the purchase money used to pay off the widow or creditor.

d) Detailed instructions precluding the orphans (or parties claiming through them) from challenging the valuation and confirming that the transfer to the buyer has an effect equivalent to any other sale. This section is the longest in each of the samples (the formulary of Rav Hai in fact seems to contain two such sections) and also shows the most variability. These facts suggest that it was the section of primary importance, and its details were drafted (and in some cases repeated) in accordance with the legal opinions of the scribes or to adapt the document to local conditions or requirements.[124]

From this structure it is reasonable to conclude that the main function of this *iggeret* was to provide the purchaser of the land with the same kind of status and protection from adverse claims that he would get from an ordinary deed of sale. Though it was important to affirm that the legal requirements, including the advertisement, were carried out correctly, this does not appear to have been the essential part of the document. The term *biqqoret*, in other words, refers to the "claim" of the widow or creditor which instigated the sale; that is, it refers to the circumstances under which the sale was made.[125]

---

124 There is also a sample quoted in the *Encyclopedia Talmudit*, from a source cited as נוסח בעל התרומות שער ג, הובא בבית יוסף סי' קג (nd); in this case the creditor has traced the land into the hands of the orphans, producing a שטרא דאדרכתא (tracing document). This sample, like those above, precludes a further variation:

ומן יומא דנן ולעלם לא יהא רשותא להאי למיתבעיה מידי בהאי ארעא

> And from that day onwards this one shall have no right to make any claim in this land.

and confirms the transfer of ownership in the following words:

ואחריות ההוא ארעא על פלוני בן פלוני דידיעא לנא דהוא מרא דארעא מן קדמת דנא

> And liability of that land on X son of Y which is known to us is that he is the owner of that land from before.

125 In much the same way, for instance, a modern municipality that seizes land and sells it for

This terminological effect is confirmed when we examine another example of an *iggeret* issued by a Beit Din, the *iggeret mazon*. Again, the *iggeret* form seems to have been used since this was not an ordinary deed of sale given by the owner to the purchaser, but a sale carried out by a Beit Din. The need for this document, as explained by Rav Yehudah,[126] arose when a wife and children were left, through the death or absence of the husband, without adequate maintenance; the Beit Din was then authorized to take some of the husband's assets held on deposit by someone else, or offer some of the husband's land for sale. Rav Yehudah's formulary gives a sample of an *iggeret mazon* issued to the purchaser in the case of a sale of land. The following sets out its operative sections:

Iggeret mazon: Formulary of Rav Yehudah Barzilai[127]

[א] ...אנו בית דין החתומים למטה כך היה דאתת קדמנא פלוניתא בת פלוני אשת פלוני וקבלת קדמנא ונתערמה על דחקה ועל צרכה ואמרת לפנינו ידיע לכון רבותי שהלך פלוני בעלה היום כמה ימים למדינת הים ולא הניח לי שיעור מזון אפי' לשלשה חדשים ואין לי סיפוק במה לזון ולהתפרנס ומעשה ידי אינן מגיעין לכלום ואני צריכה הרבה למזונות ועתה רבותי חושו לצרכי ועיינו במזונותי

[ב] ואנו בית דין ראינו דבריה נכונים וחפשנו אחר ממון בעלה ולא מצאנו דבר ראוי למכור כמו שדה פלוני או תכשיט פלוני והרשינוה למוכרה והכריזו על אותה שדה והגיעו לכך וכך דינרין ועשינו בהכרזת השדה כדבעי וכאמור רבנן

payment of arrears of taxes will issue a document called a "tax deed" to the purchaser. This document differs from an ordinary deed of sale (though it is intended to put the purchaser in the same position) and calls attention to the circumstances under which the sale was made.

126 Rav Yehudah's formulary (Halberstam, *Book of Documents*, 61-62) mentions four types of situations, which are here summarized:

...כגון שמת ראובן והניח אלמנה ויתומים והיה לו ממון אצל שמעון...כגון ראובן שהלך למדינת הים והוא במקום רחוק ויש לו מזון ביד אחרים...כגון מי שיש לו ממון אצל אחרים ונשטה (צ"ל ונשתטה)...כגון ראובן שיש לו אשה ובנים והלך למדינת הים או שמת והניח קרקעות...

For example, if Reuven died leaving a widow and orphans, and he had [left] money with Shimon [as a deposit]...[or] Reuven went abroad a great distance, and had maintenance [or possibly ממון, money] with others...[or] someone had money with others and he became demented...[or] Reuven had a wife and children and went abroad or died, and left land...

127 Hebrew text from Halberstam, *Book of Documents*, 62-63; Halberstam has indicated possible errors in round brackets.

[ג] לא יצא עליה לוקח שיתן בה כמו פלוני בן פלוני שנתן בה כך וכך דינרין וראינו אנו בית דין למוכרה להדין פלוני ופייסנוהו בכך כי היה חושש משום תרעומת שהוא במדינת הים שלא יערער עליו בכלום לכשיבוא וחזרנו על פלוני זה ופייסנוהו הרבה לקנותה ושמע ממנו וקנאה ממנו בכך וכך דינרין וצוינו לו להוציאן לאשתו במזונותיה כהוגן וכתיקון חכמים ולתת לה כל חדש וחדש כך וכך במזונותיה וכן עשה פלוני דנן

[ד] ולכך כתבנו לה מעשה בית דין זה שאנו בית דין מכרנו לו שדה זו לצורך מזון האשה ולא יהא כח לא ביד פלוני בעל האשה היום או מחר ולא ביד שום אדם לערער עליו בכלום ומעכשיו ילך פלוני זה הלוקח ויחזיק ויקנה שדה פלוני (מעשה) ויעשה בה כל חפצת נפשו הוא והבאים מכחו ויהא ראשי לירש ולהוריש לנחול ולהנחיל ולעשות בה כל חפצת נפשו מהיום ולעולם...ועל פלוני בעל האשה ועל יורשיו אחריו לפצות ולהדיח ולסלק מעל פלוני זה ומעל יורשיו אחריו כל ערעורין שבעולם ולהעמיד שדה זה שזכרנו לו בחזקתו ובחזקת הבאים מכחו בלא שום פסידא בעולם ובכן אם יצא על שדה זו שום כתב וקיום בעולם על פלוני זה בעל האשה ועל יורשיו אחריו ולסלקו ולפצתו מעל פלוני זה הלוקח ומעל יורשיו אחריו כי כן מכרנוהו לו אנו בית דין כדי שתהא אחריותו על פלוני זה ועל יורשיו אחריו כי מכיון שמכרנוהו אנו בית דין לצורך מזונות אשתו כאלו הוא מכרה בעצמו דמי ויפינו כח הלוקח שתהא אחריותו עליו ועל יורשיו כאחריות וכחומר כל שטר מכירות... כתבנו וחתמנו מעשה בית דין זה ונתננוהו ביד פלוני זה להיות בידו וביד הבא מכחו לראיה ולזכות...

Translation

(a) ...We the Beit Din who[se names are] sealed below [state] thus: X, daughter of Y, wife of Z, came before us and approached us and made plain her distress and need. She said before us: 'It should be known to you today, my lords, that Z (her husband) went abroad days ago, and did not leave me a maintenance portion for even three months; and I do not have enough to maintain or support myself, and what I earn amounts to nothing, and I require much for maintenance. Now, my lords, consider my need and look out for my maintenance.'

(b) We the Beit Din deemed her words to be correct. We sought assets of her husband and did not find anything suitable [for her] to sell [on her own], such as a particular field or jewelry, so we authorized her to sell it. They advertised this same field, and it came to such and such *dinarin*, and we conducted the advertisement as required and stated by the Sages.

(c) The only buyer who emerged who would give such and such *dinarin* was A son of B, and we the Beit Din deemed it acceptable to sell [the field] to this person. We had to persuade him about this, because he was worried about a complaint [from] the one abroad, that he did not return and make any claim against him. We went back to A and exerted much pressure on him to buy it, and he listened to us and bought it from us for such and such *dinarin*. We ordered him to take out [from the sale price] the amount of maintenance for his [i.e., the absent husband's] wife that was appropriate and prescribed by the Sages, and to give her such and such each month for her maintenance. And A did so.

(d) For this reason, we have written for her this instrument of the Beit Din, that we the Beit Din sold him this field for the wife's maintenance. Neither Z, the woman's husband, nor any person shall have the power today or in the future to claim against him [the buyer] for anything. A, the buyer, may now go and possess and acquire this field, and he, as well as anyone under his authority, may do whatever he pleases with it, and is allowed to succeed to it and transmit it, to inherit it and bequeath it, and do whatever he pleases with it, for now and for ever... Z the husband and his heirs after him must save and clear and remove from A and his heirs after him any claims in the world, and to place him, and everyone under his authority, in possession of this field that we [s]old[128] him, with no loss at all. Similarly, if any writing or attestation in the world emerges with respect to the field, [the responsibility] is on Z the husband and his heirs after him to remove [it] and deliver A the buyer and his heirs after him. For in this way we the Beit Din have sold [it] to him, that the responsibility for it shall be on [Z] and his heirs; since we the Beit Din sold it to [A] to protect [Z's] wife, it is the same as it he sold it himself. We have perfected the power of the buyer, so that the responsibility [to maintain the buyer in possession or free from claims] is on [Z] and his heirs, like the liability and substance of any deed of sale... We have written and sealed this instrument of the Beit Din and put it in the hand of this A, to be for him and anyone under his authority as evidence and right...

The structure of this document is thus seen to be quite similar to that in the *iggeret biqqoret* samples:

1) A statement of how the Beit Din came to be involved, in this case as the result of a plea by the wife that she was left without adequate support when her husband went abroad.

2) An affirmation that certain land of the husband was chosen by the Beit Din for sale and was advertised.

---

128 The Hebrew here has זכרנו, but this may be מכרנו.

3) A confirmation that the property was purchased and the purchase amount used to provide the wife with an income for her maintenance.

4) A detailed direction protecting the purchaser from any claims, particularly from the husband, and confirming that the transfer to the buyer has the same effect as if it had been made by the husband himself.

We may note, first, that advertisement is also an element in this type of sale. Second, the protection against claims is again emphasized, it being in fact stated that the *iggeret* was issued precisely because the purchaser was worried about such claims. Third, as in the case of the *iggeret biqqoret*, the term *mazon* calls attention to the circumstances under which the sale was made; though advertisement is also a feature of this sale, this fact does not figure in the name of the deed.

There are also samples of an *iggeret mered*, issued by a Beit Din in the case of a "rebellious wife." As Gulak interprets the wording of the two samples he quotes,[129] the effect of the document was to cancel the husband's obligations under the wife's *ketubbah*; the wording of the document attests to a public tearing-up of the *ketubbah* along with a declaration that the husband was now free to marry someone else.[130]

From these samples it may thus be concluded that an *iggeret* was a document issued by a Beit Din that cancelled a right that would normally be cancelled by a private document (such as a deed of sale or a *get*). Its title conventionally referred to the circumstances under which the Beit Din became involved – *biqqoret* meaning "claim," *mazon* referring to a widow's maintenance, and *mered* meaning "rebelliousness."

c) Conclusion

We may thus propose that the Mishnah and Tosefta sections quoted above are predicated upon the assumption that the *iggeret biqqoret* was equivalent to a deed of sale. Unless such a document was given to the

---

129 Asher Gulak, *A Compendium of Documents Used in Israel* [in Hebrew] (*Sifriyah Mishpatit* 5; 1926), 65-66.

130 In cases in which polygamy was allowed, any contractual restriction on taking another wife was also cancelled.

purchaser, his right to the property could be challenged on the ground of a misevaluation (within certain limits). Such a situation would leave the purchaser in a precarious position; hence the issuing of the *iggeret* might also act as an enticement to otherwise reluctant buyers. The dictum עבדים ושפחות ומיטלטלין אין להם אגרת בקרת (There is no *iggeret biqqoret* for male or female slaves or for movable property) in *yMeg.* 4:4 65b, quoted above, may be understood on its plain meaning (despite the explanations of R. Yudah and Ulla) that no deed was necessary in these cases: for מטלטלין (moveable property), deeds were not required in any event (*mQidd.* 1:5); and in this particular case, slaves were treated as מטלטלין.[131]

4.4.4.B Sanctified Property and *biqqoret*: *tArakh.* 4:3

A number of regulations in Mishnah and Tosefta discuss the case of property subject to the claim of a wife's ketubah, or to the claim of a creditor, when the property had previously been sanctified or dedicated to Temple use (*heqdesh*). The question in this case is which of the claims would take precedence. *MArakh.* 6:1 (last part) appears to give the "human" debt precedence:

המקדיש נכסיו והיתה עליו כתבת אשה רבי אליעזר אומר כשיגרשנה ידיר הנאה
רבי יהושע אומר אינו צריך...

> One who sanctifies his property and was subject to a claim for his wife's *ketubbah* – R. Eliezer says: When he divorces her, he makes her forswear any [future] benefit [from him, so that he cannot remarry her and recover the property free of the obligation of *heqdesh*]; R. Yehoshua says: It is not necessary...

MArkhin 6:2 appears to confirm this, but specifies the mechanism: the property is redeemed from *heqdesh*, by paying any additional value:

המקדיש נכסיו והיתה עליו כתבת אשה ובעל חוב אין האשה יכולה לגבות כתובתה מן ההקדש
ולא בעל חוב את חובו אלא הפודה פודה על מנת לתן לאשה כתובתה ולבעל חוב את חובו

> One who sanctifies his property and was subject to a claim for his wife's

[131] As discussed above, with respect to the legal position of slaves a question arises as to whether they were, or were always, considered "property." See also Introduction, n. 96.

ketubbah and a creditor's claim – the wife cannot claim her *ketubbah* [directly] from the *heqdesh*, nor can the creditor claim his debt, but the one who redeems [the *heqdesh*] does so on the condition of giving the wife [the amount of] her *ketubbah* and the creditor [the amount of] his debt.

Tosefta Arakhin 4 discusses the same issue, again appearing to give the "human" debt precedence (4:1). Section 4:3 provides:

המקדיש את הבהמה ומתה יש לה פדיון
המקדיש את המתה אין לה פדיון
הפודה מיד הקדש שלא ביקורת הקדש פדוי שיד הקדש על העליונה...

If one sanctifies an animal and it dies, it can be redeemed.
If one sanctifies a dead animal, there is no redemption.
If one redeems something that has been sanctified, which is not *biqqoret*, the sanctified object is redeemed, since sanctification takes precedence...

J. Neusner interprets *tArakh.* 4:3 as referring to situations in which the sanctified object is redeemed in exchange for an object of much less value; the redemption is still valid.[132] He thus translates *biqqoret* here as "without a price [specified]"; it is not clear from where this translation is derived. It can be argued, however, that an interpretation of *biqqoret* as "claim" would fit this context as well; that is, if there is no competing claim (such as a *ketubbah* or debt), the redemption is deemed valid without an accounting.

4.4.4.C *PQR* in Other Formulary Documents

Both S. Lieberman and E. Y. Kutscher[133] noted several later manifestations of the root *PQR* that they suggested would support its connection with

132 Jacob Neusner, *A History of the Mishnaic Law of Holy Things* (Leiden: Brill, 1979), 4:44. The 18th century Tosefta commentator David Pardo (Ḥasdei David) took the meaning of *biqqoret* from the traditional understanding of *iggeret biqqoret:*

פי' בלא שומא והכרזה הנקרא אגרת בקורת

The meaning is 'without valuation and advertisement,' which is called *iggeret biqqoret*.

Again, it is difficult to see why an unvalued and unadvertised item could not be redeemed.

133 Lieberman, *Tosefta KiFeshutah* 6:360, n.25; Kutscher, "Terminology of Documents," 126.

dispute or claim; this is the noun פיקאר, which Lieberman translated as תביעה וריב. This word is found, for instance, in *bTa'an.* 24b, at least in the version quoted in the *Arukh* (*s.v.* פקר I). Rabbah had sentenced someone to punishment, as a result of which the person died; the Persian King Shapur was about to interfere, but was warned by his mother: לא ליהוי פיקר בהדי יהודאי. This phrase might be translated "not to have any claim/dispute with these Jews," perhaps warning the king not to challenge Rabbah's right to impose a death sentence; but it must be noted that the version of the phrase in the standard Bavli edition has לא ליהוי עסק דברים בהדי יהודאי, which suggests more simply "not to have any dealings with these Jews."[134]

Lieberman and Kutscher also noted the appearance of the word in several later formularies, as part of a document called a שטר אביזריא. Assaf describes this document as a שטר מחילה ופצוי[135] – in other words, a document in which one person acknowledges that he is forgiving certain claims against another person. Among the lists of items forgiven are included the words ומן כל פיקר וה[ימ]ר. Though the general import of the document (as in the *iggeret biqqoret*) is that the person making the document is thereafter precluded from raising these claims again, it is difficult to know precisely what these two terms mean.[136] Thus the term פיקר, though suggestive, does not have an explicit association with the idea of "claim."

4.4.4.D The Association of *hevqer/hefqer* with "Claim"

The concept of *hevqer/hefqer*, freed or abandoned property, is not found in the Bible, as noted by Herzog;[137] much debate, however, exists around this concept in the Talmudim. Though terms such as "property" and

---

134 For the question of whether Jewish courts retained the right to impose capital penalties see Simḥah Assaf, "The Punishments after the End of the Talmud" [in Hebrew], *Sifriyah Mishpatit* 1 (1922): 16.

135 Assaf, "Sefer HaShetarot," 22 n. 2.

136 As Loewenstamm noted ("*Biqqoret Tihyeh*," 96 n. 13). The phrase quoted often appears in the formulary of Rav Hai Gaon (Assaf, "*Sefer HaShetarot*," 23); the version in the formulary of Rav Yehudah ben Barzilai is ואין לי עליו לא פיקאר ולא היאמר (Halberstam, *Book of Documents*, 10). There does not appear to be agreement as to the meaning of these terms, though Halberstam suggests that R. Yehudah's phrase means, "I have no quarrel or account with him."

137 I. Herzog, *The Main Institutions of Jewish Law* (London: Soncino, 1980), 1:289.

"ownership" are difficult to transpose from one language or legal system to another, B. Cohen[138] suggests that *hevqer/hefqer* would be included within the Roman term *derelictio*, and can be defined as נכסים שאין להם בעלים (items that have no owners). Cohen notes four types of *hevqer/hefqer*: items that have never had owners (such as wild animals), items deliberately abandoned by their current owners, and items rendered ownerless either through the effect of the law (for instance, the property of a convert who dies without Israelite heirs) or as a deliberate penalty by a court.[139] In all four cases, however, the essence of *hevqer/hefqer*, as the *Hifil* form suggests, was that it was immediately "claimable" by someone else.[140] The rabbinic debates illustrate this point, as they center around the question of when precisely one can be considered dissociated from one's property: Is this accomplished by the mere declaration of the owner, or must the property first be seized by someone else for the abandonment to be "consummated"? One may see the workings of this debate in *mNed.* 4:8, concerning the case of someone who has vowed not to receive any benefit from his friend; the issue concerns whether there is any way for the friend to give him food when he has no means of obtaining it otherwise:

1. היו מהלכין בדרך ואין לו מה יאכל נותן לאחר משם מתנה והלה מותר בה.
2. אם אין עמהם אחר מניח על הסלע או על הגדר ואומר הרי הן מובקרים לכל
3. מי שיחפוץ והלה נוטל ואוכל ורבי יוסה אוסר.

Variants:

2. מובקרים] = **ק פ ל** מופקרין = **ר**

If they [the one who vowed and his friend] were en route, and he had nothing to eat – [the friend] gives [food] to another person as a gift, and it is then permitted to [the one who vowed]. If there is no other person with them,

138 Cohen, *Jewish and Roman Law*, 2:11. Cohen suggests that the Roman *derelictio* would also include the rabbinic concept of יאוש, "resignation" or "forsaking," basically the point at which the owner of the objects that have been lost or stolen is deemed to despair of having them returned. I shall here concentrate specifically on the concept of *hevqer/hefqer*.

139 Cohen, *Jewish and Roman Law*, 2:11-12., 11-12.

140 As noted above (n. 85), Spieser, "Leviticus and the Critics," 35, and Kutscher, "Terminology of Documents," also suggested a relationship between the Akkadian *BQR/PQR* and postbiblical Hebrew *hevqer/hefqer*, but gave no explanations for this opinion.

[the friend] places [the food items] on a rock or fence and says: 'These are abandoned to anyone who wants [them],' and [the one who vowed] takes them and eats. But R. Yose forbids this.

The view of R. Yose is explained in *bNed.* 43a:

אמר ר' יוחנן מ"ט דר' יוסי קסבר הפקר כמתנה מה מתנה עד דאתיא מרשות נותן לרשות מקבל הפקר עד דאתי לרשות זוכה

R. Yoḥanan said: What is the reason of R. Yose? He was of the opinion that *hefqer* is like a gift. Just as a gift [is not effective] until it comes from the control of the giver into the control of the taker, so *hefqer* [is not effective] until it comes into the control of the acquirer.

Contrary, therefore, to the general view of the sages in the above Mishnah, R. Yose held that *hefqer* was not complete until some third party had claimed the item; such a claim could not be accomplished in this case because the vow-taker had prohibited himself any benefit from his friend.[141]

The specific issue of whether or not *hefqer/hevqer* takes effect only when the item is claimed by someone else is of particular interest as it applies to slaves. The question of when precisely the "tie" between master and slave is broken becomes especially relevant in unusual situations, such as the flight and capture of the slave, or the master's abandonment of the slave; in the latter case, is the abandonment of the slave in effect equivalent to manumission? The Talmudim grappled here with the interrelationship of the two concepts: whether *hefqer* required a transfer of control, and

141 The issue of the exact point of transfer over an item arose also in cases other than *hefqer*. We may note here one such example from *bEruv.* 71a. The issue concerns how the death of a *ger* who had no heirs would affect his share of an *eruv*, and the underlying principle of the debate is expressed in terms of the view of the two Houses regarding when transfer would pass:

אלא הכא בהא קמיפלגי דב"ש סברי ביטול רשות מיקנא רשותא הוא ומיקנא רשותא בשבת אסור וב"ה סברי אסתלוקי רשותא בעלמא הוא ואסתלוקי רשותא בשבת שפיר דמי

What is the nature of the dispute? The House of Shammai are of the opinion that a cancellation of ownership [automatically] confers the acquisition of [that] ownership [on the successor], and conferring ownership on Sabbath is forbidden; and the House of Hillel is of the opinion that it is just the giving up of ownership, and the giving up of ownership on Sabbath seems fine.

whether the slave could ever receive control of himself while still a slave. The following ruling expressed in *yGit.* 4:4 45d, it has been suggested, parallels Roman law,[142] which held that an abandoned slave remained a slave, but without an owner (*servus derelictus*).[143] According to the Yerushalmi ruling, an abandoned slave remained in a similar kind of limbo; the master who abandoned him could make no use of him, but on the other hand, could not manumit him:

ר' אבהו בשם רבי יוחנן אמר המפקיר את עבדו אינו רשאי לשעבדו
ואינו רשאי לכתוב לו גט שיחרור

> R. Abahu said in the name of R. Yoḥanan: he one who declares his slave *hefqer* may not cause him to serve, but also may not write him a deed of manumission.

The Babylonian opinion (*bGitt.* 38ab) on the other hand, appears to allow the severing of one's relationship with a slave through abandonment, though there was a dispute as to the further necessity of a *get*:

דאמר שמואל המפקיר עבדו יצא לחרות ואינו צריך גט שיחרור...
דאמר רב חייא בר אבין אמר רב אחד זה ואחד זה יצא לחירות וצריך גט שחרור...

> As Samuel said: [If] one declares his slave *hefqer*, [the slave] goes out free, and does not require a deed of manumission...
> As Rav Ḥiyya bar Avin said in the name of Rav: Both the one [the slave declared *hefqer*] and the other [the slave declared sanctified] go out free, and require a deed of manumission...[144]

---

142 Solomon Zeitlin, "*Hefqer* and *Yei'ush*," [in Hebrew], in *Studies in the Early History of Judaism,* (New York: Ktav, 1978), 4:451.

143 See, e.g., W. W. Buckland, *The Roman Law of Slavery: The Condition of the Slave in Private Law from Augustus to Justinian* (Cambridge: Cambridge University Press, 1908), 274. Buckland in fact argued that Jewish law did not admit of such a class of slaves without masters, since slavery was relative, and freedom was merely "hidden by the power of the master" (ibid., n. 7); thus without a master, there was no slave.

144 Maimonides accepted the opinion of Rav as definitive (*Hil. Avadim,* 8:13):

המפקיר עבדו יצא לחרות וצריך גט שחרור ואם מת האדון שהפקירו היורש כותב לו גט שחרור

> If one abandons his slave, he goes out free and requires a deed of manumission; and if the master who abandoned him dies, his heir writes him a deed of manumission.

The Yerushalmi commentators were aware of this discrepancy of opinion, and attempted to reconcile R. Yoḥanan's comment in *yGitt.* with the Bavli by explaining that it was not that the master was prohibited from writing a manumission deed, but that he need not do so:

ואינו רשאי: כלומר שאינו מחוייב דס"ל המפקיר עבדו א"צ גט שחרור דס"ל כשמואל בבלי דף ל"ח... [פ"מ]

'He may not [write a deed of manumission]': that is to say, he is not obligated, for he thinks that the one who declares his slave *hefqer* – he [the slave] does not need a deed of manumission, for he thinks like Shmuel in *bGitt.* 38 [Penei Moshe = Moshe Margolis, 18th century]

ה"ג ואינו צריך לכתוב לו גט שחרור... [ק"ה]

We read it this way: 'He does not have to write him a deed of manumission.' [*Qorban HaEdah* = David Fraenkel, 18th c.]

More recent opinion attempts to attribute the difference to foreign influence. S. Zeitlin argued that the two passages reflect a difference between eastern and western opinion, with the latter possibly influenced by Roman law. B. Cohen, on the other hand, seems to read all these opinions as establishing *hefqer* equal to manumission, with the main difference being whether or not a *get* was required; in his opinion, the view of Samuel in *bGitt.* possibly reflected a later, more liberal Roman attitude.[145]

In summary, there is rabbinic evidence that the concept of *hefqer*, especially as it applied to slaves, was understood as rendering something in one's possession as claimable by someone else. The literal meaning of *lehafqir,* in other words, may be taken as "to cause to claim," consistent with a *Qal* meaning of "to claim."

4.4.4.E The Proposed Meaning of *biqqoret*

Based on the analysis above, it may be argued that the word *biqqoret* in Lev. 19:20, like its postbiblical counterpart (and related *BQR/PQR* terms)

145 Zeitlin, "*Hefqer* and *Yei'ush*," 451; B. Cohen, *Jewish and Roman Law*, 2:19-20.

refers to a claim, in the general sense of a contestation of a relationship. It need not imply a return of the item claimed, but it may include a right to be compensated or a right to dispute a status.

4.5 CONCLUSION

On its surface, Lev. 19:20-22 seems to suggest that female slaves are incapable of "marriage" by deeming that a sexual transgression with such a woman, unlike that with a *be'ulat ba'al*, is not considered to be adultery. It has been proposed, however, that the concern of the Lev. 19:20 pericope is not with slave-free intermarriage, but rather to specify which of competing "users" of a *shifḥah* is to maintain control over her. This conclusion is largely based on a survey of the meanings of the *hapax*es *neḥerefet* and *biqqoret* in verse 20, as well as a functional *comparison* to LE 31. It has been argued that the term *neḥerefet* in Lev. 19:20 is the *Nifal* of the biblical verb *ḤRP I*, which carries the general connotation of a diminution of status (a connotation that can also be seen in some instances of the possible Akkadian cognate *harāpu I*). In this instance (as in other biblical occurrences of forms of *ḤRP I*, such as *ḥerpah* in Gen. 30:23), it carries the specific meaning of debasement associated with "improper" sexuality. It has also been suggested that *biqqoret* carries the general meaning of "claim." It has been argued that there are other biblical instances of *BQR* for which the meaning "claim" is appropriate, that the biblical term is cognate with Akkadian *BQR/PQR* forms, which themselves can carry the general meaning of "claim," and that the root בקר|פקר *BQR/PQR* in postbiblical Hebrew, at least in the forms *biqqoret* and *hevqer/hefqer*, continued to carry the meaning of "claim."

Lev. 19:20 may thus be translated as follows:

> If a man has carnal relations with a *shifḥah*, who has been debased by a man, but has not been redeemed or given her freedom, there shall be a claim; they shall not, however, be put to death, since she has not been freed.

The effect of Lev. 19:20-22 is thus to specify that while this situation is not one of adultery, there is recognition of a difference between an exclusive sexual relationship with a wife (where adultery does apply) and a casual relationship with a *shifḥah*. There is no hint, however, of a prohibition against "intermarriage" with slaves. Together with the analysis in chapters one and two, therefore, it may be argued that there is no direct biblical evidence that female slaves could not function as "wives."

With respect to the second element of the matrilineal principle, an assumption that a child's slave status would be inherited through its mother, it has been argued that Exod. 21:4 does not support such an assumption. The next chapter will continue analysis of the matrilineal principle in rabbinic literature.

CHAPTER 5

THE 'INHERITANCE' OF SLAVERY IN RABBINIC LAW: THE NON-LINEARITY OF THE MATRILINEAL PRINCIPLE

5.1 INTRODUCTION

As we have noted in the Introduction, *mQidd.* 3:12 sets out a matrilineal principle for the inheritance of slave status. As we have noted in previous chapters, it is unlikely that such a principle existed in the Bible. Further, a survey of other tannaitic sources leads to the conclusion that even in postbiblical law there were other principles of inheritance that competed with the matrilineal idea, especially where slavery was seen to interact with other "variables," such as ethnicity. We shall examine in particular rabbinic attitudes to the inheritance of slavery with respect to three different rules:

a) *MQidd.* 1:2 provides that a Hebrew *amah* is to be released at puberty, that is, at the appearance of two pubic hairs.[1] This rule does not have a direct biblical precedent, either in Exod. 21:7 regarding the *amah* sold by her father or in Deut. 15:12 regarding the *amah* who is to be released after six years. I propose that this was a deliberate mishnaic addition in response to the matrilineal principle, a necessary addition to the manumission list for Hebrew females. That is, given the assumption in the Mishnah of a matrilineal inheritance of slave status, it was desirable that the Hebrew female should be freed before she could give birth to any "native-born" Hebrew slaves. A review of various postbiblical sources reveals that the manumission "list" for Hebrews in general, and

1 For an overview of the issue of puberty and legal minority and majority through the end of the gaonic period see Tirzah Meacham (leBeit Yoreh), *Sefer Ha-Bagrut Le-Rav Shemu'el Ben Ḥofni Ga'on Ve-Sefer Ha-Shanim Le-Rav Yehudah Ha-Kohen* (Jerusalem: Yad ha-Rav Nisim, 5759), especially 17-25.

females in particular, had in fact several different permutations. One may demonstrate here a non-linear development in genealogical principles.

b) Leviticus 25:44-46 (with respect to the purchase of slaves "from the nations that surround you") appear to specify that "permanent" slaves may only be purchased from among non-Hebrews. An issue then arises as to a possible conflict with the provisions regarding the various "banned" nations in Deut. 7:1-3 and 20:16-17. Among the various sources to be reviewed in this chapter, one's "nationality," and hence "enslavability," appears to have been determined patrilinealy. This principle led in some cases to conflicts with the matrilineal idea.

c) We have noted in chapter one that the mishnaic matrilineal principle is asymmetric with respect to the status of the offspring in slave-free intermarriages: if the mother is a slave, the child is also a slave (*mQidd.* 3:12), while if the mother is free, the child is a *mamzer* according to some opinions (*mYev.* 7:5). There is, however, evidence of a rule according to which all children of such "mixed" marriages were considered *mamzerim*.

It may be posited, therefore, that the matrilineal principle that is reflected in *mQidd.* 3:12 was only one of a number of "genealogical" concepts that were put forward by the Sages. The above variability thus serves as evidence that attitudes regarding matrilineal inheritance of slavery were not consistent among postbiblical sages, lending further credence to the idea that this principle was not a direct, lineal derivative of biblical law.

5.2 THE FREEING OF THE HEBREW *AMAH* AT PUBERTY

5.2.1 Pentateuchal Rules on the Acquisition and Manumission of Slaves

Though mishnaic law in *mQidd.* 1:2-3 provides a systematic outline of the acquisition and manumission of slaves, this is not the case in the biblical text. The only explicit source of enslavement mentioned in the pentateuchal rules is sale: in the case of reduced circumstances (those covered by Lev.

25:10, 39 and 47, which are possibly self-sales given the use of the form *nimkar*), for theft (Exod. 22:2, though it is not clear whether the thief is sold simply as punishment or also to provide recompense for his theft), and in various unspecified circumstances (the male of Exod. 21:2, the daughter of Exod. 21:7, the males and females of Deut. 15:12, and the "foreigners" of Lev. 25:44). Various other of the conventional sources of slaves are mentioned implicitly; for instance, the enslavement of female captives after marriage to them (*yefat to'ar*) appears to be forbidden by Deut. 21:10-14, from which one may deduce that such use of captives was familiar. The *netinim* (e.g., Ezra 2:58, Neḥ. 3:26) are generally considered to be hereditary temple slaves.[2] Finally, as we have noted earlier, tradition assumes that Exod. 21:4 refers to the breeding of slaves from slave mothers.

Far more detailed among the pentateuchal provisions are the regulations regarding the manumission of slaves. There are various differences in substance among these rules, the most obvious having to do with the different terms of years in each passage and the different "ethnic" designations, especially the use of *ivri* in Exod. 21:2, *ivri/ivriyah* in Deut, 15:12, and *aḥ* in Leviticus 25. For convenience, these major differences may be summarized in table form:

TYPES OF MANUMISSION APPLICABLE TO "ETHNIC" DESIGNATION

	Female	Male	Categorization
1) Fixed Term:			
6 years (Exod. 21)	no	yes	*ivri*
6 years (Deut. 15)	yes	yes	*aḥ*, *ha-ivri/ha-ivriyah*
Jubilee (Lev. 25)	not clear	yes	*aḥ*
2) "Permanent" Service			
eved olam (Exod. 21)	no	yes	*ivri*
eved olam (Deut. 15)	yes	yes	*aḥ*, *ha-ivri/ha-ivriyah*
bequeathed (Lev. 25)	yes	yes	from the surrounding nations and *toshavim*

2 See, e.g., Haran, *Encyclopedia Miqrait* [=*EM*] (9 vols; Jerusalem: Mossad Bialik, 1968), 5:984, *s.v.* נתינים; some scholarly opinion finds a parallel between the *netinim* and the Babylonian *irkūtu* institution (ibid., 985).

3) Destruction of eye or tooth (Exod. 21:25-6)	yes	yes	none
4) Redemption			
pidyon (Exod. 21:8)	yes	no	*bat ivri**
ge'ulah (Lev. 25)	not clear	yes	*aḥ*
5) Death of Master (Lev. 25:44-5)	not clear	yes**	*aḥ*

* By implication from the previous passage, Exod. 21:2-6, which deals with the *eved ivri*
** By implication from Lev. 25:44-5: if the non-*aḥ* could be bequeathed, one assumes that the *aḥ* could not, and his service would end upon the master's death.

5.2.2 The Mishnaic Manumission Scheme for Hebrew Females

In mishnaic law significant additions and changes are apparent in the rules regarding the acquisition and manumission of slaves, including the idea that the Hebrew *amah* is to be released at puberty. These rules are found primarily in *mQidd.* 1:2-3:[3]

Mishnah Qidd. 1: 2 (acquisition and release of a Hebrew slave)

1. עבד עברי נקנה בכסף ובשטר
2. וקונה את עצמו בשנים וביובל ובגרעון כסף.

---

3 The *mishnayot* from *mQidd.* 1:2-3 here and below are are quoted from the standard printed edition. Most of the differences in the MSS appear to be minor and of the type usually found in Middle Hebrew MSS: for instance, the use of *plene* spelling (especially in Kaufmann (ק) and Lowe Cambridge 470.1 (ל), and the exchange of the final ם for the final ן in Parma 138 (פ) and ק, and Rambam Mishnah text from his commentary in Judeo-Arabic (ר) the use of abbreviations, and the use of the full antecedent in the relative clause (שהיא in line 3 of *mQidd.* 1:2, in MSS ק פ ל ר of the Mishnah codex). The latter is indicative of the *Eretz-Yisraeli* tradition while the shortened form ש – is a Babylonian development. JTS ENA 2085.1 has only minor changes from this text though its evidence is incomplete due to the fragmentary natrue of the manuscript.

3. יתרה עליו אמה העבריה שקונה את עצמה בסימנין.
4. הנרצע נקנה ברציעה וקונה את עצמו ביובל ובמיתת האדון.

Translation

1. A Hebrew *eved* is acquired by money or deed,
2. and acquires himself by [a term of six] years, or by the [occurrence of the] Jubilee or by a diminution of the [purchase] money.
3. The Hebrew *amah* is in a better position than he is, as she acquires herself with signs [of puberty].
4. The *nirtza* is acquired by piercing [of his ear], and acquires himself by the [occurrence of the] Jubilee or by the death of the master.

Mishnah Qidd. 1:3 (acquisition and release of a Canaanite slave)

1. עבד כנעני נקנה בכסף ובשטר ובחזקה
2. וקונה את עצמו בכסף על ידי אחרים ובשטר על ידי עצמו דברי ר' מאיר.
3. וחכמים אומרים בכסף על ידי עצמו ובשטר על ידי אחרים ובלבד שיהא הכסף משל אחרים.

Variants[4]: Munich 95 skips part of the Mishnah in line 3 and reads as follows:

וחכמים...אחרים] וחכמ' או' בכסף על ידי עצמו ובלבד שיהא הכסף משל אחרים

Both JTS ENA 2085.1 and Rambam add the word אף after וחכמים אומרים

Translation

1. A Canaanite slave is acquired by money, deed, or *usucaptio*,
2. and acquires himself by money given by others, and a deed given by himself—these are the words of R. Meir.
3. The Sages say: by money given by himself, and a deed given by others, as long as the money belongs to others.

4 The last line of *mQidd.* 1:3 is the subject of scholarly debate, particularly with respect to its substance and relative date. I shall simply note the variants to it here, without commenting on these issues. The manuscripts checked include Munich 95, Oxford Opp. 248 (367), and Vatican 111. Here, too, JTS ENA 2085.1 attests to the reading presented above wherever the text is present.

We may note in general that there are various differences between this and the biblical scheme, including the mishnaic distinction between the "Canaanite" and the "Hebrew" and the fact that, in contrast to Weinfeld's proposal that there was a developing tendency, as reflected in the D source, to think of the slave as an *aḥ* (brother),[5] the Mishnah still refers to these people as *eved, shifḥah*, and *amah*. The Mishnah has also added material that has no direct biblical precedent: the rules of acquisition for Hebrews, the limitation of the term of the permanent slave to the Jubilee, all the rules for "Canaanites," and most particularly, the release of the Hebrew *amah* at puberty. The Hebrew *amah* appears to get not only the modes of release of the Hebrew *eved* (the "manumission list" of שנים, יובל, גרעון כסף, – years, Jubilee, diminution of the [purchase] money), but also סימנים (signs). In effect, the provisions of Exod. 21:7-11 have been ignored.

In this regard, a question arises as to the precise meaning of יתירה עליו (in a better position than he is): does it necessarily imply that the female receives everything that the male does, plus the extra element of "signs," or does it imply merely that she is in a better position than he is because she is exempt from slavery once she reaches puberty? The definition of Ch. Kosovsky[6] suggests that it implies the receipt of something additional:

> יתר ...על: נופל על דבר שיש בו תוספת עודפת
>
> In a better position...than: One happens upon something with a preferable supplement.

Even-Shoshan, however, seems to suggest the idea of "advantageous position":

> יתר עליו: עדיף עליו
>
> In a better position than: Superior to.

Kadari notes,[7] with respect to the semantic field of the mishnaic *yeter/ yoter*, that the word can serve as the opposite to both *paḥot*, "less [than

5 Weinfeld, *Deuteronomy and the Deuteronomic School*, 283.

6 Ch. Kosovsky, *Concordance to the Mishnah* [in Hebrew] (Jerusalem: Massadah, 5713), *s.v.* יתר.

7 Menahem Zevi Kadari, *Syntax and Semantics in Postbiblical Hebrew* [in Hebrew] (Ramat-Gan: Bar Ilan University, 1995), 2:493.

x]" (which would imply the presence of x plus something additional), and *ḥaser*, "lacking [x]" (which would imply the presence of x only). There are other occurrences of *yeter … alav* in the Mishnah that suggest that when this term is used as part of a list it does not necessarily imply inclusion of all members of the list. One such instance occurs in *mKetub.* 4:4:

> האב זכאי בבתו בקדושיה בכסף ובשטר ובביאה, וזכאי במציאתה, ובמעשה ידיה, ובהפרת נדריה, ומקבל את גטה, ואינו אוכל פרות בחייה. נישאת – יתר עליו הבעל שאוכל פרות בחייה וחיב במזונותיה בפרקונה ובקבורתה...

> A father has authority over his daughter with respect to her *qiddushin* by money, deed, and intercourse, and has control over what she finds, and her handiwork, and the annulment of her vows, and receives a *get* [on her behalf], but does not have rights to the interest/produce [from her property] during her lifetime. If she is married, her husband is in a better position than he [the father] is, because he has rights to the interest during her lifetime, but is liable for her support, ransom, and burial...

The phrase יתר עליה, "in a better position than her," here would seem to refer only to the last point in the father's list, the right to receive income; it cannot imply that the husband receives all the benefits of the father, since two of elements in the list (receipt of *qiddushin* and *get* on the woman's behalf) are inapplicable to the husband. This issue, therefore, is not straightforward, and this lack of precision can be seen in various talmudic discussions.

5.2.3 The "Manumission List" in Midreshei Halakhah

As noted above, the Mishnah overlooks the provisions of Exod. 21:7-11 with respect to the Hebrew *amah. Mekhilta de R. Yishmael, Neziqin, parshah* 3 (Lauterbach)[8] appears to address this very issue, explaining how the Exodus section was to be reconciled with the provisions of Leviticus and Deuteronomy:[9]

---

8 The quotation is taken from Lauterbach's edition *Mekhilta de R. Ishmael, Neziqin*, p. 70, rather than Horovitz's edition, because the text in Horovitz has internal references with abbreviated texts in this section.

9 The other reconciliations in the *Mekhilta* include the following:

לא תצא כצאת העבדים לא תצא בראשי איברים כדרך שהכנענים יוצאים אתה אומר לא תצא בראשי איברים כדרך שהכנענים יוצאים או לא תצא בשנים וביובל כדרך שהעבדים יוצאים ת"ל כי ימכר לך אחיך העברי או העבריה ועבדך שש שנים מגיד שהיא יוצאה בשש וביובל מנין ת"ל כי עבדיי הם מכל מקום הא אין עליך לדון כלשון אחרון אלא כלשון ראשון לא תצא כצאת העבדים לא תצא בראשי איברים כדרך שהכנענים יוצאים.

She shall not go out as the avadim do [Exod. 21:7]—She shall not go out upon damage to the primary members [of the body] as the Canaanites do.[10] You say [this means] she shall not go out upon damage to the primary members as the Canaanites do, but is it that she shall not go out with [a term of] years or the Jubilee like the [Hebrew] slaves go out? Scripture states [Deut. 15:12]: *If your fellow Hebrew, male or female, is sold to you, they shall serve you six years* —this indicates she goes out in six [years]. And whence do we know she goes out in the Jubilee year? Scripture states [Lev. 25:42]: *They are my slaves*—in all cases. Therefore [since the six years and Jubilee term are already covered], you must determine the matter according to the former language, not the latter. *She shall not go out as the avadim do* [means] she shall not go out upon damage to the primary members as the Canaanites do.

Exodus 21:7 is thus interpreted as a contrast to the treatment of Canaanite slaves in Exod. 21:26-27. The latter passage in fact makes no explicit reference to the ethnicity of the slave, Canaanite or otherwise.

---

a) Exod. 21:2-6 deals with the Hebrew *eved* sold into slavery by a court as punishment for a crime.

b) The talionic-type release in Exod. 21:26-7 is taken to refer only to "Canaanite" slaves.

c) Deut. 15:17, which seems to give the female the right to remain an *eved olam*, is taken as being limited to the words העניק תעניק לו in v. 14 – that is, one also has an obligation to provide maintenance for the Hebrew *amah* upon her release, but she does not become a permanent slave.

10 This is based on the quasi-talionic provisions of Exod. 21:26-7. The restriction of these provisions to "Canaanites," though nowhere explicit in the biblical text, is also found in the *Mekhilta de R. Ishmael* (*Neziqin*, Lauterbach, p. 70), apparently based on the similar use of the terms *eved* and *amah* in Lev. 25:44:

רבי אליעזר אומר בכנעני הכתוב מדבר אתה אומר בכנעני הכתוב מדבר או אינו אלא בעברי ת"ל תקנו עבד ואמה

R. Eliezer says: Scripture [at Exod. 21:26-7] speaks of a Canaanite slave. You say Scripture speaks of a Canaanite, but perhaps it is only a Hebrew? Thus it is stated [Lev. 25: 44]: [*From them*, i.e., non-Hebrews] *you may buy an* eved *and an amah.*

Frankel[11] has argued that the tradition reflected in the Mekhilta may already be reflected in the LXX translation of Exod. 21:7, which reads: *ἐὰν δέ τις ἀποδῶται τὴν ἑαυτοῦ θυγατέρα οἰκέτιν οὐκ ἀπελεύσεται ὥσπερ ἀποτρέχουσιν αἱ δοῦλαι* (And if anyone sells his daughter as an *οἰκέτις*, she shall not depart as the *δοῦλαι* [feminine] depart.) The LXX seems to be using the two different terms, *οἰκέτις* and *δοῦλη*, to emphasize that the *amah* of Exodus 21 is an *οἰκέτις*, and she does not go out as the *female slaves* (*δοῦλαι*) do (in place of *ha-avadim* of the MT). Frankel, in fact, saw little significance in this use of the feminine form *δοῦλαι*, arguing this use was probably an unintentional reflection of the feminine *θυγατέρα*, "daughter." The primary significance of the LXX translation, in his view, lay in the use of the different terms *οἰκέτις* and *δοῦλαι*. Elsewhere in the LXX, he suggests, forms of *δοῦλος* are used for "foreign slaves" (e.g., Lev. 25:44). Thus in his opinion the LXX is making the same distinction as the *Mekhilta de R. Ishmael* above, which interpreted Exod. 21:7 as restricted to "Canaanite slaves." Like the rabbinic halakhah, therefore, the LXX has reconciled Exod. 21:7 and Deut. 15:12: as distinct from the *οἰκέτις* and her specific rules in Exodus, the *δοῦλη* in Deut. would follow the usual rule and go out, like the male, in six years; that is, all except for the *οἰκέτις* go out in six years.

Even accepting Frankel's assessment of the significance of this LXX distinction in terms, the question still remains as to the precise meaning of *οἰκέτις*. As we have noted earlier, the meaning of any of the Greek "slave" terms, both in the LXX and elsewhere, is difficult to pinpoint. In Schenker's opinion, the *οἰκέτις* in verse 7 refers specifically to someone intended for marriage.[12] Yet elsewhere in the LXX, as we have seen, *οἰκέτις* is also found for the translation of *shifḥah* (Lev. 19:20, Prov. 30:23) while in other translations of MT *shifḥah* and *amah* (including the *amah* of Deut. 15:17), one finds *παιδισκη* or *δοῦλη*. In analyzing the masculine term *οἰκέτης*, Spicq[13] notes a range of associations: it is used for *eved* in the LXX, apparently thus suggesting a "slave," but it is also used for people who do not seem "servile," and is often a synonym of *ὑπηρέτης*, the meanings of

11 Zechariah Frankel, *Über den Einfluss der palästinischen Exegese auf die alexandrinische Hermeneutik* (Leipzig: 1831; repr. Westmead: Gregg International Publishing, 1972), 91.

12 Schenker, "Affranchissement," 552. Similarly, Chirichigno, *Debt-Slavery*, 251, goes so far as to state that the MT *amah* means something other than a (chattel) slave in this case.

13 Spicq, "Le vocabulaire de l'esclavage," 218-19.

which include "assistant" and "aide-de-camp" (Liddell/Scott). Gibbs and Feldman discuss the use of *οἰκέτις* in the later books of the LXX, Josephus, and contemporary papyri, concluding that in all these sources this and other "slave" terms were increasingly regarded as synonyms.[14]

The *Mekhilta* also attempts a derivation for the association of the Hebrew *amah* with signs based on the wording of Exod. 21:11. The precise hermeneutics, however, are not at all clear:[15]

אבא חנין אומר משום רבי אליעזר ויצאה חנם בבגר אין כסף בסימנין

Aba Ḥanin said in the name of R. Eliezer: *She shall go out for nothing* [Exod. 21:11]—[This means] as an adult. *With no money* [ibid.]—With signs.

These passages thus confirm for the Hebrew *amah* a manumission list consisting of signs in addition to at least years and Jubilee. This list is at least partially confirmed in the other midrash halakhah to Exod, the *Mekhilta de R. Shimon ben Yohai* [=*Mekh. deRashbi*], *Mishpatim*, 21:7 (Epstein-Melamed p.165); in this case, however, the exegesis is presented in the name of R. Akiva:

לא תצא כצאת העבדים: שלא תהא נוטלת אחריו דלאים ובלריות למרחץ דברי ר' אל[י]עזר אמ' לו ר' עקיב' אמר לו ר' עקיבא מה אני צריך והלא כבר נאמר לא תעבד בו עבדת עבד" מה ת"ל לא תצא כצאת העבדים – שלא תהא יוצאה על השן ועל העין כעבדים שהיה בדין ומה עבד כנעני שאין יוצא בשנים וביובל ובגרעון כסף הרי הוא יוצא על השן ועל העין זו שיוצאה בשנים וביובל ובגרעון כסף אינו דין שיוצאה על השן ועל העין ת"ל לא תצא כצאת העבדים

She shall not go out like the avadim [Exod. 21:7]—[This means] that she shall not carry pails and ropes to the bath after him [the master]; these are the words of R. Eliezer [that is, v. 11 refers to the type or place of work, and

14 Gibbs and Feldman, "Josephus' Vocabulary for Slavery," 290, 294, 295. They also note that the differing patterns of use of "slave" terms throughout the LXX raises the possibility of separate authorships (ibid., 300).

15 Vermes, *Post-Biblical Jewish Studies,* 71 suggests that there were in fact two traditions of exegesis harmonizing Exod. 21:7-11 with the other provisions, both reflected in these passages of *Mekhilta de R. Yishmael*: one used the Exod. section to distinguish the Hebrew female from Canaanite slaves, and the other assumed that the section assigned to the female the special case of "signs" (two pubic hairs). He does not, however, explain the hermeneutic methods by which the concept of signs was actually derived from v. 11.

not to manumission]. R. Akiva said to him: Why do I need [v. 7 for that explanation]? Does it not already say: *Do not work him [a Hebrew] with the work of an eved* [Lev. 25:39]? [Then] what does the Torah [mean by] *She shall not go out like the avadim*—that she shall not go out [because of a destroyed] tooth or eye like the *avadim*. It would be logical that if the Canaanite *eved*, who does not go out by [term of] years, Jubilee, or diminution of price, goes out by [a destroyed] tooth and eye, she who does go out by [term of] years, Jubilee, or diminution of price, would [all the more so] go out by [a destroyed] tooth and eye. Therefore the Torah must state: *She shall not go out like the avadim* [to exclude the latter possibility].

This midrash thus confirms the manumission list for the *amah* as including the term of years, Jubilee, and diminution of price, though it contains no derivation of signs.

In contrast, *Sifrei Deut. pisqa* 118 (Finkelstein 177) restricts the female's manumission list to signs. The midrash in question addresses the reason that both males and females need to be mentioned specifically in Deuteronomy 15:

אחיך העברי או העבריה: יש בעברי מה שאין בעבריה ובעבריה מה שאין בעברי. עברי יוצא בשנים וביובל ובגרעון כסף, מה שאין כן בעבריה. עבריה יוצאה בסימנים ואינה נמכרת ונשנית ומפדים אותה על כרחה מה שאין כן בעברי. הא לפי שיש בעברי מה שאין בעבריה ובעבריה מה שאין בעברי צריך לומר בעברי וצריך לומר בעבריה.

Your brother the Hebrew male or the Hebrew female [Deut. 15:12]—There are [matters applicable] to the Hebrew male that are not [applicable] to the Hebrew female, and [matters applicable] to the Hebrew female that are not [applicable] to the Hebrew male. The Hebrew male goes out by [term of] years, the Jubilee, and diminution of price, which is not so for the Hebrew female. The Hebrew female goes out at signs [of puberty], is not sold a second time, and is redeemed against her will, which is not so for the Hebrew male. Thus since there are [matters applicable] to the Hebrew male that are not [applicable] to the Hebrew female, and [matters applicable] to the Hebrew female that are not [applicable] to the Hebrew male, it is necessary to refer [both] to the Hebrew male and to the Hebrew female.

This midrash thus specifically excludes the application of שנים, יובל, גרעון כסף (years, Jubilee, diminution of the [purchase] money) from the female, restricting her manumission to signs of puberty. In effect, contrary to the

Mishnah, the text specifically excludes the application of Deuteronomy and Leviticus to the Hebrew female, giving apparent priority to Exodus.

Further complexity is added upon an examination of *Midrash Tannaim* to Deut. 15:12 (Hoffman p.85). A passage is cited with the same format as that in *Sifrei*. Here, however, the emphasis is merely on the special case of סמנים, "signs": there is neither a reconciliation with the other mishnaic provisions nor an exclusion of them:

ולמה צריך לומר העברי או העבריה לפי שיש בעבד עברי מה שאין באמה עבריה ובאמה עבריה מה שאין בעבד עברי עבד עברי בית דין מוכרין אותו ועובד את הבן מה שאין כן באמה עבריה ואמה עבריה יוצאה בסימנין ומפדין אותה בעל כרח האב מה שאין כן בעבד עברי הא לפי שיש בזה מה שאין בזה ויש בזה מה שאין בזה צריך לומר העברי או העבריה

Why is it necessary to state *the Hebrew male or the Hebrew female*? Because there are [matters applicable] to the Hebrew *eved* that are not [applicable] to the Hebrew *amah*, and to the Hebrew *amah* that are not [applicable] to the Hebrew *eved*. The Hebrew *eved*—the Beit Din can sell him, and he works for the son [after the death of the original master], which is not so for the Hebrew *amah*. And the Hebrew *amah* goes out at signs [of puberty] and is redeemed against the will of the father,[16] which is not so for the Hebrew *eved*. Thus because there are [matters applicable] to this one and not to that one, and to that one and not to this one, it is necessary to state *the Hebrew male or the Hebrew female*.

5.2.4 The Manumission List in bQidd. 18a

A baraita in the Bavli adds yet further complexity to the issue of the manumission list:

תנו רבנן יש בעברי שאין בעבריה ויש בעבריה שאין בעברי. יש בעברי שהוא יוצא בשנים וביובל ובמיתת האדון מה שאין כן בעבריה. ויש בעבריה שהרי עבריה יוצאת בסימנין ואינה נמכרת ונשנית ומפדין אותה בעל כורחו מה שאין כן בעברי.

The rabbis taught [in a baraita]: There are [matters applicable] to a Hebrew male and not to a Hebrew female, and [matters applicable] to a Hebrew female and not to a Hebrew male. With respect to a Hebrew male, he goes out [from

16 The expected form would be בעל כרחו של האב.

slavery] after [a term of] years, the Jubilee, and the death of the master, which is not so with the Hebrew female. And with respect to a Hebrew female, the Hebrew female goes out with signs of puberty, and is not sold twice, and she is redeemed against his will, which is not so for the Hebrew male.

The baraita thus suggests, like *Sifrei Deut. pisqa* 118 (Finkelstein 177), that the *amah* is restricted to signs. Yet there are two important differences between these sources: the talmudic baraita is associated with the reading בעל כרחו (against his will), and the element מיתת האדון (death of the master) in the manumission list, whereas *Sifrei Deut.* has the reading בעל כרחה (against her will), and uses גרעון כסף (diminution of price) in the manumission list.

We may assume, given their common structure, that the talmudic baraita and *Sifrei Deut. pisqa* 118 are related. In that case, is it possible to tell which has the original readings? We shall focus on two variants in particular.

5.2.4.A "Against His/Her Will" (בעל כרחו – בעל כרחה)

The two Bavli MSS Munich 95 (ומפדין אות' בעל כרחו) and Vatican 111 (ופודין אותה בעל כורחו) support the reading of בעל כרחו (against his will). Oxford Opp. 245 (367) has an abbreviation here: כרח'. The reading בעל כרחה (against his will), however, is also attested elsewhere. Rashba, in his *Ḥidushim* to *bQidd.* 18, has:

> ת"ר יש בעברי מה שאין בעבריה ויש בעבריה וכו' שהעבריה יוצאב בסימנין ואינה נמכרת ונשנית ומפדין אותה בעל כרחה

> Our rabbis taught [in a baraita]: There are [matters applicable] to a Hebrew male and not to a Hebrew female, and [matters applicable] to a Hebrew female, etc.: the Hebrew female goes out with signs of puberty, and is not sold twice, and she is redeemed against her will.

Further in the discussion the following sentence also appears:

> ...ותנא בה מפדין אותה בעל כרחה.

> And he [the tanna] taught concerning her: They redeem her against her will.

He did, however, question the absence of גרעון כסף (diminution of price). From this it may be inferred that while he did have בעל כרחה (against her will) like the reading in *Sifrei Deut*, he did not have the complete *Sifrei* manumission list.

Finally, we may note that the *Yalqut Shimoni* attests to two readings:

ת"ר יש בעבריה מה שאין בעברי שהעבריה יוצאה בסימנין ומפדין אותה **בעל כרחה** ואינה נמכרת ונשנת. (שמות משפטים כ"ב)

Our rabbis taught [in a baraita]: There are [matters applicable] to a Hebrew female which are not [applicable] to a Hebrew male, the Hebrew female goes out with signs of puberty, and she is redeemed *against her will*, and is not sold twice. (*Exod. Mishpatim* 22)

אחיך העברי או העבריה: יש בעברי מה שאין בעבריה ובעבריה מה שאין בעברי.עברי יוצא בשנים וביובל ובגרעון כסף מה שאין כן בעבריה.עבריה יוצאה בסימנין ואין נמכרת ונשנת ומפדין אותה **בעל כרח** מה שאין כן בעברי. (דברים ראה טו, רמז תתצח)

Your brother the Hebrew [male] or Hebrew [female] —There are [matters applicable] to a Hebrew male and not to a Hebrew female, and [matters applicable] to a Hebrew female and not to a male: The Hebrew male goes out [from slavery] after [a term of] years, in the Jubilee, and with diminution of price, which is not so with the Hebrew female. The Hebrew female goes out with signs of puberty, and is not sold twice, and she is *forcibly* redeemed, which is not so for the Hebrew male. (*Deut. Re'ei* 15, *remez* 88)

Though it is thus difficult to trace the text history of this reading, it might be argued that בעל כרחה (against her will), at least from the point of view of logic, is the *lectio difficilior*, as it would imply that the redemption of the girl, presumably for her benefit, is done against her will. Yet we may note at least one citation from rabbinic literature in which this phrase is in fact used in connection with the conferring of a benefit. *Midrash ha-Gadol* on Exod. 12:36 discusses the giving to the Israelites of Egyptian plunder that is discussed in the biblical verse:

אמר ר' אמי מלמד שהשאילום בעל כרחן אמרי לה בעל כרחן דישראל ואמרי לה בעל כרחן דמצראי... ומן דאמר בעל כרחם דישראל משום משוי.

Rabbi Ami said: This teaches that they lent to them against their will. Some say [it was] against the will of the Israelites, some say against the will of the Egyptians.... Those who say [it was] against the will of the Israelites [maintain that it was] because of the burden [of carrying it].

Still, some support for the idea of בעל כרחה (against her will) as the earlier version may be derived indirectly from the talmudic discussion of בעל כרחו (against his will) that follows the baraita in *bQidd.* 18a, as between Rava and Abaye:

ומפדין אותה בע"כ סבר רבא למימר בע"כ דאדון א"ל אביי מאי ניהו דכתבנא ליה שטרא אדמיה אמאי נקים מרגניתא בידיה יהיבנא ליה חספא אלא אמר אביי בעל כרחיה דאב משום פגם משפחה אי הכי עבד עברי נמי נכפינהו לבני משפחה משום פגם משפחה הדר אזיל ומזבין נפשיה ה"נ הדר אזיל ומזבין לה הא קתני אינה נמכרת ונשנית

In Munich 95 and Oxford Opp. 248 (367) there are some errors including a homeoteleuton in Munich 95 in the last line from the word ומזבין. Vatican 111 in the last line changes ליה to לה but Oxford Opp. 248 (367) has ליה.

'And she is redeemed against his will.' Rava reasoned: Against the will of the master. Abaye said to him: What is this, we wrote him a deed for the value? Why? If he is holding a pearl, do we give him a sherd? Rather, Abaye said: Against the will of the father, on account of the shame to the family. [The stammaitic response is:] If so, for the Hebrew *eved* we could also force his family [to redeem him] on account of the shame to the family. But he could just go back and sell himself again. But here too [the father] could go back and sell [his daughter] again. Therefore the tanna teaches: She is not sold [into slavery] more than once.

The *pisqa* in the printed version of *bQidd.* 18a that introduces the dispute contains merely the acronym בע"כ (though this is expanded to בעל כרחו in both MS Munich 95 and MS Vatican 111). It may be argued that the ultimate editor of the sugya had before him only the term בע"כ, and assumed it meant בעל כרחו. Aminoaḥ in fact suggests that the entire dispute here between Rava and Abaye is actually a compilation by a later editor:[17]

ולפנינו סוגיא פומבדיתאית אבל בזמן מאוחר הניחו כי לפנינו מו"מ בין אביי ורבא.

[17] N. Aminoaḥ, *The Redaction of Tractate Qiddushin in the Babylonian Talmud* [in Hebrew] (Tel Aviv University, 1977), 113.

והגיהו בגמרא כנוסח שלפנינו.

We have before us a Pumbeditan *sugya*; at a later time, however, they assumed that before us was a discussion between Abaye and Rava, and they edited it in the Gemara according to the version that we [now] have.

Aminoaḥ suggests that the dispute actually reflects opinions of the two sages which are expressed elsewhere. A discussion in *bQidd.* 16a,[18] of the methods by which the Hebrew *eved* acquired himself cites a baraita to the effect that the element "diminution of purchase price" listed in *mQidd.* 1:2 can involve various equivalents to money:

תנא וקונה את עצמו בכסף ובשוה כסף ובשטר

Oxford Opp. 248 (367) and Vatican 111 are missing the word שטר but Vat. 111 corrects that.

It was taught in a baraita: He [the Hebrew *eved*] acquires himself by money, by an equivalent to money, and by a deed.

The *stammaim* (anonymous editors) concluded that שטר (deed) must refer to a גט שחרור (deed of manumission), since if it referred to a bond or promissory note it would be שוה כסף (equivalent to money) and that would create a repetition in the text. This opinion is supported with a statement of Rava, who argues that the giving of a manumission deed was at the option of the master:

אמר רבא זאת אומרת ע"ע גופו קנוי

Rava said: This means that the Hebrew *eved* is acquired bodily.

According to Aminoaḥ, the editor of the *sugya* in *bQidd.* 18a implied to Rava the opposite conclusion with respect to the Hebrew female: the manumission of a female by a deed was not at the option of the master. Abaye, on the other hand, is associated with the idea that the slave always has the upper hand with respect to a redemption (*bQidd.* 20a):

18 See also the discussion of this passage in chapter six, concerning the meaning of שטר.

ת"ר נמכר במנה והשביח ועמד על מתאים מנין שאין מחשבין לו אלא מנה...

Our rabbis taught: If he [the Hebrew *eved*] was sold for one *manah*, and his value increased to 200, from where [do we know that for the purposes of redemption] he is assessed at only one *manah*?

These two principles, according to Aminoaḥ, were put together by the talmudic editor to create the dispute in *bQidd.* 18a.[19] If Aminoaḥ is correct, and the dispute is a later addition, this lends support to the idea that בעל כרחו (against his will), too, is a later reading.

5.2.4.B Diminution of Purchased Price (גרעון) or Death of the Master (מיתת האדון)

It may be further suggested that the term גרעון כסף (purchase price) in the Bavli's manumission list is the *lectio difficilior*. The Rashba (*Ḥidushim, bQidd.* 18a) argued that גרעון כסף would have to be assumed to be applicable to the Hebrew female slave from the word מפדין (redeemed); this was the reason for its exclusion from the manumission list for the Hebrew *eved* in the baraita at *bQidd.* 18a:

לא בעא למתני בעברי שאין בעבריה גרעון כסף דמחזיא ברייתא דתקשי רישא אסיפא

It was not necessary to teach diminution of purchase money [as a matter applicable] to the Hebrew male and not to the Hebrew female, as the beginning of the baraita would then be seen to contradict the end [in which it is said that redemption is not applicable to the male].

Halivni[20] suggested that מיתת האדון (death of the master) was the original version, and that there was an earlier form of the Mishnah which contained the list שנים, יובל, מיתת האדון (years, Jubilee, and death of master):

מ"מ נראה שהברייתא שם מצטטת משנה קדומה שבה היתה כתובה מיתת האדון במקום גרעון כסף. ואלה שהיתה להם הגירסה במשנה כמו שהיא לפנינו גורסים בברייתא כמו

19 Aminoaḥ, *Redaction of Tractate Qiddushin*, 112.
20 Halivni, *Sources and Traditions: Seder Nashim* (Tel Aviv: Dvir, 1968) 1.

שהוא בספרי...

> In any event it seems that the baraita there [*bQidd.* 18a] quotes an earlier Mishnah in which 'death of the master' was written instead of 'diminution of purchase price.' Those who had a version of the Mishnah like ours would have read the baraita in the way it appears in *Sifrei* [Deut.]...

He suggests, however, that the reason for the substitution was the presence of a different classification scheme:

כלומר, בעוד שיתר היוצאים נשלחו היוצא בכסף שילח את עצמו.
יוצא בכסף הוא סוג אחר.

> That is, though the others [of the Hebrew *avadim*] who are released are sent out, the one who goes out with money sends himself out. One who goes out with money is [of] a different category.

One might argue, however, that מיתת האדון (death of the master) in the manumission list also reflects a different principle than שנים ויובל (years and Jubilee) as was in fact noted by a tosafist:

וממיתת האדון לא קשיא דאיכא למימר דבר שאין לו קצבה לא קתני
(תוספות הראש קידושין י"ח ע"א)

> 'Death of the master'—there is no difficulty here. It is [possible] to say that a matter which has no fixed term is not taught.

In summary, there are some indications, though not completely without difficulty, that the reading in *Sifre Deut.*, as the *lectio difficilior*, is the original.

5.2.5 Conclusion

It may be posited that there was originally a postbiblical "core" teaching that dealt merely with the special case of "signs" assigned to the Hebrew female. This core is reflected in the *Midrash Tannaim*. The question may then have arisen as to whether this special case was to operate to the exclusion of the provisions in Leviticus and Deuteronomy (the trend reflected in *Sifrei*

Deut), or in addition to them, which required reconciliation of Leviticus and Deuteronomy with Exodus (the trend reflected in the Exodus *Mekhiltot*). The Mishnah appears to summarize this debate (although, because the meaning of the term יתירה עליו (in a better position than him) is unclear, it is not certain which side of the debate the Mishnah has taken).[21] It may also be posited that there was a core "manumission list" consisting of years and the Jubilee (שנים ויובל), to which the term "dimunition" (גרעון כסף) was added.

5.3 THE INTERACTION OF SLAVERY AND NATIONALITY

As we have seen in section 5.2, the manumission pericope associated with the P [=Priestly] stratum appears to provide that only "outsiders" can be treated as permanent slaves. The precise definition of these "outsiders," however, led in later law to an apparent interaction between a matrilineal inheritance of slavery with a patrilineal inheritance of nationality.

5.3.1 Levitucus 25 and the "Ethnic" Differentiation of Slaves

Leviticus 25:44-45 specifies who may be treated as permanent slaves:

> And your *eved* and your *amah* that you shall have—from the nations that surround you – from them you shall purchase *eved* and *amah*. And also from the sons of the *toshavim* who reside with you—from them you shall buy, and from their families who are with them whom they sired in your land; and they will be a holding to you.

Among the many issues with respect to the implications and language of these verses, there appears to be no agreement as to who precisely is

21 One might argue, in contrast, that the midreshei halakhah are variously interpreting an ambiguous Mishnah, at least with respect to the question of "signs" for the female. The parallel versions of the baraita in *Sifrei*, *Midrash Tannaim*, and the various Bavli passages, however, reflect differences in the corresponding manumission list for males, which cannot be straightforwardly explained as different interpretations of the Mishnah. I think it is thus more logical to assume, at least in the case of this baraita, that it was a teaching independent of the Mishnah.

intended in this pericope, particularly with respect to the term *toshav* (resident). Thus, for instance, the *EM* defines this term as יושב בבית אחר וסמוך על שלחנו, אבל אינו נחשב לבן ביתו (one resident in another's house, and dependent on his table, but not considered his *ben bayit*); Chirichigno assumes that like the *sakhir* (hired laborer) it referred to people who had to seek dependency and protection from an Israelite because they had no land of their own.[22]

From Exod. 12:45 it is clear that neither the *toshav* (resident) nor the *sakhir* (hired laborer) were considered close enough to the household to share in the Passover sacrifice. All the appearances of the term in the Pentateuch happen to be associated with verses belonging to the P source. One might therefore posit a postexilic referent for this term:[23] perhaps the religiously suspect remnant of Judeans left behind; or the foreign deportees relocated to Israel and Judea (although the deportees of Esarhaddon in Ezra 4:4 are called *am ha-aretz*, "people of the land"); or the offspring of intermarriage between the returnees and foreigners (we may note that in Ezra 10:14 the text describes one who takes in foreign wives as *ha-hoshiv nashim nokhriyot*, "those who brought back foreign women"). In other words, *toshav* might have described one who was not a member of the surrounding nations, but who also could not be clearly identified as an "Israelite." Targum Onkelos and TY both translate *toshavim* with *totavya arelya* (uncircumcised *toshavim*), perhaps to emphasize their non-Israelite status. The apparently superfluous words in verse Lev. 25:45, *asher holidu be-artzekhem* (whom they sired in your land), may also have been intended to emphasize the fact that such "unidentifiables" were not to be regarded as Israelites despite having been born in the land of Israel.

An issue arises, however, as to whether *toshav* might refer to the seven "banned" nations described in Deut. 7:1-3 and 20:16-17 (including the "Canaanites"), who are subject to the *ḥerem*, "ban". This institution was

22 *EM s.v.* תושב; Chirichigno, *Debt Slavery*, 133 n. 2.

23 Following the argument of Deller, "Assyrisch um/nzarḫu," *ZA* 74 (1984): 238, with respect to the term אזרח. Noting that this term, too, is associated with the P source, Deller suggests that the word derives from Neo-Babylonian *um/nzarḫu,* which he translates as "homeborn". He posits that the Israelite deportees might have been influenced by Babylonian concepts of "nationality" and attempted to apply such ideas to their own situation.

assumed to involve the complete destruction of the offending nation, and rendered its property off-limits;[24] this would seem to preclude even the taking of slaves. The dilemma is discussed by certain of the biblical commentators and seems to have been a matter of controversy. Rashbam's commentary on Deut. 29:7, for instance, assumes that even Canaanite slaves were allowed in certain circumstances:

> לא תחיה כל נשמה: כשתבא להלחם עליהם לא תקרא להם לשלום...אבל אם יבואו אליך מדעתם להיות עבדיך קודם שתלך עליהם כמו הגבעונים יכול אתה להחיותם

> *You shall leave no soul alive* [Deut. 20:16]: If you come to war with them, do not welcome them (call to them for peace) ... but if they come to you consciously to be your slaves before you go out to [attack] them, like the Gibeonites [Josh. 9:21], you may spare them.

In contrast, Ibn Ezra, commenting on this apparent biblical contradiction as well as on the use of the term Canaanite slave in the Mishnah (commentary to Lev. 25:45), assumed that *toshav* must refer to any resident foreigner with the exception of the banned nations:

> וגם מבני התושבים הדרים בארץ כנען... והם מהגוים הנזכרים או מצרים וכל עם חוץ משבעת הגוים...ויתכן שחז"ל אמרו עבד כנעני כל הגר הגר בארץ כנען ואינני [איננו] כנעני בייחוסו או הם ידעו להוציא זה הדבר לאמתו כי דעתנו נקלה כנגד דעתם

> *And also from the children of the toshavim* [Lev. 25:45]—those who reside in the land of Canaan... And these are from the nations mentioned or Egypt or any nation, except the seven [banned] nations... It is likely that the Sages spoke of the Canaanite slave [meaning] any stranger living in the land of Canaan but not a Canaanite in origin; or they knew how to derive this correctly [as an exception], since our knowledge is weak compared to theirs.

Further, the use of resident "foreigners" as slaves would also create difficulties if they were members of the particular nations whose right to join the Israelite community was affected by the prohibitions and restrictions in Deut. 23:4 and 8-9 (Ammonites, Moabites, and Edomites). Could such slaves have then participated in the cultic rituals ordinarily

---

24 *EM, s.v.* חרם.

open to slaves, though not to members of these three nations? If such slaves were manumitted, would they become Israelites? We may gather the extent of the complexities involved in these competing prohibitions by noting the simplifying solution of Maimonides (*Hil. Issurei Biyah*, 12:25): after the mass deportations of Sennaḥerib, one would no longer have been able to distinguish a member of the banned or prohibited nations, and such issues could no longer be relevant:

כשעלה סנחריב מלך אשור בלבל כל האומות וערבם זה בזה והגלה אותם ממקומם... לפיכך כשנתגיר הגר בזמן הזה בכל מקום, בין אדומי בין מצרי בין עמוני בין מואבי בין כושי בין שאר אומות - אחד הזכרים ואחת הנקבות מתרין בקהל מיד.

When Sennaḥerib the king of Assyria arose he scrambled all the nations and intermixed them and deported them... Therefore when someone converts today in any place—whether Edomite, Egyptian, Ammonite, Moabite, Kushite, or from any other nation—both males and females are permitted to come into the community immediately.

5.3.2 Sifra Behar parshah 6 and its Parallels

Attempts to sort through the various prohibitions with respect to "foreign" slaves and nationality were nonetheless put forward by the sages. Sifra *Behar parsha* 6:4 (Weiss p.109d-110a) on Lev. 25:44-45 (MS Vatican 31) reveals one such solution: an appropriate interpretation of the biblical text is used to permit the enslavement of one whose mother was a Canaanite, as long as the father was of "one of the nations":

1. וגם מבני התושבים הגרים עמכם מהם תקנו בניהם ובנותיהם
2. הן עצמן מנ' תל מהם תקנו
3. וממשפחתם אש' עמ' מה תל' מנ' אתה או אחד מכל משפחות הארצו'
4. שבא על אחת מן הכנענ' וילדה ממנו בן מותר אתה לקנותו עבד
5. תל' לו' ממשפח אש עמהם
6. או אחד מכל הכנענים שבא על אחת מכל משפחות הארץ וילדה ממנו בן
7. מותר אתה לקנותו עבד תל' לו' אשר הולידו בארצכם

1. *And also from the children of the toshavim who live with you, from them you may acquire*—their sons and daughters.
2. From where [do we learn that one may acquire the *toshavim*] themselves?

Scripture says: *you may acquire them.*
3. *And from their families who are with them*—What is the meaning of this? From where do you learn: [If] a member of any of the nations
4. has intercourse with a Canaanite [woman], and she gives birth to his son, you may acquire him as a slave?
5 Scripture says: *from their families who are with them.*
6. Or: Any Canaanite who has intercourse with a female of any of the nations, and she gives birth to his son,
7. can you acquire him as a slave? Scripture says: *whom they sired in your land.*

The last statement, it may be noted, is equivocal. Further, there are some variants for כנענים such as אומות in the tertiary witnesses with respect to line 6 of the passage.25[25]

Further permutations of this passage appear in the Bavli, each with its own twist. In *bYev.* 78b we find a version of the passage is clearly being used to support the principle, attributed to R. Yoḥanan, that nationality ("אומות-hood") is inherited through the father:

כי אתא רבינא א"ר יוחנן באומות הלך אחר הזכר נתגיירו הלך אחר הפגום
שבשניהם באומות הלך אחר הזכר כדתניא מנין לאחד מן האומות שבא על הכנענית
והוליד בן שאתה רשאי לקנותו בעבד שנאמר וגם מבני התושבים הגרים עמכם מהם תקנו
יכול אפי' אחד מן הכנענים שבא על אחת מן האומות והוליד בן שאתה רשאי לקנותו בעבד
ת"ל אשר הולידו בארצכם מן הנולדים בארצכם ולא מן הגרים בארצכם

When Ravina came, R. Yoḥanan said: [With respect to] nations, it [inheritance of status] followed the male. If they converted, it followed the [parent] with any taint [in status]. Nations followed the male, as it was taught [in the baraita]: From where do we know that if a member of one of the nations had intercourse with a female Canaanite and sired a son, you are allowed to buy him as a slave? As it is said: *And also from the sons of the toshavim who reside with you, from them you may buy.* Is it possible that if a

25 The witnesses include only Vatican 31 (as Assemani 66 is incomplete and lacking this section) Breslau ב, and the first edition of Venice and tertiary witnesses, Midrash HaGadol and Yalqut Shimoni. As will be discussed below (n. 26), the Midrash HaGadol seems to have been influenced by Maimonides. In the ב MS, either the word מכל was accidentally dropped, so that we may take משפחות as "families," or there is some sort of influence here from the version of this passage in *bQidd.* 16b (to be discussed below), and משפחות means "of the female slaves."

male Canaanite had intercourse with a female of one of the nations and sired a son, you would be allowed to buy him as a slave? Scripture thus states: *that they sired in your land* —from those who are born in your land, but not from those who live in your land.

Again, however, the last statement is equivocal. Rashi (*bYev.* 78b *s.v.* מן הנולדים בארצכם) rationalizes the rule by postulating that it is always the female who remains in her own land:

...דרך אשה להיות במקומה ודרך איש לגלות הלכך הנולדים בארץ ודאי אמו משבעה אומות אבל הנולדים במקום אחר ודאי אמו משאר אומות...

The woman's way is to stay in her place, and the man's way is to leave. Thus, for those born in the land, their mother is certainly from one of the seven [banned nations], but for those born elsewhere, their mother is certainly from one of the other nations...

In other words, if a *toshav* and a female Canaanite have a child, this is assumed to take place in Israel; the offspring would thus be included within the words ממשפחתם אשר עמכם (from their families who are with them) and would therefore also be a *toshav*. Conversely, if a male Canaanite has a child with a female of one of the other nations, it is assumed that the birth would take place outside Israel, wherever the mother is, and thus the offspring would not be אשר הולידו בארצכם (that they sired in your land). This "proves" that "nationality" is inherited through the father.

A version which on the surface appears similar to the text in *bYev.* 78b is found in *bSotah* 3b. The context is a discussion of biblical hermeneutics between the schools of R. Ishmael and R. Akiva:

דתנא דבי רבי ישמעאל כל פרשה שנאמרה ונישנית לא נישנית אלא בשביל דבר שנתחדש בה לעולם בהם תעבדו רשות דברי ר' ישמעאל ר"ע אומר חובה מאי טעמא דרבי ישמעאל איידי כתיב לא תחיה כל נשמה איצטריך נמי לכתיב לעולם בהם תעבדו *למשרי אחד מכל האומות שבא על הכנענית והוליד ממנה בן שאתה רשאי לקנותו * דתניא ** מנין לאחד מן האומות שבא על הכנענית והוליד ממנה בן שאתה רשאי לקנותו בעבד ת"ל וגם מבני התושבים הגרים עמכם מהם תקנו יכול אף הכנעני שבא על אחת מן האומות והוליד ממנה בן שאתה רשאי לקנותו בעבד ת"ל אשר הולידו בארצכם מן הנולדים בארצכם ולא מן הגרים בארצכם **

(* and ** added to text, to be discussed below)

> As it was taught from the school of R. Ishmael: If a passage is repeated, this is because the repetition has something novel. *You may work them forever* [Lev. 25:46]—[This is] a permission, in the words of R. Ishmael. R. Akiva says: It is an obligation. What is the reason of R. Ishmael? Since it is written [Deut. 29:7]: *Do not allow any soul to live*, it was necessary also to write *you may work them forever*, to permit [the following]: A member of one of the nations who has intercourse with a female Canaanite and sires a son, you are allowed to purchase him, as it was taught: How do we know that if a member of one of the nations has intercourse with a female Canaanite and sires a son, you are permitted to buy him as a slave? Scripture states: *and also from the sons of the toshavim who reside with you, from them you may buy*. Is it also possible that if a Canaanite who had intercourse with a female of one of the nations sired a son, you are permitted to buy him as a slave? Scripture states: *whom they sired in your land*—from those who were born in your land, and not from those who reside in your land.

R. Ishmael interprets the words in Lev. 25:46 as permissive: their purpose is to show that, despite the broad wording of Deut. 20:16, one is permitted to take Canaanites as slaves. If, however, we examine the words marked * in the text, it is clear that the talmudic editor assumed that the issue of a female Canaanite and a male non-Canaanite was a Canaanite (and thus the necessity for the phrase in Lev. 25:46). Thus the supporting baraita seems to have been interpreted in a manner completely contrary to that in *bYev.*—it is the mother who determines nationality, and the child of a Canaanite mother may be enslaved. It would then follow that in the second element of the baraita the child of a non-Canaanite mother would be excluded from slavery, and it is not clear why this would be so. We may propose, therefore, that either the talmudic editor misunderstood the baraita, or that it was susceptible to several interpretations.

A further permutation of this baraita appears in *bQidd.* 16b. Again there is the statement of R. Yoḥanan that nationality is inherited through the father. In this version, however, the second element of the baraita raises a further complexity: it deals not simply with people of two nationalities, but with slaves of two nationalities:

> כי אתא רבי אמר רבי יוחנן באומות הלך אחר הזכר נתגיירו הלך אחר הפגום שבשניהם מאי באומות הלך אחר הזכר כדתניא מנין לאחד מן האומות שבא על הכנענית והוליד בן שאתה רשאי לקנותו בעבד ת"ל וגם מבני התושבים הגרים עמכם מהם תקנו יכול אף עבד שבא

על שפחה מן האומות והוליד בן שאתה רשאי לקנותו בעבד ת"ל אשר הולידו בארצכם מן הנולדים בארצכם ולא מן הגרים בארצכם

When Rabbi came, R. Yoḥanan said: [With respect to] nations, it [inheritance of status] followed the male. If they converted, it followed the [parent] with any taint [in status]. What is the meaning of 'nations followed the male'? As it was taught: From where do we know that if a member of one of the nations had intercourse with a female Canaanite and sired a son, you are allowed to buy him as a slave? Scripture states: *And also from the sons of the toshavim who reside with you, from them you may buy*. Is it possible that if a male slave had intercourse with a female slave from one of the nations and sired a son, you would be allowed to buy him as a slave? Scripture states: *that they sired in your land* — from those who are born in your land, but not from those who live in your land.

Rashi noted the difference and attempted to explain why the child of slaves would not be enslavable: they are *garim* (those who reside) but not *noladim* (born) (*bQidd.* 16b, *s.v.* מן הגרים בארצכם):

שהולידו בני ארצכם במקומות אחרים מבנות שאר אומות ובאו הבנים לגור כאן אצל אבותם ובתורת כהנים גרסינן ולא מן הכנענים שבארצכם כלומר שנולדו מן הכנענים

[Sons] that natives of your land sired in other places by women from the other nations, and the sons came here to live with their fathers; and in Sifra we read 'and not from the male Canaanites' in your land, which is to say, who were born of the Canaanites.

Finally, we may note that Maimonides extended the slave-nationality issue to the first element of the baraita as well (*Hil. Avadim* 9:3):[26]

אחד מן האומות שבא על שפחה כנענית שלנו הרי הבן עבד כנעני שנאמר 'אשר הולידו בארצכם' אבל העבד שלנו שבא על אחת מן האומות אין הבן עבד שנאמר 'אשר הולידו בארצכם' ועבד אין לו יחס

A member of one of the nations who has intercourse with our female Canaanite slave, the son is a Canaanite slave, as it is said: *that they sired in your land*. But if our male slave has intercourse with a female of one of the nations – the son is not a slave, as it is said: *that they sired in your land*, and a slave has no kinship.

---

26 Midrash HaGadol **מ** has obviously been influenced by Maimonides (see n. 25 above).

5.3.3 Conclusion

In a case in which a question of the nationality of a potential slave arose (specifically, whether the individual would be considered a member of the seven banned nations), we find evidence that nationality was considered to be inherited through the father. Attempts to reconcile this principle with the idea of a matrilineal inheritance of slavery led to a variety of results, which seem to depend on whether the nationality principle or the slavery principle was given precedence.

5.4 *TOSEFTA QIDDUSHIN* 5:11: "SYMMETRICAL" INHERITANCE OF MAMZERUT?

As noted, in the mishnaic rule of *mYev.* 7:5 it is only the child of a free female and slave male who would be treated as a *mamzer*. There is some hint, however, that in the complex working out of the principles of genealogy, *mamzerut* was the fate of any issue that resulted from impaired *qiddushin*. Of particular interest is a baraita attributed to R. Meir (which we may term the "five nations" baraita), found in *tQidd.* 5:11, *y. Qidd.* 3:13 64d, and *bYev.* 99a. It concerns a working out of the inheritance of status among various "peoples" (*umot*): slaves, gentiles, converts, freedmen, *mamzerim*, and Israelites. The versions in each source differ; of special interest is the fact that the Tosefta version suggests that offspring of any slave-free Israelite relationship, and not just the child of a slave male and free Israelite female, would have been a *mamzer*.[27]

tQidd. 5:11 (Lieberman p. 297)

1. היה ר' מאיר אומ' יש איש ואשה שמולידין חמש אומות כיצד

2. גוי שיש לו עבד ושפחה ולהם שני בנים נתגייר אחד מהן הרי אחד גר ואחד גוי

3. נתגייר רבן וגיירן לעבדים והולידו בן והולד עבד

27 For reasons of brevity, only the relevant sections of the baraita have been quoted. There are numerous variations in the sources, but these do not directly affect the argument.

4. (נשתחרר אחד מהן הרי אחד והולידו בן הולד ממזר)
נשתחררה שפחה ובא אליה אותו עבד והולידו בן הולד משוחרר

5. נשתחררו שניהם והולידו בן הולד עבד משוחרר

yQidd. 3:13 64d

1. תני משום ר' מאיר יש איש ואשה שמולידין חמש אומות כיצד

2. מי שיש לו עבד ושפחה והולידו בנים הרי גוים נתגייר אחד מהן הרי אחד גר ואחד גוי

3. נתגייר רבו וגיירו לשני עבדים והולידו בנים הרי אילו עבדים
אמר ר' זעירא הדא אמרא גוי שבא על שפחה והוליד בן הוולד עבד

4. שיחרר שפחה והולידה הוולד ממזר

5. ואחר כך שיחרר העבד והוליד בן הרי זה בן עבד משוחרר

bYev. 99a

1. תניא היה ר"מ אומר איש ואשה פעמים שמולידין חמש אומות כיצד

2. ישראל שלקח עבד ושפחה מן השוק ולהן שני בנים ונתגייר אחד מהן נמצא אחד גר ואחד עובד כוכבים

3. הטבילן לשם עבדות ונזקקו זה לזה הרי כאן גר ועובד כוכבים ועבד

4. שחרר את השפחה ובא עליה העבד הרי כאן גר ועובד כוכבים ועבד וממזר

5. שחרר שניהם והשיאן זה לזה הרי כאן גר ועובד כוכבים ועבד וממזר וישראל
מאי קמ"ל עובד כוכבים ועבד הבא על בת ישראל הולד ממזר

Translations
tQidd. 5:11

1. R. Meir used to say: One man and one woman [can] sire five nations [*umot*]. How?

2. A gentile who has a male and female slave, and they produce two sons,

[and] one of them [i.e., the sons] converted, the result is that one [son] is a convert [*ger*] and one a gentile.

3. [If] their master converted, and they [i.e., the parents] converted to slaves [that is, until they became the slaves of Jews, they were simply gentiles], and they sired [another] son, the child is a slave.

4. [a] [If] one of them [the male or female] was freed, that is one, and they sired [another] son, the child is a *mamzer*.

[b] [If] the female slave was freed, and the same male slave had intercourse with her, and they sired a son, the child is a freedman [*meshuḥrar*].

5. [If] both [the male and female slave] were freed and sired a son, the child is a freedman.

yQidd. 3:13 (64d)

1. It was taught in the name of R. Meir: One man and one woman [can] sire five nations [*umot*]. How?

2. [If] one has a male and female slave, and they produce sons, these are gentiles. If one converted, one is a convert and one is a gentile.

3. His master converted and caused the two slaves to convert, and they produced sons: these are slaves.

R. Zeira said: This means that if a gentile has intercourse with a female slave and sires a son, the child is a slave.

4. [If] he freed the female slave and she gave birth, the child is a *mamzer*.

5. And [if] he then freed the male slave and he sired a son, this is the son of a freedman.

bYev. 99a

1. It was taught: R. Meir used to say: One man and one woman [can] sometimes sire five nations [*umot*]. How?

2. An Israelite who bought a male and female slave from the market, who had two sons, and one converted, there results one who is a convert and one who is a gentile.

3. [If] he caused them to be immersed as slaves [i.e., to take the first step of conversion], and they were put together [and another child resulted], there is now a convert and a gentile and a slave.

4. [If] he freed the slave woman and the male slave had intercourse with her [and another child resulted], there is now a convert and a gentile and a slave and a *mamzer*.

5. [If] he freed both and caused them to marry [and another child resulted], there is now a convert and a gentile and a slave and a *mamzer* and an Israelite.

What does this teach? A gentile and a male slave who have intercourse with an Israelite women—the child is a *mamzer*.

For our purposes we may concentrate on element number 4, dealing in each case with the offspring of a slave partner and a freed partner. In the Tosefta version, parts 4[a] and 4[b] seem to be two inconsistent versions of the rule in such a case. Part [a], though grammatically difficult, suggests that the child would be a *mamzer* regardless of which parent was free and which remained a slave. Part [b] deals only with the case in which the female had been freed; inconsistent with part [a] (and with the Mishnah), the child here is a "freedman." Part [a] which is marked in parentheses in the text is missing in the Erfurt Tosefta MS. It is also missing in the versions of this baraita in the Talmudim; the latter directly reflect the mishnaic rule that the offspring of a free woman and slave man is a *mamzer*:

Can the Tosefta version in [a] be relied upon as evidence of an extant rule that the offspring of any slave-free relationship was a *mamzer*? In his toseftan commentary, Lieberman considered this version to be corrupt;[28] section (a) is missing in the Ehrfurt MS and this is a doubled section so he considers the correct reading to be section (b) only, but with והולד ממזר instead of הולד משוחרר in line with the Bavli and Yerushalmi:

28 Lieberman, *Tosefta kipeshutah tQidd.*, loc. cit., 980-81.

> [If] the slave woman were freed and a slave had intercourse with her and she birthed [their] child, the child is a *mamzer*.

Yet its very difficulty may argue in favor of its originality (as the *lectio difficilior*). We may further argue that it is the Talmudim that have summarized as well as edited an earlier version; evidence of this procedure is seen, for instance, in the summary in *bYev.* and the amoraic comments.[29]

Finally, we may note that both Josephus and Philo seem familiar with a rule that the offspring of a slave female would also normally have been considered simply "illegitimate" or base-born (Greek *νόθος*), rather than specifically a slave. Josephus, for instance, describes Avimelekh, the *ben amah* of Judg. 9:18, as a *νόθος* (*Ant.* 5:233), as opposed to the son of an *οἰκέτις*, or similar phrase. Philo similarly discusses the children of the *amahot/shefaḥot* Bilhah and Zilpah:

> The base-born sons (*νόθοι*) of the handmaids [Bilhah and Zilpah] received the same treatment as the legitimate, not only from the father... since his paternity extends to all alike, but also from the stepmothers.[30]

---

29 There is a puzzling comment by the Karaite commentator *Yaqub al-Qirqisani* on this "five nations" baraita, translated as follows (B. Chiesa and W. Lockwood, *Ya'Qub al-Qirqisani, Abu Yusuf: On Jewish Sects and Christianity; A Translation of* "Kitab al-anwar," [Judentum and Umwelt 10; Frankfurt: Peter Lang, 1984] 1:119) :

> They [Rabbanites] maintain that if a man's wife gave birth to a child by a non-Jew [גוי] or a Jewish slave, the child is legitimate [כשר], provided that the woman had been the victim of force or deceit. They regard a Jewish slave as being on the same footing as a non-Jew, who comes under the Commandments and deserves: "To be put to death together with the adulteress" <Lev. 20, 10>, and whose status is the same as that of a citizen [אזרח]. They say that R. Meir, speaking of the "five peoples," said that if a non-Jew and a slave, have intercourse with a Jewish woman and the woman bear a child, that child is a bastard [ממזר]. Those who came after them said: "The *halakhah* is in accordance with R. Meir," while those who preceded them said: "The words of the scribes need confirmation from the Torah, but the words of the Torah do not need confirmation." This is like the saying of Scripture: "Let them bring their witness, that they may be justified" <Isa. 43, 9>. Of course, this also renders void the claim of those who assert that their teachings have been transmitted from the prophets.

The version of the rule cited here follows that found in the Talmudim. The precise nature of his criticism of Rabbanite law is unclear; he seems, however, to suggest that there are other rules with respect to the inheritance of slave status besides the one he has quoted.

30 Philo, *On the Virtues* (tr. F.H. Colson), 224. S. Cohen notes (*The Beginnings of Jewishness*

5.5 VARIABILITY IN GENEALOGICAL THINKING

This chapter has reviewed certain tannaitic traditions that relate to the issue of the inheritance of slave status. It has been argued that two of the cases reviewed reflect rabbinic attempts to reconcile a matrilineal inheritance of slavery with biblical provisions. The considerable variation shown in these attempts is taken as an indication that the implications of matrilineal inheritance of slavery were neither commonly agreed upon among postbiblical sages, nor based on long-held traditions. It was proposed that the rule of "signs" for the Hebrew *amah*, which has no direct biblical precedent, was devised as a necessary adjunct to the matrilineal inheritance of slavery, so as to prevent a "native"-born slave class; it was further proposed that the "signs" rule as it stands in the Mishnah reflects a debate, the elements of which are in turn reflected in various midreshei halakhah and baraitot, as to how "signs" were to be reconciled with the biblical manumission provisions in Exodus and Deuteronomy with respect to the *amah*. It has also been argued that with respect to the question of slaves from the biblically banned seven nations, there is evidence in rabbinic sources of a patrilineal determination of the "nationality" of potential slaves, and in turn a variety of attempts to reconcile this rule with matrilineal inheritance of slavery.

It was also argued that there is evidence of a tannaitic opinion, in one version of *tQidd.* 5:11, that the offspring of any slave-free union would have *mamzer* status, contrary to the mishnaic rule that *mamzer* status would apply only to the offspring of a slave father and Israelite mother.

271-72) that Philo also uses *νόθος* to describe the offspring of Jewish-gentile marriages, regardless of whether the male or the female was the gentile, and thus argues that Philo was not familiar with a rule of matriliny regarding either gentiles or slaves.

CHAPTER 6

RABBINIC INTERPRETATIONS OF LEVITICUS 19:20-22

6.1 THE SIGNIFICANCE OF PARALLEL BARAITOT

In tannaitic sources Lev. 19:20 serves as the basis of a rule regarding "sex right" to the *shifḥah neḥerefet*. That is, the status of the *shifḥah* of Lev. 19:20 is constructed in these sources, through a comparison of the legal effect of the sexual offence in Lev. 19:20 with the legal effects of other prohibited sexual liaisons. This comparison is found, with considerable variation, in *mKer.* 2:4b-6, *tKer.* 1:16-18, Sifra *Qedoshim pereq* 5, a baraita in *yQidd.* 1:1 59a and a baraita in *bKer.* 11a. Given the difficulties in the text of Lev. 19:20, some of which were examined above, such variation in the sources is not surprising. I propose, however, that such differences indicate significant variations in opinion regarding the status of the *shifḥah neḥerefet* and the matter of slave-free intermarriage. The net result is the creation of a new sort of offence with a female slave woman, one akin in some respect to the incest prohibitions, but so unclear as to its protagonists and punishments as to make it virtually unworkable in practice.

The nature of the relationship implied by the biblical term *neḥerefet* is taken in two of the sources to mean either marriage (Tosefta) or betrothal (Sifra) between a slave woman (or a woman who is "half-slave, half-free") and a free man. The Mishnah, in contrast, avoids mentioning the relationship at all, and this attitude is also reflected in the two Talmudim. The question then arises: can this difference be accounted for as simply the result of scribal error or oral transmission, or does it require a more substantive explanation, such as a difference in opinion? To state the issue from another perspective: Does the Tosefta passage simply comment on the associated Mishnah passage, or does it reflect a distinct viewpoint?

Similarly, does the Sifra passage merely reflect the midrashic derivation of the Mishnah rules, or does it too reflect a different opinion?

These questions are of interest, not merely with respect to the development of ideas concerning slave-free intermarriage, but also with respect to the issue of parallels among the various tannaitic sources. Neusner, for instance, in commenting on such parallels, has argued that versions of a shared item in different sources show only alternate wordings of a single text, not a history of ideas.[1] I shall argue in contrast that the parallel passages on the *shifḥah neḥerefet* do reflect differences in ideas concerning slavery. I shall argue further that the Tosefta version of the parallel was likely the original (or "more" original). This conclusion, while contrary to the conventional assumption that Tosefta is later than, and comments upon, Mishnah, is in accord with recent observations that suggest a priority for Tosefta in certain cases.[2] Finally we may question the existence of a "half-slave, half – free" status as one of the proposed meanings of *neḥerefet;* does this represent a real status or is it merely a convenient contruct?

To address these questions, I shall first set out the relevant passages in Mishnah and Tosefta, noting briefly significant textual variations in the sources. I shall then discuss in detail the Sifra passage, especially its numerous variants with respect to the crucial issue of intermarriage between slave and free, as this source contains the most extensive discussion of the law of the *shifḥah neḥerefet.* I shall then propose an explanation of the relationship among these passages and those in the two Talmudim. Finally, I shall propose various ideas concerning the meaning of "half-slave, half-free."

6.2 *MISHNAH KEREITOT* 2:4B-6

The base text is taken from MS Parma deRossi 138 (פ).[3] Comparisons were made to MSS Kaufmann A50 (ק), Lowe (Cambridge Add. 470.1) (ל),

1 Jacob Neusner, "The Synoptic Problem in Rabbinic Literature: The Cases of the Mishna, Tosepta, Sipra and *Leviticus Rabba*," *JBL* 105 (1986) 506.

2 See, e.g. Harry Fox, "Introducing Tosefta: Textual, Intratextual and Intertextual Studies" 28; Shamma Friedman, "The Primacy of Tosefta to Mishnah in Synoptic Parallels," in *Introducing Tosefta*, 100.

3 MS Kaufmann A50 (ק) has some errors and several corrections making it easier to use MS Parma as the base text.

Maimonides (**ר**), Munich 95 (**מ**), London British Museum Add. 25, 717 (**L**), Vatican Ebr. 120 (**V120**), Vatican Ebr. 119 (**ו**), Firenze Nationale Central Biblioteca II.1.7 (**F**) and the following geniza fragments: Cambridge TSE II 88 (**ג**), TS NS 329.270 and TS F II (2) 60. No relevant material was found in the latter two witnesses. After the quotation of the text according to MS Parma with some minor corrections, significant variants will be noted but not abbreviations, obvious errors or minor changes in orthography. An asterisk * indicates that all manuscripts except those indicated have the reading in the lemma. When a significant variant has changes in orthography or an error but still attests to a particular reading, the word and the relevant MS will be underlined.

1. ומה בין שפחה לשאר כל העריות

2. שלא שווה להם לא בעונש ולא בקרבן

3. שכל העריות בחטאת והשפחה באשם

4. כל העריות אחד האיש ואחד האישה שווים במכות ובקרבן

5. ובשפחה לא הישווה את האיש לאשה במכות

6. ולא את האשה לאיש בקרבן

7. כל העריות עשה בהן את המערה כגומר וחייב על כל ביאה וביאה

8. החמיר בשפחה שעשה בה את המזיד כשוגג

9. אי זו היא שפחה

10. כל שחציה שפחה וחציה בת חורין

11. שנ' והפדה לא נפדתה כדברי ר' עקיבה

12. ר' ישמעאל אומר זו היא שפחה וודיי

13. ר' לעזר בן עזריה או' כל העריות המפורשות משייור אין לנו אלא שחציה שפחה וחציה בת חורים

14. כל העריות אחד גדול ואחד קטן הקטן פטור

15. אחד ער ואחד ישן הישן פטור

16. אחד שוגג ואחד מזיד השוגג בחטאת והמזיד בהיכרת

1. לשאר כל] = **פ**   לבין כל = **קלג**   לכל = **רו** F   לבין = **מ** V^{120} L

3. באשם] = **פקלר**   באשם כאחד = **ג**   באשם כל העריות בנקבה ושפחה בזכר
= **מ** V^{120} F L   באשם כל העריות בחטאת בנקיבה ושפחה בזכר = **ו**

5. הישווה] = *   הושווה = **ק**   את] = **פקלגמ** L V^{120} חסר = **רו**   לא = F

7. וביאה] = *
ובשפחה לא עשה בה את המערה כגמור ודינו חייב על כל ביאה וביאה = L V^{120}

12. וודיי] = **פק**   ודאי = **גמ** V^{120} ודאית = **לרו** F

13. משייור] = **פקל**   ומשיור = **ג**   ושיור = **ר**   שיור = F
משוייר = L V^{120} **מ**   חסר = **ו**

Translation

1. What is the difference between [the] *shifḥah* and [the] rest of the forbidden relationships?

2. That they are not treated equally with respect to punishment or sacrifice;

3. that all the [other] forbidden relationships require a *ḥattat* sacrifice, and the [offence with the] *shifḥah* [requires] an *asham* sacrifice.

4. [With] all the [other] forbidden relationships the man and the woman are equal with respect to lashes and sacrifice,

5. with respect to the *shifḥah* the man is not made equal to the woman with respect to lashes,

6. and the woman is not made equal to the man with respect to sacrifice.

7. [With] all the [other] forbidden relationships the one who is [merely] aroused is like the one who consummates intercourse, and is liable for each act of intercourse,

8. it is stricter with respect to the *shifḥah*, as with respect to her the one who acts intentionally is like the one who acts inadvertently.

9. Who is a *shifḥah* [in this case]?

10. Anyone who is half-slave, half-free,

11. as it is said *redeemed she has not been redeemed* [a literal translation of the infinitive absolute form in Lev. 19:20] – according to the words of R. Akiva [who interprets each element of the infinitive absolute form separately].

12. R. Ishmael says: This is a certain/definite *shifḥah*.

13. R. Lazar ben Azaria says: All the forbidden relationships [are] stated explicitly; there is none remaining except [that regarding] the woman who is half-slave, half-free.

14. [With] all the [other] forbidden relationships, if one is an adult and one a minor, the minor is exempt [from punishment];

15. if one is awake and one asleep, the one asleep is exempt;

16. If one acts intentionally and the other inadvertently, the one who acted inadvertently [is liable for] a *ḥattat* sacrifice, and the one acting intentionally [is liable to] excision.

A number of comments may be made on the variants illustrated. In line 1, Mishnah codices MSS – **קל** and BT geniza fragment **ג** seem to have the correct reading because each word serves as the basis of the variants in Maimonides and in the BT MSS while the reading in **פ** seems to be an error.

The MSS of BT have an addition to the Mishnah in line 3. This addition is also found in the printed edition of Mishnah in *bKer.* 10b but is erased by R. Shmuel Kaidenover (Rashaq). This phrase does appear in *tKer.* 1:16 and in Sifra *Qedoshim pereq* 5:10. Another addition less thoroughly attested in the BT MSS is at the end of line 7 which seems to be an attempt to fill in the parallel situation concerning the slave woman which is absent in the Mishnah.

The original reading in line 12 is according to codex MSS **פ ק ל** (with some orthographic differences) and this is supported by fragment **ג** with the addition of וי"ו and by **ר** with the same addition but without the initial מ"מ and by BT MS **F** without any prefix. It is possible that the initial מ"מ vocalized with a *hiriq* may have been a contraction of the question "who" (מי) with the meaning "who is left/who is remaining" which would be appropriate for the continuation which answers the question. The reading in the printed edition is ומה שיור which is translated "and what remains" but we have no evidence in the manuscripts for a separate word מה. The majority of the BT MSS have a verb form, a *pu'al* participle, instead of the noun. The other possibility to explain the מ"ם is the addition of a phoneme to imitate nearby words such as מפורשות. In any case the question is clear.

The precise intention of the term וודיי (line 13) is not clear, either in its form in MSS **ק פ** and **ג מ** with a different spelling, or the declined form ודאיית in MSS **ר ל̲ F ו** V^{120}. If it is intended as the opposite of ספק[4] it may simply reflect an opposition to R. Akiva's identification of the *shifḥah* as חציה שפחה חציה בת חורין. There is also the possibility, as will be discussed in a comparison of this section to its parallels in other sources, that the term refers to a "Canaanite" slave. MS **ק** adds the interrogative particle אי to the start of the clause זו היא שפחה in line 12 creating a question. This reading is an error because the structure calls for a statement rather than a question.

The only other place with great variation is the gender and the spelling of the word ודיי. It is either an abstract noun in the masculine meaning "something which is clear and certain" or an adjective describing שפחה in which case it should be in the feminine. Since the best manuscripts have mixed readings it is difficult to decide which is original.

6.3 *TOSEFTA KEREITOT* 1:16-18

The base text is from the Zuckermandel edition (p. 562) which he based on MS Erfurt (**ע**), with line numbers added for convenience though not according to Zuckermandel's line numbers. The variants underlined in lines 13 and 20 and the homeoteleuton in line 17 filled in with brackets are taken from Vienna MS Cod. Hebr. 20 (**ב**). The remaining changes between Zuckermandel's edition from the Erfurt MS and the Vienna MS are minor, chiefly differences in orthography, definite article and abbreviation.

1. אלו דברים שבין שפחה חרופה לכל עריות

4 Kadari, 1:96 Syntax and Semantics [Hebrew]. Kadari confirms that וודיי as an appositive can appear either declined or not, even with respect to the same noun; there appears to be no semantic significance in the difference. He also cites instances in which it is used as a subject paired with the term ספק (e.g. *mQidd.* 4:3).

2. כל עריות שבתורה הרי אלו חייבין על זדונן כרת ועל שגגתן חטאת ועל לא הודע אשם תלוי

3. מה שאין כן בשפחה חרופה

4. כל עריות שבתורה עושה אונס כרצון שאין מתכוין כמתכוין מערה כגומר ישינה כעירה כדרכה ושלא כדרכה חייבת על כל ביאה וביאה

5. מה שאין כן בשפחה חרופה

6. כל עריות עשה קטן כגדול לחייב על הגדול

7. ובשפחה אם היה קטן הרי אלו פטורין

8. כל עריות שניהן לוקין ובשפחה היא לוקה והוא אינו לוקה

9. כל עריות שניהם מביאין קרבן ובשפחה הוא מביא והיא אינה מביאה

10. כל עריות בחטאת בשפחה באשם

11. כל עריות בנקבה ושפחה בזכר

12. כל עריות חייב על כל ביאה וביאה בשפחה אחת על ביאות הרבה

13. כל עריות שבתורה בית דין חייב על הוראתן מה שאין <u>כן</u> בשפחה חרופה

14. כל עריות כהן משיח שהורה ועשה חייב ובשפחה עשה אף על פי שלא הורה מביא אשם ודאי

15. ר' ישמעאל אומר בשפחה כנענית הכתוב מדבר נשואה לעבד כנעני

16. אחרים אומרים משמו זו נשואה לבן חורין

17. ר' עקיבא אומר מן התורה חצייה שפחה וחצייה בת חורין [ר' אלעזר בן עזריה אומ' מן התורה חצייה שפחה חצייה בת חורין] [5] נשואה לבן חורין

[5] Lieberman, (תוספת ראשונים: פירוש מיוסד על כתבי יד התוספתא וספרי ראשונים ומדרשים בכתבי יד ודפוסים ישנים, ניו יורק וירושלים: בית המדרש לרבנים באמריקה, תשנ"ט, 594) was surprised that Zuckermandel had not corrected MS Erfurt here but placed it in the apparatus. Lieberman held that the text in brackets is the original reading and that it was dropped by a scribal error in the Erfurt MS on which Zuckermandel's edition is based. This homeoteleuton is due to the repetition of the phrase בת חורין. The reading בן in line 13 is a graphic error.

18. הבא על אחת מכל עריות האמורות בתורה הוא בהעלם אחד והיא בחמשה העלמות הוא מביא חטאת אחת והיא מביאה חמש חטאות היא בהעלם אחת והוא בחמשה העלמות היא מביאה חטאת אחת והוא מביא חמש חטאות

19. כל עריות אחד גדול ואחד קטון הקטן פטור

20. אחד נעור ואחד ישן הישן פטור

21. אחד שוגג ואחד מזיד השוגג בחטאת והמזיד בהכרת

Variants

13. כן] = **ב** בן = **ע**

17. ר' אלעזר בן עזריה אומ' מן התורה חצייה שפחה חצייה בת חורין] = **ב** ∩ = **ע**.

20. נעור] = **ב** נוער = **ע**

Translation

1. These are the [different] matters between the *shifḥah ḥarufah* and the forbidden relationships:

2. All those [who transgress] the forbidden relationships in the Torah if they act intentionally are liable to excision, if they act in error for a *ḥattat* sacrifice, and if they were not aware [that they transgressed] for a conditional *asham* sacrifice,

3. which is not the case for the *shifḥah ḥarufah*.

4. [With respect to] all the forbidden relationships in the Torah, [it is the same for the woman whether] the male forces [her] or there is acquiescence, whether the male acts with intention or not, whether the male is merely aroused or consummates intercourse, whether she is awake or asleep, whether the intercourse is "normal" or "abnormal," and she is liable for each act of intercourse,

5. which is not the case for the *shifḥah ḥarufah*.

6. [With respect to] all the forbidden relationships the minor is treated like the adult, to render the adult liable,

7. but with respect to the *shifḥah*, if the male is a minor, both are exempt.

8. [With respect to] all the forbidden relationships both receive lashes, but with respect to the *shifḥah*, she receives lashes but the male does not.

9. [With respect to] all the forbidden relationships both bring a sacrifice, but with respect to the *shifḥah*, the male brings a sacrifice but she does not.

10. [With respect to] all the forbidden relationships [the sacrifice is] a *ḥattat*, with the *shifḥah* it is an *asham*.

11. [With respect to] all the forbidden relationships [the sacrifice is] a female [she-goat], with the *shifḥah* it is a male [ram].

12. [With respect to] all the forbidden relationships [the male] is liable for each [separate] act of intercourse, with the *shifḥah* [he is liable one *ḥattat*] for [any] number of acts [with the same *shifḥah*].

13. [With respect to] all the forbidden relationships in the Torah a Beit Din is liable for [an incorrect] decision, which is not the case for the *shifḥah ḥarufah*.

14. [With respect to] all the forbidden relationships, an Annointed [=High] Priest who made [an incorrect] decision and acted on it is liable, but with respect to the *shifḥah* if he acted even without making [an incorrect] decision he is liable for an *asham vadai*.

15. R. Ishmael says: Scripture is speaking of a Canaanite *shifḥah* married to a Canaanite *eved;*

16. Others say in his name: This one [who] is married to a free man.

17. R. Akiva says: From [the words of] the Torah she is half-slave half-free. [R. Elazar ben Azaria says: She is half-slave half-free] married to a free man.

18. One who engages in any act of intercourse forbidden by the Torah – [if] he is in a state of unawareness [as to the fact that the act is prohibited] once, and she five times, he brings one *ḥattat* sacrifice and she brings five *ḥattat* sacrifices; [if] she is in a state of unawareness once and he five times, she brings one *ḥattat* sacrifice and he brings five *ḥattat* sacrifices.

19. [With respect to] all the forbidden relationships, if one is an adult and one a minor, the minor is exempt;

20. if one is awake and the other asleep, the one asleep is exempt;

21. if one acts inadvertently and one intentionally, the one who acts inadvertently [is liable for] a *ḥattat*, the one acting intentionally [is liable to] excision.

6.4 *SIFRA QEDOSHIM PEREQ* 5

6.4.1 Overview of the Text

i. Text Witnesses

The section under consideration is designated in the printed editions as 'קדשים פרק ה פר'ש פר'קי ב) in Assemani 66 (p. 401 in Finklestein's edition), פרק ג in Vatican 31), covering Lev. 19:20-22 (Weiss 89c). Four main text witnesses have been examined and variants from a number of additional MSS used by Finkelstein[6] in the partial apparatus in his introduction to Assemani 66 are also noted where relevant.

Primary
א = Assemani 66
ר= Vatican 31
ב = Breslau (Zuckerman 108)
ד = Venice Edition 1445
ג = Parma De Rossi 139
ה = Oxford Neubauer 151
ל = London (Margaliot 341 Part II)

Secondary
מ = Midrash HaGadol
ח = Midrash Ḥakhamim
ש = Yalkut Shimoni

Tertiary
ר"ה = Rabbenu Hillel
ראב"ד = Rabad

The Sifra citations in Yalqut Shimoni are questionable as they seem to have been taken apart, reassembled and paraphrased. Therefore the variants found in Midrash HaGadol, Midrash Ḥakhamim, and Yalqut Shimoni will be presented in the apparatus in angled brackets < > along with the readings in the commentators ר' הלל ראב"ד, קרבן אהרון, רש"י, הגר"א.[7]

6 Finkelstein, תורת כהנים על פי כתב יד רומי מנוקד: אסמאני מספר 66, ניו יורק: בית המדרש לרבנים באמריקה, תשי"ז, נ-סג. [= *Torat Kohanim*] It should be noted that not all the *sigla* are those used by Finkelstein.

7 Based on Louis Finkelstein, 1989 (ניו יורק: בית המדרש לרבנים באמריקה) ספרא דבי רב [= *Sifra deVei Rav*] 1:119, text witnesses of Sifra can be divided into four geographical groups,

Assemani 66 is taken as the base text for the section; this follows the opinion of Finkelstein, who maintained that Assemani 66 was overall the "best" manuscript.[8] Variants considered relevant to the discussion are listed following each unit but some units have no significant variants as these generally do not include variations in spelling.[9] For ease of reference, the section has been divided into nine sections (A-I), based on subject matter. The biblical citations are italicized in the translation and indicated with quotation marks in the Hebrew, and line numbers have been added. The signs {} indicate that a word is only partially readable.

ii. Structure

The passage shows an unusual combination of styles. In its first part it shows the conventional form of citing a biblical lemma and deriving its interpretation. These consist either of a straightforward *derash* (word X means Y), occasionally with the use of רבוי-מיעוט logic, though with no express formulae, or the use of hermeneutical principles to derive a rule, particularly הקש and גזרה שוה. The end of the passage, however, is in a non-typical form, consisting in effect of a summary of many of the previously derived rules. Unlike the usual midrash form, it contains no citations of the biblical text. It is this part that appears to be parallel to, and perhaps derived from, baraitot or the Mishnah and Tosefta.

---

which all ultimately relate back to one original version (p. 71): Eastern, including Vatican 31, and the versions used by the Midrash Hagadol and the Mishneh Torah; North African, including Assemani 66; Spanish, including the versions used by the ספר מצוות גדול and Rabad, and by Maimonides in his Mishnah commentary; and other Western, including the printed editions, and the versions used by the Yalqut Shimoni and R. Hillel.

8 Finkelstein, *Sifra deVei Rav* 1:18.

9 Such as כתיב מלא versus כתיב חסר, exchanges between ן-ם, and differences in any vocalization and short forms. On the use of a separate apparatus for spelling variants, abbreviations and errors, see Tirzah Meacham, משנת מסכת נידה עם מבוא, מהדורה ביקורתית עם הערות בנוסח, בפרשנות ובעריכה, ופרקים בתולדות ההלכה ובראליה (ירושלים: האוניברסיטה העברית, 1989 [= Meacham, "Mishnat Niddah"] 1:24 Finkelstein has apparently ignored short forms and spelling changes in his apparatus.

6.4.2 Sifra's Interpretation of Lev. 19:20

6.4.2.A The Age of the Parties

1. "איש" פרט לקטן

2. או יכול שני מוציא בן תשע שנים ויום אחד תל לו "ואיש"

3. "כי[10] ישכב את אשה" פרט לקטנה

1. *Man* – except a minor.

2. Or perhaps I exclude a boy of nine years and a day? It is thus stated *And a man* [thus one includes any male of at least nine years].

3. *Who lies with a woman* – except a minor female.

This section seems to be restricting the application of the transgression to those who are physically mature. The age of nine years plus a day as the boundary of sexual capability for the male is found elsewhere in Sifra with regard to sexual transgressions, using a similar structure as in this case: the setting up of a possible exclusion of a male of nine-twelve years (i.e. one who is sexually capable but legally not responsible) from a general rule with the words יכול ש[א]ני מוציא and then the rejection of this exclusion based on some type of inclusion – רבוי often based on the letter *vav*, as in this case.[11] This is found, for instance, in Sifra *Metzora pereq* 7:1 (Weiss 78c) with respect to the בועל נדה – *bo'el niddah* (one who has intercourse with a menstruant) based on the words ואם שכב ישכב in Lev. 15:24 using the doubling of the verb; and in Sifra *Metzora pereq* 6:1 (Weiss 77d) with respect to the זב – *zav* (a male with an abnormal genital discharge) based on the *vav* in the word ואיש in Lev. 15:16. A law in mNid. 5:5 similarly differentiates between sexual capability and legal responsibility:[12]

בן תשע שנים ויום אחד...ואם בא על אחת מכל העריות האמורות בתורה,
מיתות על ידיו, והוא פטור

10 Assamani 66 misquotes the verse which begins with כי instead of אשר. Vatican 31 has the correct version and that is what appears as the text quoted above.

11 Midrash HaGadol (MS מ) seems to base the inclusion on the words כי ישכב, perhaps making the logical assumption that איש is to include any male deemed capable of שכיבה.

12 The Mishnah texts here and below from Tractate Niddah are quoted from Tirzah Meacham, "Mishnat Niddah" 2:53

A boy of nine years plus a day ... if he engages in one of the sexual relationships prohibited in the Torah, [the women in this case] are put to death on his account, and he is exempt.

With respect to the female, we may assume that the boundary of sexual capability is set at three years plus a day as it is elsewhere in Sifra with respect to sexual offences. For instance, Sifra *Metzora pereq* 6:7 (Weiss 78a) uses רבוי to specifically include a girl of three years plus a day with respect to the offence of engaging in one of the sexually prohibited relationships, based on the word ואשה in Lev. 15:18. Again, there is a similar rule in mNid. 5:4:[13]

בת שלש שנים ויום אחד... בא עליה אחד מכל העריות בתורה,
מתים על ידיה, והיא פטורה. פחות מיכן - כנותן אצבע בעין

A girl of three years plus a day ... if one has intercourse with her in one of the sexual relationships prohibited in the Torah, [the men in this case] are put to death on her account, and she is exempt. If she is younger than this, it is like a finger in the eye [i.e. there is deemed to have been no sexual intercourse].

Thus both Sifra and the Mishnah exclude the minors, קטן and קטנה, from liability for punishment in their respective rules. While the Mishnah, however, explicitly states that the other party is still liable, this is not explicit in the case at hand in Sifra. A controversy is apparent on this issue among certain *Rishonim* (Medieval commentators). Maimonides (*Hil. Issurei Biyah* 3:17) held that both parties in such a case were liable to their respective punishments:

בן תשע שנים ויום אחד שבא על שפחה חרופה היא לוקה והוא מביא קרבן

A boy of nine years and a day who has intercourse with a *shifḥah ḥarufah* – she is whipped and he brings a sacrifice.

The anti-Maimonidean commentator Rabad, R. Avraham ben David, (12th century, Provence), in contrast, held that neither party in a Lev. 19:20 transgression was liable to punishment if one was a קטן:

---

13 Meacham, "Mishnat Niddah" 2:50

א"א זה שבוש שלא מצינו קטן בר עונשין וקרבן זה מן העונשין הוא
והיא כמו כן פטורה דהא מיקשו אהדדי

Avraham said: It [the Sifra text] is an error, as we have not found that a minor boy is liable to punishment, and this sacrifice is a punishment. She [the minor girl] is similarly exempt, for they are similar to one another.

The principle expressed here suggests that the punishment of the male is dependent on the liability of the female. The Mishneh Torah commentator Magid Mishneh supported Maimonides against the existence of such a principle:[14]

ורבינו סבור שהכל תלוי באשה...ולא אמרו בזמן שהוא אינו מביא
קרבן היא אינה לוקה

Our Rabbi [Maimonides] was of the opinion that all depended on the female ...they did not say that whenever he does not bring a sacrifice, she is not whipped.

6.2.4.B The Nature of the Offence

1. "שכבת זרע" פרט למערה

[In] a lying of seed – except one who is merely in a state of arousal.

Because Lev. 19:20 specifies the word זרע (*zera* – semen) this passage is interpreted to mean that there must actually be an emission of semen, thus excluding the מערה (one who engages in sexual activity but not to the point of ejaculation). In contrast, for instance, Sifra *Metzora pereq* 7: 1 (Weiss 78c) includes the מערה (*me'areh*) in the offence of intercourse with a menstruant, based on the doubled language אם שכב ישכב in Lev. 15:24. What is not clear here, however, is whether ejaculation without penetration is counted as an offence. The Sifra commentary is elsewhere aware of the possibility of different types of intercourse; on the issue of a male lying with a male in

14 Such a rule does occur in some legal systems; see, e.g., LH section 129 which provides that a male adulterer is not punished by the king if his co-adulterer is not punished by her husband.

Lev. 20:13, for instance, Sifra *Qedoshim pereq* 9:14 (Weiss 92b) states:

"משכבי אשה" מגיד הכתוב ששתי משכבות באשה

> [*If a man lies with a man in*] *the lyings* [plural] *of a woman* – Scripture [by the use of the plural] indicates that there are two types of intercourse with a woman.

The Tosefta passage (*tKer.* 1:16-18), as noted above (lines 4-5), does specifically exclude the situation of לא כדרכה ("abnormal" intercourse) from Lev. 19:20, among other situations not mentioned in Sifra. This is probably relating to sexual expression without the possibility of conception based on the word זרע in the sense of offspring.

6.2.4.C The Identity of the *shifḥah neḥerefet* (the "Intermarriage Baraita")

1. "והיא שפחה" יכול בשפחה הכנענית הכתוב מדבר תל' לו' "והפדה"

2. או "והפדה" יכול כולה תל' לו' "לא נפדתה"

3. הכייצד בפדויה ובשאינה פדויה ושחיציה שפחה וחיציה בת חורין

4. במאורסת לבן חורים הכתוב מדבר דברי ר' עקיבה

5. ר' ישמעאל או' בשפחה הכנענית הכתוב מדבר המאורסת לבן חורין

6. ר' לעזר בן עזריה אומר כל העריות כבר אמורות

7. מישיור אין לנו אילא שחיציה שפחה וחיציה בת חורים

There are several differences in orthography, abbreviations and especially use of prepositions in the MSS (and even some errors in tertiary witnesses) which will not be brought in the apparatus. Only variants reflecting significant differences in meaning will be brought unless there is some issue to be discussed. The sigla for the MSS can be found above on page 260. A word underlined in the lemma indicates the underlined witnesses support the reading but have changes in orthography, abbreviations, prepositions, etc.[15]

3. בפדויה] = **א**   פדויה] = **א°° ר ב ג ל ד ה <מ ח>**

4. במאורסת] = *   המאורסת = **ה**   מאורסת = **<ח>**

5. הכתוב מדבר המאורסת לבן חורין] = **א ב**   הכתוב מדבר במאורסת לבן חורין = **ר ג ל ד**
המאורסת לבן חורין הכתוב מדבר = **<ח>**   הכתוב מדבר המאורסת לעבד עברי = **ה <ש>**
במאורסת לעבד עברי הכת' מדבר = **א°° <ר"ה>**   המאורסת לעבד עברי = **<ראב"ד>**

7. מישיור] = **א ר ב**   ושיור = **ה**   משאר = **ד**   משוייר = **<מ ח ר"ה>**

שחיצה] **א ר ג**   את שחציה = **ב ה**   שפחה שחציה = **ל**   מי שחציה = **<מ>**
זו שחציה = **<ראב"ד>**

חורים] *   חורין והיא שפחה לחייב על כל שפחה ושפחה = **<מ>**
חורין המאורסת לעבד עברי אחרים אומ' לא יומתו כי לא חופשה בשפחה כנענית ומאורסת לעבד (עברי) כנעני = **<ש** והגירסא דומה **בווייס>**

Translation

1. *And she is a female slave.* Is it possible that Scripture is speaking of a Canaanite slave? [No, because] it is stated *caused to be redeemed.*

2. Or [another possibility]: does *caused to be redeemed* mean she is totally redeemed? [No, because] it is stated *she is not redeemed.*

3. How [is this to be interpreted]? Concerning one who is redeemed and not redeemed, [that is] of whom half is slave and half is free,

4. [and] concerning one engaged to a free man Scripture is speaking – according to R. Akiva.

5. R. Ishmael says: Scripture speaks of a Canaanite female slave, who is engaged to a free man.

6. R. Lazar ben Azariah says: All [those who have] forbidden sexual practices have already been stated;

15 See Finkelstein, *Torat Kohanim* p. 50ff for a more complete apparatus.

7. there is nothing left over except one who is half-slave and half-free.

The key point in this *Sifra* section is the attribution to three different sages of a ruling that accepts as a possibility a betrothal between a partial slave female and "free" male. There is also considerable variation in the MSS with respect to these lines, as well as a number of difficulties in logic:

1. In contradiction to the view of R. Ishmael which is cited further on, the *Sifra* editors state explicitly that the *shifḥah neḥerefet* could not be a Canaanite slave. This is based on the reference to פדיון – redemption in Lev. 19:20, and the apparent assumption that Canaanite slaves would not be redeemed by anyone. (This is in part confirmed by Lev. chapter 25, in which the idea of redemption seems to apply only to people referred to as אחיך *your brother*).
   It is not clear, however, whether this means the *shifḥah neḥerefet* is a Hebrew female (as Ibn Ezra in fact assumed in his commentary to Lev. 19:20). Based on *mQidd.* 1:2, the only type of Hebrew female slave would be a minor, since the Hebrew *amah*, according to that section, goes free at the onset of puberty. Yet based on the *Sifra* section above, if the female is a minor, the offence is deemed not to have occurred.[16] In effect, if *Sifra* presupposes knowledge of Mishnah, it has argued itself into an impossibility, since the conditions of Lev. 19:20 would never be met.

2. R. Akiva identifies the *shifḥah neḥerefet* with one who is "half-slave, half-free." The possible intention, though it is not stated explicitly, may have been to refer to one who was originally a Canaanite slave but was now half-free, thus putting her into a different category, and resolving the above dilemma. Rashi, at least, assumed that this was the case (commentary to Lev. 19:20)

16 The text here may refer to minor girl of less than three years and a day whose intercourse in not considered intercourse in *mNiddah* 2:4. Over that age but before majority (the appearance of two pubic hairs and reaching the age of twelve years and six months and a day) there would be the issue of fines for rape or seduction of a virgin and if she were married or betrothed to another man, he would be liable for adultery if she were a Hebrew slave. According to Rashi on Deut. 15:12, the court may sell the debtor's entire family into slavery including his wife and minor daughters.

ובשפחה כנענית חציה שפחה וחציה בת חורין...הכתוב מדבר

Scripture is speaking of...a Canaanite *shifḥah* who is half-slave half-free.

R. Akiva's justification for this status is based on his usual method of interpreting each element of the text separately, and thus deriving from both parts of the infinitive absolute construction הפדה לא נפדתה (in Lev. 19:20) the condition of redemption and non-redemption. The opinion of his contemporary R. Elazar ben Azariah, which appears to support him, is based on logic: since Scripture, in his opinion, has already covered all other forbidden sexual relationships (as in Lev. chapters 18 and 20), the only remaining type involves the half-slave half-free woman.

This additional support seems unusual, if merely for the reason that, as noted by Frankel,[17] R. Elazar b. Azariah and R. Akiva did not see eye to eye in the matter of דרשה. In particular, R. Elazar seems not to have accepted the method of interpreting separately each element of an infinitive absolute. This attitude is confirmed in the reaction attributed to him in the following baraita in *bQidd.* 17b, with respect to the obligation העניק תעניק in Deut. 15:14, concerning the provision of maintenance to persons one has freed:

ר' אלעזר בן עזריה אומר ככתבן נתברך בית בגללו מעניקים לו לא נתברך בית בגללו אין מעניקים לו אם כן מה ת"ל "הענק תעניק" דברה תורה כלשון בני אדם

R. Elazar ben Azariah says: [Matters are] as they are written. [If] the household was blessed on his [the slave's] account, he is supported; [if] it was not blessed on his account, he is not supported. Then why does Scripture [repeat the verb in the infinitive absolute form and state] הענק תעניק [*bestow you shall bestow*]? The Torah speaks in ordinary language.

3. One may also question on what basis R. Elazar argued that all other types of forbidden relationships were already covered in Scripture; that is, since these other prohibitions do not explicitly include slaves, it is possible that Lev. 19:20 was in fact referring to one who is totally

17 Zechariah Frankel, דרכי המשנה (Warsaw 1923) 98-99.

a slave, as in the opinion of R. Ishmael. This question apparently occurred to R. Hillel, who argued that forbidden relationships with slaves had in fact already been covered in Scripture:

ואי אמרת הא איכא שפחה דלא כתיבה בתורה הא כת'
"לא תהיה קדשה מבנות ישראל" ושפחה קדשה היא

If you were to say that this is a *shifḥah* who has not [already] been written about in the Torah, it is written [Deut. 23:18] *There shall not be a qedeshah from the daughters of Israel*, and a *shifḥah* is a *qedeshah.*

This unusual interpretation of Deut. 23:18 is reminiscent of the translation of this verse found in Targum Onkelos, which, in a departure from its usual word-for-word rendering of the MT, assumed this verse was a condemnation of slave-free intermarriage:

לא תהי אתתא מבנת ישראל לגבר עבד ולא יסב גברא מבני ישראל אתתא אמה

There shall be no woman of the daughters of Israel [as wife] to a man [who is an] *eved*, and no man of the sons of Israel shall take a woman [who is an] *amah.*

On the question of sexual relationships with slaves, *Sifra* itself seems to reflect some disagreement. In Lev. 18:26, in the general conclusion to the incest prohibitions, we find the words:

ולא תעשו מכל התועבת האלה האזרח והגר בתוככם

You shall not commit any of these abominations, [neither] the citizen nor the stranger who lives among you.

Using רבוי logic, Sifra *Aḥarei Mot pereq* 13:18 (Weiss 86c) comments:

גר זה הגר הגר לרבות נשי הגרים בתוככם לרבות נשים ועבדים

Stranger – it is *the stranger. The stranger* – to include the wives of the strangers. *Among you* – to include women and slaves.[18]

18 This same midrash on these words to include women and slaves is in *Sifra* see for example

Such language would imply that slaves were included in the general prohibitions against incest. In two sections of *Sifra*, however, which are deemed to be part of the interpolation known as the מכילתא דעריות, the opposite opinion is expressed. Regarding the prohibition against one's כלה (daughter-in-law) in Lev. 20:12, *Sifra Qedoshim* 9: 13 (Weiss 92b), reflecting an assumption against intermarriage with slaves, states:

אי כלתך אפילו שפחה אפילו נכרית תלמוד לומר אשת בנך היא לא אמרתי
אלא באשה שיש לה אישות עם בנך יצאו השפחה והנכרית שאין לה אישות עם בנך

If [Scripture prohibits] your *daughter-in-law* [you might think it includes] even a *shifḥah* or gentile woman. It is thus stated *She is the wife of your son* [Lev. 18:15]; I spoke only of a woman who has wifehood with your son, [thus] the *shifḥah* and gentile woman are excluded, since she has no wifehood with your son.

Similar logic is applied to the prohibition against אחות (one's sister) in Lev. 20:17; the statement at *Sifra Qedoshim pereq* 10:13 (Weiss 92d-93a) is:

אי אחותך אפילו שפחה אפילו נכרית תלמוד לומר בת אשת אביך.

If [Scripture prohibits] *your sister* [you might think it includes] even a *shifḥah* or gentile woman. It is thus stated *the daughter of your father's wife* [Lev. 18:11].

There is further attestation in tannaitic sources that the female slave was assumed to be freely available, as in the following passage from *tHor.* 2:11:

מפני מה הכל קופצין לישא את הגיורת ואין הכל קופצין לישא את המשוחררת
מפני שהגיורת היא היתה בחוקת המשתמרת והשפחה המשוחררת היא היתה בכלל
המופקרת

Why does everyone jump to marry a female convert, but not to marry a freed female slave? Because the female convert was considered observant [i.e. of all sexual rules], while the freed *shifḥah* was considered someone made freely available.

Aḥarei Mot pereq 7:9 (Weiss 83a) concerning Yom Kippur and *pereq* 12:1 (Weiss 84c) concerning the prohibition of eating blood.

Thus there is no consistent evidence as to whether incest prohibitions "crossed" between slave and non-slave groups. R. Elazar's point may have been that the only way in which such "crossing" between groups could be a sexual transgression (ערוה) is if there were some element of freedom about the woman in question.

4. The attribution to R. Akiva is complicated by the existence of the following variants in lines 3-5:

3. בפדויה ובשאינה פדויה]	פדויה ושאינה	פדויה
4. במאורסת]	המאורסת	מאורסת
5. המאורסת]	במאורסת	

The effect of these variations in or absence of the particles ב and ה, as Finkelstein notes,[19] is to make it unclear exactly how much of lines 3-4 are to be attributed to R. Akiva. The reading in the base text (Assemani 66) gives the impression that there are two prepositional phrases (בפדויה...במאורסת) which are the subject of הכתוב מדבר, the first describing who the slave woman is, and the second describing to whom she is connected and how, and it is only the second which is to be attributed to R. Akiva. In contrast, in line 5, in which there are two similar types of phrases, the reading המאורסת joins the two elements together much more clearly.

It is likely that the two elements in each case are intended to be joined and attributed to each of the respective sages. Some support for this may in fact be found in the Yerushalmi version of this citation (MS Leiden, to be cited in full further below), in which R. Akiva's position contains the words בשחצייה ... במאורסת. The significance of these variants, though on the surface seemingly trivial, becomes apparent when compared with *mKer.* 5:5. There the assumption that the two elements in each case were actually said by each sage may be questioned, because the second element in each case is missing (that is, according to the Mishnah, the sages had nothing to say about the slave's relationship). This issue will be explored further below, when

19 Finkelstein, *Sifra deVei Rav* 1:60.

the various parallels are compared.

5. The existence of variants that replace בן חורין with עבד עברי raises a question as to which term is original, and whether the *Sifra* passage can be used as evidence of a trend in favor of slave-free intermarriage. The majority of the primary witnesses attest to בן חורין being the second party in the relationship, in the opinion of both R. Akiva and R. Ishmael. The term עבד עברי appears in a marginal gloss in the Assemani 66 text, regarding the opinion of R. Akiva, and seems to be in a different hand than the main text. It also appears in MS ה regarding the opinion of R. Ishmael, and in some of the tertiary witnesses. As will be more fully discussed below, the idea that the עבד עברי is the second party was likely influenced by the Babylonian Talmud.

6.2.4.D The Creation of a "Half-Slave"

1. (ג) "והפדה לא נפדתה" בכסף ובשוה כסף

2. מנ' אף בשטר תל' לו' "או חפשה לא נתן לה"

3. ולהלן הוא אומר "וכתב לה"

4. מה "לה" אמור להלן בשטר אף כן בשטר

5. (ד) אין לי אילא כסף בחציה ושטר בכולה מנ' אף בשטר בחציה

6. תל' לו' "או חפשה לא נתן לה" מה כסף בחציה אף בשטר בחציה

1. *And she has not been redeemed* – with money or a money equivalent.

2. How do we know that even a deed [releases her]? Scripture therefore states: *And her freedom has not been given to her.*

3. Below [Deut. 24:1] it says: *And he writes her* [*a deed of divorce*].

4. Just as *to her* is written below concerning a deed, so *to her* is written here concerning a deed.

5. I know only that money [can release] half of her, [but] a deed [releases] all of her. How do we know that even a deed can release half of her?

6. It is thus stated: *And her freedom has not been given her* – just as money [can release] half of her, so can a deed [release] half of her.

The question underlying this section is the technical possibility of creating half a slave. The section begins by confirming that a slave can be released by both money and the equivalent of money (implied in the use of the term פדה in Lev. 19:20), and a "deed" (implied in the use of the term חפשה לא נתן לה). The latter association is derived by a גזירה שוה with Deut. 24:1 concerning divorce, based on the word לה; just as there a woman is released from marriage by having a document given to her, so here she is released from slavery by having a document given to her. The Malbim commentary to the Torah (19th century) explains why the word לה attracts attention in Lev. 19:20:

> ומ"ש או חופשה לא נתן לה לשון שלא השתמש בו בשום מקום שתמיד יאמר "משלח חפשי" "לחפשי ישלחנו"...
>
> What [Scripture] wrote, *freedom has not been given to her*, is language that it does not use elsewhere; it will always say *sending free*, *he shall send him free* [Exod. 21, Deut. 15, Jer. 34]...

The section now confirms that half of a slave can be released, by both money and a deed. The latter is derived by the logical assumption that both methods should have the same effect. A version of this baraita in *bGitt.* 41b makes this relationship clear:

> ת"ש "והפדה" יכול לכל ת"ל "לא נפדתה" אי לא נפדתה יכול לכל ת"ל "והפדה" הא כיצד פדויה ואינה פדויה בכסף ובשוה כסף ואין לי אלא בכסף בשטר מנין ת"ל "והפדה לא נפדתה או חופשה לא נתן לה" ולהלן הוא אומר "וכתב לה ספר כריתית" מה להלן בשטר אף כאן בשטר אין לי אלא חציו בכסף או כולו בשטר חציו בשטר מנין ת"ל "והפדה לא נפדתה או חופשה לא נתן לה" מקיש שטר לכסף מה כסף בין כולו בין חציו אף שטר נמי בין כולו בין חציו
>
> Come and hear: *redeemed* – with respect to all [of her]? [No,] it is stated: *she had not been redeemed*. If she has not been redeemed, does this mean

all [of her]? [No,] it is stated *redeemed*. How can she be redeemed and not redeemed? With money and something equivalent to money. I know only with money, whence with a deed? [In Lev. 19:20] it states: *redeemed she has not been redeemed or her freedom given her*, and there [Deut. 24:1] it states: *and he writes her a bill of divorce*. Just as there is a deed in that case, there is a deed in this case. I know only half [redeemed] with money, and all with a deed; whence half with a deed? It is stated: *redeemed she has not been redeemed or her freedom given her* – it compares a deed to money. Just as money [is effective] for all or half, so a deed [is effective] for all or half.

The significance of this *Sifra* section lies in several points:

1. The term שטר does not seem to be used consistently in rabbinic sources with respect to slaves. The שטר in this *Sifra* section appears to imply a גט שחרור, a deed of manumission, particularly given its analogy to the ספר כריתות of Deut. 24:1. The slave's שטר in the Mishnah, however, seems to be a bond or promissory note – that is, something of value is given to the master, either by the slave or others: in *mQidd.* 1:3, referring to the שטר by which the Canaanite slave acquires himself, and the references in *mGitt.* 4:4-5 to שטר על דמיו or על חצי דמיו given in exchange for a forced manumission. This is to be distinguished from the גט שחרור, mentioned periodically throughout *Mishnah Gittin*, which seems to imply something done by the master, whether or not in return for value (as in *mGitt.* 9:3, גופו של גט שחרור: הרי את בן חורין, הרי את לעצמך – "The body of a deed of manumission [states]: Behold, you are free; behold, you belong to yourself"). The following baraita in *bQidd.* 16a, and its corresponding discussion, confirm that later sages also perceived this confusion, and, like *Sifra*, assumed that the שטר as it applied to slaves was a גט שחרור:

> תנא וקונה את עצמו בכסף ובשוה כסף ובשטר בשלמא כסף דכתיב מכסף מקנתו שוה כסף נמי ישיב גאולתו... אלא האי שטר ה"ד אילימא דכתב ליה שטרא אדמיה היינו כסף אלא שיחרור שטר למה לי לימא ליה באפי תרי זיל א"נ באפי בי דינא זיל אמר רבא זאת אומרת עבד עברי גופו קנוי והרב שמחל על גרעונו אין גרעונו מחול

> It was taught: He [presumably a Hebrew slave, from the context below] acquires himself with money, with something equivalent to money, or with a deed. Money is reasonable, as it is written [Lev. 25:51, with respect

> to a Hebrew] *with the money of his purchase.* Similarly, for something equivalent to money , [it is written, ibid.] *he shall return [the value of] his redemption...* But what is the case for this deed? If we say [the slave] writes [the master] a note for his value, this is [the same thing as] money. Rather, it is a manumission. [But] why a deed – let [the master] tell him, "Go out" before two [witnesses], or before the Beit Din. Rava said: This means that a Hebrew slave is acquired bodily, and if a master forgives the remainder owing on him, the remainder is not forgiven.

The three Jewish Targumim also accept the association of חופשה in Lev. 19:20 with a deed; Pseudo-Jonathan and Neofiti specifically identify this deed as a שטר שחרורה (deed of manumission) or a כתב חרותה (document of freedom) while Onkelos simply has שטר.

2. The above baraita confirms another point raised by the *Sifra* section: the גט שחרור was a valid method of manumission. In that case, it must be asked why this method is not specifically listed among the types of manumission for either the Hebrew or Canaanite slave in *mQidd.* 1:2-3. The answer may lie in the use of the phrase קונה את עצמו in these mishnayot. This phrase suggests that the types of manumission listed in these mishnayot are perceived to be at the instance of the slave, rather than that of the master; that is, they are either invoked by the slave or others on his behalf (such as through payment of money), or operate automatically for the benefit of the slave (such as the passage of time or appearance of puberty signs). The deed of manumission, on the other hand, based on various sources including the two mentioned above, appears to have been at the instance of the master.

   If this distinction is correct, then we can understand the *Sifra* section as confirming that a half-slave can be created at the instance of either the slave or the master: the slave can buy a partial manumission (a situation which appears to be consistent with Hellenistic practice, to be discussed below), or the master himself can create a situation of partial freedom.

3. This leads to the final issue: is this *Sifra* section discussing a slave owned by a single master, or by partners? That is, could a single owner release half his ownership, or did the half release apply only in a case in

which one partner released all of his share? Amoraic discussion reveals an assumption that this issue was a matter of dispute, between R. Judah [the Patriarch] and others. The following discussion in *yGitt.* 4:5 46a (with respect to releasing a male half-slave) suggests that only R. Judah [the Patriarch] accepted that a single owner could free half his slave:

> היאך איפשר חציו עבד וחציו בן חורין תיפתר או כרבי דרבי אומר אדם משחרר חצי עבדו או דברי הכל עבד של שני שותפין ועמד אחד מהן ושיחרר חלקו

> How is it possible for someone to be half-slave half-free? Explain this either according to Rabbi [Judah the Patriarch], as Rabbi [Judah the Patriarch] says a man may free half his slave, or [according to] the opinion of all, [this is] a slave of two partners, and one frees his portion.

Certain of the Babylonian Amoraim , however, thought that the issue might depend on the type of manumission (*bGitt.* 41b):

> ת"ר המשחרר חצי עבדו רבי אומר קנה וחכ"א לא קנה אמר רבה מחלוקת בשטר דרבי סבר והפדה לא נפדתה או חופשה לא נתן לה מקיש שטר לכסף מה כסף בין כולו בין חציו אף שטר נמי בין כולו בין חציו ורבנן גמרי לה לה מאשה מה אשה חציה לא אף עבד נמי חציו לא אבל בכסף דברי הכל קנה... ורב יוסף אמר מחלוקת בכסף דרבי סבר והפדה לא נפדתה פדויה ואינה פדויה ורבנן סברי דברה תורה כלשון בני אדם אבל בשטר דברי הכל לא קנה מיתיבי המשחרר חצי עבדו בשטר רבי אומר קנה וחכ"א לא קנה תיובתא דרב יוסף תיובתא

> The sages taught: If one frees half his slave, Rabbi [Judah the Patriarch] says [the slave] has acquired [half of himself], and the sages say he has not acquired [half of himself]. Rabbah said: This is a dispute with respect to a deed, as Rabbi [Judah the Patriarch] is of the opinion that *she has not been redeemed or her freedom given her* [Lev. 19:20] compares a deed to money; just as money [is effective to acquire] all or half [of the slave], so a deed is also [effective] for all or half. The sages learn *her* [in Lev. 19: 20] from *her*, a wife [*he shall write her a bill of divorce* – Deut. 24:1]; just as one cannot [divorce] half a wife [with a bill of divorce], one cannot [free] half a slave [with a deed of manumission]. But all agree that money acquires [half]... Rav Yosef said: This is a dispute with respect to money, as Rabbi [Judah the Patriarch] is of the opinion that [the infinitive absolute] *she has not been redeemed* [is unbundled to mean] she is redeemed and not redeemed, while the sages are of the opinion that the Torah speaks in plain language. But all agree that

a deed does not acquire [half]. They object [as it was taught above]: If one frees half his slave, Rabbi [Judah the Patriarch] says [the slave] has acquired [half of himself], and the sages say he has not acquired [half of himself]. [Is this] a refutation of Rav Yosef? [It is] a refutation.

The talmudic editor thus confirms that R. Judah the Patriarch would accept a partial release by a single owner in any case.

The significance of this position may be understood by comparing it with with Roman law. Pre-Justinian, not only could a single owner not release half his ownership, but a co-owner of a slave could not free the "entire" slave. As Buckland explains:[20]

> ... the owner of half cannot free the other half. Hence the classical jurists held that if one of co-owners purported to free the slave, the manumission did not take effect. The act was not, however, a mere nullity. If the manumission was formal ... the effect was to vest the share of the freeing owner in the other owner by accrual.

Under Justinian, there was pressure in favor of freeing the slave; thus, other co-owners were forced to sell their shares to any co-owner who wanted to free the slave (C 7.7.1.1, translated and quoted by Buckland):[21] "If one owner desires to free *inter vivos* or by will the others shall sell their shares to him or his *heres* who shall then free."

This difficulty with half-slave status may be understood on examination of the Roman concept of manumission. The essence of Roman manumission, according to Buckland,[22] was not a conveyance of what the master owned in the slave back to the slave; it was a *cessio in iure* of the master's rights in the slave, and the creation of a new status:

> [Manumission] is not in strictness transfer of *dominium*. A man has no *dominium* in himself or his members. Nor is it an alienation of liberty. The right received is not that of the master....Manumission is an act emanating from the holder of ownership removing the man (by the authority of the State, which is present in all formal manumission) from that class... It does

20 W.W. Buckland, *The Roman Law of Slavery* 575.

21 Buckland, *The Roman Law of Slavery* 577.

22 Buckland, *The Roman Law of Slavery* 714.

> indeed confer rights and capacities on him, but it is from the notion of destroying capacities for rights over him that the conception starts.[23]

Enslavement in this system, in other words, implied that one person possessed certain powers over another, and such powers could not be given up in half-measures. In the tannaitic system, in contrast, which did accept a half-slave status, we might thus infer that enslavement was seen as ownership by the master of something ordinarily belonging to the slave, and that this "something" could be given back in whole or in part.[24] This idea is consistent with the language used in the Mishnah regarding manumission: קונה את עצמו ("he acquires himself," *mQidd.* 1:2-3); הרי את לעצמך ("you belong to yourself," *mGitt.* 9:3).[25] It is also consistent with the mishnaic rule that slaves became liable for torts they had committed during their enslavement, after they have become free (*mB.Bat.* 8:4); such a rule implies that the slave had some sort of legal "essence" which continued to incur liabilities even while it was in the possession of another. One did, in other words, have *dominium*, or something like it, in one's self, which could be conveyed to others.

Finally on this point, it may be noted that Maimonides (*Hil. Avadim*, 7:1-2) accepted that a single owner could free half a slave only upon receipt of money (the view of the חכמים above, and against the view of both R. Judah the Patriarch and *Sifra*):

> גט שחרור צריך שהיה ענינו דבר הכורת בינו לבין אדוניו ולא ישאר לאדון בו זכות...
> המשחרר חצי עבדו בשטר לא קנה העבד חציו והרי הוא עבד כשהיה אבל אם שחרר חציו
> בכסף...קנה ונמצא חציו עבד וחציו בן חורין

> It is necessary that a deed of manumission be in essence something that cuts off [the relationship] between [the slave] and his master, and no right in him remains with the master...if one frees half his slave with a deed, the slave does not acquire half of himself and is still a slave as he was; but if he frees half of

23 Buckland, *The Roman Law of Slavery* 437-438.

24 The creation of a half-slave status will be examined more fully in the Excursus in 6.6 of this chapter.

25 This wording in *mGitt.* is similar to that found in certain Mesopotamian manumissions, in which the manumitted person was required to serve or support the manumitter until the latter's death; at that point one finds language such as *ša ramānīša šī* (see, e.g. the OB manumission document UAZP 29, line 14). The relationship between half-slavery and conditional manumission will be explored more fully in the Excursus in 6.6 of this chapter.

him with money...he acquires [half of himself] and is half-slave half free.

6.4.2.E The Punishment of the Woman

1. "בקורת" מכות מלמד שהיא לוקה
2. יכול אף הוא ילקה תל לו "תהיה"
3. היא לוקה והוא אינו לוקה

1. *Biqqoret* – lashes. This teaches that she is whipped.
2. Is it possible that he too is whipped? It is thus stated *tihyeh* [i.e. the verb is 3 f.s.]
3. [implying] she is whipped and he is not whipped.

The text here accepts *biqqoret* as lashes, and confirms that only the woman is punished in this way. No derivation is given here, but the various *Sifra* commentators, such as R. Hillel and Rabad, accept the amoraic opinion in *bKer.* 11a, which cites this midrash on *tihyeh*.

6.4.2.F The Necessity of a Deed of Manumission

1. "לא יומתו כי לא חפשה" הא אם חפשה הרי אילו חייבין מיתה
2. ר' שמעון אמר משום ר' עקיבה יכול יהא הכסף גומר בה
3. תל לו "לא יומתו כי לא חופשה" ערה את כל הפרשה ל"כי לא חפשה"
4. מלמד שאינו גומר בה אילא בשטר

1. *They shall not die because she has not been freed*. Thus if she has been freed, they would be liable to death.
2. R. Shimon said in the name of R. Akiva: Does money finish with her [manumit her]?
3. Scripture says: *They shall not die because she has not been freed*; it intertwines the

entire section with the words *because she has not been freed.*

4. This teaches that he [the master] does not finish with her [i.e. she is not manumitted] except by deed.

The issue in this case appears to be the circumstance in which the *shifḥah* would be free, so that both parties would be liable to death for adultery (assuming the woman is otherwise betrothed). The meanings of both גומר and ערה[26] in this context are vague, and one might argue that they are intended as a play on the same terms which were used earlier in the passage in a sexual sense. Despite the fact that an earlier section confirmed that either a payment or a deed of manumission can release part or all of the slave woman, this section appears to be stating that a final manumission can be effected only by a deed of manumission. As the Malbim commentary explains, the *Sifra* passage is reacting to the fact that only the term חפש is repeated at the end of v. 20:

> וסיים ב"לא חופשה" לבד ולא אמר "לא יומתו כי לא נפדתה ולא חופשה"
> מבואר שפדיון כסף לבדו אינו גומר לעשותה ב"ח
>
> It concludes with *she had not been freed* only; it did not say: *they shall not die because she has not been redeemed and has not been freed.* It is explained that a monetary redemption alone does not make her completely free.

Further, this *Sifra* passage contradicts the position in *mGitt.* 4:5, in which the male half-slave and half-free seems to be released upon writing of a bond (that is, a money equivalent).

1. One possibility is that the more stringent formality was applicable specifically to the *shifḥah neḥerefet* to keep her sexually available for the maximum possible time without penalty of death.

2. An alternative possibility is that the necessity of a deed of manumission may have been a later development. From certain amoraic debates in

26 ערה appears to be the *Pi'el* 3 m.s. perf. of ערי "to intertwine" (Jastrow). The reading אורעה in the witness ש is the form found in *bGitt.* 39b (as will be seen below), and appears to be the *Afel* 3 m.s. perf. of ארע "to join" (Jastrow). Even-Shoshan *s.v.* ערה .ב has the same definition for a Hebrew word.

the Talmudim, it seems that the deed of manumission was thought to be a special requirement in certain cases. In such cases, it was clear that the master had otherwise severed connection with the slave – for instance, declaring him הקדש (sanctified property) or rendering him הפקר (abandoned property), or when יאוש (abandoning hope of recovery) was deemed to have occurred regarding a stolen or runaway slave. The issue was then whether the slave was automatically free, or whether he remained simply a slave without a master until someone wrote him a deed of manumission. We may note first a controversy in *bGitt.* 39b on the matter of יאוש, which contains a slightly different version of the *Sifra* section. Here it is acknowledged that the limitation to a deed of manumission that is expressed in this midrash would not apply in the case of a slave dedicated as sanctified property; in the latter case there is in effect someone to accept the redemption money:

אמרו לפני רבי אמר נתייאשתי מפלוני עבדי מהו אמר להם אומר אני אין לו תקנה אלא בשטר...והתניא רבי אומר אומר אני אף הוא נותן דמי עצמו ויוצא מפני שהוא כמוכרו לו הכי קאמר או בכסף או בשטר והאי פקע ליה כספיה ולאפוקי מהאי תנא דתניא ר' שמעון אומר משום רבי עקיבא יכול יהא כסף גומר בה כדרך ששטר גומר בה ת"ל והפדה לא נפדתה אורעה כל הפרשה כולה ללא חופשה לומר לך שטר גומר בה ואין כסף גומר בה

It was posed before Rabbi [Judah the Patriarch]: If one said: I have abandoned hope [of recovering] a certain slave of mine – what is [the rule]? He said to them: I say that [the slave] has no remedy except a deed [of manumission]...

But was it not taught [with respect to a slave who was dedicated as sanctified property]: Rabbi [Judah the Patriarch] says: I say that he [the slave] also gives his value and goes out [free], because it is as if [the Temple treasurer] sells him to himself. Thus he says that either money or a deed [manumits a slave], and in this case his money releases him. This is to exclude [this situation from the view of] the following *tanna*, as it was taught: R. Shimon says in the name of R. Akiva: Could it be that money finishes with her in the way a deed finishes with her? It is stated [in the doubled infinitive absolute form]: *redeemed she has not been redeemed*. The entire passage is joined to *because she has not been freed*, to tell you that a deed finishes with her and money does not finish with her.

3. Finally, it may be noted that Maimonides (*Hil. Avadim*, 7:6) again

appears to have ignored this *Sifra* section:

שפחה חרופה אם רצה לשחרר חציה הנשאר ותעשה אשת איש גמורה הרי זה משוחרר בין בכסף בין בשטר שאף הכסף גומר שחרורה

[With respect to] a *shifḥah ḥarufah* – if one wants to free the half of her that remains [enslaved], and she will be made a "complete" wife, he can manumit her with either money or a deed, because even money completes her manumission.

It is possible that Maimonides had a different text of *Sifra*; it will be noted that the witness **מ**, which Finkelstein assigns to the same geographical group, is missing the citation of R. Shimon. In that case, however, we might also expect the same lacuna in MS Vat. 31. A more likely explanation of Maimonides' view (which then influenced **מ**) is the fact that in *bGitt.* 39b there is an Amoraic dispute about whether the view of R. Shimon was correct:

אמר רמי בר חמא א"ר נחמן הלכה כר' שמעון
ור' יוסף בר חמא א"ר יוחנן אין הלכה כר' שמעון

Rami bar Ḥama said in the name of Rav Naḥman: The halakhah is according to R. Shimon. Rav Yosef bar Ḥama said in the name of R. Yoḥanan: The halakhah is not according to R. Shimon.

The Talmud then goes on to cite a case which appears to support R. Shimon. Rav Naḥman had disallowed a manumission in which a dying master had given his slave woman his own cap to effect an acquisition of herself. The Talmud concludes, however, that R. Shimon's dictum was irrelevant to the case:

מאן דחזא סבר משום דהלכה כר' שמעון ולא היא אלא משום דהוה ליה כליו של מקנה

One who saw [this] thought [the reason for Rav Naḥman's decision was] that the halakhah is according to R. Shimon. But this is not so; it was because [the master] owned the items [used] for the purchase [i.e. the woman was in effect handing him back his own property, and thus there was no redemption].

6.4.2.G The Punishment of the Male

1. "והביא את אשמו ליי וג"

2. נא' כן "איל אשם" ונא' להלן "איל אשם"

3. מה "איל אשם" אמור להלן בכסף שקלים אף כן בכסף שקלים

1. *And he shall bring his guilt offering to God*, etc.

2. *A guilt offering ram* is said here, and *a guilt offering ram* is said below [Lev. 5:15, according to the various *Sifra* commentators].

3. As *a guilt offering ram* is said below to be in silver [i.e. money is given to purchase the sacrifice, rather than the individual actually bringing the sacrificial animal], so here too it is in silver.

Using another verse as a parallel, it is derived that the *asham* sacrifice here was also to be paid in money.[27] The גזירה שוה analogy on the word אשם is based, according to the Malbim, on the fact that this word is superfluous in Lev. 19:21:

שהיל"ל "והביא את אשמו" וכו' "איל"

...it should have said *and he shall bring his asham sacrifice* etc. – *a ram*

This is brought out more clearly in the fuller quotes in ד and ר; the more focused wording in ש (Yalkut Shimoni), on the other hand, seems to base the גזירה שוה on the phrase איל אשם.

6.4.2.H Further Specification of the Nature of the Offence

1. "וכפר עליו הכהן באיל האשם לפני יי על חטאתו אשר חטא"

2. מלמד שהוא מביא אחת על ביאות הרבה

3. "ונסלח לו מחטאתו אשר חטא" לעשות את המיזיד כשוגג

27 As Noth also argued (see chapter 3, section 3.2), though on other grounds.

1. *And the priest will atone for him with the guilt offering ram before God on the sin which he sinned.*

2. This teaches that he brings one [sacrifice] for many acts of intercourse.

3. *And he shall forgive him for the sin which he sinned* – to render the one who acts intentionally like the one who acts inadvertently.

Both of the rules in this *Sifra* section are also found in the Mishnah:

1. *mKer.* 1:2 sets out a general rule regarding those acts which require a punishment of excision (these are listed in *mKer.* 1:1, including various types of sexual transgressions). The rule requires a difference in punishment according to the mental state of the offender:

על אלו חיבים על זדונם כרת ועל שגגתם חטאת ועל לא הודע שלהן אשם תלוי

On [the following types of offences] they are liable for excision if they acted intentionally, and for a sin offering if they acted in error, and for a conditional guilt offering if they were not uncertain [that they had sinned]...

mKer. 2:2, however, provides a contrasting rule for the *shifḥah neḥerefet* offence:

...וארבעה מביאין על הזדון כשגגה...הבא על השפחה...

... and four [types of sinners] bring [the same type of sacrifice] whether they acted intentionally or in error... [including] the one who has intercourse with the *shifḥah* [*neḥerefet*]...

2. *Mishnah Ker.* 2:3 provides a further special rule regarding the *shifḥah neḥerefet*, in the case in which one commits many acts of the same nature (presumably with the same *shifḥah*):

חמשה מביאין קרבן אחד על עברות הרבה...הבא על השפחה ביאות הרבה...

Five persons bring one sacrifice for many transgressions... [including] one who has intercourse with a *shifḥah* [*neḥerefet*] many times...

As explained by the Malbim commentary, *Sifra* supports these rules based on the apparently superfluous wording in Lev. 19:22:

מ"ש על חטאתו אשר חטא מיותר וכפול פי' חז"ל שמכפר באיל האשם הא' על כל מה שחטא...וכפל שנית...לעשות את המזיד כשוגג

What [Scripture] stated *on his sin that he sinned* is superfluous and repetitive. The sages' interpretation is that he is forgiven with the ram of the *asham* that is stated with respect to everything he has sinned...and it is repeated...to render the one who acts intentionally like the one who acts in error.

A parallel citation to *Sifra* appears in *bKer.* 9a; here, however, the last phrase is "corrected" to its more logical order:

ונסלח לו מחטאתו אשר חטא לעשות מזיד כשוגג והא קרא כי כתיב במזיד כתיב אלא אימא לעשות שוגג כמזיד

...and the sin that he committed will be forgiven him [Lev. 19:22] – to render the one who transgresses intentionally like the one who transgresses in error. But Scripture writes of one who transgresses intentionally. Say rather: to render the one who transgresses in error like the one who transgresses intentionally.

There also appears to be an issue as to whether the offence described in Lev. 19:20 concerns the מזיד (intentional sinner) or the שוגג (inadvertent sinner). Rashi states (*bKer.* 9a, ד"ה ונסלח):

והא עיקר קרא במזיד כתיב דכתיב בקורת תהיה והיינו מלקות ואין מלקות אלא במזיד

The object of Scripture is written with respect to the מזיד, because it is written *there will be a biqqoret*, and this is lashes, and lashes apply only to the מזיד.

The Malbim commentary, however, concludes:

...שעיקר הקרבן על השוגג...ובזה נכונה גם גי' הספר' "לעשות המזיד כשוגג"

...the object of the sacrifice is on the שוגג... and in this respect the version in *Sifra* "to make the מזיד like the שוגג" is also correct.

6.4.2.I The Summary Section

1. (ט) כל העריות לא עשה בהם את המערה כגומר

2. והשפחה עשה בה את המערה כגומר.

3. (י) כל העריות לא עשה בהן את הקטן כגדול

4. והשפחה עשה בה את הקטנה כגדולה.

5. (יא) כל העריות אחד האיש ואחד האשה שוין במכות ובקורבן

6. והשפחה היא לוקה והוא אינו לוקה הוא מביא קרבן והיא אינה מביאה קרבן

7. כל העריות בחטאת והשפחה באשם

8. כל העריות בנקבה ושפחה בזכר

9. כל העריות חייב על כל ביאה וביאה והשפחה לא חייב אילא אחת על ביאות הרבה.

10. כל העריות לא עשה בהם את המיזיד כשוגג והשפחה עשה בה את המי{זיד כ}שוגג

Variants

1. לא עשה] = **א**   עשה = **ר ב ד <מ ש ר"ה וייס>**

2. והשפחה] = **א ב**   ובשפחה = **ר <מ>**   ושפחה = **ד**
עשה] = **א**   לא עשה = **ר ב ד <מ ש וייס>**

3-4 כל-כקטנה]*   ∩ = **ב**

3. לא עשה] = **א ד <וייס>**   עשה = **ר ב <מ ר"ה ראב"ד>**

4. והשפחה] = **א**   ובשפחה = **ר <מ>**   ושפחה = **ד**   עשה] = **א ד**
לא עשה = **ר ב <מ ר"ה ראב"ד וייס>**   בה את] = *   חסר = **ד <וייס>**

6. והשפחה] = **א**   ובשפחה = **ר ב ד <מ>**

7. והשפחה] = *   ושפחה חרופה] = ד <וייס>

9. והשפחה] = א   ובשפחה = ר ב ד <מ>   לא] = *   אינו] = ד

10. את] *   חסר = ד   המיזיד] = *   מזיד = ד   והשפחה] = א
ובשפחה = ר ב <מ>   ושפחה = ד

Translation

1. Concerning all the forbidden relationships, [Scripture] has not made the one who is merely aroused like the one who completes intercourse,

2. while concerning the slave, it has made the one who is merely aroused like the one who completes intercourse.

3. Concerning all the forbidden relationships, [Scripture] has not made the minor male like the adult male,

4. while concerning the slave, it has made the minor female like the adult female.

5. Concerning all the forbidden relationships, both the man and woman are equal with respect to lashes and sacrifice,

6. [while concerning] the slave, she is whipped and he is not whipped, he brings a sacrifice and she does not bring a sacrifice.

7. All the forbidden relationships [require] a *ḥattat* (sin offering), [while] the slave [requires] an *asham* (guilt offering).

8. All the forbidden relationships [require] a female [sacrifice, while] the slave [requires] a male [sacrifice].

9. Concerning all the forbidden relationships, one is liable for each and every act of intercourse, while concerning the slave, one is liable only once for many acts of intercourse.

10. Concerning all the forbidden relationships, [Scripture] has not made the one who acts intentionally like the one who acts in error, while concerning the slave, it has made the one who acts intentionally like the one who acts in error.

From a stylistic point of view, these lines are in effect a continuation of the idea of R. Elazar that Lev. 19:20 constitutes the one remaining ערוה; they list the ways in which this forbidden relationship differs from all others, by summarizing all the points which have just been proved in the first part of the section. Yet, as noted above, the summary form without biblical citations is not characteristic of this halakhic midrash, a feature that is rendered more significant by the fact that this summary section has parallels in the Mishnah and Tosefta. Further, there are a number of elements in the *Sifra* summary that explicitly contradict the midrashic derivations in the first part of the section:

1. The wording in lines 1 and 2 of this section is clearly reversed with respect to the midrashic derivation in section (a) above: with respect to the *shifḥah*, the גומר is not like the מערה. Thus the wording in the remaining witnesses (which reverse the order of the עשה – לא עשה) seems to be correct; yet as the *lectio difficilior*, the reading in Assemani 66 might be considered original.

   It is also possible that the reading in Assemani 66 was a deliberate scribal change. In the following passage in *bKer.* 11ab, it appears that the Amoraim had before them a simple statement to the effect that the גומר is considered equal to the מערה, with no specification as to whether this referred to the *shifḥah neḥerefet* or all *arayot*. Rav Sheshet manages to argue both cases. With respect to the slave, he considers additional elements regarding the nature of the act (elements that are present in Tosefta), and argues in essence that the גומר is exempt, like the מערה, if his גמירה occurs with respect to something which is not a שכבת זרע:

   > תני תנא קמיה דרב ששת עשו גומר כמערה מתכוין כשאין מתכוין כדרכה כשלא כדרכה ניעור כישן...א"ל...הכי קתני עשו גומר שלא כדרכה בשפחה חרופה דלא מיחייבי כמערה כדרכה דשכבת זרע כתיב מתכוין שלא כדרכה בשפחה דפטורין כאינו מתכוין דשכבת זרע כתיב ניעור שלא כדרכה בשפחה דפטורין כישן מ"ט דשכבת זרע כתיב נמצא מתכוין והמערה בשפחה כשאין מתכוין בכל עריות ישן כדרכה כישן דעריות נמצא ניעור שלא כדרכה בשפחה כישן דכל עריות

   A *tanna* repeated before Rav Sheshet: They rendered one who completes his act like one who is merely aroused, one who acted intentionally like one who acted unintentionally, 'normal' intercourse like 'abnormal' intercourse, the one who was awake like the one who was asleep... He said to him... This is what is taught: They rendered one who completed 'abnormal' intercourse with a *shifḥah ḥarufah*, who is not liable, like one who is merely aroused during 'normal' intercourse, as it is written *in a lying of seed* [i.e. a completed act of ejaculation during vaginal intercourse]; [they rendered] one who committed an intentional act of 'abnormal' intercourse with a *shifḥah*, who is exempt, like one who did not act intentionally, as it is written 'in a lying of seed'; [they rendered] one who is awake while engaging in 'abnormal' intercourse with a *shifḥah*, who is exempt, like one who is asleep. What is the reason? It is written: *in a lying of seed*. Thus it was found that one who acts intentionally and one is merely aroused with respect to a *shifḥah* is like one who acts unintentionally with respect to other prohibited sexual relations; one who is asleep during 'normal' intercourse [with a *shifḥah*] is like one who is asleep with respect to other prohibited sexual relations; it was found that one who is awake during 'abnormal' intercourse with a *shifḥah* is like one who is asleep with respect to other prohibited sexual relations.

It is thus possible that Assemani 66 was corrected to reflect the passage but it is also possible that the reading in Assemani 66 was the reading before the editors of the Babylonian Talmud.

2. Lines 3 and 4 again seem to be a mistake in Assemani 66; here, however, the wording in ד also follows Assemani 66. Possibly attempting to reconcile these differences in the witnesses, the Sifra commentator Qorban Aharon was able to propose a logical interpretation for both this reading and the reverse, and thus to see them as paraphrases of the same idea. For כל העריות עשה והשפחה לא עשה (the reading in ר and מ) he explained:

צריכין אנו לפרש אותה על זה האופן כל העריות עשה בהם הקטן לחייב פה החוטא בו כגדול שכמו שהבא על הגדולה חייב כך הבא על הקטנה חייב... ובשפחה חרופה לא עשה הקטנה כגדולה אלא דהבא על הגדולה חייב ואם בא על קטנה דהיא פטור אף הוא פטור

We must interpret it in this manner: for all the transgressions the minor is made like the adult, to render liable the one who sins with him, so that just as one who has [wrongful] intercourse with an adult female is liable, so one who has [wrongful] intercourse with a minor female is liable...but with the *shifḥah ḥarufah* the minor female is not like the adult female; rather, one who has intercourse with an adult [*shifḥah*] is liable, but if he has intercourse with a minor, who is exempt, he is also exempt.

For the opposite wording the explanation is as follows:

ואם נרצה לקיים גרסת הספרי' דגרסי' כל העריות לא עשה והשפחה עשה... כלומר שלא תלה עונש הגדול בקטן... אבל בעריות [צ"ל בשפחה] עשה הקטנה כגדול, שהשוה את הגדול לקטן ופטר הגדול אם בא על הקטנה

If we want to give effect to the version where we read "for all the transgressions it does not render [the minor like the adult] and for the *shifḥah* it does render [the minor like the adult]"...that is to say, [generally] the punishment of the adult is not dependent on [the punishment of] the minor...but for all the transgressions [*sic;* probably *shifḥah*], the minor female is like [i.e. has the same effect on] the adult male, as the adult male is made equal to the minor male and is exempt if he has intercourse with a minor [*shifḥah*].

In other words, both readings are saying the same thing from a different angle. The second explanation is somewhat weak, in that, as Weiss notes, we would have expected the end phrase to be עשה את הגדול כקטנה. We may therefore posit that the reading in ר and also found in Midrash HaGadol (מ) is original; this is supported by the fact that the parallel baraita in Tosefta has the same structure.

6.5 ASSESSING THE PARALLEL TEXTS

As we have noted, both Mishnah and Tosefta contain parallel texts to that in *Sifra*, though not in the same order as *Sifra*. Of particular interest is the part of the citation outlining the views of the sages concerning the identity and relationship of the *shifḥah neḥerefet*, as both *Sifra* and Tosefta give evidence of support to intermarriage, in complete contradiction to the Mishnah. There are further appearances of this particular intermarriage section in each of the Talmudim, again with a certain amount of variability. The question thus arises as to which version, particularly of the intermarriage section, is original (or, perhaps, "more" original).

I propose that the version in Tosefta is the "most" original, in effect by default:

1) *Sifra* contains internal contradictions, evidence of amendment according to the Bavli, and an unusual summary section that does not appear to be original to it;

2) Mishnah is streamlined to conform with its other slave rulings.

While this argument does not preclude changes having been made to the Tosefta text over time (as is evident from variants in the Tosefta MSS that are quoted by Zuckermandel), it will be argued that the versions in the Mishnah and Sifra have been based on a text most similar to Tosefta; in some cases these versions have been deliberately edited, and in other cases they show changes which are consistent with the streamlining which occurs during a period of oral transmission.

6.5.1 General Considerations Between Mishnah and Tosefta

It might be argued on the one hand that the Tosefta passage shows the characteristics expected of it, particularly if one accepts the contention of those (such as Frankel and Neusner) who argue that the Tosefta is a commentary, or form of Talmud, upon the Mishnah:

a) It adds details which appear to explain or extend the application of the Mishnah's rules, and this would include details concerning the status of the *shifḥah* as married to a slave or free man;

b) It follows the structure of the Mishnah exactly. This structure consists of three parts:

i. a list of the differences between the *shifḥah* and כל העריות ("differences" pericope)

ii. a discussion of the identity of the *shifḥah* ("intermarriage" pericope)

iii. a list of common principles which apply to כל העריות ("summary" pericope).

I shall argue, however, that in this case it is more logical to treat the Mishnah pericope as commentary on the material found in Tosefta. In other words, the Mishnah's editor had before him (in writing or orally) a block of material similar to that in the Tosefta (though not necessarily the version in the current Tosefta), including a list of the differences between the שפחה and כל העריות. He then summarized this material into certain basic principles. This contention is based on two main arguments:

1. The three pericopes of the citation bear only a loose relationship to one another; in other words, there is no particular reason why they should be connected to chapter 2 of *mKer.* in this particular order. They do fit generally within the context of the first two chapters of *mKer.*, which consist of groupings of offences which share similar characteristics. We might, however, have expected the definition of the *shifḥah* to have been added after *mKer.* 2:2, which has the first mention of the *shifḥah*; and we might have expected general principles concerning עריות to have been part of *mKer.* 1:1, which contains a list of עריות. It may be argued, in other words, that the three pericopes have been lifted as a whole from somewhere else and tacked on to the end of chapter 2, because there happens to have been a previous mention in this chapter of the *shifḥah.*

   In contrast, this kind of loose arrangement of material on a similar subject matter is consistent with the style of Tosefta, where the jumping from subject to subject would cause no particular concern.

   Consistent with the assumption that this citation was originally a loose collection of materials which had circulated independently, and was at some point brought together in a Tosefta-like collection, is the fact that the "intermarriage" pericope and the "summary" pericope appear as separate items in Sifra, and the "intermarriage" pericope appears as a separate item (with variations) in each Talmud.

2. The Mishnah citation shows signs of editing. In particular, conclusions are drawn which go beyond a mere list of cases. Examples of such conclusions are:

   A. The phrase לא שווה להם לא בעונש ולא בקרבן. That is, this is one general difference between the שפחה and כל העריות, and the text then goes on to give examples of such differences: the type of sacrifice, and the fact that with respect to the שפחה the male and female are treated separately.

B. The phrase החמיר בשפחה, which is stated to be the effect of making the מזיד כשוגג – the intentional [sinner] like the inadvertent [sinner]. (The precise nature of the חומרה – stringency is unclear; it may be from the point of view of the *shifḥah*, in that she is punished regardless of the intention of the male).

Further, the last section in the Mishnah, starting כל העריות אחד גדול ואחד קטן – [with] all the [other] forbidden relationships, if one is an adult and one is a minor, needs a context to be fully understood. In particular, it is not clear whether the Mishnah is still dealing with differences between the *shifḥah* and כל העריות, or whether it has moved to a new subject. From the Tosefta, it is clear that the latter is the case; we are now dealing with a baraita on כל העריות, with no interest in the *shifḥah*, and are listing rules regarding different protagonists (man-woman, minor-adult, asleep-awake etc.). The Mishnah has thus merely abstracted some of these rules.

The BT also understood that this part of the Mishnah required a context. The editors, however, chose to see this part of the Mishnah as a continuation of the list of differences between the *shifḥah* and כל העריות and interpreted the Mishnah accordingly (*bKer.* 11a):

והכא חייב קטן א"ר יהודה הכי קתני כל עריות אחד גדול ואחד קטן קטן פטור וגדול חייב והכא גדול נמי פטור מ"ט דהא מקשין אהדדי...

Is a minor male liable with [respect to a *shifḥah]*? Rav Judah said: This is what is taught: For all the transgressions, if one is a minor and one is an adult, the minor is exempt and the adult liable, but here the adult is also exempt. What is the reason? They are made comparable to each other...

(In effect, this conclusion sounds similar to the wording found in the Assemani 66 text concerning the קטן, as discussed in section b):

כל העריות לא עשה בהן את הקטן כגדול, והשפחה עשה בה את הקטנה כגדולה

[Concerning] all the forbidden relationships, [Scripture] has not made the male minor like the adult male, while [concerning] the slave, it has made the minor female like the adult female.

6.5.2 General Considerations between Sifra and Tosefta

It is reasonably clear that the "summary" pericope is the same baraita in both *Sifra* and Tosefta, based on the resemblance in both subject matter and structure. As noted above, however, its overall structure is unusual to the midrashic form. Further, the version of the baraita in Sifra shows certain signs which are consistent with an independent baraita having been modified to serve the needs of the midrashic context:

1. The *Sifra* version lacks the introductory question or context-setting terminology found in Tosefta (אלו דברין שבין שפחה... – These are the [different] matters between the *shifhah*...).

2. The *Sifra* version appears to have streamlined many of the additional details found in Tosefta, and possibly subsumed several cases under one general rule (for instance, the מערה may include the לא מתכוון and the לא כדרכה). The effect of this streamlining is to make the *Sifra* version of the differences pericope relate more closely to the biblical text, as is consistent with the midrashic form.

3. Further to the last point, the *Sifra* version follows the order of the biblical proof texts somewhat more closely than Tosefta:

Biblical phrase & proof	Sifra	Tosefta
1. ואיש-קטן	2. גומר	5.מזיד|שוגג
2. זרע-גומר	1. קטן	2. גומר
3. בקרת-לוקה	3.לוקה-קרבן	1.קטן
	3a. אשם-חטאת	3a. אשם-חטאת
	3b. זכר-נקבה	3b. זכר-נקבה
4.אשר חטא-ביאות הרבה	4. ביאות הרבה	3.לוקה-קרבן
5. אשר חטא-מזיד|שוגג	5.מזיד|שוגג	4.ביאות הרבה

(As noted in section h above, the **ד** witness of *Sifra* also reversed the order of 2 and 1, possibly to make it even more consistent with the biblical text.)

6.5.3 The "Intermarriage" Pericope

We have noted that this pericope in the *Sifra* section (section c) associates the biblical term **נחרפת** with **מאורסת**; the parallel Tosefa passage (lines 15-17) similarly uses the term **נשואה**. The parallel Mishnah passage (lines 9-13), in contrast, though comparable in other respects, leaves out any mention of a slave-free betrothal or marriage. The versions of this pericope found in the two Talmudim add further variations. *Bavli Ker.* 11a provides for a betrothal between two slaves, one Canaanite and one Hebrew:

א1. ת"ר והפדה יכול כולה ת"ל לא נפדתה

ב1. יכול לא נפדתה ת"ל והפדה

2. הא כיצד פדויה ואינה פדויה חציה שפחה וחציה בת חורין ומאורסת לעבד עברי דברי ר"ע

3. ר"י אומר בשפחה כנענית הכתוב מדבר ומאורסת לעבד עברי א"כ מה ת"ל והפדה לא נפדתה דברה תורה כלשון בני אדם

4. ר' אלעזר בן עזריה אומר כל עריות מפורשות לנו משוייר לנו חציה שפחה וחציה בת חורין ומאורסת לעבד עברי

5. אחרים אומרים לא יומתו כי לא חופשה בשפחה כנענית הכתוב מדבר ומאורסת לעבד עברי

Significant Variants

MSS: Munich 95 (**מ**), Florence II-I-7 (**F**), London – BL Add. 25717(402) (**L**), Vatican 120 (**V120**), Vatican 119 (**ו**). The text quoted above is the Vilna edition which serves as the base text in the apparatus below.

א1. ת"ר] = *   שנ' = **L**   יכול כולה] = **F V120**   מניין יכולה כולה = **ו**
יכול לא כולה = **מ**   לא לא נפדתה = **L**

ב1. יכול לא נפדתה] יכול כולה = **L מ**   אי לא נפדתה יכול כולה = **V120**
יכול מקצתה = **F ו**

2. ומאורסת] = **מ** V^{120} L   ומחורפת = F **ו**

3. רבי ישמעאל...לעבד עברי] = *   חסר = L

4. כלשון] = F L   בלשון = **מ ו** V^{120}

5. בשפחה כנענית] = *   בעבד עברי = **מ**

Translation

1. The sages taught: *...redeemed* [Lev. 19:20] – does this mean all of her? Scripture [also] says: *She is not redeemed* [*ibid.*] – does this mean she is not redeemed? [But] Scripture says *...redeemed* [*ibid.*].

2. How can she be redeemed and not redeemed? She is half-slave and half-free and betrothed to a Hebrew slave – these are the words of R. Akiva.

3. R. Ishmael says: The Bible speaks of a female slave who is Canaanite, and is betrothed to a Hebrew slave. Then why [in his view] does Scripture say *redeemed she is not redeemed*? The Bible speaks in ordinary language.

4. R. Elazar b. Azariah says: All the forbidden relationships are set out explicitly for us; there remains to us only the woman who is half-slave, half-free and betrothed to a Hebrew slave.

5. Others say: *They shall not die because she was not free [ibid.]* – the Bible speaks of a female slave who is Canaanite, and betrothed to a Hebrew slave.

Yerushalmi Qidd. 1:1 59a, in contrast, attributes a slave-free betrothal to R. Akiva, and a betrothal between two slaves to R. Ishmael. The discussion takes place after a question is posed as to how a woman who is half-slave half-free would "acquire herself" – that is, can she be divorced, like a wife, or does she follow the usual rules with respect to the manumission of slaves?

6. מהו שתקנה עצמה במיתת רבה ובהשלים שש

7. מה צריכה ליה כרבי עקיבה דרבי עקיבה אמר בשחצייה שפחה וחצייה בת חורין

במאורסת לבן חורין הכתוב מדבר

8. ברם כרבי ישמעאל צריכה ליה דרבי ישמעאל אמ׳ שפחה כנענית הנשואה לעבד עברי הכתוב מדבר

9. אם נישואי תורה הן אם אדניו יתן לו אשה

10. לא צורכה דלא מהו שתקנה עצמה במיתת רבה ובהשלים שש וכמאן דאמר אין עבד עברי עובד את היורש

<u>Variant (MS Leiden)</u>

8. דרבי ישמעאל...מדבר] ∩ = **ל** דר׳ ישמעאל אומר שפחה כנענית הנשואי לעבד עברי הכתוב מדבר = **ל**°°

The homeotoleuton in **ל** is filled in by another hand.
Translation

6. Can she [the *shifḥah neḥerefet*] acquire herself on the death of her master, or upon serving six years [like a Hebrew slave]?

7. Why is this [issue] necessary? [Not for] R. Akiva, as R. Akiva said the Bible speaks of a woman half-slave half-free betrothed to a free man [and therefore presumably can be divorced].

8. It is necessary, however, for R. Ishmael, as R. Ishmael said the Bible speaks [of] a Canaanite *shifḥah* married to a Hebrew *eved*.

9. Is this not a marriage according to the Torah law [i.e. Exod. 21:4]: *If his master gives him a wife....*

10. No, the question is still necessary, can she acquire herself on the death of her master, or upon serving six years, according to one who stated that a Hebrew slave does not serve the heir [i.e. even if this is a "real" marriage, the Hebrew male might go free on the death of the master, but it is not clear that his Canaanite wife would as well].

The differences among the sources (using the base texts in each case, except where otherwise noted) may be summarized as follows; for each source the first element (the identity of the *shifḥah*) and the second element (the relationship) of the opinion attributed to each sage are listed:

	Mishnah	Tosefta	Sifra	Bavli	Yerushalmi
R. Akiva					
1st element	חציה-חציה	same	same	same	same
2nd element	——	נשואה	מאורסת	מאורסת	מאורסת
		לבן חורין	לבן חורין	לע"ע	לבן חורין
R. Ishmael					
1st element	שפחה	כנענית	כנענית	כנענית	כנענית
2nd element	——	נשואה	מאורסת	מאורסת	נשואה
		לעבד כנע'	לבן חורין	לע"ע	ל'ע"ע
אחרים[28]		**(בשם ר"י)**			
1st element		כנענית		כנענית	
2nd element		נשואה		מאורסת	
		לבן חורין		לעבד כנעני	
R. (E)lazar		**(כ"י וויען)**			
1st element	חציה-חציה	same	same	same	——
2nd element	--	נשואה	---	מאורסת	
		לבן חורין		לע"ע	

Certain general observations may be made:

1. All sources seem consistent in identifying the slave as either a half-slave/half-free (ר"ע, ר"א) or a Canaanite (ר"י, ר"מ). (The identification as an עבד עברי in Bavli MS Munich 95 is likely a mistake).

2. The type of relationship is also reasonably consistent among the sages in the various sources: in the Mishnah it is absent, in Tosefta it is נשואין, and in *Sifra*, Bavli and Yerushalmi it is ארוסין (Yerushalmi in one instance has נשואה, however, it must be noted that in MS Leiden,

28 As Finkelstein notes (Finkelstein, *Sifra deVei Rav* 1:54) אחרים may be ר' מאיר, as he is described in *bHorayot* 13b:

...לרבי מאיר אחרים ולר' נתן יש אומרים

...R. Meir has [the opinion of] others and R. Natan has [the opinion of] others say.

the only witness available, this citation is written in the margin in a different hand).

3. It is the object of the relationship which shows the most variability; however, it may be argued that the עבד עברי is prominent only in the Bavli. There are also hints in the Bavli (*bKer.* 11a) that its editors were aware there was another version of the baraita with בן חורין:

> לר' ישמעאל בשלמא והפדה לא נפדתה כדקתני דברה תורה כלשון בני אדם
> אלא דקתני מאורסת לעבד עברי מנלן דכתיב כי לא חופשה מכלל דהוא חופש...

> With respect to R. Ishmael [who according to the Bavli maintains that the *shifḥah neḥerefet* is a Canaanite woman betrothed to a Hebrew slave], his opinion is reasonable with respect to [his non-deconstruction] of *redeemed she has not been redeemed* [Lev. 19:20], as he states: The Torah speaks in the language of humans. But as to what he states, 'betrothed to a Hebrew slave,' where do we derive this? As it is written [*ibid.*]: *she has not been freed* – this implies that he was freed...[emphasis added]

In other words, there is an attempt to assimilate an *eved ivri* to free man. Finkelstein, among others, assumes[29] that this is because:

> אין משפטו של ע"ע שונה מזה של בן חורין. הוא בן חורין שנמסר לזמן קצוב לעבודה

> The law regarding a Hebrew slave does not differ from that of a free man. He is a free man who is given over to work for a fixed period.

This seems, however, to be stretching the point. The commentators do not seem to address this point.

The question therefore arises as to whether Tosefta and *Sifra* simply reflect a slipshod approach to terminology, or whether they in fact reflect different attitudes to slave-free marriages. Finkelstein assumed that the differences in terminology might be explained by assuming that the different terms reflected different marriage customs.[30] Noting the discussion of the

29 Finkelstein, *Sifra deVei Rav* 1:56.
30 Finkelstein, *Sifra deVei Rav* 1:60-61.

term *ḥarufah* in *bQidd.* 6a quoted above,[31] he argued:

בוודאי יש קשר בין השימוש במלה חרופה ביהודה ומנהג בני יהודה להתיר יחוד קודם החופה (יבמות ד'י')...אם כן המלה נחרפת פירושה כמו שאמרו בירושלמי, כתושה... בתוספתא השתמשו במלה נשואה מפני שארוסה בגליל אין פירושה מותרת לבעילה ומיוחדת לאישות...

Undoubtedly there is a connection between the use of the word *ḥarufah* in Judah and the custom in Judah to permit private meeting [between an engaged man and woman] before the *ḥupah* ceremony (*mYev.* 4:10)...if so, the meaning of the word *neḥerefet* is as stated in the Yerushalmi, "crushed" [i.e. a reference to sexual intercourse]... in Tosefta the word *nesu'ah* was used because in the Galilee the meaning of *arusah* would not have encompassed permission for intercourse and designated for wifehood...

While such an explanation might explain the difference in terminology between Sifra and Tosefta, it does not, however, resolve the conflict with the Mishnah,[32] and another solution must be looked for beyond a simple difference in terminology. Having proposed the possibility that *mKer.* 2:4-6 has in general been edited from a previous, Tosefta-like source, we may now explore the possibility that the intermarriage pericope in the Mishnah has also been edited, to reflect the general mishnaic attitude against slave-free intermarriage.

Though there is in fact no *direct* prohibition of "intermarriage" between slave and free in the Mishnah, such a prohibition can be inferred from a number of provisions:

1. *MGitt.* 4:5, (which has a parallel in *mEduyot* 1:13), which addresses

---

31 איבעיא להו: חרופתי מהו? תא שמע, דתניא: האומר חרופתי מקודשת, שכן ביהודה קורין לארוסה חרופה...

It was asked of them [the sages]: What is *ḥarufati* ? Come [and] hear: the one who says *ḥarufati* is betrothed since in Judah they call a betrothed woman *ḥarufah*...

32 Another possibility is that a situation of אירוסין was seen by the editors of Sifra as a compromise between the two positions in Mishnah and Tosefta: less than full marriage, but a way of fitting certain *de facto* relationships, such as those between slaves and free, or the situation of the concubine, into a more normalized system. This solution, however, would imply that the editors of *Sifra* were aware of both positions in Mishnah and Tosefta and deliberately took a position between them.

the problem of the male who is half-slave, half-free. Being partially a slave, he is forbidden to marry a free woman; being partially free, he is forbidden to marry a slave woman:

מי שחציו עבד וחציו בן חורין עובד את רבו יום אחד ואת עצמו יום אחד דברי בית הלל אמרו להם בית שמאי תקנתם את רבו ואת עצמו לא תקנתם לשא שפחה אי אפשר שכבר חציו בן חורין בת חורין אי אפשר שכבד חציו עבד יבטל והלא לא נברא העולם אלא לפריה ורביה שנאמר לא תהו בראה לשבת יצרה אלא מפני תקון העולם כופין את רבו ועושה אותו בן חורין וכותב שטר על חצי דמיו וחזרו בית הלל להורות כדברי בית שמאי

One who is half-slave and half-free works one day for his master and one day for himself – the words of Beit Hillel. Beit Shammai said to them: You have set in order his master['s position] but not his [the slave's]; he cannot marry a *shifḥah* because he is already half-free, and he cannot marry a free woman since he is already half-slave. Shall he be exempt [from marriage]? Was the world not created for propagating, as it is said [Isa. 45:18]: [*God*] *did not create* [*the earth as*] *a wasteland, He formed it to be dwelt in*?[33] Rather, for the sake of worldly order we pressure his master and he frees him, and he [the slave] writes a note for half his value. Beit Hillel reversed themselves to teach according to the words of Beit Shammai.

2. The closest formulation to direct prohibition of "intermarriage" refers to a full female slave and the prohibition is to be inferred from the last element of *mQidd.* 3:12, which, as noted in the Introduction, denies her *qiddushin*:

And whoever has no *qiddushin* with this or any man, the child follows her [status]. What child is this? The child of a *shifḥah* or gentile woman.

The following points support the idea that the Mishnah version of the *shifḥah neḥerefet* passage in *mKer.* was edited to support this anti-intermarriage stance:

1. In the commentary on section (c) of the *Sifra* passage above, a question

33 There is evidence that females were deemed not to be subject to the commandment "to be fruitful and multiply"; see, e.g. Tosafot, *bB.Bat.* 13a, שנאמר ה"ד, which repeats the maxim: דאיתתא לא מפקדא אפריה ורביה (That the woman is not commanded concerning being fruitful and multiplying).

was raised as to whether the sages actually said all that was attributed to them – in particular, whether both R. Ishmael and R. Akiva identified the *shifḥah*, and then specified to whom she was related and how. It was further noted that there is a discrepancy between Mishnah and Tosefta: both these elements are present in Tosefta (and *Sifra*), whereas only the first is present in the Mishnah. In other words, if we were to accept the position that Tosefta is a commentary on the Mishnah, the Tosefta editor has added words which imply that the Sages ignored the position of both Houses (as reflected in *mGitt.* 4:5) that נשואין was impossible for slaves and half-slaves.

It is more logical to argue the opposite case: the Mishnah editor, in citing a version of the intermarriage pericope similar to that in Tosefta, deleted any reference to the second element, so as to make the views of the Sages consistent with *mGitt.* 4:5. This situation would imply that, despite the references to the views of the Houses in *mGitt.* 4:5, the idea attributed to them that נשואין were unavailable to a slave or half-slave was actually a later development. With respect to *mGitt.* 4:5 being a later development, it is interesting to note that Tosefta appears to contain no material corresponding to *mGitt.* 4:4-5, or the corresponding *mEduyot* 1:13; that is, there is no material regarding the hypothecated slave or the general legal status of the half-slave half-free. This is, of course, an argument from silence; this silence, however, is also consistent with the mishnayot having been added after Tosefta's compilation, whenever this compilation took place.

It must also be questioned whether R. Elazar's view was part of the original intermarriage pericope in either Mishnah or Tosefta, as this attribution does not appear in all witnesses – for instance, the Mishnah contained in MS Munich, and the witness which served as the base text for Zuckermandel's *Kereitot*. The most likely explanation for the omission, however, is an error based on *homeoteleuton*, with respect to the words בן חורין.

2. The degree of variation in the Mishnah text at this point may also be noted, since it makes interpretation difficult – in particular, אי זו היא versus זו היא, and the fact that the word ודאי is masculine in all but the Maimonides text. In MS Munich, the effect of the variant readings is

to make an anonymous *tanna* answer R. Ishmael's question איזוהי שפחה with וודאי כל העריות מפורשות.

3. There is also the discrepancy, noted above, between the view of R. Elazar ben Azaria expressed in this Mishnah and his usual attitude toward R. Akiva. It may be noted that the editors of the Bavli also seem aware of this discrepancy, and reconcile it by providing him with another biblical interpretation (*bKer.* 11a):

> ר' אלעזר בן עזריה היינו ר"ע לר' ישמעאל קאמר לדידי בעלמא כוותיך סבירא ליה דדברה תורה כלשון בני אדם והכא שאני מכדי כתיב ליה קרא כי לא חופשה, והפדה לא נפדתה ל"ל ש"מ להכי אתא לחציה שפחה וחציה בת חורין
>
> R. Elazar ben Azariah – is this [not like the opinion of] R. Akiva? [One could suppose that in this case] he said to R. Ishmael: Generally it is like your opinion; he holds that the Torah speaks in human [i.e. plain] language. But here it is different; when Scripture writes *because she has not been freed*, why do I [also] need *she has not been redeemed*? Derive from this that [that phrase] came [to teach about] one who is half-slave, half-free.

4. We may note also that R. Ishmael's identification of the *shifḥah* in the Mishnah version of this pericope describes her as a שפחה וודיי, as opposed to a שפחה כנענית. The meaning of the term וודיי is not clear – that is, whether it is intended as the equivalent of the latter term, or as the opposite of ספק,[34] seemingly in contrast to R. Akiva's identification of the *shifḥah* as חציה שפחה חציה בת חורין. In any event, the impression is that this is a deliberate editorial change in the Mishnah, given that Tosefta and Sifra agree on the reading שפחה כנענית.

5. In summary, it is possible that a version similar to that represented in Tosefta was the basis upon which the mishnaic editor took his outline, edited to fit within the general principles of the Mishnah. The earlier form of the intermarriage pericope had the sages expressing the view that נישואין were possible for both the שפחה כנענית and the half-slave; this point of view had changed by the time of the redaction of the Mishnah.

---

34 See n. 4 *supra*.

6.5.4 The Priority of the Tosefta Passage

The following sequence of events may be proposed as consistent with the evidence: Tosefta represents the earliest version of the intermarriage pericope, which was later assimilated into a larger unit. This earlier intermarriage pericope attests to the possibility of intermarriage between slaves and free persons. As changes in the law occurred (possibly under Roman influence), the baraita was assimilated into the Mishnah in edited form according to its general system of prohibiting *qiddushin* to slaves. Some schools, however, allowed a compromise situation, that of ארוסין, which is reflected in *Sifra* and the Talmudim. The change to עבד עברי in the Bavli represents an attempt to reconcile the earlier baraitot with the Mishnah, according to the tradition that the עבד עברי[35] is the only one permitted to a שפחה כנענית under Exod. 21:4.

6.5.5 Conclusion

The mishnaic rules state, at least indirectly, a prohibition against intermarriage between slave and free. This is seen in *mQidd.* 3:12, which denies the ability of the *shifḥah* to form *qiddushin*, and *mGitt.* 4:5, which attests to the inability of the male who is "half-slave, half-free" to form *qiddushin*. Other tannaitic sources, however, do make reference to intermarriage between female slaves and free males. This is seen, for instance, in a passage found in *tKer.* 1:16-18 and *Sifra Qedoshim pereq* 5, which are parallel to *mKer.* 2:4b-6. These passages discuss the law of the *shifḥah neḥerefet* in Lev. 19:20-22. The Mishnah passage refers to various opinions as to the identity of the *shifḥah neḥerefet*, as either half-slave, half-free (R. Akiva) or a "real" slave (R. Ishmael). The Tosefta and *Sifra* passages contain expanded versions of these opinions; Tosefta refers to a half-slave, half-free female married (נשואה) to a free man, or a Canaanite female slave married to either a free man or Canaanite *eved*, while the *Sifra* passage refers to a half-slave, half-free female betrothed (מאורסת) to a free man, or a Canaanite female slave betrothed to a free man. These

35 As reflected, e,g. in the *Mekhilta de R' Ishmael*, *Neziqin*, *parshah* 2 (ed. Jacob Lauterbach, *Mekilta de-Rabbi Ishmael* [Philadelphia: Jewish Publication Society of America, 1976]), 10.

differences, it is argued, are significant, and reflect the existence of rabbinic opinions that did not prohibit intermarriage between slave and free. It has also been argued, contrary to traditional opinion, that the toseftan version of the passage, rather than the mishnaic version, is the original (or "more" original). Foreign influence was suggested as one possibility to explain the change of opinion reflected in the Mishnah.

The *Sifra* passage, however, also discusses manumission methods, and in particular the method for creating someone who is "half-slave, half-free." It was noted that this concept seems to be contrary to theories of slave ownership that formed part of Roman law; such a contradiction would, of course, complicate any question of foreign influence.

A more likely explanation of the variations, which are so complex as to be rendered as ineffectual, is that these simply reflect the complexity of tannaitic thought and its myriad exegetical methods. I wish to examine in depth the question of a half-slave half-free status, in an attempt to ascertain whether this was a convenient construct or an actual status.

6.6 EXCURSUS: THE EXISTENCE OF A HALF-SLAVE, HALF-FREE STATUS

As we have noted in 6.5.3 the necessity of correcting the impediment to marriage for a male who is half-slave half-free (*mGitt.* 4:5) is one of the few indirect references in the Mishnah to a prohibition against intermarriage between slave and free. We have also noted that in the Roman legal system, contrary to the discussions in *Sifra*, the creation of a half-slave half-free status was a legal impossibility. The question arises as to whether this status was simply a theoretical construct within the rabbinic legal system.[36]

[36] The fondness of the mishnaic editor(s) for classifications and for discussing the theoretical boundaries between classes has been noted by Judith Romney Wegner (Wegner, *Chattel or Person* 7). She argues that the Mishnah shares the "Hellenistic dislike of the excluded middle"; to avoid creating hybrid categories for items that cannot be easily classified (such as the *koy* of *mBikk.* 2:8), the Mishnah will describe them as "like X" in some respects and "not like X" in others. As a further example of a situation that appears to be such theorizing, we may note *mGitt.* 8:2; if a husband has thrown his wife her bill of divorce so that it lands halfway between the two of them, she is described as מגרשת ואינה מגרשת (divorced and not divorced). Likely this did not describe an actual status, particularly as the situation could be easily remedied.

In support of a contention that such a situation of partial freedom actually existed, we may note briefly that something resembling such a "half" status is found in various slave systems, and seems to arise in various ways:

a) One of several partners freeing his share in a slave, as suggested in the *Sifra* section above. Biezunska-Malowist cites examples among the Greco-Roman papyri in Egypt of ownership of partial shares in slaves. She notes that partial manumission was viable in these legal systems, contrary to the situation in Roman law.[37]

b) Someone who was viewed as a slave with respect to one person but free with respect to another. We may note, for instance, the situation set out in *mGitt.* 4:4, the mishnah (perhaps not coincidentally) preceding that discussing the situation of the half-slave; here a debtor has pledged a slave as security to a creditor, and the debtor has freed the slave while he is still pledged:[38]

...עבד שעשאו רבו אפותיקי לאחרים ושחררו שורת הדין אין העבד חייב כלום
אלא מפני תקון העולם כופין את רבו ועושה אותו בן חורין וכותב שטר על דמיו...

A slave whose master makes him a hypothec to others and frees him – the strict law is that the slave owes nothing, but for the sake of social order we put pressure on his master, and he frees him, and he writes him a note for his value...

The interpretation of this passage is quite difficult (in particular, the precise kind of security implied by "hypothec," whether it is the creditor who is the "master" being pressured to free the slave, and who

37 Biezunska-Malowist, *L'esclavage* 123, n. 1. She cites, among others, the case of a woman receiving rights to a half-share in a number of slaves whom her brother had freed. She speculates (ibid. 129) that where several slaves were co-owned among several people, there might have been a tendency to maintain the legal co-ownership, even if the slaves were in fact divided up among the various owners, both to minimize the tax paid by each co-owner, and to spread the risk of loss.

38 One assumes, first, that the slave has remained in the debtor's possession, and second, that there is no concept of differentiated ownership, in which a creditor might ensure that his rights had priority.

is to write the note); for our purposes, however, we may conclude that the issue is whether the pledged but freed person still remains a slave with respect to the creditor.

c) A slave allowed to purchase his manumission over time, so that he gains his freedom by degrees. Such is one of the situations considered by Westermann to underlie an edict dating to the Second Temple period and applicable to Syria-Phoenicia.[39] The precise function of the edict is unclear,[40] but seems to require the registration (for tax purposes) of various types of holdings, such as cattle and slaves. Of interest for our purposes is an unusual reference in this edict to *σωματα λαικα ελευθερα*. This term, as Westermann notes, implies "enslaved persons who are free"; one of the purposes of the edict, in his opinion, was to free those persons who were not considered legally complete slaves, because, among other possibilities, they had been partially manumitted.[41] He suggests further, based on literary similarities, that the author of the Letter of Aristeas, in which there is a reference to an alleged freeing of Hebrew slaves by Ptolemy II, may have used a document resembling this edict as a model for the freeing of those wrongfully enslaved.[42]

d) Conditional manumission, in which the slave is freed if he or she agrees to continue to provide some service to the master until some future point. Scholars studying the various ways of providing for the elderly in the ancient Near East note (among other methods) an arrangement made with a slave to serve the master in return for manumission upon the master's death.[43] In certain cases this arrangement might include the

39 The edict is the Rainer Papyrus (PER) Inv. 24, 552, dated by William L. Westermann, "Enslaved Persons Who are Free," *American Journal of Philology* 59 (1938) 2 to the 3rd century BCE during the reign of Ptolemy Philadelphus.

40 Westermann, "Enslaved Persons," 7, argued in contrast to earlier opinion that this was not in itself a fiscal edict, but presumed an earlier edict requiring registration of "slaves"; as too many people had avoided registration on the assumption that their human holdings were not slaves, this edict was an inquiry into status.

41 "Enslaved Persons," 1, 14. For a somewhat more recent example of manumission by installments, see the discussion of the Cuban institution of *coortación* in Herbert S. Klein, *Slavery in the Americas. A Comparative Study of Virginia and Cuba* (Chicago: University of Chicago Press, 1967) 196-200.

42 Westermann, "Enslaved Persons" 19-20.

43 See, *e.g.*, the sources cited in Marten Stol and Sven Vleeming, *The Care of the Elderly in*

provision of a mate for the slave (whether another slave, or a free person), with both partners undertaking the responsibility of caring for the master; in some cases such an arrangement might also have been a way to provide for a daughter with "limited prospects."[44] In certain of these cases the verb *palāḫu* might be used to describe the obligation of the slave or couple. Variations on this type of *palāḫu* arrangement involving slaves are found in documents of different eras, including NA redemption agreements, in which a person redeemed from slavery is called on to repay his redeemer through service,[45] and NB/LB *širkūtu* documents, in which a slave is dedicated to a god on the condition that he continue to serve his master in some capacity.[46] The slave's freedom in such cases may be described as tenuous or ambiguous, taking effect immediately yet dependent on the future fulfillment of a condition that might not occur. The situation has been described as reminiscent of the Greek institution of *παραμονη*, and creating a situation of "*halbfreiheit.*"[47]

---

the Ancient Near East. Studies in the History and Culture of the Ancient Near East 14 (Leiden: E.J. Brill, 1998) 51-53 (Neo-Sumerian), 83-84 (Old Babylonian), 183-184 (Neo-Babylonian). A similar example from Nuzi can be found in Aapeli Saarisalo, "New Kirkuk Documents Relating to Slaves," *Studia Orientalia* 3 (1934) 13, in which an adopted male slave is to serve the adopter (*ipallaḫšu*).

44 Stol and Vleeming, *Care of the Elderly* 83, 193.

45 See, e.g. SAAS V, 16, BM 103206, lines 11-12, in which it appears that two men have redeemed their brother from slavery, and he is to repay them by serving them:
kūm KU'.BABBAR 3 MU.AN.NA.MEŠ
[x IT]U.MEŠ-*ni ipallahšunu*
for the silver [probably interest], 3 years
x months he shall serve them.

46 See, e.g. Yale Babylonian Texts [= YBT] Vol. VII 17, lines 8b-14, cited in Raymond Dougherty, *The Shirkûtu of Babylonian Deities*. YOS Researches 5/2 (New Haven: Yale University Press. Reprinted New York: AMS Press, 1923) 40-41. In this instance a husband PN1 and wife PN2 dedicate their slave PN3 to Ishtar "for the preservation of their lives" (*ana balāṭ napšatīšunu*), though retaining him in lifelong service; Dougherty suggests this is possibly the first stage of a manumission:

ūmū mala	During the days that
PN1 *u*	PN1 and
PN2 *balṭunū*	PN2 are living,
PN3 *ipallaḫšunūtu*	PN3 shall serve them.
ina ūmu ina šīmat ittallkū	On the day they go to their fate,
PN3 *šimki*	PN3 a *sirku*(?)
ša Ištar iššû	of Ishtar shall be.

47 Paul Koschaker, *Über einige griechische Rechtsurkunden aus den östlichen Randgebieten des*

Such an arrangement may in fact be hinted at in biblical references to the עבד עולם in Exod. 21:5-6 and Deut. 15:17, despite the suggestion of permanent servitude implicit in this phrase.[48] In support of this interpretation of the biblical term we may note, first, that the two non-pentateuchal instances of עבד עולם also hint at a relationship of a client-patron nature. In 1Sam. 27:12, Akhish refers to David as his *eved olam*; in Job. 40:28, there is an interesting apposition of *eved olam* with ברית, as part of a description of the power of Leviathan:

היכרת ברית עמך תקחנו לעבד עולם

Will he make a covenant with you, will you take him as an *eved olam*?

Second, we may note that the Onkelos Targum to Exod. 21:6 and Deut. 15:17 has עבד פלח לעלם ("a slave who serves/works forever," as opposed to the biblical "a slave forever").[49] This Targum generally uses פלח to translate the Hebrew עבד in all its range of meanings, including "to work" and "to worship," as well as for other situations of slave's labour, including the idea of the Hebrew רדה , as in Lev. 25:43. It can, however, also bear the meaning of "to serve."[50] We may note that PLḤ is used in a variety of post-biblical agreements, often as part of a list of mutual obligations undertaken by the parties to the agreement.[51] Most relevant for

---

Hellenismus (Leipzig: S. Hirzel, 1931) 74.

48 We may note that the ritual described, particularly in the Exod. passage in which the slave is brought אל האלהים, is reminiscent of the slave's dedication to a god in the *širkūtu* arrangement cited in Dougherty, *The Shirkûtu of Babylonian Deities* supra n. 39.

49 Targum Neofiti has עבד משתעבד לעלם – a slave who is enslaved permanently, and in Deut. 15:17 עבד משעבד עוד לעולם — a slave enslaved forever, while TY in Exod. 21:6 reflects the rule in *mQidd.* 1:2, by limiting this slave's term to the Jubilee: עבד פלח עד יובלא – a slave works/serves until the Jubilee.

50 See, *e.g.* Dalman, *s.v.* פלח, who gives *dienen* as one of the meanings for both the Hebrew and Aramaic forms.

51 The terms אפלח and פלחה are found in certain marriage contracts of the geonic period. Mordechai Friedman, *Jewish Marriage in Palestine. A Cairo Genizah Study* (Tel Aviv: Jewish Theological Seminary of America, 1980) 1:172 notes that אפלח appears as one of the husband's obligations in non-Palestinian style *ketubbot*, as in the following instance :

...ואנא אפלח ואיזון ואיסובר ואפרנס ואכלכל ומיקר...

And I will serve, feed, support, sustain, maintain

our purposes is a conditional manumission document from Elephantine. In this document (Porten and Yardeni, B.3.6), one Meshullam frees his *amah* Tapamet and her daughter; Tapamet had previously married the man Anani. Though in line 4 of the document the release from slavery seems to take place as of Meshullam's death (Porten and Yardeni in fact characterize the document as a "Testamentary Manumission"), lines 8-12 suggest that the release takes place immediately, on the condition that the two women continue to *PLḤ* Meshullam and then his son:

...ואנתי שביקה מן טלא לסמשא ויהישמע ברתכי וגבר אחרן לא שליט עליכי
ועל יהישמע ברתכי ואנתי שביקה לאלהא ואמרת תפמת ויהישמע ברתה אנחן
יפלחנך זי יסבל בר וברה לאבוהי בחייך ועד מותך נסבל לזכור ברך...

...[Meshullam states:] You are let go from the shade to the sun, and your daughter Yehoyishma, and no other man has authority over you and over Yehoyishma your daughter, and you are let go to God. And Tapamet said, and her daughter: We will *PLḤ* you as a son or daughter supports its father, in your lifetime and until your death, [and then] we will support your son Zakur...

(Friedman Vol II. p. 62, line 9)

A similar set of obligations appears in the formulary of R. Hai Gaon :

...[ואנא] במימרא דשמיא אפלח ואוקיר ואיזון ואפרנס ואכלכל ואכבי יתיכ[י]...

And I in the name of heaven shall serve and honor and maintain and support and sustain and clothe you

(Assaf, 1st document, p. 13)

פלחה appears as one of the wife's obligations in Palestinian-style *ketubbot*:

וקב[ל]ת דתהוי מוקרה ומיקרה ומשמשה ו[פלחה קמיה]...

And she undertook to honor, esteem, attend and [serve him]..

(Friedman Vol. II. p. 39, line 11)

Falk (in Ze'ev Falk, "Mutual Obligations in the Ketubah," *JJS* 8 [1957] 217) would translate these forms of *PLḤ* as meaning "to cherish," arguing that, with respect to the husband's אפלח, this was a "moral" obligation, added relatively late to supplement the legal obligations. Friedman, on the contrary, takes both forms of *PLḤ* in these contracts to refer to "service." Whatever the precise nuance, we may argue that as in the conditional manumissions *PLḤ* suggests an obligation undertaken within a mutual set of benefits.

Such conditional status changes were recognized as creating difficulties regarding the precise situation of the person subject to the condition. The Mishnah speaks of the circumstances under which a bill of divorce (גט)[52] can be given conditionally, and questions the status of the woman in such a case (*mGitt.* 7:3-4):

זה גטך אם מתי זה גטך אם מתי מחלי זה זה גטך מאחר מיתה לא אמר כלום
מהיום אם מתי מעכשיו אם מתי הרי זה גט...מה היא באותן הימים רבי יהודה אומר
כאשת איש לכל דבריה רבי יוסי אומר מגרשת ואינה מגרשת

> [If one gives a bill of divorce conditionally, such as] 'This is your *get* if I die' [or] 'this is your *get* if I die of this disease' – [this is like saying] 'this is your *get* after [my] death – he has said nothing. [If he says, 'This is your *get*] from today, if I die' [or] 'from now, if I die' – this is a [valid] *get*... What [status] is she during this time? R. Yehudah says she is like a married woman in all respects; R. Yosi says she is divorced and not divorced.

The Mishnah thus confirms that a conditional change of status must be effective immediately, even if the condition does not materialize until the future; we note also that there is a question as to the woman's precise status during this time, with R. Yosi's "divorced/not divorced" suggesting something like the "half-slave/half-free" situation.

The difficulty inherent in these future conditions is again discussed in the formulary of Rav Yehudah Barzilai with respect to a conditional manumission. The specific concern is a situation in which a slave is freed on condition he serve the master until the master's death; if the slave happens to die before the master, the condition is not fulfilled, and the status of any marriage contracted in the meantime, and that of any children, are in doubt. A number of ingenious proposals are made to avoid this difficulty, including the following:[53]

...וכן תקנתי שיכתו' לו שטר שחרור שלם ויאמר לו הרי זה שחרור ע"מ שתכתו' לי עליך
שטר מוחזק שתמשני כל ימי חיי בכך וכך נמצא זה שחרור תלוי בכתיבה ולא בשימוש
מאלתר... הרי הוא מותר בבת ישראל...

---

52 Aside from its name, this document bears other similarities to a deed of manumission (גט שחרור), such as its operative wording. See, *e.g.*, *mGitt.* 1:4, 9:3.

53 Halberstam, *Book of Documents* 127 (document of conditional slave).

> ...thus I have established that he [the master] write him a complete deed of manumission, and say to him, 'Here is a manumission, on the condition that you write for my benefit a secure deed that you will serve me all my life [by doing] this and that.' The manumission is thus conditional on the writing [of the deed of service] forthwith and not on the service [itself]...then he is permitted to an Israelite woman...

In this way the slave does not have to wait until the master's death to marry, and fulfillment of the condition is easier to assess.

In summary, it is possible that the concept of "half-slavery" was associated with practical situations – conditional manumission or partial manumission among them. Yet, as the *Sifra* section discussed above indicates, there was a difference of opinion concerning how a partial manumission could be effected. It seems that again we are dealing with a concept that is incapable of application.

CHAPTER 7

LITERATURE IN SUPPORT OF LAW: THE PROBLEM OF BILHAH AND ZILPAH

7.1 THE DILEMMA

The biblical narratives regarding Hagar, Bilhah and Zilpah, the slave-wives of Abraham and Jacob who bear children on behalf of Sarah, Rachel, and Leah, closely reflect the "surrogacy" contracts that are found in various eras and locations in the ancient Near East.[1] These arrangements generally involved a slave woman provided to the husband by the wife, or bought by the couple, who was to bear children on behalf of the wife. Apparently typical of such arrangements was the rather ambiguous status of the "surrogate," as is attested, for instance, in an OB contract (CT VIII 22b, UAZP 77) that refers to the purchase of a girl by a male, PN3, and female, PN4 (presumably husband and wife):

> PN1 *mārat* PN2 *itti* PN2 *abīša* PN3 *u* PN4 *išāmūši*
> *ana* PN3 *aššat ana* PN4 *amat*
> *ūm* PN1 *ana* PN4 *bēltīša ul bēltī attī iqtabu ugallabši ana kaspim inaddišši*

> PN1 is the daughter of PN2; from her father, PN2, PN3 and PN4 have bought her.
> To PN3 [husband] she is (in the status of) a wife, to PN 4[wife] she is (in the status of) a slave.
> On the day that PN1 says to PN4 her mistress: "You are not my mistress," she (may) shave her and sell her.

1 For discussions of these contracts, see, e.g., A. K. Grayson and J. van Seters, "The Childless Wife in Assyria" (NA documents); Westbrook, *Old Babylonian Marriage Law* chap. 6, esp. 106 (OB documents); and Tikva Frymer-Kensky, "Patriarchal Family Relationships and Near Eastern Law," *Biblical Archeologist* 44 (1981): 209-14 (OB documents).

The biblical accounts of Bilhah and Zilpah also reflect this ambiguity, as we will see below. Further, their status and the status of their offspring present an interesting dilemma with respect to the matrilineal principle. Under mishnaic law (*mQidd.* 3:12) these women would be deemed incapable of *qiddushin,* and their four offspring (Dan, Naftali, Gad and Asher) would legally be slaves. We have noted the inconsistency in reaction to slave status in various legal sources. I suggest that postbiblical narratives of Bilhah and Zilpah in so-called literary sources—such as found in apocrypha, Targumim, aggadic midrash, and within some of the legal sources—show the same sort of inconsistency in their reactions to the status of these women. Thus, for instance, discomfort with the women's slave origins is explicitly revealed in the Bavli and Targum references, as well as in certain later midrashim associated with the school of R. Moshe haDarshan; other references, however, seem indifferent to the question of their slave status. These competing traditions suggest that the mishnaic disapproval of slave-free intermarriage, and the consequent effects on a child's status, did not constitute a unanimous, linear tradition.

7.2 BIBLICAL REFERENCES TO BILHAH AND ZILPAH

The biblical passages regarding the origins of these two "slave-wives" reveal them as women of apparently dubious ancestry and limited deeds; they are described simply as *shefaḥot* belonging to Lavan and given in turn to his daughters Rachel and Leah when each married Jacob (Gen. 29:24, 29). As a result of an apparent competition between the two daughters to bear children, each daughter donates her *shifḥah* to Jacob, in a repetition of Sarah's donation of her *shifḥah* Hagar to Abraham (Gen. 16:2ff). Bilhah gives birth to sons Dan and Naphtali, and Zilpah to sons Gad and Asher. A review of the relevant passages in Gen. 30:3-13 indicates the terseness of the narrative, which is careful to keep the two women marginal to the action:

ותאמר הנה אמתי בלהה בא אליה ותלד על ברכי ואבנה גם אנכי ממנה.
ותתן לו את בלהה שפחתה לאשה ויבא אליה יעקב.
ותהר בלהה ותלד ליעקב בן.
ותאמר רחל דנני אלהים וגם שמע בקלי ויתן לי בן על כן קראה שמו דן.
ותהר עוד ותלד בלהה שפחת רחל בן שני ליעקב...ותקרא שמו נפתלי.
ותרא לאה כי עמדה מלדת ותקח את זלפה שפחתה ותתן אתה ליעקב לאשה.

ותלד זלפה שפחת לאה ליעקב בן...ותקרא את שמו גד.
ותלד זלפה שפחת לאה בן שני ליעקב...ותקרא את שמו אשר.

> [Rachel said]: Here is my *amah* Bilhah; lie with her, and she shall give birth on my knees, and I will be built up from her. She gave him [Jacob] Bilhah her *shifḥah* as a wife, and Jacob lay with her. Bilhah conceived and bore Jacob a son. Rachel said: God has judged me, and also heard my voice and gave me a son; therefore she called his name Dan. [Bilhah] conceived again, and Bilhah the *shifḥah* of Rachel bore a second son to Jacob...and she [Rachel] called his name Naftali. Leah saw that she had left off giving birth; she took Zilpah her *shifḥah* and gave her to Jacob as a wife. Zilpah the *shifḥah* of Leah bore Jacob a son...and she [Leah] called his name Gad. Zilpah the *shifḥah* of Leah bore Jacob a second son...and [Leah] called his name Asher.

Like Hagar, the women are variously described as *amah, shifḥah,* and *ishah.* Unlike Hagar, however, these two *shefaḥot* have no period of rebellion or speech of their own.[2] They are little more than surrogate wombs, deliberately dissociated from the biological fact of motherhood: Rachel says (Gen. 30:3), "I will be built/have children through [Bilhah]" (the Hebrew אבנה can be taken as a play on the words בן (son/child), and בנה (build)); it is Rachel and Leah who actually name the children borne by the other women. The inherent ambiguity of the surrogate is further reflected in the fact that some of the biblical chronologies do emphasize Bilhah and Zilpah as the mothers—for instance, Gen. 33:2 (Jacob's meeting with Esau, albeit in a position of greater danger which may indicate lesser status), Gen. 35:25-6 (a listing of the sons of Jacob), and Gen. 46:18, 25 (describing the migration to Egypt). Yet in Ruth 4:11, it is only Rachel and Leah who are said to have "built the house of Israel" (אשר בנו שתיהן את בית ישראל).

Further, though the Genesis 30 passage quoted above clearly describes Bilhah and Zilpah as "wives" of Jacob, this description is not maintained consistently. Genesis 32:23, for instance, expressly distinguishes between the two groups of women:

2 Bilhah in one instance is also called a *pilegesh* (Gen. 35:22). As I suggest in chapter 1, a) the word *pilegesh* should be translated as "consort" rather than "concubine," and does not indicate a particular legal status; b) the word *pilegesh* may have been added to the account of the Bilhah-Reuven incident in Gen. 35:22, so as to avoid any suggestion that Bilhah was Jacob's wife and thus that Reuven was guilty of incest; thus even within the biblical text itself there may have been an uncertainty regarding her status.

...ויקח את שתי נשיו ואת שתי שפחתיו ואת אחד עשר ילדיו...

...and he [Jacob] took his two wives and his two *shefaḥot* and his eleven sons...

Genesis 35:25 and 26 similarly refer to Bilhah and Zilpah as the *shefaḥot* of Rachel and Leah respectively, while 46:18 and 25 refer to Zilpah and Bilhah as being given by Lavan to Leah and Rachel. Further, Bilhah and Zilpah and their children are clearly placed closest to the danger at Jacob's meeting with Esau (Gen. 33:1, 2, 6). Yet despite these indications of their subordinate rank, it is only Bilhah who is explicitly mentioned by name as a wife of Jacob in the genealogies of Chronicles (1Chr. 7:13).

This "scheme" of surrogate and diverse motherhood may reflect, as has been suggested by scholars,[3] an "awareness of unequal degrees of kinship" among the founding groups of Israel; yet there is nothing in the Bible to suggest that any of the tribes was regarded as of lower status than the rest. Genesis 37, recounting the situation leading up to Joseph's abduction by his brothers, may suggest some ill-feeling on the part of the sons of Bilhah and Zilpah, whose דבה רעה (evil talk), was reported by Joseph to his father Jacob (v. 2).[4] Yet their mothers are still referred to in this verse as the *nashim (*wives), of Joseph's father.[5]

---

3 See, e.g., John Bright, *A History of Israel* (Philadelphia: Westminster Press, 1959), 142-43.

4 Such ill-feeling was read into this story by the author of the apocryphal story "Joseph and Aseneth" (C. Burchard, "Joseph and Aseneth," in *The Old Testament Pseudepigrapha* [ed. J.H. Charlesworth; New York: Doubleday, 1985], 177-247). The story describes a plot against Joseph by the Pharaoh's son, who attempts to enlist the aid of the sons of the "handmaids" (24:2):

> And his servants said to him into the ear, saying, "Behold, the sons of Bilhah and the sons of Zilpah, Leah's and Rachel's maidservants, Jacob's wives, are hostile to Joseph and Aseneth and envy them...."

The story continues at vv. 7-9:

> And Pharaoh's son lied to them [the sons] and said, "... I heard Joseph your brother saying I will blot them out from the earth and all their offspring lest they share the inheritance with us, because they are children of maidservants...."

5 We may note also that in 1Chr. 2:1-2, the order of the sons is different from the order of their births in Gen. 29ff and the order of the lists in chaps. 35 and 46. In chap. 35 all of Leah's sons are listed first, followed by Rachel's sons and then the "surrogate" sons Dan, Naphtali, Gad, and Asher of Bilhah and Zilpah, while in chap. 46 all of Leah's sons are followed by Zilpah's sons and then Rachel's and Bilhah's sons.

7.3 EARLY POSTBIBLICAL REFERENCES

An examination of the terms used to describe Bilhah and Zilpah in early literature reveals two distinct trends. Most of the Targumim translate *amah* and *shifḥah* in reference to Bilhah and Zilpah with the usual אמתא and *ishah* with אתתא; the LXX similarly has *παιδίσκη* and *γυνή*. Another trend is evident, however, which implies that the women were some sort of subordinates, rather than outright slaves. This indicates, it seems to me, a sensitivity to the problems that would be created by *mQidd.* 3:12.

First, we may note that Josephus, as well as three of the Targumim, are careful to avoid the suggestion that Jacob had married "slaves." In *Ant.* 1:303, Josephus states that the women were not "slaves" (*δοῦλαι*) but rather *ὑποτεταγμέναι*, "subordinates" (Liddell / Scott). Targum Pseudo-Jonathan adds explicitly that Bilhah and Zilpah were "freed" before Rachel and Leah gave them to Jacob:

ושחררת ליה ית בלהה אמתה ומסרה ליה לאנתו ועל לוותה יעקב
וחמת לאה ארום קמת מלמילד ושחררת ית זלפה ויהבת יתה ליעקב לאנתו

> And [Rachel] freed her handmaid Bilhah for him and gave her for wifehood, and Jacob went in unto her. (TY to Gen. 30:3)
> And Leah saw that she had ceased to bear children and she freed Zilpah her handmaid and gave her to Jacob for wifehood. (TY to Gen. 30:9)

There is as well an interesting pattern of translation in Onkelos, which I would argue is also an attempt to suggest that Bilhah and Zilpah were "subordinates," and thus to get away from any suggestion of slavery. Like the other Targumim, Targum Onkelos generally uses אמתא to translate

[In Gen. 37:2, they are simply referred to as "his (Joseph's) father's wives," but Joseph brings to his father Jacob "bad reports of them." According to Targum Pseudo-Jonathan the sons of the slave wives are accused of eating the limbs of living animals, a serious transgression of the dietary laws. Targum Neofiti uses a root signifying "character, nature" intimating that the sons of the slave wives were inherently evil. According to *Ber. Rab.* (Theodor-Albeck) 84:2, Joseph brings reports from his brothers of them eating the limbs of living animals, casting their eyes on the women of the land, scorning them and referring to them as "sons of the slave women, slaves." Martin McNamara brings the relevant bibliography for this reading in *Targum Neofiti 1: Genesis* (Collegeville, Minn.: Liturgical Press, 1992), 171 n. 3. TM]

shifḥah and *amah*; in addition, it uses the term לחנה as a translation for the Hebrew *pilegesh*. In five instances, however, לחנה is also used by Onkelos to translate *amah* or *shifḥah*. These instances (Gen. 31:33; 32:23; 33:1, 2, 6) exhibit a particular pattern: (i) they relate only to Bilhah and Zilpah, (ii) they are used only after these women have been taken as wives by Jacob, and (iii) they are used only when the text describes them in relation either to Jacob or to his camp, and not in relation to Rachel and Leah. This pattern, which is also followed in Neofiti and Pseudo-Jonathan, suggests that Targum Onkelos is deliberately departing from its usual word-for-word translation in order to emphasize that the women, though likely subordinate to the other wives, were not slaves in their relationship to Jacob.

7.3.1 לחנה in Onkelos as a Cognate of the Akkadian laḫḫi/anatu, "Female Subordinate"

The forms of לחנה found in the Targumim are generally assumed to mean "concubine;"[6] Dalman (*s.v.* לחינה, לחינתא) argued that there were two forms, לחינה, meaning *Magd* (maid) and לחינתא, meaning both *Magd* and *Kebsweib* (concubine). Despite this often-found association with concubines (or maidservants), S. Kaufman[7] in fact accepts לחנה as a loanword from the Akkadian *laḫḫi/anatu*, a female "official at the queen's court" (*CAD*) or simply *eine Angestellte* (female employee) (*AHW*).[8] Kaufman contends that Onkelos misunderstood לחנה as "concubine" and hence incorrectly applied it to translate the Hebrew *pilegesh*. Yet the argument is circular, as there is nothing to suggest that Onkelos understood either *pilegesh* or the Bilhah-

6 Sokoloff and Jastrow give "concubine" as the translation; Mandelkern similarly has *pellex*. Even-Shoshan notes that the word has entered Hebrew as equivalent to *pilegesh*, based on the following statement in *Exod. Rab.* 40:4, a point regarding the offspring of Bilhah and Zilpah:

> אמר ר' חנינא בן פזי אין לך גדול משבט יהודה ואין לך ירוד משבט דן שהיה מן הלחנות
>
> R. Ḥanina ben Pazi said: There is no tribe greater than Judah, and no tribe lower than Dan, which was [descended] from the *leḥeinot*.

(A similar quote appears in Midrash Tanḥuma *pereq Ki Tissa siman* 13; there, however, the word *shefaḥot* is used).

7 Kaufman, *Akkadian Influences*, 66.

8 The masculine form *laḫḫinu* is given in *AHW* as *ein Angestellter in Tempeln usw* (temple employee).

Zilpah verses as implying a concubinage relationship; the deliberate pattern of translation in Onkelos suggests a more subtle understanding, and the idea of an "official" though subordinate status would fit well with the status of Bilhah and Zilpah.

Further, there are several instances of masculine and feminine forms of *LḤN* in Imperial Aramaic sources in which the translation "concubine" is doubtful.[9] While there is no scholarly agreement on the meaning of the term in these sources, we may argue that "subordinate" would provide a suitable translation in at least two of the instances:

a) The biblical book of Daniel (5:2, 3, 23) has a version of the root *LḤN* among the list of those involved in the desecration of the Temple vessels at the feast of Belshatzar:

(5:2) ...וישתון בהון מלכא ורברבנוהי שגלתה ולחנתה
(5:3)...ואשתיו בהון מלכא ורברבנוהי שגלתה ולחנתה
(5:23)...ואנתה ורברבניך שגלתך ולחנתך חמרא שתין בהון

The לחנתה of these verses is assumed by various scholars, as well as most English translations, to mean "concubines," as the KJV translation makes clear:

> (5:2)...that the king, and his princes, his wives, and his concubines could drink from them
> (5:3)...and the king, and his princes, his wives, and his concubines drank from them
> (5:23)...you and your princes, your wives, and your concubines drank wine from them

This association of לחנה with some sort of sexual partner seems to have begun with the LXX translation of these verses; yet it is to be noted that in this translation it is the term שגלתה that is translated by παλλακαι, "concubines" (Liddell/Scott),[10] while לחנתה is translated as παρακοιτοι,

9 There is also an instance of *LḤN* in the Canaanite Keret Epic (Driver, *Canaanite Myths and Legends* (Old Testament Studies 3; Edinburgh: T&T Clark, 1956), K III iv 13: *lḥn s*[...]*md*[...] *tsm 'mly* [*h*]*ry*. This is translated by Driver as "the wench Harray shall obey."

10 B. Landsberger, "Akkadisch-Hebräische Wortgleichungen," *Supplements to VT* 16

"female bedfellows" or simply "wives" (ibid.). Among those who accept the meaning here as "concubine," there is no agreement as to the derivation, though there are various attempts to associate the term with an idea of lasciviousness.[11] A further difficulty with this translation is that it does not suit the various other Imperial Aramaic instances of the root *LḤN*, as will be discussed below.

b) Elephantine contract from the archive of Anani son of Azariah: Anani and his wife Tapamet, who was apparently married to him while still the *amah* of another man,[12] are parties to several contracts. Anani is identified in each of these contracts as a לחן (det. form לחנא); in one contract only his wife is identified as a לחנה:[13]

...אמר ענני בר עזריה לחן זי יהו ונשין
תפמת אנתתה לחנה זי יהו אלהא שכן יב ברתא...

(1967): 196, argued that the term שגלתה is derived from the Akkadian *ša ekalli*, translating the Sumerian formula MI.ŠÀ.É.GAL.MEŠ; this term has the range of meanings "queens," "harem," "personnel surrounding the queen" (*CAD*). In Deut. 28:30, however, the verbal form ישגלנה is replaced in the public Torah reading by ישכבנה. There is also a replacement of this root by the root שכב in Isa. 13:16, Jer. 3:2 and Zech. 14:2, where the reference is rape or fornication as it was considered too vulgar. In Ps. 45:10 and Neḥ. 2:6 the meaning appears to be "consort" and there is no replacement.

11 Several argue that the word is cognate with Arabic root לח'נ (ערווה nakedness) according to Even-Shoshan, ריח רע (bad smell) according to anonymous sources quoted by Kohut, or, metaphorically, "obscene" (B. Davidson, *Analytical Hebrew and Chaldee Lexicon* [London: Bagster, 1970], 423). Landsberger, "Akkadisch-Hebräische," 204, took the term in Daniel as "prostitutes," supposedly reflecting the Bible's dim view of women. Others, however, took the root as חנן, and thus related to חננא, used in Onkelos for חנון in Exod. 22:26 (I. Kosovsky, *Concordance to Targum Onkelos* [in Hebrew] (Jerusalem: Hebrew University, 1986), or לחן, used in Pseudo-Jonathan for חן in Exod. 12:36 (E. G. Clarke, *Targum Pseudo-Jonathan of the Pentateuch: Text and Concordance* [Hoboken: Ktav, 1984]). Still others see a cognate in the Arabic לחנ (נגון tune) and thus assume some relation to court singers (the explanation preferred by Kohut).

12 Porten and Yardeni, *Aramaic Documents*, 2:B.3.3., records a marriage between Anani and Ta[pa]met, who is also described as אמתך with respect to one Meshullam; B.3.6. records the manumission of Ta[pa]met by Meshullam. Porten and Yardeni (ibid., 73) describe the latter document as a "testamentary manumission," to take effect only at Meshullarn's death; as has been discussed in chapter 6, however, this document may be an example of conditional manumission.

13 Porten and Yardeni, *Aramaic Documents*, B.3.12, lines 1-2.

> ...Anani son of Azariah, *laḥan* of YHV, and the woman Tapamet his wife, *leḥana* [or *leḥeina*] of YHV, the God [who] resides at Yeb the fortress, said...

Some scholars assume that both Anani and Tapamet were temple singers, or "cantors."[14] It seems from the document, however, that they are not associated with the temple, but rather with the Deity YHV; Porten and Yardeni thus identify them as "servitors of YHW."[15] The term may thus be describing an occupation, an attendant of this Deity; but it is also possible that it is identifying the "proper law" of the parties—that is, the law applicable to such "YHV-ians."[16] The term may thus be an ethnic identifier, similar to other terms of nationality found in the witness descriptions in these documents.[17]

c) Notation on the back of a Behistun fragment:
The profession of a certain Azaria appears to be described. Some would identify this person as the father of Anani above:

עזריה לחנא נגרא תנ...
זכרן על עז[ר]יה לחנא זי...

---

14 C. C.Torrey, "More Elephantine Papyri," *JNES* 13 (1954): 149-53, at 151; B. Couroyer, "LHN: Chantre?" *VT* 5 (1955): 86, who notes a cognate Arabic term and suggests a comparison to contemporaneous Egyptian temple practice.

15 Porten and Yardeni, *Aramaic Documents*, 96. One may note that according to Serge Sauneron, *The Priests of Ancient Egypt* (trans. Ann Morrissett; New York: Grove, 1968), 60, it was customary to refer to Egyptian cult personnel at a particular temple as "servants of the god." If לחן is describing a specific function within the Jewish temple at Yeb, a further issue is raised concerning the position of Ta[pa]met: was her title לחנה simply an honorific based on her husband's position, like the נביאה of Isa. 8:3 (E. G. Kraeling, *The Brooklyn Museum Aramaic Papyri* [New York: Arno Press, 1969], 145; contra, Couroyer, "LHN," 85), or did Ta[pa]met herself have a specific function within the temple?

16 The existence of the "proper law" of a contract—that is, the rules of a specific legal system that are to be used in interpreting that contract—is an issue familiar in modern occurrences in which the parties to the contract (or other aspects of the contract) "belong to" different jurisdictions. Z. Falk, "Mutual Obligations in the Ketubah," *JJS* 8 (1957): 215-17, has suggested that such concerns are also evident in ancient documents; the use of the phrase כדת משה וישראל (according to the law of Moses and Israel), for instance, is intended to specify the appropriate legal system for interpreting a marriage contract.

17 While the usual description of a witness in these documents is PN1 *bar* PN2, there are certain instances of ethnic identifiers, with or without a father's name. See, e.g., Porten and Yardeni, *Aramaic Documents*, B.2.2, line 19 (הדדנורי בבליא); B.3.5, line 24 (מתרסה מגשיא תת מגשיא); and B.3.6, lines 16-47 (אתרפרן בר ניסי מדי).

Azaria, maker of wooden bowls
Memorandum concerning Azaria, *leḥana* who...
(Cowley, *Aramaic Papyri* 63 lines 9 and 12)

This לחן is taken as a "maker of wooden bowls,"[18] based on the Akkadian *laḫannu*, "bowl," and the association with נגרא, "carpenter" (Jastrow). Otherwise, there is nothing in the context that gives any clue as to the meaning.

d) There may be a fourth instance in an Aḥiqar papyrus from Elephantine, apparently concerning the discipline of underlings:

מחאה לעלים כא[יה] לחנת אף לכל עבדיך אל[פנא] איש זי
קנה עבד פר[יץ ו]אמה גנבה ...

A blow for a slave, re[buke] for a maid, and for all thy servants [dis]cipline.
A man who buys a li[centious] slave or a thievish maid

(Cowley, *Aramaic Papyri* lines 83-84)

Since the ל of לחנת might be a preposition, Cowley considered the noun to be חנת; Kraeling, however, considered this form to be a "haplological ellipsis" of ללחנת[19]. ללחנת is translated by some as "maidservant"[20] or "slave-girl."[21] Yet the word appears to be paired with עלים (young men), and not עבדים (slaves), so that the general sense may be young male and female underlings; in this case the form may be plural, with the expected ה left off.

Given that some idea of "subordinates" or "attendants" seems appropriate for the instances of *LḤN* in the Elephantine and Aḥiqar documents, we might also posit a similar meaning for the term in Daniel, and translate the lists as "nobles, consorts, and (female) attendants."

18 Driver, *Canaanite Myths and Legends,* 59.
19 Cowley, *Aramaic Papyri*, 234; Kraeling, *Brooklyn Museum* 144.
20 For instance, Kraeling, *Brooklyn Museum*, 144; Koehler and Baumgartner, *Hebrew and Aramaic Lexicon*, 1090.
21 Lindenberger, "Ahiqar," 498.

An issue is then raised as to whether these various attestations are related both to each other and to terms used in the Targumim, and further, whether Dalman is correct in arguing for two forms of the word. We would argue that all the forms above, with the possible exception of Cowley 63, are consistent with the expected Imperial Aramaic forms[22] of a feminine noun לח[י]נה and a masculine noun לחן :

	feminine		masculine	
singular				
abs	לחנה	Ananiah archive	לחן	Ananiah archive
cstr	לחנת	Aḥiqar(?)	לחן	-
det	לחנתא	Targumim	לחנא	Behistun fragment
plural				
abs	לחנן	Targumim	לחנין	-
cstr	לחנת	-	לחני	-
det	לחנתא	Targumim, Aḥiqar(?)	לחניא	-
Suffix (3ms)	לחנתה	Daniel	לחניה	-

Dalman's distinction may be based solely on context, if he assumed that the Targum form must equal "concubine" but believed that this meaning would be inappropriate in other instances. There are also several instances in which the Targumim do use the form לחינתא to translate an apparently absolute form in the Hebrew text, thus giving the impression that it actually is a separate absolute form; Targum Onkelos to Gen. 36:12, for instance, has לחינתא לאליפז for the Hebrew [ותמנע היתה] לאליפז פילגש (Timna was a *pilegesh* of Eliphaz), and the Targum to 2Sam. 3:7 has ולשאול לחינתא for the Hebrew ולשאול פלגש ושמה רצפה (Saul had a *pilegesh* named Ritzpah). Rather than this being a separate absolute form, however, it may simply be an appropriate use of the Aramaic definite form, in which a definite article might be assumed as in English[23] ("Timnah was *the pilegesh* of Eliphaz"), or a case in which the definite form in Aramaic does not necessarily retain its definite meaning.[24]

---

22 See F. Rosenthal, *A Grammar of Biblical Aramaic* (Weisbaden: O. Harrasowitz, 1968), 23, 26.

23 Rosenthal, *Grammar of Biblical Aramaic*, 24.

24 W. B. Stevenson, *Grammar of Jewish Palestinian Aramaic* (Oxford: Oxford University Press,

It may thus be postulated that either the masculine *laḫḫinu* first entered Aramaic as לחן, from which developed the feminine form לחנה, or the *laḫḫi/annatu* form entered and then underwent a "backformation" to לחנה (the Akkadian feminine final "t" being subject to Aramaic morphological rules[25]).

It may then be further proposed that לחנה as understood by Onkelos meant some sort of subordinate or underling and was used in connection with Bilhah and Zilpah to avoid a suggestion that they were slaves. That this choice of words was deliberate is confirmed by the existence of the same pattern in Neofiti[26] and Pseudo-Jonathan, particularly as the latter otherwise uses פלקה rather than לחנה to translate the biblical *pilegesh*.[27]

7.3.2 The Relationship between Targum Onkelos and Josephus

The influence of Onkelos on other Targumim has been noted by scholars.[28] What is also curious in this instance is the choice by both Onkelos and Josephus to render the women as "subordinates." It is difficult to say whether there is any interrelationship between these two sources. It must be noted, however, that Onkelos departs from its usual word for word rendering in another instance involving slave marriages and appears to cite a rabbinic law that was also known to Josephus. Deut. 23:18 reads:

לא תהיה קדשה מבנות ישראל ולא יהיה קדש מבני ישראל.

1962), 23.

25 Kaufman, *Akkadian Influences*, 145.

26 There is one exception; as noted in chapter one, Neofiti to Gen. 35:22 does not translate the Hebrew פילגש אביו but has a marginal note with פלגש אבוי. In the Yemenite tradition, in which the reader recites Targum Onkelos with the Torah reading, this section is skipped in the Targum in accordance with *mMeg.* 4:10.

27 Pseudo-Jonathan also uses לחנה for the barren *amahot* of Avimelekh in Gen. 20:17. It is thus not completely clear whether this Targum understood the Aramaic term in the same way as did Onkelos.

28 See, e.g., Abraham Tal, "Ms. Neophyti I: The Palestinian Targum to the Pentateuch," *Israel Oriental Studies* 4 (1974): 31-43, with respect to the influence of the vocabulary of Targum Onkelos on Targum Neofiti. On p. 41, he mentions specifically the use of the term לחינא in Neofiti as an example of this phenomenon. This phenomenon seems confirmed (at least in this instance) given that Neofiti follows the pattern of use of this term in Onkelos with respect to Bilhah and Zilpah.

> There shall not be a *qedeshah* from female Israelites, and there shall not be a *qadesh* from male Israelites.

The precise meaning of *qadesh/qedeshah* is unclear, and it is usually translated as a male or female prostitute. As noted in chapter six, Targum Onkelos renders the verse:

> לא תהי אתתא מבנת ישראל לגבר עבד ולא יסב גברא מבני ישראל איתא אמה

> An Israelite female shall not be a wife to a male slave, and an Israelite male shall not marry a female slave.[29]

Josephus at *Antiquities* 4:8:23 has:

> ...nor let free men marry slaves, although their affections should strongly bias any of them so to do; for it is decent, and for the dignity of the persons themselves, to govern those their affections. And further, no one ought to marry a harlot, whose matrimonial oblations, arising from the prostitution of her body, God will not receive...[30]

---

29 Ellinson, *Nissuin,* 66, notes that later rabbinic opinion was divided as to the source of this opinion: Maimonides (*Hil. Issurei Biyah* 12:11, 13; 15:4) argued it was rabbinic, while Rashi (*bQidd.* 69a *s.v.* או דיעבד קאמר) argued it was biblical.

30 Philo, faced with the same need to explain the slave wives of Abraham and Jacob, is equivocal on the question of intermarriage between slave and free. In his allegorical explanation of the difference between the "wife" and the "handmaid," the latter represents the "lower instruction given by the lower branches of school lore" (*On Mating with the Preliminary Studies,* 14, trans. F. H. Colson and G. H. Whitaker). Yet Philo recommends espousing both the wife and the handmaid (ibid., 24):

> ...anyone whose mind is set on enduring to the end the weary contest in which virtue is the prize, who practises continually for that end, and is unflagging in self-discipline, will take to him two lawful wives and as handmaids to them two concubines.

In another passage Philo in effect equates certain handmaids with wives:

> There were women born beyond the Euphrates, in the extreme parts of Babylonia, who were handmaids and were given as dowry to the ladies of the house at their marriage. But when they were thought worthy to pass on to the wise man's bed, the first consequence was that they passed on from mere concubinage to the name and position of wedded wives, and were treated no longer as handmaids, but as almost equal in rank to their mistresses, who indeed, incredible as it seems, promoted them to the same dignity as themselves. (*On the Virtues,* 223, trans. F. H. Colson)

7.4 BILHAH AND ZILPAH AS "MATRIARCHS"

We have noted the inconsistency in the biblical text with respect to the "wifely" status of Bilhah and Zilpah.[31] A further issue that arises in the postbiblical traditions is the question of "matriarch status." In modern, western tradition the title אמהות (Matriarchs), is reserved for four of the Genesis women: Sarah, Rebecca, Leah, and Rachel.[32] The origin of the word אמהות (which is simply a plural of אם (mother)) as an honorific is difficult to determine, but we may trace the term at least as far back as the extracanonical *Tractate Semaḥot*, chap. 1, halakhot 13-14. These rules follow a list of mourning customs, in which it is stated that the usual mourning customs are not to be observed on the death of one's slaves; rather, one treats such deaths like the loss of an animal. An exception, however, was made for certain slaves, including the man named Tevi who belonged to Rabban Gamliel,[33] who is described here as *kasher*. The text continues with a further exception made for the slaves of Rabban Gamliel and then adds a general statement regarding the use of honorifics:

אין קורין לעבדים ולשפחות אבא פלוני ואמא פלונית
של בית רבן גמליאל היו קורין לאבא טבי ולאימא טביתא.
אין קורין לאבות אבינו אלא לשלשה האבות ולא לאימהות אמנו אלא לארבעה האימהות

---

31 Not surprisingly, this inconsistency continues in the postbiblical tradition. *Gen. Rab.* 66:4 (Rom), for instance, refers explicitly to Jacob's "four wives: Leah and Rachel, Zilpah and Bilhah," while the version in Theodor-Albeck has: "that Jacob took four."

32 This theme of four matriarchs is familiar especially in the liturgy. We may cite as two familiar examples the refrain in אחד מי יודע, found in the Passover Haggadah:

ארבע מי יודע? ארבע אני יודע. ארבע אמהות...

Who knows four? I know four. Four are the matriarchs...
and the Yizkor prayer in *Tiqun Meir*:

...תהא נפשה [נפשו] צרורה בצרור החיים עם נשמות אברהם יצחק ויעקב שרה רבקה רחל ולאה...

...Let his/her soul be bound in the bond of life with the souls of Abraham, Isaac, and Jacob, Sarah, Rebecca, Rachel, and Leah...

33 There are various references in the rabbinic literature to Tevi and Tevita, the unusual slaves of Rabban Gamliel; see, e.g., *mSukkah* 2:1. For a justification of this vocalization of the name, see Harry Fox, "Critical Edition of Mishnah Tractate Succah," 2:41-42, who argues that these names are likely Aramaic rather than Greek.

(13) We do not call male and female slaves "Father so-and-so" or "Mother so-and-so." Those of the house of Rabban Gamliel [however] were called Father Tevi and Mother Tevita.
(14) We do not use the term "our fathers" except for the three patriarchs, or the term "our mothers" except for the four matriarchs.

These rules are also stated in a baraita reported in *bBer.* 16b, again within the context of mourning customs with respect to slaves. *MBer.* 2:7 refers to the exception made for Tevi, here too described as *kasher*. The Gemara then appears to "add" the further rules concerning honorifics, and to explain some apparent contradictions raised by them:

ת"ר אין קורין אבות אלא לשלשה ואין קורין אמהות אלא לארבע אבות מאי טעמא אילימא משום דלא ידעינן אי מראובן קא אתינן אי משמעון קא אתינן אי הכי אמהות נמי לא ידעינן אי מרחל קא אתינן אי מלאה קא אתינן אלא עד הכא חשיבי טפי לא חשיבי תניא אידך עבדים ושפחות אין קורין אותם אבא פלוני ואמא פלונית ושל ר"ג היו קורים אותם אבא פלוני ואמא פלונית מעשה לסתור משום דחשיבי

Our Sages taught [in a baraita]: We call only three men "patriarchs" [Abraham, Isaac and Jacob, according to Rashi, and this is the accepted tradition] and only four women "matriarchs" [i.e., Sarah, Rebecca, Leah, and Rachel]. Patriarchs: what is the reason [for instance, why not include Jacob's sons]? If you say it is because we do not know [from which son we are descended, i.e.,] whether we come from [the tribe of] Reuven or Shimon [etc.], the same is true for the [last two matriarchs]—we do not know whether we come from [the tribe of] Rachel or Leah. Rather, [the reason] is because up to [Jacob] they are worthy of consideration, and the rest are not.
It was further taught: We do not *call* male and female slaves "Father so-and-so" or "Mother so-and-so." Those of Rabban Gamliel [however] were called "Father so-and-so" and "Mother so-and-so." [Does this] fact [not] contradict [the above rule]? [No], because they were worthy of consideration.

The terms אמא and אמהות (matriarch[s]) and their masculine counterparts אבא and אבות (patriarch[s]) are clearly considered here to be honorifics, reserved to a limited few; as Rashi explains, the terms are equivalent to calling someone מר or מרת ("sir" or "madam"). From the context (that is, the first discussion regarding matriarchs and patriarchs is immediately followed by a prohibition against using similar honorifics for slaves), it may be assumed that it was the slave origins of Bilhah and Zilpah that came to exclude them from entitlement to the term "matriarch." This connection is in fact made explicit in a post-tannaitic, anonymous exegesis found in *Num. Rab.*, a work attributed to R. Moshe haDarshan of Narbonne (11th century C.E.). The exegesis is based on Numbers 7, specifically the list of animals brought by the tribal leaders for a peace offering at the consecration of the Tabernacle altar (two oxen, five rams, five he-goats, and five yearling lambs, repeated for each leader in vv. 17, 23, 29, 35, 41, 47, 53, 59, 65, 71, 77, 83). The midrash at 14:11 (ed. Rom) provides:

ולזבח השלמים בקר שנים כנגד יצחק ורבקה שהיו תמימים ובני מלכים.
אילים חמשה עתודים חמשה כבשים בני שנה חמשה למה היו ג' מינים
אילים ועתודים וכבשים כנגד יעקב לאה ורחל למה היו של חמשה
חמשה חמשה לפי שחשבונם עולה ט"ו כנגד יעקב ולאה ורחל וי"ב
שבטים והאמהות לפי שקראו האמהות שפחות לכך לא נכנסו לחשבון

> *For the peace offering: two oxen*—corresponding to Isaac and Rebecca, who were pious and children of kings; *five rams, five he-goats, five yearling lambs*—Why were there three kinds, rams, he-goats, and sheep? Corresponding to Jacob, Leah, and Rachel. Why were there five of each? Because this sums up to fifteen, corresponding to Jacob and Leah and Rachel and the twelve tribes. And the two *amahot* [here as the plural of *amah,* "handmaid, i.e. Bilhah and Zilpah]? Since they were called *shefaḥot,* they did not enter into the calculation.

Despite this apparently straightforward tradition, however, there is evidence that this "matriarchal quartet" was not fixed until relatively late. *Song of Songs Zuta* 1:15 (Buber, p. 16)[34] contains a midrash on the name Qiryat Arba that states:

...שנקברו שם ארבע אמהות חוה שרה רבקה ולאה

> ...since there were buried there four matriarchs: Eve, Sarah, Rebecca, and Leah

34 This work is dated by some to the 10th century C.E. (H. L. Strack and G. Stemberger, *Introduction to the Talmud and Midrash*, 347).

More particularly, there are several earlier-redacted midrashim that refer to six matriarchs, explicitly including Bilhah and Zilpah as אמהות. One such midrash in *Pesiqta de Rav Kahana* (ca. 5th century C.E.) is another exegesis based on Numbers 7 and the consecration of the desert Tabernacle; in this case it is a parable on the number six, reflecting the six carts brought by the tribal leaders (v. 3):

ויביאו את קרבנם לפני ה' שש עגלות וגו' - כנגד ששת ימי בראשית.
שש כנגד שש ערכי המשנה. שש כנגד שש האימהות. ואלו הן, שרה רבקה רחל ולאה בלהה וזלפה

And [the leaders] brought their offering before the Lord: six carts ... [Six] for the six days of creation, six for the orders of the Mishnah, six for the six matriarchs. And these are: Sarah, Rebecca, Rachel and Leah, Bilhah, Zilpah. (ed. D. Mandelbaum, *pisqa* 1:7)

Variations of this "six" parable are also found in later midrashim. An expanded version found in *Esth. Rab.* to 1:2 (ca. 6th century C.E.) is based on the six steps of King Solomon's throne (2 Chr 9:18). The midrash at 1:12 (ed. Rom) provides:

ר' הושעיא רבה אומר שהיה עשוי כטירכי מרכבו של מי שאמר והיה העולם הקב"ה וכה"א שש מעלות לכסא שש כנגד ששה רקיעים ולא שבעה הן אמר ר' אבון הן דמלכא שארי טיטיון שש כנגד ארצות ארץ אדמה ארקא גיא ציה נשיה תבל וכתיב והוא ישפוט תבל בצדק שש כנגד ששה סדרי משנה זרעים מועד נשים נזיקין קדשים וטהרות שש כנגד ששת ימי בראשית שש כנגד שש אמהות שרה רבקה רחל ולאה בלהה זלפה

R. Hoshaya Rabba says that it [the throne] was made like the chariot[35] of the One who declared and the world came into being—the Holy One, Blessed Be He. He would say thus: *six steps to the throne* [2 Chr 9:18]—six for the six levels of heaven. Are there not seven? R. Abun said: The one in which the King rests is imperial domain[36] [i.e., off-limits]. Six for the six [levels of] earth:[37] *eretz, adamah, arqa, gai, tziah, neshiah, tevel.* And it is written

35 According to Jastrow (*s.v.* טירכי), כטירכי מרכבתו is a tautography for כמרכבתו.

36 According to Jastrow (*s.v.* טיטיון), טיטיון is a corruption of טמיקון, the form found in *Song of Songs Rabbah* (*infra*), and both are related to *ταμιαχος*, *tamiacus*, "imperial domains."

37 There are actually seven levels listed. Shimon Dunsky, *Midrash Rabba to Song of Songs* (Jerusalem: Dvir, 1980), 193 n. 3 notes a midrash in *VaYiqra Rab.* (Margoliot) 29:11 on the phrase "In the seventh month" in Lev. 23:24, in which a listing of the levels of heaven

[Ps. 98:9]: *He will rule tevel justly.* Six for the six orders of the Mishnah: *Zeraim*, *Moed*, *Nashim*, *Neziqin*, *Qodashim*, and *Taharot*. Six for the six days of creation. Six for the six matriarchs: Sarah, Rebecca, Rachel and Leah, Bilhah, Zilpah.

Song of Songs Rab. to 6:4 (ca. 6th century C.E.), again based on Num. 7:3, also contains this expanded version. The midrash at 6:4 (ed. Rom) provides:

ד"א יפה את רעיתי כתרצה כשאת רוצה כד את בעייה לית את צריכה בעייה מכלום
מילף מכלום מי אמר להם להביא עגלות ובקר לטעון המשכן לא מהן ובהן הביאו אותן
הה"ד ויביאו את קרבנם לפני ה' שש עגלות צב כנגד ששה רקיעים ולא שבעה הם
א"ר אבון הן דמלכא שרי טמיקון שש כנגד שש ארצות ארץ ארקא אדמה גיא ציה נשיה
תבל וכתיב ישפוט תבל בצדק ו' כנגד ו' ערכי משנה שש כנגד ששת ימי בראשית
ו' כנגד ו' אמהות שרה רבקה רחל לאה זלפה בלהה

Another matter: *You are beautiful, my beloved, like Tirzah* [6:4]. When you desire [a word play on *tirzah*]: when you want [something], you need not ask from anyone or learn from anyone. Who told them [the princes] to bring carts and cattle for the requirement of the Tabernacle? Did they not bring them of their own accord? As it is said: *And [the leaders] brought their offering before the Lord: six covered wagons*—for the six heavens. Are there not seven? R. Abun said: The one in which the King rests is imperial domain [i.e., off-limits]. Six for the six [levels of] earth: *eretz, arqa, adamah, gai, tziah, neshiah, tevel.* And it is written [Ps. 98:9]: *He will rule tevel justly.* Six for the six orders of the Mishnah; six for the six days of creation; six for the six matriarchs: Sarah, Rebecca, Rachel, Leah, Zilpah, Bilhah.

---

and earth is in fact based on the number seven:

בחדש השביעי לעולם שביעי חביב למעלה שביעית חביבה וילון רקיע שחקים זבול מעון מכון
ערבות סולו לרוכב בערבות ביה שמו בארצות שביעית חביבה ארץ אדמה ארקא גיה צייה נשייה
תבל והוא ישפוט תבל בצדק...

> *In the seventh month*—The seventh is always beloved. The seventh above is beloved: *vilon, raqi'a, shehaqim, zevul, ma'on, makhon, aravot* [=the seven different heavens]; *Extol the One who rides upon the heavens* [=*aravot*] *in His name Yah* [Ps. 68:5]; in the lands seventh is beloved: *eretz, adama, arqa, gai, tziyya, neshiyya, tevel* [=the seven types of land]; *And He shall judge tevel righteously* [Ps. 96:13]...

The midrash continues with other examples of sevenths: Enoch, Moses, David, Asa, and the seventh sabbatical. This makes it likely that the listing in the *Esth. Rab.* midrash is based on this (or a similar) "seven" parable.

We may note a further reference to six matriarchs in an expanded commentary in Targum Pseudo-Jonathan to Exod. 14:21, concerning the parting of the sea:

וארכין משה ית ידיה על ימא בחוטרא רבא ויקירא דאיתברי מן שירויא וביה חקיק
ומפרש שמא רבא ויקירא ועישרתי אתוותא די מהא ית מצראי ותלת אבהת עלמא ושית
אימהתא ותריסר שיבטוי דיעקב ומן יד דבר ה' ית ימא ברוח קידומא תקיף כל ליליא ושוי
ית ימא נגיבא ואתבזעו מיא לתריסר בזיען כל קבל תריסר שיבטוי דיעקב

And Moses stretched his hand over the sea with the great and precious staff that was created from the beginning, and in which was engraved and specified the great and precious Name, and the ten signs that dispersed the Egyptians, and the three fathers of the world, and the six mothers, and the twelve tribes of Jacob; and immediately God moved the sea with a powerful east wind all the night, and made the sea like dry land, and the water was split into twelve parts alongside the twelve tribes of Jacob.

A final example from *Gen. Rab.* (ca. 5th century C.E.) is interesting in that it attributes the relevant opinion to R. Meir, a tanna who preceded the Mishnah redaction. The passage records a dialogue between R. Meir and a Samaritan on an apparent contradiction between a pentateuchal statement and one in a prophetic book, which was not included in the Samaritan biblical tradition *Gen. Rab.*(Rom) 70:7:

ר' יהושע דסכנין בשם ר' לוי אמר כותי אחד שאל את ר' מאיר אמר לו אין אתם אומרין
יעקב אמתי דכתיב תתן אמת ליעקב אמר לו הין א"ל ולא כך אמר וכל אשר תתן לי עשר
אעשרנו לך א"ל הין אמר לו הפריש שבטו של לוי אחד מעשרה למה לא הפריש א' מי"
לשנים שבטין אחרים אמר לו וכי י"ב הן והלא י"ד הן אפרים ומנשה כראובן ושמעון יהיו
לי א"ל כ"ש אוסיפתא מיא אוסיף קמחא אמר לו אין את מודה לי שהם ארבע אמהות א"ל
הין אמר לו צא מהם ד' בכורות לד' אמהות הבכור קודש ואין קודש מוציא קודש אמר לו
אשריך ואשרי אומתך שאת שרוי בתוכה

R. Yehoshua of Sakhnin said in the name of R. Levi: A Samaritan asked a question of R. Meir. He said [to R. Meir]: Do you not say, "Jacob is my truth," as it is written: *You will show truth to Jacob* [Micah 7:20]? [R. Meir] replied: Yes. He said [to R. Meir]: And did Jacob not say, *And of all that You give me I will give a tenth to you* [i.e., a tithe; Gen. 28:22]? [R. Meir] replied: Yes. He said [to R. Meir]: [Jacob] separated the tribe of Levi [for divine work. But a tithe of twelve tribes should be 1.2 tribes, whereas this tithing of Levi represents only] one out of ten [tribes]; why did he not [also] separate one-tenth of the other two tribes? [R. Meir] replied: [You say] there are 12 [tribes]. But are there not 14, [as Jacob said]: *Ephraim and Menasheh [Joseph's sons] are like Reuven and Shimon to me* [Gen. 48:5]? He said [to R. Meir]: All the more so! More water, more flour [i.e., you have strengthened my point; there should have been 14 tribes dedicated]. [R. Meir] said to him: Would you not agree there were four matriarchs? He said [to R. Meir]: Yes. [R. Meir] said to him: Remove from [the calculation] the four firstborn sons of the four matriarchs: the firstborn is holy, and a holy object does not have a [further] holy object taken from it [i.e., the tithe calculated as 1/(14-4); 1 of 10 tribes is thus correct]. He replied: Happy are you and happy is the nation in which you exist.

From the context, it is to be understood that the four matriarchs from whom four firstborn sons have descended must refer to Jacob's wives, including Bilhah and Zilpah.

We might have concluded, based only on the baraita in *Berakhot* and the later midrash of R. Moshe haDarshan, that the tradition of exclusion of Bilhah and Zilpah is relatively late. The precise dating of *Semaḥot*, however, puts this conclusion in doubt. Strack/Stemberger assert that this tractate might date from as early as the third century.[38] The priority of *Semaḥot* to tractate *Berakhot* seems also to be suggested by the awkward language of halakhah 1:14, thus rendering it the *lectio difficilior;* this seems to be in effect the opinion in the commentary *Naḥalat Ya'aqov*:

הלשון בהלכה זאת אינו מדוקדק אבל בגמרא דברכות גרסי' הכי אין קורין אבות אלא לשלשה דהיינו אברהם יצחק ויעקב ואין קורין אמהות אלא לארבע שרה רבקה רחל ולאה עכ"ל וכן ראויה להיות הכא

The language in this halakhah [14] is not precise, but in the Gemara of *Berakhot* we read: "We call only three men patriarchs"—that is, Abraham, Isaac, and Jacob—"and we call only four women matriarchs"—Sarah, Rebecca, Rachel, and Leah. Until here is its language, and it seems suitable in this instance [as well].

If the halakhot of *Semaḥot*, and thus the attitude of exclusion toward Bilhah

38 Strack and Stemberger, *Talmud and Midrash*, 249.

and Zilpah, are dated early, it seems that rival opinions toward the women had co-existed. It can be argued that the midrash in *Num. Rab.* 14:11 was in fact intended as a deliberate contrast to the earlier parable based on Numbers 7, with the express purpose of excluding Bilhah and Zilpah. The numbers are manipulated to arrive at fifteen, not usually a particularly significant figure,[39] and the exegesis is also compelled to ignore Sarah and Abraham.

7.5 THE GENEALOGY OF BILHAH AND ZILPAH

Finally, we may note two major traditions concerning the origins of Bilhah and Zilpah. As we will see below, such origin tales are unusual for women, let alone slave women. Both of these traditions provide the women with a paternal link to Abraham, one through Lavan[40] and one through an extrabiblical figure, possibly named Aḥiyot or Aḥoti. It has been suggested that the rabbinic sages were concerned to provide all twelve tribes with Abrahamic connections through their mothers as well as their father Jacob,[41] yet we must still question the unusual existence of not one, but two genealogies for these slave women. I propose that the Lavan version was an explicit attempt to explain away the slave origins; the Aḥiyot version reflects the same kind of emphasis on inclusion and kinship and indifference to slave-free intermarriage that we have noted with respect to Exod. 21:4-11.

The Lavan tradition is discernible in brief references in various midrashim and Targumim. The Aḥiyot tradition, in contrast, is part of a detailed "genealogical" record concerning Bilhah. This genealogy is found

39 See, however, *mSukkah* 5:4, which does refer to the number 15 in connection with the Temple:

> חמש עשרה מעלות היורדות מעזרת ישראל לעזרת נשים כנגד חמשה עשר שיר המעלות שבתהילים
>
> Fifteen steps going down from the Israelites' [i.e., men's] area to the women's area, corresponding to fifteen "Step Songs" in the Psalms [120:34].

40 Lavan was the grandson of Naḥor, Abraham's brother (see, e.g., Gen. 24:15, 24, 29), but in Gen. 29:5 he is called "Lavan son of Nahor." The classical Jewish commentator Nachmanides claims that Naḥor was more important than his son Betuel and that this is why Lavan was called his son. Rabbenu Baḥya consider this a case of grandchildren being the same as children.

41 Louis Ginzberg, *The Legends of the Jews* (7 vols.; Philadelphia: Jewish Publication Society, 1938), 5:295 n. 167.

in a Qumran fragment in Hebrew as well as within a larger apocryphal document in Greek, known as the Testament of Naphtali (one of Bilhah's sons, according to the biblical record);[42] of particular interest for our purposes, in addition to the genealogical data "added" to the biblical record for these apparently marginal biblical women, is a "naming speech"[43] for Bilhah. As well, there is a partial repetition of some of the elements of both the Lavan and the Aḥiyot traditions in the late midrashic work *Bereshit Rabbati,* again attributed to the school of R. Moshe haDarshan. The existence of two genealogical traditions, one apparently sectarian in origin and the other of a more "mainstream" background, is not in itself surprising. As will be noted in a brief review of these sources, however, the lines of transmission are not straightforward.

7.5.1 The Aḥiyot *Tradition*

The Hebrew version of the Bilhah genealogy is found in Qumran fragment 4Q215, dated between 30 B.C.E. and 20 C.E.:[44]

1. עם אחיות אבי בלהה א[חי*]ה דבורה אשר הניקה את רב[קה

2. וילך בשבי וישלח לבן ויפרקהו ויתן לו את חנה אחת מאמהותי [ותלד*]

3. ראישונה את זלפה ויתן את שמה זלפה בשם העיר אשר נשבה אל[יה

4. ותהר ותלד את בלהה אמי ותקרא חנה את שמה בלהה כי כאשר נולדה [היתה*]

5. מתבהלת לינוק ותואמר מה מתבהלת היאה בתי ותקרא עוד בלהה [

6. [...]

---

42 The Hebrew version of a Testament of Naphtali found in mediaeval MSS (such as that set out in R. H. Charles, *The Greek Versions of the Testaments of the Twelve Patriarchs* [Oxford: Oxford University Press, 1960] Appendix II), does not contain any genealogical information.

43 This term will be explained below.

44 The Hebrew text is taken from the reconstruction by Michael Stone, "Testament of Naphtali," in *Qumran Cave 4, XVII, Parabiblical Texts, Part 3,* (DJD 22; Oxford: Clarendon, 1996b), 73-82, at 78-79, 804; further reconstruction (marked *) is by Prof. H. Fox. Prior treatments of this fragment are listed on p. 73 of the Stone article.

7. וכאשר בא יעקוב אבי אל לבן בורח מלפני עישיו אחיהו וכאשר [מת*]

8. אבי בלהה אמי וינהג לבן את חנה אם אמי ואת שתי בנותיה [ויתן אחת]

9. [ללאה*] ואחת לרחל וכאשר היתה רחל לוא ילדה בנים [

10. [יעקו]ב אבי ונתון לו את בלהה אמי ותלד את דן אח[י

11. [ ]תי אח ש ל לש]

1. with Aḥiyot the father of Bilhah [brother of] Deborah who nursed Reb[ecca

2. and he went into captivity and Lavan sent and redeemed him and gave him Ḥanah, one of [his] *amahot* [and she gave birth to]

3. Zilpah first and he gave her name (as) Zilpah after the name of the city [to] which he was taken captive

4. and she conceived and gave birth to Bilhah my mother, and Ḥanah called her name Bilhah because when she was born [she was]

5. in a hurry to nurse, and she said: How she[45] hurries, she is my daughter, and again called her Bilhah[...]

6. [....]

7. And when Jacob my father came to Lavan fleeing from Esau his brother and when [he died]

8. the father of Bilhah my mother—Lavan led away Ḥanah my mother's mother and her two daughters [and he gave one]

9. [to Leah] and one to Rachel, and when Rachel was not son-bearing[46] [...]

10. to Jaco]b my father, and gave[47] him Bilhah my mother, and she gave birth to Dan [my] brother[...]

11. [...

---

45 היאה is Qumranic orthography for היא. See, e.g., Tov, *Textual Criticism*, 108-9.

46 Stone takes ילדה here as the participle יולדה following a perfect of היתה.

47 Stone takes נתון as an infinitive absolute.

The Greek Testament of Naphtali, whose *terminus ad quem* is given as the third century C.E.,[48] contains genealogical data similar to that in the Qumran fragment. Chapter 1:6-12 reads:

> I was born from Bilhah,
> and because Rachel dealt craftily and gave Bilhah to Jacob in place of herself,
> and she bore me on Rachel's knees,
> therefore I was called Naphtali.
> And Rachel loved me because I was born upon her knees;
> and as I was tender in appearance, she used to kiss me, saying: May I see a brother of yours from my own womb like you. Therefore also Joseph was like me in all things,
> according to the prayers of Rachel.
> And my mother is Bilhah,
> the daughter of Rotheus, a brother of Deborah, Rebecca's nurse
> who was born on the same day as Rachel.
> And Rotheus was of the family of Abraham,
> a Chaldean, god-fearing, freeborn and noble.
> And after having been taken captive he was bought by Laban, and he gave him Aina his servant to wife
> who bore him a daughter
> and she called her name Zilpah,
> after the name of the village where he had been taken captive. Next she bore Bilhah, saying:
> My daughter is eager for what is new;
> for immediately after she was born she was eager to suck.

The midrashic work *Bereishit Rabbati,* in its commentary to Gen. 29:24, contains elements of both the Aḥiyot tradition and the Lavan tradition:[49]

> ויתן לבן [לה] את זלפה [שפחתו] וכי שפחותיו היו, אלא בנימוס הארץ בנותיו של אדם מפגלשיו נקראו שפחות. ואית דאמר אבי בלהה וזלפה אחיה של דבורה מינקת רבקה היה ואחותי היה שמו, וטרם שנשא אשה נשבה שלח לבן ופדאו ונתן לו שפחתו לאשה וילדה לו בת וקרא שמה זלפה על שם העיר שנשבה לשם, ילדה עוד בת וקרא שמה בלהה, כשנולדה היתה מתבהלת לינק, אמר מה בהולה בתי. וכאשר הלך יעקב אצל לבן מת אחותי אביהן

48 The English translation is from H. W. Hollander and M. de Jonge, *The Testaments of the Twelve Patriarchs: A Commentary* (Leiden: Brill, 1985) 297-98.

49 The Hebrew text is from the edition of C. Albeck, *Midrash Bereshit Rabbati* [in Hebrew] (Jerusalem: Meqitse Nirdamim), 119.

ולקח לבן לחוה שפחתו ולשתי בנותיה ונתן זלפה הגדולה ללאה בתו הגדולה לה לשפחה, ובלהה הקטנה לרחל בתו הקטנה.

And Lavan gave [to her, to Leah his shifḥah] Zilpah [Gen. 29:24]. Were they his *shefaḥot?* Rather, by the law of the land the daughters of a man by his *pilagshim* were called *shefaḥot*. And there are those who say that the father of Bilhah and Zilpah was the brother of Deborah, Rebecca's nurse, whose name was Aḥoti. Before he married, he was taken captive, and Lavan sent and redeemed him and gave him his *shifḥah* as a wife, and she gave birth to a daughter to him, and he called her Zilpah, after the name of the city to which he was taken captive. She gave birth to another daughter, and he called her Bilhah, since when she was born she hurried to nurse, and he said: How my daughter hurries. When Jacob was at Lavan's, Aḥoti their father died, and Lavan took his *shifḥah* Ḥavah [could be read Ḥanah, according to Albeck] and her two daughters, and gave Zilpah the elder to his elder daughter Leah as a *shifḥah,* and Bilhah the younger to his younger daughter Rachel.

These documents have been of particular interest to scholars who wish to trace the transmission of non-rabbinic works from the Second Temple period, particularly works now known from the apocryphal and pseudepigraphic collections, to mediaeval Jewish literature. It is useful to list in table form the various elements of this genealogy; in this way, those elements not present in the biblical text are highlighted, as well as the variations in each source upon which scholars have relied to establish their theories of transmission:

	MT	4QTNaph	Greek	Ber. Rabbati
Relationship of Bilhah/Zilpah	none	sisters	sisters	sisters
Elder sister	n/a	Zilpah	Zilpah	Zilpah
Father's name	none	אחיות/Aḥiyot	Rotheus	אחותי/Aḥoti
Father's relationship to Abraham	n/a	not explicit	explicit	not explicit
Redemption terminology	n/a	פרק	bought	פדה

	MT	4QTNaph	Greek	Ber. Rabbati
mother's name	none	חנה	Aina	חוה-חנה
mother's status	n/a	one of the *amahot* of Lavan	maidservant (παιδισκην) of Lavan	*shifḥah* of Lavan
aunt's name	none	דבורה	Deborah	דבורה
"Zilpah" origin	none	city to which father taken	city in which father captive	city to which father taken
"Bilhah" origin	none	– play on מתבהלת – eagerness to suck	eagerness to suck	– play on מתבהלת – eagerness to suck
Giving of Bilhah and Zilpah to Rachel and Leah	explicit	explicit	absent	explicit

Prior to the availability of the Qumran fragment, scholars had focused on the evident structural similarities between the Greek Testament and *Ber. Rabbati*. Himmelfarb, for instance, concluded that the degree of similarity between the Greek Testament (and certain other apocryphal units) and *Ber. Rabbati* is such that a literary relationship has to be assumed; she suggests that differences between the sources might simply be revisions by R. Moshe to conform to contemporary Jewish practice.[50] Addressing the issue of the channel of transmission between these sources, Himmelfarb suggested that R. Moshe may have had access to a Byzantine Italian Christian version or the Greek Testament, probably translated into Hebrew.[51] The publication of the Qumran fragment allowed a reconsideration of the relationship between the sources. Stone considered it unlikely that the Greek Testament was an intermediary in the transmission of this source, given the details

50 Martha Himmelfarb, "R. Moses the Preacher and the Testaments of the Twelve Patriarchs," *AJS Review* 9 (1984): 55-78, at 62, 63.

51 Himmelfarb, "R. Moses the Preacher," 73-74.

shared between the Qumran fragment and *Ber. Rabbati*, as against the Greek document:[52] the difference in both the father's[53] and mother's names in Greek, the use of "in which" instead of "to which" in the Zilpah story, the fact that the Greek contains an explicit reference to the relationship with Abraham but lacks any reference to the two women being given as maidservants, and most particularly, the fact that the Bilhah wordplay works only in Hebrew and thus could not have originated in the Greek. Stone posits a Second Temple "original Naphtali" from which both the Hebrew sources drew.[54]

7.5.1.A The Naming Speech

Pardes has explained the naming speech as a literary genre found throughout the Bible, among other sources, in which someone, usually a woman, provides a name for a child, often developing the name from a play on words. The naming speech, in her opinion, is usually reserved for significant people; it "accentuates the importance of a given birth."[55] The naming speech format found in both the Hebrew and Greek formats can thus be considered significant, raising an issue as to why the birth of Bilhah was emphasized. Further, one may question why the naming traditions for the two "slave wives" are not equivalent: that of Zilpah is a simple appropriation of a place name.

One proposal, as suggested by Stone, is that the emphasis on Bilhah's genealogy is actually intended to accentuate the prominence of her descendants. Stone notes in particular the mention of Tobit as a descendant of the tribe of Naphtali (1:1). Given the apparent emphasis in this book on reclaiming Tobit as a "good" Israelite, in contrast to his apostate ancestors (e.g. 1:3-5), one might posit the origins of both the Bilhah lineage and

52 Michael Stone, "The Genealogy of Bilhah," *DSD* 3 (1996a): 20-36, at 28-32.

53 In contrast to Stone's view of the Greek name Rotheus as anomalous, Albeck suggests in his notes to the *Ber. Rabbati* passage (p. 119) that it is possible to read the Hebrew in that passage as Aroti and not Aḥoti, that is, as a Hebraicized Rotheus with an extra *aleph;* it would then be the name Aḥiyot in the Qumran fragment that is anomalous.

54 Stone, "Genealogy of Bilhah," 33.

55 Ilana Pardes, *Countertraditions in the Bible: A Feminist Approach* (Cambridge: Harvard University Press, 1992), 40-43, 153. The narrative in Gen. 29:32-30:24, for instance, in which Leah and Rachel name their own sons as well as those of Bilhah and Zilpah, contains a series of such speeches.

the book of Tobit in a sectarian group anxious to affirm their respectable lineage. Against the sectarian idea, however, is the fact, noted above, that the Bilhah lineage seems already to have been emphasized in the biblical text itself, as she is the only one of Jacob's four wives mentioned by name in the genealogies of 1Chr. 7:13. There are also various traditions linking Bilhah closely to Joseph, suggesting that she in fact raised him after the death of his mother (*Gen. Rab.* [Rom] 84:11), and that her death was precipitated by the news that he had supposedly perished (*Jub.* 34:15). There is also the possibility that naming speeches, or at least naming wordplays, were more common than is reflected in written sources. Philo, for instance, gives explanations for the names Bilhah and Zilpah, as he does for certain other names:[56]

> Moses has given us the names of these two handmaidens, calling them Zilpah and Bilhah. Zilpah by interpretation is "a walking mouth," which signifies the power of expressing thought in language and directing the course of an exposition, while Bilhah is "swallowing," the first and most necessary support of mortal animals.

These explanations occur within the context of Philo's allegorical interpretation of the relationships between the patriarchs and their wives and handmaids. What is interesting, however, is that the explanations appear to be Hebrew/Aramaic, rather than Greek, word-plays: "a mouth going forth" is probably זיל, the imperative of the Aramaic אזל (go), plus פה, (mouth); while "a swallowing" is possibly from בלע (swallow), with ע-ה exchange. This suggests that Philo had access to some Hebrew/Aramaic traditions regarding biblical names.

7.5.1.B Channels of Transmission

Despite the various similarities among the texts, there are still several issues that suggest that the lines of transmission were not straightforward.

a) We may agree that, at the very least, the naming speech of Bilhah likely had a Hebrew original, given the nature of the wordplay. With

56 *On Mating with the Preliminary Studies,* 30, trans. F.H. Colson and G. H. Whitaker. In this work Philo also gives explanations for, among others, the names Sarah, Rachel and Ephraim.

respect to the other elements, however, there is no compelling reason to accept a Hebrew over a Greek original. Moreover, even if we posit an "original Naphtali" in Hebrew (and the positing of such an original still gets us no further in explaining the channel of transmission to the midrashic source), we must still explain why the three sources differ among themselves with respect to the identity of Bilhah's name-giver, and why the Greek source would have changed the identity of Zilpah's name-giver, as summarized below:

	MT	4QTNaph	Greek	Ber. Rabbati
name-giver to Zilpah	n/a	father	mother	father
name-giver to Bilhah	n/a	mother	mother	father

b) Another point of difference among the versions is that the connection to Abraham is not explicit in either of the Hebrew versions of this genealogy. Stone suggests, however, that such a relationship may be derived from the use of the term *paraq* to describe Lavan's redemption of Aḥoti, arguing that this term is unusual in the Qumran texts,[57] though it is found in Lam. 5:8, where it is used with respect to a slave. Lavan's motive for this action may thus have been the obligation in Lev. 25:47-50 to redeem a relative taken into slavery; hence there is a suggestion that Lavan and Aḥoti were related and thus of Abrahamic stock. There is, however, another tradition which connected Deborah, the sister of Aḥoti according to the Hebrew genealogies, with Naḥor, Abraham's brother,[58] a possibility of which the Hebrew versions may also have been aware.

---

57 Stone, "Testament of Naphtali," 81. An Aramaic form of *paraq* is found as part of a required condition in the marriage contract that a husband is obligated to redeem his wife if she is taken captive (*mKet.* 4:8): אם תשתבאי אפרקניך. The Akkadian term *pirqu* is found at Nuzi (interestingly, the *AHW* suggests this is actually a metathesis of the root *PQR*).

58 There is another tradition that may identify Deborah as a great-niece of Abraham. The midrash *Sefer ha-Yashar* (Dan), p. 114, mentions a Deborah as the daughter of Utz, the son of Abraham's brother Naḥor: ויהיו בני עוץ בכור נחור אביחרף וגדין ומילום ודבורה אחותם (And the children of Utz, the firstborn of Naḥor: Aviḥeref and Gadin and Milon and their sister Deborah). This genealogy, however, is not mentioned in the Bible, and it is not clear from the context whether this is the same Deborah who was Rebecca's nurse. The midrash itself is dated relatively late, anywhere from the 11th to the 16th century C.E. (see the summary in Strack and Stemberger, *Talmud and Midrash*, 359).

c) Though the Qumran fragment mentions the disposition of Bilhah and Zilpah, it does not specifically describe them as *shefaḥot,* as does *Ber. Rabbati* (this may, however, be due to the fragmentary nature of the material).

d) The three sources agree that Zilpah was the elder sister. Rashi, however, explicitly states the opposite. At Gen. 30:10 he cites a midrashic source (found at *Gen. Rab.* 71:9) that detected something unusual in the wording used in Genesis 30 to describe Zilpah's giving birth to Gad and Asher. In both verses 10 and 12 the phrase used is "And Zilpah the handmaid of Leah gave birth":

בכולם כתיב ותהר וכאן ותלד אלא בחורה היתה ולא היתה ניכרת בעיבורה

With all [the other women in this chapter—Leah, Bilhah and Rachel] —it is written: *and she conceived [and gave birth]*, and here just *she gave birth*—she was a young girl, and her pregnancy did not show.

From this unusual idea, it followed that Zilpah was younger and that this was the reason she was given to Leah:

...וכדי לרמות יעקב נתנה לבן ללאה שלא יבין שמכניסין לו את לאה שכך מנהג ליתן שפחה הגדולה לגדולה וקטנה לקטנה

In order to trick Jacob, Lavan gave [Zilpah] to Leah, so that he would not know that they were giving him Leah. This was the custom, to give the older *shifḥah* to the older woman and the younger to the younger.

This reversal is also suggested, though not explicitly, in the 11th century *Midrash Aggadah*, a source also attributed to the school of R. Moshe haDarshan:

והיתה קטנה והיתה ראויה לרחל ונתנה ללאה ברמאותו כדי להראות ליעקב שזו שפחת רחל

And she [Zilpah] was small, and suited to Rachel; and she was given to Leah as part of his [Lavan's] deception, to show Jacob that this was Rachel's *shifḥah.*

It is difficult to explain the existence of this contradiction in two sources apparently belonging to the school of R. Moshe haDarshan. Further, though Rashi was familiar with and quoted some of the work of this school, it is difficult to tell from his comments in this case whether he was unaware of all or part of the Aḥoti tradition, or whether he was deliberately choosing to ignore it.

7.5.2 The Lavan Tradition

Bereishit Rabbati, unlike the two versions of the Testament, gives a tradition naming Lavan as the father of Bilhah and Zilpah, thus making them half-sisters to Leah and Rachel. The earliest attestation of this tradition seems to be in *Gen. Rab.* 74:14 (redacted 5th century C.E.), in a midrash in the name of the third generation amora R. Reuven. This midrash is based on Gen. 31:50, in which Lavan exacts from Jacob an oath after the latter has fled from Lavan's household with his wives and children: *If you torment my daughters or take other wives over them... God is the witness between me and you.* [emphasis added] If Lavan meant here to protect his daughters Leah and Rachel from being supplanted by further wives, surely he was aware that Jacob had already been given "other wives"—Bilhah and Zilpah. According to the midrash, the solution was obvious:

א"ר ראובן כולהון בנותיו היו

Rabbi Reuven said: All of them [that is, Leah, Rachel, Bilhah, and Zilpah] were [Lavan's] daughters.

Targum Pseudo-Jonathan (redacted 7-8th cent. C.E.)[59] on Gen. 29:24 was a similar wording for Bilhah in Gen. 29:29 adds to this identification that the mother of each woman was a "concubine":

ויהב לבן ליה ית זלפה ברתיה דילידת ליה פילקתיה ומסרה ללאה ברתיה לאמהו

And Lavan gave her[60] Zilpah, his daughter borne to him by his concubine, and gave her to Leah as her *amah.*

---

59 Despite its late redaction date, the Targum likely contains earlier material.

60 The Clarke Targum has ליה, but presumably this is an error for לה.

This notion of the mother as a "concubine" seems also to be recognized in the following midrash in *Pirqei de R. Eliezer* (8-9th century), *pereq* 37, which posits the idea that the daughters of a *pilegesh* are called *shefaḥot* (the midrash repeated in the later *Ber. Rabbati*):

לקח לבן את שתי שפחותיו ונתנן לשתי בנותיו. וכי שפחותיו היו והלא בנותיו היו,
אלא ללמדך שבנותיו של אדם מפלגשו נקראו שפחות שנאמר ויתן וגו' בלהה שפחתו

> Lavan took his two *shefaḥot* and gave them to his two daughters. Were they his *shefaḥot?* Were they not his daughters? This teaches you that the daughters of a man from his *pilegesh* are called his *shefaḥot,*[61] as it is said: *And he gave,* etc., *Bilhah his shifḥah....*

7.6 CONCLUSION

A review of various references to Bilhah and Zilpah suggests that there were competing traditions regarding them from an early period; already in the biblical text there is evident uncertainty as to their precise status. In postbiblical sources we find two traditions regarding their genealogy, both of which were possibly familiar to the editor of Jubilees. Early midrashim accept the women as matriarchs. Targum Onkelos and TY "correct" their status by referring to them as "subordinates" or by claiming they were freed (a tradition also reflected in Josephus); the Bavli (and the Tractate *Semaḥot*), as well as certain later midrashim, reject them as matriarchs, apparently because of their slave origins. It is thus primarily the "mainstream" sources that are conditioned by the same sensitivity to slave-free intermarriage that is reflected in the Mishnah.

---

61 Betsy Halpern-Amaru, "Bilhah and Naphtali in Jubilees: A Note on 4QNaphtali," *DSD* 6 (1999): 1-10, at 5-6, notes that, contrary to the biblical text, in which Zilpah is always called a *shifḥah,* in *Jubilees* she is called an *'amato,* the Ge'ez equivalent of *amah.* She suggests that this change indicates that the author of *Jubilees* may have been aware of (and rejected) the idea that Zilpah was the daughter of a concubine. This would imply that the tradition that daughters of concubines were called *shefaḥot* was known relatively early. It is possible, however, that the *Jubilees* author is simply using *'amato* as a generic term for female slave, much as אמתא is used in Aramaic.

CONCLUSION

The terms *shifḥah* and *amah* were used in the Bible as synonyms, where the use reflects differences in ethnic origin or source. These female slaves were dependents, but some slave terminology was used for non-slave situations where the reference was to an aide, steward, assistant, consort, or other faithful dependent. The same woman could be both wife and slave, and there is material evidence of a wife-like status for some *amahot.* Great effort was made to place these women in some kind of family or kinship structure, most likely where marriage was allowed. There is no evidence that the primary use of the *shifḥah* and *amah* was exploitation either as a concubine or breeder, although both uses were made. Their sexual use was carefully regulated. The epigraphic evidence concerning *amah* suggests that the term was used in pre- and postexilic Israel for a woman of relatively high social status, as demonstrated by the fact that the term for "wife," *ishah*, is also applied to women who are elsewhere referred to as *shifḥah* and *amah*.

Hezser's functional analysis of rabbinic and Roman law regarding slaves is an in-depth synchronic analysis of postbiblical slavery. My study continues such a study as an individual diachronic analysis of a particular aspect of slavery, namely sex right, and analyzes its evolution from the ancient Near East to the Greco-Roman context.

In contradistinction, Flesher focuses on the genealogical distinctions between Israelite debt-servants who are temporarily indentured and will return to Israelite society proper and the non-Israelite slaves who are permanent slaves or whose masters may release them to become part of Israelite society. The primary system in the Mishnah according to Flesher defines slavery in terms of male Israelite householders' control over the slaves regardless of their ethnicity. Sometimes the slave is categorized as property, sometimes as dependent household member (like, for example, women and minors) and sometimes as citizen. Flesher presents the system as gender neutral. He considers the *shifḥah* and *amah* of Exod. 21:7-11 and Lev. 19:20 as concubines rather than slaves, while the *amah* of Deuteronomy is the female counterpart of *eved*. In his view, as opposed to mine, the Mishnah's primary system of slavery considers slave women more like slaves than women with the added attribute of sexual use.

I have argued that the different halves of the matrilineal principle in *mYev.* 7:5 and *mQidd.* 3:12 cannot be explained by householder control. Moreover, Flesher's ethnic and primary slave systems are not complementary with respect to female slaves. In the non-ethnic system there are provisions for the *shifḥah* who gives birth and in the ethnic system the female Hebrew slave must be released before puberty — neither of which can be explained by householder control. Flesher's underlying systemic approach assumes that the Mishnah is a homogeneous code. I have argued that the Mishnah is a collection of specific rules, but not a complete codification in the modern sense. Urbach and others have demonstrated layers in the Mishnah and divergent opinions, making it unlikely that the Mishnah represents a consistent worldview. I treat the inconsistencies in the Mishnah as reflective of different schools' traditions, which can be compared and contrasted to provisions in other canonical texts, particularly the Tosefta and midreshei halakha. I have found that these represent a multiplicity of quite distinct and often contradictory halakhic positions.

Methodologically, biblical law, like Mesopotamian law collections, may be considered "internormative" — rules sharing certain moral, ethical, and religious norms, civil and economic regulations, or political goals, rather than statute law in the modern sense. My definition is an anthropological definition of law as a complex phenomenon rather than a discrete set of rules.

Furthermore, I have used diachronic philological examination (words and terms in a variety of contexts) and comparison of terms and provisions of other legal systems to uncover a history of concepts. Comparison, especially of Hebrew and Akkadian terms, assumed that nuances of meaning in one language may suggest similar nuances in the other. I have made use of comparison with "functionally equivalent" acts and remedies from other legal systems as a basic method of comparative law. Although this is largely subjective, it has proven to be quite fruitful. In my opinion the strength of the method is that linkage between particular legal systems need not be demonstrated before arguing for functional equivalence.

I have thus made use of a multi-factor model of halakhic development of the type proposed by B. Jackson. This allows for both historical causes and inherent logical development in the analysis of any legal decision. The halakhic construction of "female slave" status was neither consistent nor linear, and historical causes offer only a partial explanation of the dominance of certain principles. Hence, I have focused on the different reasoning methods used by sages in the same general time frame. P. Heger's pluralistic model attributes to each decisionmaker logical and environmental influences which are in a certain degree of tension with the deep belief in the immutability of the Torah. This allows, in my opinion, for a nuanced view of halakhic development. Positivist models such as Neusner's or Flesher's assume or demand consistency throughout the legal canon, a proposition which denies the multiplicity of rabbinic positions so obviously a part of Jewish legal discourse. I have argued that legal concepts change over time. The issue of the authority of a sage must then be investigated historically and not merely dogmatically to uncover the motives of an authority and various influences on it. Inconsistencies in various rabbinic texts are significant, and even if the texts are firmly established philologically on the basis of their variant readings in the extant manuscripts, the texts once established may remain internally inconsistent — demonstrating a variety of conflicting positions.

There is no universal agreement of scholars on an appropriate model. The evolutionary approaches used hitherto tend to obscure the specific differences that relate to females. Thus, I have argued that the use of functional equivalence may serve as a "corrective" in this respect, since it allows scholars to compare how such problems were addressed in different sources.

Various approaches have been put forth by scholars concerning the three sets of biblical slave legislation (Exod. 21:2-11 — *eved ivri, amah*; Lev. 25:39-46 — *aḥ*; Deut. 15:12-18 — *eved ivri, amah*). Mendelson filled in the gaps of Hebrew slave legislation on the basis of Mesopotamian parallels. Westbrook argued for a common, fairly static law in the entire Near East for 1500 years, which allowed cross-referencing between Bible and cuneiform law collections. Nonetheless, it is difficult to assume that the law remained static even for hundreds, much less thousands, of years in the Near East given contact between different civilizations, either by peaceful means such as trade or violent ones involving warfare, conquests, and frequent dislocation or relocation. This synchronous approach of Westbrook and Mendelson fails to posit the mechanism responsible for the widespread dissemination of "common law." J. J. Finkelstein rejects the *a priori* assumption of a common law in the Near East, but he acknowledges the closeness of cases and language. There was perhaps a scribal connection between Eastern and Western Semites, though not necessarily a "common law" in the ancient Near East. Heger, Finkelstein, and others have argued that biblical legislation faced the same problems as other legal systems did but developed solutions in accordance with its own unique theology.

I argue that reproductive capacity makes comparison of the female slave to the *ishah*, wife, more relevant than comparison to male slaves. Sexual access, sex right, and its consequences depend on where a woman is on the dependence continuum evident in the Israelite household, with the legitimate wife bound by laws of adultery in the strict sense at one extreme end. Sex right may be used as a marker to show how female slaves were differentiated from wives and other women in Jewish law. Legal marriage and the resultant status of the offspring created class differences while adultery laws protected a man's sex right to a particular woman. Differential legal provisions concerning sexual activity result in at least some legal recognition of what is otherwise status inequality. Legal status is assigned by a legal system and therefore is constructed; it is not an inherent condition.

As such, it was proposed that an essential factor in defining "female slave" is the notion of sex right – that is, the regulation of sexual access to such females. This study has looked at two facets of sex right in connection with slaves: the notion that a female slave has no *qiddushin*, with the correlative idea that her offspring will also be slaves (the matrilineal principle), and the question of whether one can commit adultery with a female slave.

It was shown that the biblical notion of "female slave" placed her on a continuum with wives. Such women could marry (in fact, the provision of Exod. 21:7-11 may be a species of a fitting-out-for-marriage contract), and their children would not necessarily be slaves (though they might be inferior with respect to inheritance). Adultery with the female slave of Lev.

19:20-21 seems to consist of a kind of treason or betrayal.

In contrast, mishnaic law provides for a clearly articulated matrilineal principle, though it was noted that there were likely a number of different views of slave marriage extant postbiblically, as reflected in other tannaitic works. As to adultery with the female slave of Lev. 19:20-21, it was noted that a variety of exegeses reflected in tannaitic material led to a plethora of conflicting definitions of this crime, with the result that the crime, though vaguely resembling transgression of an incest prohibition, ended up as virtually unenforceable, for want of a clear definition of the protagonists. Far from the slave-wife continuum reflected in the biblical texts, the postbiblical material studied reflected distancing with a far more complete separation between slave and family.

The development in slave definition from Bible, where a slave woman was dependent and placed in the family continuum and her reproductive capacity would be utilized, forms a sharp contrast with the Mishnah, where she is marginalized and sexual relations with her are either prohibited or without legal consequence. Biblical slaves were part of the dependence continuum, while in the tannaitic period concepts like *ben/bat ḥorin* (free person) and *meshuḥrar/meshuḥreret* (freed slave) apparently are far closer to Greek and Roman legal categories.

In short, there is a leap (at least in these elements) in the definition of female slave between biblical and postbiblical texts. Why did this occur? As for the multitude of definitions of Lev. 19:20, this may at first blush be explained simply by the pluralism extant in the tannaitic era. Each sage has his own view of the crime contemplated in Lev. 19:20, and each view is supported by the sage's particular form of exegesis – some show influence of foreign (i.e., Greco-Roman) law, particularly with respect to notions of "property," while others seem to be reacting more to important different referents in the biblical text. In general, postbiblical contact with Greco-Roman law, with its precise distinctions between property and person, overcame the biblical idea of a dependence continuum. The resulting conditions, such as "half-slave, half-free," became too tenuous to be put into practice, another example of the marginalization of the slave class.

I have argued that there is no conclusive evidence of a prohibition of legal marriage for female slaves, nor is there automatic inheritance of slave status in the Bible. The asymmetry in the rulings depending on which parent is a slave demonstrates for S. Cohen that there was no unified matrilineal principle in Mishnah. In contradistinction, I argue that the variety of opinions concerning inheritance of slave status in postbiblical literature gives no firm basis for arguing a linear development of the matrilineal principle in Jewish law. Rather, the evidence is consistent with the difference between dependence and marginalization in biblical and postbiblical texts. In the case of the *shifḥah neḥerefet*, the unfree status of the woman seems to preclude the possibility of adultery. In what seems to be a conflict between sex right and some idea of property rights, the case was resolved according to property rights. In nearly all slave systems, there is a conflict between slave as person and slaves as property, yielding inconsistent treatment of slaves. In Exod. 21:20 a kind of *talion* is given to the slave killed by his master—"he shall surely be avenged"—and in Exod. 21:26-27 slaves injured by the master are manumitted. This seems to indicate that they were not considered solely as property. The *shifḥah neḥerefet* may be understood as an upset of the dependence continuum. For the slave it is a crime of trespass and for the wife a crime of adultery. Adultery constitutes treason against the husband. Although the slave was not formally married, this sexual crime is nevertheless considered to be a trespass.

The matrilineal principle as it developed in postbiblical Judaism consists of two elements: restriction on "legal" marriage and the interdependence of the child's status with its mother's status. As opposed to what appears to be the case in the Bible, legal marriage was often not available to female slaves. The status of slave women is not changed by intercourse, that is, they do not become legal "wives" and therefore their children remain slaves. Jewish-gentile and free-slave sexual connections do not yield marriage. In *mQidd.* 3:12 if the woman is a gentile her child is a gentile; if she is a slave, her child is a slave regardless of the nationality of the father. If the mother is an Israelite and the father is a slave or gentile, the offspring is a *mamzer* according to *mYev.* 7:5.

The matrilineal principle and its development in mishnaic law, at least with respect to slaves, I believe is due more to foreign influence and the demands of the Greco-Roman administrative system on householders to keep detailed lists of household elements, probably for purposes of taxation. In particular, I suggest that tax law would account for this change from the previous biblical model. It is in the Ptolemaic era that I think we first notice the taxation of slaves as commodities. This system should be contrasted with the taxation of *transactions* involving slaves, in which the slave would be defined as such by the parties to a sale or a general poll or head tax. Under these new conditions a slave, like other household members, would be taxed according to the definitions of slavery by an administrative ruling. That is, this increase in commodity taxation would likely necessitate the greater existence of a poll or census with a clearly defined notion of slavery. There likely would be considerable pressure to adopt such formal definitions.[1]

Assuming for the moment that these conclusions have some plausibility, should they have any effect on halakhah in modern times? The construct of slaves and slavery is supported by certain legal, political, economic, and social definitions, only some of which have relevance in the Western world. I return in particular to the halakhic possibility of acquiring a female slave described at the beginning of the Introduction. One proposed solution for "curing" the offspring of a *mamzer* would be for him to purchase a non-Jewish woman as a slave. The offspring would be slaves who could then be freed without carrying the status of *mamzer*; the woman could then be freed as well with manumission constituting conversion to Judaism. This raises the question as to whether legal actions which are to a large extent symbolic should be permitted despite their abeyance and in this case repugnant nature in the modern world.

Many of us today would view contemporaneous reliance on such an antiquarian model as this as a morally dangerous position. Under a positivist characterization of Jewish law, such as that proposed by Englard and

---

1 Certain general observations on the need to maintain extensive lists to justify commodity taxation may be made:
In ancient Athens it was considered irreconcilable with a person's dignity to impose a tax on one's person, income, or capital; therefore there were generally direct taxes only on metics and indirect taxes and liturgies; *eisphora* was an extraordinary direct tax for extraordinary demands such as war (Thomsen, p. 11).
In Roman Egypt, there were poll taxes on persons already from Ptolemy IV Philopater (Wallace, p. 96); for this purpose, slaves, sons, and freedmen followed their master (Wallace, 119). Documentation was required to show the relationship of all persons to an owner (Wallace, 102). Exact information was also important with respect to capitation taxes imposed by Romans (Wallace, 96), from which people fled (Wallace, 97, 136; and possibly Luke 2:1-4 which was either a tax or census registration possibly for taxation purposes). Given the nature of this increased administrative attention, detailed rules were required for commodity transactions.

Roth,[2] such a position is legally acceptable if pronounced by a recognized authority. Both scholars, as noted above, would seem to exclude factors in the historical development of a particular halakhah from consideration by any *poseq* (legal decisor), and this would appear to render irrelevant any data that show that particular rules were time– and circumstance-specific. From the texts studied above it is evident that sex right is an outmoded model inextricably linked to female status. Such a connection, through such axioms as *shinnui ha-itim* (changing times),[3] might now be easily ruptured by a *poseq*. Yet this type of connection also reflects a flawed view of positivism, in my opinion, even if one concedes that this is the correct model with which to assess modern halakhah. It is a static view that would preclude the formation of new norms based directly on the Torah. It puts the strongest emphasis on the continuity of precedent (Englard) or the existence of so-called systemic principles (Roth), over recognition of the significance of differences in decisions and principles that have always been a feature of the halakhic system. It fails to acknowledge the fact that the decision makers' values and circumstances inevitably influence their acceptance of particular trends of Torah interpretation. Even using a positivist model, there is room for a dynamic viewpoint, under which new norms can be derived from the Torah (law) and there can be open acceptance of differing interpretations, rather than a static viewpoint under which all norms have already been derived. Hence we would argue for a new dynamic model based on a continuum in which we see sex rewarded or sex punished depending on our contemporaneous interpretations of good and evil. A static model is, in my opinion, a dying model.

---

2 Englard, "Research in Jewish Law," 36; J. Roth, "An Halakhic Perspective on an Historical Foundation," *Judaism* 133 (1985):, 62-67, at 63. Roth argues that the historical sources of a norm are legally significant only if a) they remain the sole justification for the norm, and b) they are judged to be inaccurate or inapplicable. While b) would seem to give a wide allowance for the introduction of historical data, a) gives a wide allowance for the positing of a variety of justifications for any particular norm. Under the latter, Roth rejects the relevance of historical data regarding the matrilineal principle (p. 67).

3 See explanations of this term in Roth, "An Halakhic Perspective," 251, 254, 285.

BIBLIOGRAPHY

Albeck, Chanoch (חנוך אלבק).

1940 מדרש בראשית רבתי. ירושלים: מקיצי נרדמים.

[*Midrash Bereishit Rabbati*]

Alexander, P.S.

1976 "The Rabbinic Lists of Forbidden Targumim." *JJS* 27, 177-91.

Aminoaḥ, N. (נ. עמינח).

1977 עריכת מסכת קידושין בתלמוד הבבלי. אוניברסיטת תל אביב, תשל"ז.

[*The Redaction of Tratate Qiddushin in the Babylonian Talmud*]

Amit, Yairah (יאירה אמית).

1991 "פרשת פילגש בגבעה בפולמוס סמוי נגד מלכות שאול ואהדיה

(שופטים י"ט-כ"א)." בית מקרא 37, 109-118.

["The Story of the *Pilegesh* in Givea in the Hidden Dispute against the Kingship of Shaul"]

Ariel, Yaqov (יעקב אריאל).

1989 "הפילגש ומעמדה ההלכתי במקרא." מגדים ח (תשמ"ט), 57-67

["The *Pilesgesh* and her Halakhic Status in the Bible"]

Assaf, Simḥah (שמחה אסף).

1922 "העונשין אחרי חתימת התלמוד." ספריה משפטית א. ירושלים, תרפ"ב.

["The Punishments after the End of the Talmud"]

1930 "ספר השטרות לרב האיי גאון." מוסף-התרביץ א. ירושלים: תר"ץ.

["Sefer HaShetarot of Rav Hai Gaon"]

Atwood, Margaret.

1985 *The Handmaid's Tale*. Toronto: McClelland & Stewart.

Aufrecht, Walter.
1989 *A Corpus of Ammonite Inscriptions.* Ancient Near Eastern Texts and Studies. Lewiston: Edwin Mellen.

Avigad, Naḥman.
1946 "A Seal of a Slave Wife." *Palestine Exploration Quarterly,* 125-32.
1953 "The Epitaph of a Royal Steward from Siloam Village." *IEJ* 3, 137-52.
1976 *Bullae and Seals from a Post-Exilic Judean Archive. Qedem* 4. Translated by R. Grafman. Jerusalem: Magnes.

Axworthy, Thomas S.
2005 "Sexual Slavery Seen as World's Greatest Crime." *The Toronto Star*, 25 September 2005, A-17.

Bal, Mieke.
1988 *Death and Dissymmetry: The Politics of Coherence in the Book of Judges.* Chicago: University of Chicago Press.

Ben-Ḥayim, Ze'ev (זאב בן-חיים).
1935 66-362 (תרצ"ו) לשונינו ז ".(ויקרא י"ט כ') "והוא שפחה נחרפת לאיש
["And She is a Shifḥa *Neḥerefet* to Man (Leviticus 19:20)"]

Bergmann, Aaron.
1912 *The Old Testament in Hebrew and Yiddish.* London: British and Foreign Bible Society.

Berger, Adolph.
1991 *Encyclopedic Dictionary of Roman Law.* Transactions of the American Philosophical Society n.s. 43/2 (1953). Repr., Philadelphia.

Bernstein, Moshe.
1994 "4Q252: From Re-Written Bible to Biblical Commentary." *JJS* 45, 1-27.

Biezunska-Malowist, Iza.
1968 "Les esclaves en copropriété dans l'Egypte gréco-romaine." *Aegyptus* 48, 116-29.
1974 *Periode ptolémaïque.* Part 1 of *L'esclavage dans l'Égypte Gréco-Romaine.* Translated by J. Wolf and J. Kasinska. Wroclaw.

Blok, Josine.
1987 "Sexual Asymmetry: A Historiographical Essay." In *Sexual Asymmetry: Studies in Ancient Society,* 1-57. Edited by Josine Blok and Peter Mason. Amsterdam: J. C.Gieben.

Boggs, Ralph S. et al.
1946 *Tentative Dictionary of Medieval Spanish.* 2 vols. Chapel Hill, N.C.

Boling, Robert.
1975 *Judges.* Anchor Bible 6A. Garden City, N.Y.: Doubleday.

Bowen, Donna Lee.
1981 "Muslim Juridical Opinions Concerning the Status of Women as Demonstrated by the Case of *'AZL* [coitus interruptus]." *JNES* 40, 323-28.

Breuer, Mordechai (מרדכי ברויאר).
1992 "אמה עברייה ושפחה חרופה." מגדים טז (אדר ב' תשנ"ב) 19-36.
["*Amah Ivriah* and *Shifḥa Neḥerefet*»]

Breneman, J. Mervin.
1971. "Nuzi Marriage Tablets." Ph.D. dissertation, Brandeis University.

Brenton, L.
1986 *The Septuagint Version: Greek and English.* Grand Rapids, Mich.: Zondervan.

Bright, John.
1959 *A History of Israel.* Philadelphia: Westminster.

Brinkman, J.A.
1980 "Forced Laborers in the Middle Babylonian Period." *JCS* 32, 17-22.

Brooke, G.
1996 "4Q Commentary on Genesis A." In *Qumran Cave 4, XVII, Parabiblical Texts, Part 3,* 185-207. *DJD* 22. Oxford: Clarendon.

Brown, John Pairman.
1995 *Israel and Hellas.* ZAW Supplements 231. Berlin: De Gruyter.

Brown, Lesley.
1993 *The New Shorter Oxford English Dictionary on Historical Principles.* Oxford: Clarendon.

Buber, Solomon (שלמה בובר).
1924 . מדרש זוטא. ברלין, תרנ"ד. נדפס מחדש בתל אביב[=*Midrash Zuta*]
1891 מדרש תהילים, וילנא [=*Midrash Tehilim*]

Buckland, W. W.
1908 *The Roman Law of Slavery: The Condition of the Slave in Private Law from Augustus to Justinian.* Cambridge: Cambridge University Press.

Burchard, C., trans.
1985 "Joseph and Aseneth." In *The Old Testament Pseudepigrapha,* 177-247. Edited by J. H. Charlesworth. New York: Doubleday.

Burke, Martin J.
1995 *The Conundrum of Class.* Chicago: University of Chicago Press.

Came, Barry.
2000 "Freeing the Slaves of Sudan." In *Maclean's,* 10 April 2000, 20-27.

Cardascia, Guillaume.
1951 *Les archives des Murasu, une famille d'hommes d'affaires babyloniens a l'epoque perse.* Paris: Imprimerie Nationale.
1958 "Le statut de l'etranger dans la Mesopotamie ancienne." *Recueils de la Société Jean Bodin* 9, 105-17.
1959 "Le concept babylonien de la propriété." *RIDA* (3e serie) 6, 19-32.

Cardellini, Innocenzo.
1981 *Die biblischen "Sklaven"-Gesetze im Lichte des keilschriftlichen Sklavenrechts.* Bonner Biblische Beiträge 55. Bonn: Peter Hanstein.

Cassin , E. M.
1938 *L'adoption à Nuzi.* Paris: Adrien Maisonneuve.

Charles, R. H.
1908 *The Greek Versions of the Testaments of the Twelve Patriarchs.* Repr., Oxford: Oxford University Press, 1960.

Chiesa, B. and W. Lockwood.
1984 *Ya'Qub al-Qirqisani, Abu Yusuf.* Book I of *On Jewish Sects and Christianity: A Translation of "Kitab al-anwar."* Judentum and Umwelt 10. Frankfurt: Peter Lang.

Chirichigno, Gregory C.
1993 *Debt-Slavery in Israel and the Ancient Near East.* JSOT Supplement Series 141. Sheffield: JSOT Press.

Clarke, E.G.
1984 *Targum Pseudo-Jonathan of the Pentateuch: Text and Concordance.* Hoboken: Ktav.

Cogan, Mordechai and Hayim Tadmor.
1988 *II Kings.* Anchor Bible 11. Garden City, N.Y.: Doubleday.

Cohen, Boaz.
1966 *Jewish and Roman Law: A Comparative Study.* 2 vols. New York: JTSA.

Cohen, Shaye D.
1985 "The Origins of the Matrilineal Principle in Rabbinic Law." *AJS Review* 10/1, 19-53.
1999 *The Beginnings of Jewishness: Boundaries, Varieties, Uncertainties.* Berkeley: University of California Press.

Cooke, G. A.
1903 *A Text-Book of North-Semitic Inscriptions.* Oxford: Clarendon.

Couroyer, B.
1955 "LHN: Chantre?" *VT* 5, 83-88.

Cowley, A.
1923 *Aramaic Papyri of the Fifth Century B.C.* Oxford: Clarendon.

Dahood, Mitchell.
1968 *Psalms II, 51-100.* Anchor Bible. Garden City, N.Y.: Doubleday.
1981 *Psalms III, 101-150.* Anchor Bible. Garden City, N.Y.: Doubleday.

Dalman, Gustaf H.
1967 *Aramaisch-neuhebraisches Handworterbuch zu Targum, Talmud und Midrasch.* Hildesheim: Georg Olms.

Dan, Yosef (יוסף דן).
1986 .ספר הישר. ירושלים: מוסד ביאליק, תשמ"ו
[*Sefer HaYashar*]

Dandamaev, M.
1984 *Slavery in Babylonia: From Nabopolassar to Alexander the Great (626-331 BC).* Revised edition. Translated by Victoria Powell. Edited by Marvin Powell. DeKalb: Northern Illinois University Press.

Davidson, B.
1970 *Analytical Hebrew and Chaldee Lexicon.* London: Samuel Bagster.

Deller, K.
1984 "Assyrisch um/nzarḫu und Hebraisch 'azraḥ." *ZA* 74, 235-39.

Diakonoff, I. M.
1972 "Socio-Economic Classes in Babylonia and the Babylonian Concept of Social Stratification." *RAI* 18, 41-49.
1976 "Slaves, Helots and Serfs in Early Antiquity." In *Wirtschaft und Gesellschaft im alten Vorderasien,* 45-78. Edited by J. Harmatta & G. Komoróczy. Budapest: Akadémiai Kiadó.
1987 "Slave Labour versus Non-Slave Labour: The Problem of Definition." In *Labor in the Ancient Near East,* 1-3. AOS 68. Edited by Marvin A. Powell. New Haven: American Oriental Society.

Dias, R.W.M.
1970 *Jurisprudence.* 3rd edition. London: Butterworths.

Diez Macho, Alejandro.
1970 *Neophyti I.* 5 vols. Madrid: Consejo Superior de Investigaciones Cientificas.

Donner, Herbert and Wolfgang Rollig.
1962-64 *Kanaanäische und aramäische Inschriften.* 3 vols. Wiesbaden: O. Harrassowitz.

Dougherty, Raymond.
1923 *The Shirkûtu of Babylonian Deities.* YOS Researches 5/2. New Haven: Yale University Press. Repr., New York: AMS.

Douglass, Frederick.
1994 "Narrative of the Life of Frederick Douglass, an American Slave." In *Autobiographies,* 1:1-102. New York: Library Classics of the United States.

Driver, G. R.
1956 *Canaanite Myths and Legends.* Old Testament Studies III. Edinburgh: T&T Clark.

Driver, G.R. and J.C. Miles.
1952 *The Babylonian Laws.* 2 vols. Oxford: Clarendon.

Dunsky, Shimon (שמעון דונסקי).
1980 מדרש רבה שיר השירים. ירושלים: דביר, תש"מ.
[*Midrash Rabba to Song of Songs*]

Eisenman, Robert and Michael Wise.
1992 *The Dead Sea Scrolls Uncovered.* New York: Penguin.

Elliger, Karl.
1966 *Leviticus.* Handbuch zum Alten Testament Erste Reihe 4. Herausgegeben von O. Eissfeldt. Tübingen: Mohr.

Ellinson, Elyaqim (אליקים ג'. אלינסון).
1975 נישואין שלא כדת משה וישראל. תל אביב: דביר, תשל"ו .
[*Nissuin Not in Accordance with the Law of Moses and Israel*]

Ellis, Maria de J.
1975 "An Old Babylonian Contract from Tel Harmel." *JCS* 27, 130-51.

Elon, Menachem.
1994 *Jewish Law: History, Sources and Principles.* Philadelphia: Jewish Publication Society.

Englard, I.
1980 "Research in Jewish Law." In *Modern Research in Jewish Law*, 21-65. Edited by B. Jackson. Leiden: Brill.

Epstein, J. N. (י.נ. אפשטיין).
1962 מבואות לספרות האמוראים. ערוך ע"י ע. מלמד. ירושלים: מאגנס.
[*Introductions to Amoraic Literature*]

Epstein J.N. and E.Z. Melamed (י.נ. אפשטיין וע.צ. מלמד).
1955 מכילתא דרבי שמעון בן יוחאי. ירושלים: מקיצי נרדמים.
[*Mekhilta deR. Shimon ben Yoḥai*]

Epstein, Louis.
1934-5 "The Institution of Concubinage Among the Jews." *PAAJS* 6, 153-88.
1942 *Marriage Laws in the Bible and the Talmud.* Harvard Semitic Series 12. Cambridge, Mass.: Harvard University Press.
1973 *The Jewish Marriage Contract.* JTSA, 1927. Reprinted New York: Arno.

Epstein-Halevi, E. (א.א. הלוי).
1972 עולמה של האגדה: האגדה לאור מקורות יוונים. תל-אביב: דביר .
[*The World of the Aggada: The Aggada in Light of Greek Sources*]

Even-Shoshan, A. (אברהם אבן-שושן).
1988 המלון העברי המרכז. ירושלים: קרית ספר, תשמ"ח.
[*The Concise Hebrew Dictionary*]

Exum, J. Cheryl.
1993 *Fragmented Women.* Valley Forge, Penn.: Trinity Press.

Fales, F. M. and J. N. Postgate.
1995 *Imperial Administrative Records, Part II.* SAA XI. Helsinki: Helsinki University Press.

Falk, Ze'ev.
1957 "Mutual Obligations in the Ketubah." *JJS* 8, 215-17.

Fensham, F. Charles.
1969 "The Son of a Handmaid in Northwest Semitic." *VT* 19, 312-321.

Fernández, Miguel Perez.
1997 *An Introductory Grammar of Rabbinic Hebrew.* Translated by John Elwolde. Leiden: Brill.

Fields, Weston.

1992 "The Motif 'Night as Danger' Associated with Three Biblical Destruction Narratives." In *Sha'arei Talmon: Studies in the Bible, Qumran and the Ancient Near East Presented to Shemaryahu Talmon,* 17-32. Edited by M. Fishbane and E. Tov. Winona Lake, Ind.: Eisenbrauns.

Finkelstein, J. J.

1961 "Ammiṣaduqa's Edict and the Babylonian Law Codes." *JCS* 15, 91-104.
1981 *The Ox That Gored.* Transactions of the American Philosophical Society 71/2. Philadelphia: American Philosophical Society.

Finkelstein, Louis (אליעזר פינקלשטין).

1957 תורת כהנים על פי כתב יד רומי מנוקד: אססמאני מספר 66. ניו יורק : בית המדרש לרבנים באמריקה, תשי"ז.
[*Torat Kohanim Romi* 66]
1969 *Sifre on Deuteronomy.* Repr., New York: JTSA, 1993.
1989 ספרא דבי רב. 6 כרכים. ניו יורק: בית המדרש לרבנים באמריקה, תשמ"ט.
[*Sifra deVei Rav*]

Finley, Moses I.

1976 "A Peculiar Institution?" *Times Literary Supplement,* 2 July 1976, 819-21.

Flesher, Paul V. M.

1988 *Oxen, Women or Citizens? Slaves in the System of the Mishnah.* Brown Judaic Studies 143. Atlanta: Scholars Press.

Fokkelman, Jan.

1992 "Structural Remarks on Judges 9 and 19." In *Sha'arei Talmon: Studies in the Bible, Qumran and the Ancient Near East Presented to Shemaryahu Talmon,* 33-45. Edited by M. Fishbane and E. Tov. Winona Lake, Ind.: Eisenbrauns.

Fox (leBeit Yoreh), Harry ((מנחם צבי פוקס (לבית יורה).

1979 מהדורה ביקורתית של משניות מסכת סוכה עם מבוא והערות. חיבור לשם קבלת תואר דוקטור לפילוסופיה, האוניברסיטה העברית. 2 כרכים.
["A Critical Edition of Mishnah Tractate Succah with Introduction and Notes"]
1995 "יש אם למקרא." סיני 611, 53-131
["There is a Source to the Verse"]
1999 "Introducing Tosefta: Textual, Intratextual and Intertextual Studies." In *Introducing Tosefta: Textual, Intratextual and Intertextual Studies,* 1-37. Edited by H. Fox (leBeit Yoreh) and T. Meacham (leBeit Yoreh). Jersey City, N.J.: Ktav.

Frankel, Zechariah.

1831 *Über den Einfluss der palästinischen Exegese auf die alexandrinische Hermeneutik.* Leipzig. Repr., Westmead: Gregg International, 1972.

1923 .דרכי המשנה. וורשה, תרפ"ג

[*Darkei HaMishnah*]

Friedman, Mordechai.

1980-81 *Jewish Marriage in Palestine: A Cairo Genizah Study.* 2 vols. Tel Aviv: JTSA.

Friedman, Shamma.

1999 "The Primacy of Tosefta to Mishnah in Synoptic Parallels." In *Introducing Tosefta: Textual, Intratextual and Intertextual Studies,* 99-121. Edited by H. Fox (leBeit Yoreh) and T. Meacham (leBeit Yoreh). Jersey City, N.J.: Ktav.

Friedmann, Daniel.

1972 "The Unmarried Wife in Israeli Law." *Israel Yearbook on Human Rights* 2, 287-316.

Frymer-Kensky, Tikva.

1981 "Patriarchal Family Relationships and Near Eastern Law." *Biblical Archeologist* 44, 209-14.

Fuller, Lon.

1967 *Legal Fictions.* Stanford: Stanford University Press.

Garelli, Paul.

1972 "Problèmes de stratification sociale dans l'empire assyrien." *RAI* 18, 73-79.

Gelb, I. J.

1972a "From Slavery to Freedom." *RAI* 18, 81-92.

1972b "The Arua Institution." *RA* 66, 1-32.

1982 "Terms for Slaves in Ancient Mesopotamia." In *Societies and Languages of the Ancient Near East: Studies in Honour of I. M. Diakonoff,* 81-98. Edited by J. N. Postgate. Warminster: Aris & Phillips.

Gibbs, John and Louis Feldman.

1986 "Josephus' Vocabulary for Slavery." *JQR* 76, 281-310.

Ginzberg, Louis.
1938 *The Legends of the Jews*. 7 vols. Index by Boaz Cohen. Philadelphia: Jewish Publication Society.

Glueck, Nelson.
1959 *Rivers in the Desert: A History of the Negev*. Philadelphia: The Jewish Publication Society.

Goitein, S.D.
1967-1993 *A Mediterranean Society*. 6 vols. Berkeley: University of California Press.

Grace, E.
1973 "Status Distinctions in the Draconian Law." *Eirene: Studia Graeca et Latina* 11, 5-30.

Grayson, A.K. and J. Van Seters.
1975 "The Childless Wife in Assyria and the Stories in Genesis." *Orientalia* n.s. 44, 485-86.

Graveson, R.H.
1953 *Status in the Common Law*. London: Athlone.

Greenberg, Moshe.
1997. *Ezekiel 21-37*. Anchor Bible 22A. Garden City, N.Y.: Doubleday.

Grivsky, A.L. (א.ל. גרייבסקי).
1959 "פילגשות בישראל." מולד (תשי"ט) 666-70.
["Concubinage in Israel"]

Gruber, Mayer.
1995 "Matrilineal Determination of Jewishness: Biblical and Near Eastern Roots." In *Pomegranates and Golden Bells: Studies in Biblical, Jewish and Near Eastern Ritual, Law and Literature in Honor of Jacob Milgrom*, 437-43. Edited by D. Wright et al. Winona Lake, Ind.: Eisenbrauns.

Gulak, Asher (אשר גולאק).
1926 אוצר השטרות הנוהגים בישראל. ספריה משפטית ה. ירושלים: תרפ"ז.
[*A Compendium of Documents Used in Israel*]

Gulak, Asher (אשר גולאק).

1994 השטרות בתלמוד לאור הפפירוסים היוונים ממצרים ולאור המשפט היווני והרומי. ערך והוסיף הערות: רנון קצוף. ירושלים: מאגנס, תשנ"ד.
[*The Documents in the Talmud in Light of the Greek Papyri from Egypt and in Light of Greek and Roman Law*] Rev. from the German edition of 1935.

Halberstam, Shlomoh (שלמה האלברשטאם).

1967 ספר השטרות להרב הנשיא רבינו יהודה בר' ברזילי הברצלוני ז"ל. ברלין: איטצקאווסקי, 1898. נדפס מחדש ירושלים: תשכ"ז
[*The Book of Documents of the Rabbi and Patriarch Rabbenu Yehuda bar R. Barzilai of Barcelona*]

Halbertal, Moshe (משה הלברטל).

1997 מהפכות פרשניות בהתהוותן: ערכים כשיקולים פרשניים במדרשי הלכה. ירושלים: מאגנס
[*Interpretive Revolutions in the Making*]

Halivni, David (דוד וייס הלבני).

1959-60 "פירושים במשנה ובברייתא: מסכת כתובות." תרביץ 92 (תש"ך), 46-32
["Commentaries on Mishnah and Baraita"]
1968 מקורות ומסורות. כרך 1. ביאורים בתלמוד לסדר נשים. תל-אביב: דביר, תשכ"ט.
[*Sources and Traditions: Seder Nashim*]
1986 *Midrash, Mishnah and Gemara: The Jewish Predilection for Justified Law.* Cambridge, Mass.: Oxford University Press
1991 *Peshat and Derash: Plain and Applied Meaning in Rabbinic Exegesis.* New York: Oxford University Press.

Haran, Menahem (מנחם הרן).

1968 *Encyclopedia of the Bible* (אינצקלופדיה מקראית, 9 כרכים, ירושלים: מוסד ביאליק) *s.v.* נתינים

Halpern-Amaru, Betsy.

1999 "Bilhah and Naphtali in Jubilees: A Note on 4QNaphtali." *DSD* 6, 1-10.

Harkavy, A. (אברהם אליהו הרכבי).

1903 לקוטי קדמוניות: לקורות דת בני מקרא וספרותם, חלק שני. חוברת ראשונה: השריד והפליט מספרי המצות הראשונים לבני מקרא. זכרון לראשונים ח. ס"ט פטרבורג, תרס"ג
[*Collections from Early Writings*]

Harper, Robert Francis.

1892-1914 Assyrian and Babylonian Letters belonging to the Kouyunjik Collections of the British Museum. 14 vols. Chicago: University of Chicago Press.

Harrington, D.J., trans.
1985 "Pseudo-PhiloPhilo." In *The Old Testament Pseudepigrapha,* 2:298-377. Edited by J. H. Charlesworth. New York: Doubleday.

Harris, R.L. et al., eds.
1981 *Theological Wordbook of the Old Testament.* 2 vols. Chicago: Moody.

Heger, Paul.
1999a *The Three Biblical Altar Laws.* BZAW 279. Berlin: Walter de Gruyter.
1999b "The Law of the Hebrew Slave." *ZAW* 108, 138-141.
2003 *The Pluralistic Halakhah: Legal Innovations in the Late Second Commonwealth and Rabbinic Periods.* Berlin: De Gruyter.

Henshke, David (דוד הנשקה).
1999 "לטיב זיקתו של התרגום המיוחס ליונתן למדרשי ההלכה: לפרשיות אמה עברייה."
תרביץ סח, ב (תשנ"ט) 187-210.

["On the Nature of the Relationship of Targum Pseudo-Jonathan to Midreshe Halakha"]

Herzog, I.
1980 *The Main Institutions of Jewish Law.* 2 vols. London: Soncino.

Hezser, C.
2003 "Introduction." In *Rabbinic Law in its Rabbinic and Near Eastern Context,* 1-16. Texts and Studies in Ancient Judaism 97. Tübingen: Mohr Siebeck.

Himmelfarb, Martha.
1984 "R. Moses the Preacher and the Testaments of the Twelve Patriarchs," *AJS Review* 9, 55-78.

Hoffmann, David Tzevi (דוד צבי האפפמאנן).
1962 מדרש תנאים על ספר דברים. נדפס מחדש תל אביב: מפעלי ספרים ליוצא.
[*Midrash Tannaim on Deuteronomy*]

Hoftijzer, J. and K. Jongeling.
1995 *Dictionary of the North-West Semitic Inscriptions.* 2 parts. Leiden: Brill.

Hollander, H. W. and M. de Jonge.
1985 *The Testaments of the Twelve Patriarchs: A Commentary.* Leiden: Brill.

Homer.

1971 *The Iliad of Homer*. Translated by Richmond Lattimore. Chicago: University of Chicago Press.

Horovitz, H.S. (חיים שאול הורביץ).

1992 ספרי על ספר במדבר וספרי זוטא. ירושלים: שלם.
[*Sifre on Numbers and Sifre Zuta*]

Hugenberger, Gordon.

1994 *Marriage as a Covenant: A Study of Biblical Law and Ethics Governing Marriage Developed from the Perspective of Malachi.* VT Supplements LII. Leiden: Brill.

Hunter, Virginia.

1997 "Status Distinctions in Athenian Law." Paper presented at conference "Law and Social Status in Classical Athens," University of Toronto, April 1997.

Hyamson, Moses.

1913 *Mosaicarum et Romanorum Legum Collatio.* London: Oxford University Press.

Jackson, Bernard S.

1975 *Essays in Jewish and Comparative Legal History.* Leiden: Brill.
1980a "History, Dogmatics and Halakhah." In *Jewish Law in Legal History and the Modern World,* 1-26. Edited by B. S. Jackson. Leiden: Brill.
1980b "Towards a Structuralist Theory of Law." *Liverpool L. Rev.* 2, 5-30.
1981 "On the Problem of Roman Influence on the Halakah and Normative Self-Definition in Judaism." In *Jewish and Christian Self-Definition.* Vol. 2: *Aspects of Judaism in the Graeco-Roman Period,* 157-203. Edited by E. P. Saunders, with A. I. Baumgarten and A. Mendelson. Philadelphia: Fortress.
1988 "Can One Speak of the 'Deep Structure' of Law?" In *Theory and Systems of Legal Philosophy*, 250-61. ARSP Supplementa III. Edited by S. Panow et al. Stuttgart: Franz Steiner. 1991 "Analogy in Legal Science: Some Comparative Observations." In *Legal Knowledge and Analogy,* 145-64. Law and Philosophy Library 13. Edited by P. Nerhot. Dordrecht: Kluwer Academic Publishers.

Jastrow, Marcus.

1950 *Dictionary of the Targumim, Talmud Babli, Yerushalmi and Midrashic Literature.* New York: Pardes.

Jepsen A.

1958 "*Amah* and Schiphchah." *VT* 8, 293-97.

Jolowicz, H. F.

1978 *Roman Foundations of Modern Law*. Oxford University Press, 1957. Repr., Westport, Conn.: Greenwood.

Joösten, Jan.

1998 "The Function of the Semitic D Stem: Biblical Hebrew Materials for a Comparative-Historical Approach." *Orientalia* 67, 202-31.

Josephus, Flavius.

1926-1965 Josephus. 9 vols. Translated by H. St. Thackeray. London: Heinemann.

Joüon, Paul.

1996 *A Grammar of Biblical Hebrew*. 2 vols. Translated and revised by T. Muraoka. Subsidia Biblica 14/I, II. Rome: Pontificio Instituto Biblico.

Just, Roger.

1989 *Women in Athenian Law and Life*. London: Routledge.

Kadari, Menahem Zvi (מנחם צבי קדרי).

1995 תחביר וסמאנטיקה בעברית שלאחר המקרא. 2 כרכים. אוניברסיטת בר אילן, תשנ"ה.
[*Syntax and Semantics in Post-Biblical Hebrew*]

Kafaḥ, Yosef D. (יוסף ד. קאפח)

1965 משנה עם פירוש רבינו משה בן מימון. תרגם מערבית ע"י י. ד. קאפח. ירושלים: מוסד הרב קוק, תשכ"ה.
[Mishnah with Maimonides' Commentary]

Katz, David.

1994 "The Mamzer and the Shifcha." *JHCS* 28, 73-104.

Katzoff, Ranon.

2003 "The Children of Intermarriage: Roman and Jewish Conceptions." In in *Rabbinic Law in its Roman and Near Eastern Context*, 276-86. Texts and Studies in Ancient Judaism 97. Edited by C. Hezser. Tübingen: Mohr Siebeck.

Kaufman, S.

1974 *The Akkadian Influences on Aramaic*. Chicago: University of Chicago Press.

Kaufman, S. and M. Sokoloff.

1993 *A Key-Word-in-Context Concordance to Targum Neofiti: A Guide to the Complete Palestinian Aramaic Text of the Torah*. Baltimore: Johns Hopkins University Press.

Kautzsch, E.

1970 *Gesenius' Hebrew Grammar.* Second English Edition, 1910. Revised by A. E. Cowley. Oxford: Clarendon.

Keukens, K.

1983 "Die rekabitischen Haussklaven in Jeremia 35," *Biblische Zeitschrift* n.s. 27, 228-35.

Kleiman, Ephraim.

1987 "Opportunity Cost, Human Capital, and Some Related Economic Concepts in Talmudic Literature." *History of Political Economy* 19, 261-87.

Klein, Herbert S.

1967 *Slavery in the Americas: A Comparative Study of Virginia and Cuba.* Chicago: University of Chicago Press.

Koehler, L. and W. Baumgartner.

1995 *The Hebrew and Aramaic Lexicon of the Old Testament.* 5 vols. Translated and edited by M. E. J. Richardson. Leiden: Brill.

Kohler, J. and A. Ungnad.

1913 *Assyrische Rechsturkunden.* Leipzig: Eduard Pfeiffer.

Kohler, J. and F. E. Peiser.

1891 *Aus dem Babylonischen Rechtstleben.* Part II. Leipzig: Eduard Pfeiffer.

Kohut, A., ed.

1892 Natan ben Yehezqel. *Supplement to Aruch Completum.* New York: Ginsberg.

1926 Vindobona ,הערוך השלם [=*Arukh*]

Kopytoff, Igor and Suzanne Miers.

1977 "African 'Slavery' as an Institution of Marginality." In *Slavery in Africa: Historical and Anthropological Perspectives,* 3-81. Edited by S. Miers and I. Kopytoff. Madison, Wisc.: University of Wisconsin Press.

Koschaker, Paul.

1911 *Babylonsich-Assyrisches Burgschaftsrecht.* Leipzig: B. G. Teubner.

1917 *Rechtsvergleichende Studien zur Geseztgebung Hammurapis, Königs von Babylon.* Leipzig: Von Veit.

1931 *Über einige griechische Rechtsurkunden aus den östlichen Randgebieten des Hellenismus.* Leipzig: S. Hirzel.

Kosovsky, Ch. (חיים קוסובסקי).

1953 אוצר לשון המשנה. ירושלים: מסדה, תשי"ג
[*Concordance to the Mishnah*]
1971 אוצר לשון התלמוד. ירושלים: משרד החנוך והתרבות של ממשלת ישראל, תשל"א
[*Concordance to the Talmud*]

Kosovsky, I. (י. קוסובסקי).

1986 אוצר לשון תרגום אונקלוס. ירושלים: האוניברסיטה העברית.
[*Concordance to Targum Onkelos*]

Kosovsky, M. (משה קוסובסקי).

1982 *Concordance to the Talmud Yerushalmi.* New York: JTSA.

Kraeling, E. G.

1953 *The Brooklyn Museum Aramaic Papyri.* Repr., New York: Arno, 1969.

Kraus, F.R.

1958 *Ein Edikt des Königs Ammi-Ṣaduqa von Babylon.* Leiden: Brill.

Kriger, Diane.

2010 "A Re-embracement of Judges 19: Challenging Public-Private Boundaries." In *Vixens Disturbing Vineyards: Embarrassment and Embracement of Scriptures, Festschrift in Honor of Harry Fox leBeit Yoreh*, 53-64. Edited by Tzemah Yoreh *et al.* Boston: Academic Studies Press.

Krückmann, O.

1931 *Babylonische Rechts – und Verhaltungs-Urkunden aus der Zeit Alexanders und der Diadochen.* Leipzig: Hof-Buchdruckerei.

Kutscher, E. Y. (יחזקאל קוטשר).

1977 "למונחי שטרות בתלמוד ובספרות הגאונים." in *Hebrew and Aramaic Studies,* Hebrew section, pp. תיז-תל. Jerusalem: Magnes.
["On the Terminology of Documents in the Talmud and in Geonic Literature"]

Lambdin, Thomas.

1953 "Egyptian Loan Words in the Old Testament." *JAOS* 73, 145-55.

Lanfranchi, G. and S. Parpola.

1990 *The Correspondence of Sargon II, Part II.* SAA V. Helsinki: Helsinki University Press.

Landsberger, B.
1937 *Die serie ana ittišu*. Rome: Sumptibus Pontifici Instituti Biblici.
1939 "Bemerkungen zu San Nicolo und Ungnad, Neubabylonische Rechts – und Verwaltungsurkunden, Bd. I." *ZA* 39, 277-94.
1967 "Akkadisch-Hebräische Wortgleichungen." *Supplements to VT* 16, 176-204.

Lauterbach, Jacob, ed.
1976 *Mekilta de-Rabbi Ishmael.* 3 vols. Philadelphia: Jewish Publication Society.

Lautner, J.G.
1922 *Die richterliche Entscheidung und die Streitbeendigung im altbabylonischen Prozessrechte.* Leipzig: Theodor Weicher.

Lerner, Gerda.
1986 *The Creation of Patriarchy.* New York: Oxford University Press.

Leshem, Yosi (יוסי לשם).
1994-95 "אמה ושפחה בסיפורי המלוכה שבמקרא." אסופות זיכרון לשושנה בהט, 47-5. מ. בר אשר, עורך. ירושלים: האקדמיה ללשון העברית, תשנ"ז.
["*Amah* and *Shifḥa* in the Kingship Stories of the Bible"]

Levin, Saul.
1983 "Hebrew {pi(y)légeš} Greek παλλακη, Latin *paelex:* The Origin of Intermarriage Among the Early Indo-Europeans and Semites." *General Linguistics* 23, 191-97.

Levine, Baruch.
1989 *The JPS Torah Commentary: Leviticus.* Philadelphia: Jewish Publication Society.

Levinson, Bernard.
1994 "The Case for Revision and Interpolation within the Biblical Legal Corpora." In *Theory and Method in Biblical and Cuneiform Law: Revision, Interpolation and Development,* 37-59. JSOT Supplement Series 181. Sheffield: Sheffield Academic Press.
1997 *Deuteronomy and the Hermeneutics of Legal Innovation.* New York: Oxford University Press.

Lewy, Hildegard.
1952 "Nitokris Naqi'a." *JNES* 11, 264-86.

Lidzbarski, Mark.

1898 *Handbuch der nordsemitischen Epigraphik nebst ausgewählten Inschriften.* Weimar: Felber.

Lieberman, Saul.

1937-39 תוספת ראשונים: פירוש מיוסד על כתבי יד התוספתא וספרי ראשונים ומדרשים בכתבי יד ודפוסים ישנים. ניו יורק וירושלים : בית המדרש לרבנים באמריקה, תשנ"ט. 4 כרכים. ירושלים תרצ"ז-תרצ"ט.

[*Tosefet Rishonim*]

1955-88 תוספתא כפשוטה. 10 כרכים. ניו יורק: בית המדרש לרבנים באמריקה.

[*Tosefta KiFshutah*]

1962 *Hellenism in Jewish Palestine.* New York: JTSA.

1965 *Greek in Jewish Palestine.* New York: JTSA.

Liddell, H.G. and R. Scott.

1996 *A Greek-English Lexicon.* 9th edition with revised supplement. Oxford: Clarendon.

Lindenberger, J. M., trans.

1985 "Ahiqar." In *The Old Testament Pseudepigrapha,* 2:479-507. Edited by J. H. Charlesworth. New York: Doubleday.

Loewenstamm, Shmuel (שמואל לונשטם).

1980 "בקרת תהיה." שנתון ד, 94-97

["*Biqqoret Tihyeh*"]

Lowe, William H.

1883 *The Mishnah on which the Palestinian Talmud Rests,* Cambridge: Cambridge University Press.

Luria, Solomon (שלמה בן יחיאל לוריא).

1766 ים של שלמה על מסכת קדושין. ברלין: איצק שפייאר. תקכ"ו.

Macho, Alejandro Diez, ed.

1968-1979 *Neophyti 1, Targum Palestinense ms. de la Biblioteca Vaticana.* Edición príncipe, introducción y versión castellana [por] Alejandro Díez Macho. Traducciones cotejadas de la versión castellana: francesa: R. Le Déaut; inglesa: Martin McNamara y Michael Maher. Madrid: Consejo Superior de Investigaciones Científicas. [=*Neofiti*]

Maimonides, Moses.
1963 *The Guide of the Perplexed.* Translated by Shlomo Pines. Chicago: University of Chicago Press.

Mandelbaum, Bernard.
1987 פסיקתא דרב כהנא. 2 כרכים. ניו יורק: בית המדרש לרבנים באמריקה.
[=*Pesikta deRav Kahana*]

Mandelkern, S. (שלמה מאנדעלקערן).
1955 קונקורדנציא לתנ"ך. ירושלים: שוקן.
[*Concordance to the Bible*]

Margoliot, M. (מרדכי מרגליות).
1993 מדרש ויקרא רבה. 2 כרכים. ירושלים: בית המדרש לרבנים באמריקה, תשנ"ג.
[*Midrash VaYiqra Rabba*]

Maris, Cees W.
1991 "Milking the Meter." In *Legal Knowledge and Analogy,* 71-104. Law and Philosophy Library 13. Edited by P. Nerhot. Dordrecht: Kluwer Academic Publishers.

Marx, Victor.
1902 "Die Stellung der Frauen in Babylonien gemäss den Kontrakten aus der Zeit von Nebukadnezar bis Darius." *Beitrage zur Assyriologie* 4, 1-77.

McCarter, P. Kyle, Jr.
1980 *I Samuel.* Anchor Bible 8. Garden City, N.Y.: Doubleday.

McComiskey, Thomas.
1965 "The Status of the Secondary Wife: Its Development in Ancient Near Eastern Law, A Study and Comprehensive Index." Ph.D. dissertation, Brandeis University.

McNamara, Martin.
1966 *The New Testament and the Palestinian Targum to the Pentateuch.* Rome: Pontifical Biblical Institute.
1992 *Targum Neofiti 1: Genesis.* Collegeville, Minn.: Liturgical Press.

Meacham (leBeit Yoreh), Tirzah ((תרצה מיטשם (לבית יורה).
1989 משנת מסכת נידה עם מבוא, מהדורה ביקורתית עם הערות בנוסח, בפרשנות ובעריכה, ופרקים בתולדות ההלכה ובראליה. חיבור לשם קבלת תואר דוקטור לפילוסופיה, האוניברסיטה העברית. 2 כרכים.

Meacham (leBeit Yoreh), Tirzah (תרצה מיטשם (לבית יורה)).
["Mishnah Tractate Niddah with Introduction: A Critical Edition with Notes on Variants, Commentary, Redaction and Chapters in Legal History and Realia"]
1997 "The Missing Daughter: Leviticus 18 and 20." *ZAW* 109, 254-59.
1999 ספר הבגרות לרב שמואל בן חפני גאון וספר השנים לרב יהודה הכהן ראש הסדר, ירושלים: יד הרב נסים.
[*Sefer HaBagrut*]

Meillassoux, Claude.
1986 *Anthropologie de l'esclavage: Le ventre de fer et d'argent.* Paris: Presses Universitaires de France.

Mendelsohn, Isaac.
1935 "The Conditional Sale into Slavery of Free-Born Daughters in Nuzi and the Law of Ex. 21:7-11." *JAOS* 55, 190-5.
1949 *Slavery in the Ancient Near East.* New York: Oxford University Press.

Milgrom, Jacob.
1976 *Cult and Conscience: The* Asham *and the Priestly Doctrine of Repentance.* Studies in Judaism in Late Antiquity 18. Leiden: Brill.
1977 "The Betrothed Slave-girl, Lev. 19, 20-22." *ZAW* 89, 43-50.

Minow, Martha.
1990 *Making All the Difference: Inclusion, Exclusion, and American Law.* Ithaca: Cornell University Press.

Moreshet, Menahem (מנחם מורשת).
1981 לקסיקון הפועל שנתחדש בלשון התנאים. רמת גן: אוניברסיטת תל אביב, תשמ"א.
[*Lexicon of the New Verbs in Middle Hebrew*]

Morgenstern, Julian.
1929 "*Beena* Marriage (Matriarchat) in Ancient Israel and its Historical Implications." *ZAW* 47 (=n.s. 6), 91-110.
1931 "Additional Notes on *Beena* Marriage in Ancient Israel." *ZAW* 49 (=n.s. 8), 46-58.

Morwood, James, ed.
1994 *The Pocket Oxford Latin Dictionary.* Oxford: Oxford University Press.

Muffs, Yohanan.
1969 *Studies in the Aramaic Legal Papyri from Elephantine.* Leiden: Brill.

Muntingh, L. M.

1967 "The Social and Legal Status of a Free Ugaritic Female." *JNES* 26, 102-13.

Neufeld, E.

1944 *Ancient Hebrew Marriage Laws.* London: Longmans, Green.

Neusner, Jacob.

1979 *A History of the Mishnaic Law of Holy Things.* Part Four. Leiden: Brill.

1986a "The Synoptic Problem in Rabbinic Literature: The Cases of the Mishna, Tosepta, Sipra and *Leviticus Rabba.*" *JBL* 105, 499-507.

1986b *The Oral Torah.* San Francisco: Harper and Row.

1987 *First Principles of Systemic Analysis.* Lanham, Md.: University Press of America.

1988 *Wrong Ways and Right Ways in the Study of Formative Judaism.* Brown Judaic Studies 145. Atlanta: Scholars Press.

2002 "The Mishnah in Historical and Religious Context." In *The Mishnah in Contemporary Perspective, Part Two*, pp. 81-109. Edited by A. J. Avery-Peck and J. Neusner. Leiden: Brill.

Noth, Martin.

1962 *Exodus: A Commentary.* Old Testament Library. Translated by J. S. Bowden. London: SCM.

1965 *Leviticus: A Commentary.* Old Testament Library. Translated by J. E. Anderson. Philadelphia: Westminster.

Novak, David.

1998 *Natural Law in Judaism.* Cambridge: Cambridge University Press.

Oppert, J.

1888 "*Une femme gardienne de son mari.*" *ZA* 3, 17-22.

Pardes, Ilana.

1992 *Countertraditions in the Bible: A Feminist Approach.* Cambridge, Mass.: Harvard University Press.

Parpola, S.

1987 *The Correspondence of Sargon II, Part I.* SAA I. Helsinki: Helsinki University Press.

1993 *Letters from Assyrian and Babylonian Scholars.* SAA X. Helsinki: Helsinki University Press.

Pateman, Carole.

1988 *The Sexual Contract.* Stanford: Stanford University Press.

Patai, Raphael.

1959 *Sex and Family in the Bible and the Middle East.* New York: Doubleday.

Paul, Shalom.

1969 "Exod. 21:10: A Threefold Maintenance Clause." *JNES* 28, 48-53.

Patterson, Orlando.

1982 *Slavery and Social Death: A Comparative Study.* Cambridge, Mass.: Harvard University Press.

1991 *Freedom in the Making of Western Culture.* Vol. 1 of *Freedom.* New York: Basic Books.

Petschow, Herbert.

1939 *Die neubabylonischen Kaufformulare.* Leipzig: Theodor Weicher.

1956 *Neubabylonisches Pfandrecht.* Abhandlungen der sächsischen Akademie der Wissenschaften zu Liepzig Philologisch-historische Klasse, band 48/1. Berlin: Akademie.

Philo of Alexandria. (trans. F.H. Colson and G.H. Whitaker).

1968[2] *On Mating with the Preliminary Studies.* Vol. 4 of *Philo in Ten Volumes.* London: Loeb Classical Library.

Pope, Marvin H.

1965 *Job.* Anchor Bible 15. Garden City, N.Y.: Doubleday.

Porten, Bezalel and Ada Yardeni.

1989 *Contracts*, vol. 2 of *Textbook of Aramaic Documents from Egypt.* Jerusalem: Hebrew University.

Postgate, J.N.

1974 *Taxation and Conscription in the Assyrian Empire.* Studia Pohl: Series Major 3. Rome: Biblical Institute.

Rabin, C.

1974 "The Origin of the Hebrew Word Pilegeš." *JJS* 25, 353-64.

Radner, Karen.

1997 *Die neuassyrischen Privatrechtsurkunden als Quelle für Mensch and Umwelt.* SAAS VI. The Neo-Assyrian Text Corpus Project. Helsinki: Helsinki University Press.

Reifenberg, Adolf.
1950 *Ancient Hebrew Seals*. London: East and West Library.

Revell, E. J.
1996 *The Designation of the Individual: Expressive Usage in Biblical Narrative*. Contributions to Biblical Exegesis and Theology 14. Kampen: Kok Pharos.

Riesener, Ingrid.
1978 *Der Stamm* עבד *im Alten Testament*. *BZAW* 149. Berlin: De Gruyter.

Rosenthal, F.
1968 *A Grammar of Biblical Aramaic*. Weisbaden: O. Harrasowitz.

Roth, Joel.
1985 "An Halakhic Perspective on an Historical Foundation." *Judaism* 34, 62-67.
1986 *The Halakhic Process: A Systemic Analysis*. New York: JTSA.

Roth, Martha.
1995 *Law Collections from Mesopotamia and Asia Minor*. Atlanta: Scholars Press.

Roth, Martha, editor-in-charge.
1956-2006 *The Assyrian Dictionary of the Oriental Institute of the University of Chicago*. Chicago: University of Chicago Press. [=*CAD*]

Rouland, Norbert.
1994 *Legal Anthropology*. Translated by P. Planel. London: Athlone.

Saarisalo, Aapeli.
1934 "New Kirkuk Documents Relating to Slaves." *Studia Orientalia* 3.

San Nicolo, M.
1922 *Die Schlussklauseln der altbabylonische Kauf– und Tauschvertrage*. Munich: Oskar Beck.

San Nicolo, M. and A. Ungnad.
1929 *Neubabylonische Rechts – und Verwaltungsurkunden*. Band I. Leipzig: J. C. Hinrichs.

Sauneron, Serge.
1968 *The Priests of Ancient Egypt*. Translated by Ann Morrissett. New York: Grove.

Scarry, Elaine.
1985 *The Body in Pain: The Making and Unmaking of the World.* New York: Oxford University Press.

Schenker, Adrian.
1988 "Affranchissement d'une esclave selon Ex 21,7-11." *Biblica* 69, 547-56.

Schiffman, L.
1985 "Jewish Identity and Jewish Descent." *Judaism* 34, 78-84.

Schorr, M.
1913 *Urkunden des Altbabylonischen Zivil – und Prozessrechts.* Leipzig: J. C. Hinrichs.

Schulz, Fritz.
1967 *History of Roman Legal Science.* Oxford: Clarendon.

Schumpeter, Joseph.
1966[2] "The Problem of Classes." In *Class, Status and Power,* 42-46. Edited by R. Bendix and S. M. Lipset. New York: Free Press.

Schwartz, Baruch.
1986 "A Literary Study of the Slave-Girl Pericope – Leviticus 19: 20-22." In *Studies in Bible,* 241-55. Scripta Hierosolymitana 31. Edited by S. Japhet. Jerusalem: Magnes.

Shifman, Pinhas.
1981 "Marriage and Cohabitation in Israeli Law." *Israel Law Review* 16, 439-60.

Siegel, Bernard J.
1947 "Slavery During the Third Dynasty of Ur." *American Anthropologist* n.s. 49. Repr., Millwood, N.Y.: Kraus Reprint Co., 1969.

Sokoloff, Michael.
1992 *A Dictionary of Jewish Palestinian Aramaic.* Ramat-Gan: Bar Ilan University Press.

Soloveitchik, Haym.
2004 "Halakhah, Hermeneutics, and Martyrdom in Medieval Ashkenaz (Pt I of II)." *JQR* 94, 77-108.

Speiser, E. A.
1960 "Leviticus and the Critics." In *Yehezkel Kaufmann Jubilee Volume,* 29-45. Edited by M. Haran. Jerusalem: Magnes.

Sperber, Alexander.
1959-1973 *The Bible in Aramaic.* 5 vols. Leiden: Brill.

Spicq, C.
1978 "Le vocabulaire de l'esclavage dans le nouveau testament." *Revue Biblique* 85, 201-26.

Stec, David.
1994 *The Text of the Targum of Job: An Introduction and Critical Edition.* Leiden: Brill.

Stern, Ephraim.
1982 *Material Culture of the Land of the Bible in the Persian Period 538-332BC.* Warminster: Aris & Phillips.

Stevenson, W. B.
1962 *Grammar of Jewish Palestinian Aramaic.* Oxford: Oxford University Press.

Stol, Marten and Sven Vleeming.
1998 *The Care of the Elderly in the Ancient Near East.* Studies in the History and Culture of the Ancient Near East 14. Leiden: Brill.

Stone, Ken.
1995 "Gender and Homosexuality in Judges 19: Subject-Honor, Object-Shame?" *JSOT* 67, 87-107.

Stone, Martin.
1995 "Focusing the Law: What Legal Interpretation is Not." In *Law and Interpretation,* 31-96. Edited by A. Marmor. Oxford: Clarendon.

Stone, Michael.
1996a "The Genealogy of Bilhah." *DSD* 3, 20-36.
1996b "Testament of Naphtali." In *Qumran Cave 4, XVII, Parabiblical Texts,* 3:73-82. DJD 22. Oxford: Clarendon.

Strack, H. L. and G. Stemberger.
1992 *Introduction to the Talmud and Midrash.* Minneapolis: Fortress.

Tal, Abraham.

1974 "Ms. Neophyti I: the Palestinian Targum to the Pentateuch." *Israel Oriental Studies* 4, 31-43.

1988 התרגום השומרוני לתורה. 3 כרכים. אוניברסיטת תל אביב.
[*The Samaritan Targum to the Torah*]

2000 *A Dictionary of Samaritan Aramaic*. Leiden: Brill.

Talmon, Shemaryahu.

1966 *'Pisqah Be'emṣa Pasuq' and 11QP5^{a}*. *Textus* 5, 11-21.

Taubenschlag, Raphael.

1955 *The Law of Greco-Roman Egypt in the Light of the Papyri, 332 B.C. – 640 A.D.* 2nd ed. Warsaw: Panstwowe Wydawnictwo Naukowe.

Thomsen, Rudi.

1964 *Eisphora: A Study of Direct Taxation in Ancient Greece*. Copenhagen:

Gyldendalske Bogttandel.

Thureau-Dangin, F.

1921 *Rituels Accadiens*. Repr., Osnabrück: Otto Zeller, 1975.

Torrey, C. C.

1954 "More Elephantine Papyri." *JNES* 13, 149-53.

Tov, Emanuel.

1992 *Textual Criticism of the Hebrew Bible*. Revised and enlarged from the Hebrew edition of 1989. Minneapolis: Fortress.

1997 *The Text-Critical Use of the Septuagint in Biblical Research*. Jerusalem Biblical Studies 8. Jerusalem: Simor.

Tsevat, Matitiahu.

1958 "Marriage and Monarchical Legitimacy in Ugarit and Israel." *JSS* 3, 237-43.

Unterman, Jeremiah.

1980 "The Literary Influence of 'The Binding of Isaac' (Genesis 22) on 'The Outrage at Gibeah' (Judges 19)." *Hebrew Annual Review* 4, 161-66.

Urbach, Efraim E. (א.א. אורבך).

1964 "The Laws Regarding Slavery as a Source for Social History of the Period of the Second Temple, the Mishnah and Talmud." In *Papers of the Institute of Jewish Studies, London*, 1:1-94. Edited by J. G. Weiss. Jerusalem: Magnes.

Urbach, Efraim E. (א.א. אורבך).
1984 ההלכה: מקורתיה והתפתחותה. גבעתיים, ישראל: יד לתלמוד – מסדה בע"ם
[*The Halakha: Its Sources and Development*]

van den Branden, A.
1956 "*Notes phéniciennes. Bulletin du Musée de Beyrouth*" 13, 87-95.

Van Seters, John.
1996 "The Law of the Hebrew Slave." *ZAW* 108, 534-46.

Veenhof, K.R.
1982 "A Deed of Manumission and Adoption from the Later Old Assyrian Period." in *zikir šumim—Assyriological Studies Presented to F.R. Kraus on the Occasion of his Seventieth Birthday,* 359-85. Leiden: Brill.

Vermes, G.
1975 *Post-Biblical Jewish Studies.* Leiden: Brill.

Von Soden, W.
1965 *Akkadisches Handwörterbuch.* 3 vols. Wiesbaden: Otto Harrassowitz. [=*AHW*]

Wallace, Sherman L.
1938 *Taxation in Egypt from Augustus to Diocletian.* Princeton: Princeton University Press.

Ward, William.
1983 "Reflections on Some Egyptian Terms Presumed to Mean 'Harem, Harem-Woman,Concubine.'" *Berytus* 31, 67-74.

Waterman, Leroy.
1930 *Royal Correspondence of the Assyrian Empire.* Ann Arbor, Mich.: University of Michigan Press.

Watson, Alan.
1974 *Legal Transplants: An Approach to Comparative Law.* Edinburgh: Scottish Academic Press.
1985 *The Evolution of Law.* Baltimore: Johns Hopkins University Press.
1987 *Roman Slave Law.* Baltimore: Johns Hopkins University Press.

Weber, Max.
1952 *Ancient Judaism.* Translated by H. Gerth and D. Martindale. New York: Free Press.

Wegner, Judith Romney.
1988 *Chattel or Person? The Status of Women in the Mishnah.* New York: Oxford University Press.

Weinberger, Theodore.
1997 "'And Joseph Slept with Potiphar's Wife': A Re-Reading." *Literature and Theology* 11, 145-151.

Weinfeld, Moshe.
1972 *Deuteronomy and the Deuteronomic School.* Oxford: Clarendon.

Welch, Bryan.
2007 "Putting a Stop to Slave Labor: A Moral Solution to Illegal Immigration." *UTNE Reader*, March-April 2007, 42-44.

Westbrook, Raymond.
1988a *Old Babylonian Marriage Law.* Horn: Ferdinand Berger.
1988b *Studies in Biblical and Cuneiform Law.* Paris: J. Gabalda.
1991 *Property and the Family in Biblical Law.* JSOT Supplement Series 113. Sheffield: JSOT Press.
1994 "What is the Covenant Code?" in *Theory and Method in Biblical and Cuneiform Law: Revision, Interpolation and Development,* 15-36. JSOT Supplement Series 181. Edited by B. Levinson. Sheffield: Sheffield Academic Press.

Westermann, William L.
1938 "Enslaved Persons Who are Free." *American Journal of Philology* 59, 1-30.

Wevers, John, W.
1990 *Notes on the Greek Text of Exodus.* SBL Septuagint and Cognate Studies Series 30. Atlanta: Scholars Press.

Wiedemann, T.
1981 *Greek and Roman Slavery.* London: Croom Helm.

Wigmore, John H.
1897 "I. The Pledge-Idea: A Study in Comparative Legal Ideas." *Harvard Law Review* 10, 321-50.

Wintermute, O. S., trans.
1985 "Jubilees." In *The Old Testament Pseudepigrapha,* 2:52-142. Edited by J. H. Charlesworth. New York: Doubleday.

Wright, Marcia.
1993 *Strategies of Slaves & Women: Life-Stories from East/Central Africa.* New York: Lilian Barber.

Xenophon
1970 *Xenophon's Socratic Discourse: An Interpretation of the Oeconomicus.* Translated by C. Lord. Commentary by Leo Strauss. Ithaca: Cornell University Press.

Yaron, Reuven.
1958 "On Defension Clauses of Some Oriental Deeds of Sale and Lease, From Mesopotamia and Egypt." *BiOr* 15, 15-22.
1961 *Introduction to the Law of the Aramaic Papyri.* Oxford: Clarendon.
1988[2] *The Laws of Eshnunna.* 2nd Revised Edition. Jerusalem: Magnes.

Yoreh, Tzemaḥ.
2010 *The First Book of God.* Berlin: De Gruyter.
2009- www.biblecriticism.com

Zakovitch, Yair (יאיר זקוביץ).
1977 "הדגם הספרותי שלושה-ארבעה במקרא." חיבור לשם קבלת תואר דוקטור לפילוסופיה, האוניברסיטה העברית, תשל"ח.
["The Literary Paradigm Three-Four in the Bible"]

Zakovitch, Yair and Avigdor Shinan (יאיר זקוביץ ואביגדור שנאן).
1984 מעשה ראובן ובלהה. מפעלי המחקר של המכון למדעי היהדות, ג. ירושלים: האוניברסיטה העברית, תשמ"ד.
[*The Story of Reuven and Bilhah*]

Zeitlin, Solomon.
1963 "Slavery During the Second Commonwealth and the Tannaitic Period." *JQR* 53, 185-218.
1978 "הפקר ויאוש." In *Studies in the Early History of Judaism,* Volume IV, 438-53 New York: Ktav.
["*Hefqer* and *Yei'ush*"]

Ziegler, Ignaz.
1903 *Die Konigsgleichnisse des Midrasch beleuchtet durch die römanische Kaiserzeit.* Breslau: Schlesische Verlage-Anstalt.

Zucrow, Solomon.
1932 *Women, Slaves and the Ignorant in Rabbinic Literature.* Boston: Stratford.

Zweigert, K.
1972 "Methodological Problems in Comparative Law." *Israel Law Review 7,* 465-74.

CITATIONS INDEX

1. Bible

Gen.

9:21 49
12:16 36, 41, 42, 157
14:14 63, 64, 68, 78, 79
15:2 79, 80
15:3 79, 80
16:1 36, 42, 170
16:2 42
16:2ff 314
16:3 36, 42
16:5 42
16:6 42
16:8 42
Ch. 17 65, 68, 76, 93
17:12 62, 68, 78
17:20 55
17:21 55
17:23 62
17:27 62, 68
Ch. 19 113
19:8 113
19:30-38 100
20:14 36, 42, 157
20:17 42, 324
21:2 56
21:9-10 54
21:10 36, 42, 54
21:12 36, 42
21:13 36, 42, 54
22:3 113
22:10 113
22:24 89, 115
24:15 333
24:24 333
24:29 333
24:35 36, 42, 157
25:1 90, 99
25:6 92, 93 99
25:9 54
25:12 42, 56
25:19 56
25:32 101
28:8 135
28:22 331
Ch. 29 335
29:5 333
29:24 40, 42, 314, 336, 337
29:29 36, 40, 42, 314
29: 32-30:24 339
Ch. 30 315, 342
30:3 36, 41, 42, 315, 317
30:3-13 314
30:4 36, 42, 157
30:5 56
30:7 42
30:9 36, 42, 317
30:10 42, 342
30:12 42, 342
30:18 42
30:23 164, 217
30:43 36, 42, 167
31:15 67, 68
31:33 36, 42, 318
31:50 343
32:5 42
32:6 36, 42
32:23 36, 41, 42, 315, 318
33:1 42, 316, 318
33:2 42, 315
33:6 42, 316
34:14 164
34:25 100
Ch. 35 35
35:22 89, 90, 95, 97, 99, 104, 105, 107-109, 119, 315
35:25-6 42, 315, 316
36:12 89, 108, 323
Ch. 37 316
37:2 56,317
39:10 109
42:22 176
42:27 67
43:9 163
Ch. 46 335
46:18 315, 316
46:25 315, 316
48:5 332
Ch. 49 106, 109
49:3-4 99
49:4 106, 108, 109,111
49:5-7 100

Exod.

1:13 126
2:4-11 127
2:5 42
11:5 42
12:29 113

12:36 232, 320
12:43-45 67
12:43 68
12:44 68
12:45 238
20:10 36, 42, 60, 61
20:14 36, 42
Ch. 21 12, 23-25, 124, 128, 140, 155, 227
21:2 28, 129, 221
21:2-6 20, 129, 222, 226
21:2-11 33, 53, 121, 122, 127, 130, 132-134, 137, 141, 150, 347
21:2-27 134
21:3 132
21:4 9, 33, 127, 132, 150, 152, 218, 221, 297, 304
21:4-5 37
21:4-6 141
21:4-11 153, 333
21:5-6 309
21:6 128, 129, 309
21:7 42, 43, 169, 219, 221, 226-228
21:7-11 21, 22, 23, 29, 37, 128, 132, 138, 139, 141, 142, 150, 160, 224, 225, 228, 346, 349
21:8 37, 66, 68, 129, 139, 143, 144, 148, 160, 222
21:9 128
21:10 139, 150
21:11 228
21:12 12
21:19 67
21:20 13, 36, 350
21:20-21 12, 67
21:21 66, 67
21:23-27 12
21:25-26 222
21:26-27 4, 36, 123, 152, 226, 350
21:32 36, 42
22:2 221
22:4 192, 193
Ch. 23 61
23:11 192
23:12 42, 60, 61, 62
23:24 193
31:17 60
32:1-20 109
32:2 193
32:11 84

Lev.

5:6 156
5:14-16 175
5:15 156, 283
5:17-19 175
5:20-25 175
5:20-26 175
5:22 175
5:50 166
13:36 176
15:18 109, 263
15:24 262, 264
17:1-26:46 128
Ch. 18 103
18:3 103
18:9 68
18:11 270
18:15 131, 270
18:20 156
18:26 269
Ch. 19 40, 153, 156, 157
19:20 13, 14, 22-24, 29, 40, 41, 42, 43, 94, 109, 133, 152, 154, 155, 158-161, 162, 163, 166, 168, 169, 172-175, 177, 181, 183, 216, 217, 227, 251, 255, 262-265, 267, 268, 273-276, 285, 288, 296, 299, 346, 349
19:20-21 10, 13, 14, 33, 34, 349
19:20-22 37, 151, 156, 158, 175, 217, 251, 260
19:21 283
19:22 285
19:23 157
20:12 270
20:13 265
20:17 270
22:11 65, 75, 76
23:24 329
Ch. 25 28, 221, 222
25:6 36, 42
25:10 221
25:39 13, 221, 229
25:39-46 21, 125,347
25:42 66, 226
25:43 13
25:44 36, 129, 221, 226, 227
25:44-45 222, 237, 240
25:44-46 220
25:45 238, 239
25:46 243
25:47-50 128, 341
25:47-55 127
25:51 274
25:55 3
26:30 193
27:33 176

Num.

1:18 78
5:6-7 158, 159
5:6-8 175
5:13 109, 156

6:24-26 110
Ch. 7 329
7:3 330
12:5 85
12:7 86
12:7-8 42
13:22 68
13:28 68
21:20 87

Deut.

5:12-18 163
5:14 36, 46
5:18 36, 46
7:1-3 220, 238
7:3 78
7:4 78
12:12 36, 42
12:18 36, 42
Ch. 15 128, 129, 132, 140, 142, 229
15:1-3 24
15:12 129, 219, 221, 226, 227, 229, 230, 267
15:12-18 21, 121, 124, 127, 136, 347
15:14 268
15:17 36, 37, 42, 128, 226, 227, 309
16:11 36, 42
16:14 42
20:16 39, 243
20:16-17 220, 238
21:10-14 221
21:14 66, 136
Ch. 22 156
22:9-11 156
22:14ff 156
22:22 151, 153, 160
22:23 133, 152, 160
22:25-27 161
23:4 239
23:8-9 239
23:18 269, 324
24:1 272-276
25:19 108
28:30 320
28:68 42
29:7 239, 243
33:6 107
34:5 42

Josh.

5:9 164
9:21 239
15:14 68

Judges

1:1-2 117
5:18 168
8:31 57, 94
9:2 58
Ch. 9 58, 121
9:15-20 58
9:18 57, 90, 94 249
9:19 37
11:31 117
Ch. 18 114
Ch. 19 94, 111, 113-116
Ch. 19-20 98
Ch. 19-21 90, 99, 100, 101, 111, 114, 117
19:1 90, 99, 115, 116
19:1-3 111
19:3 90, 115, 116
19:4 90, 96, 116
19:5 116
19:7 116
19:9 116
19:19 37, 116
19:27 115, 116, 117
19:27-28 112
20:4 115
20:18 117
21:25 115
22:23 152

1Sam.

1:11 37
1:16 37
1:18 37
8:16 37
10:26 115
11:7 113
14:48 109
15:3 109
15:7 109
17:10 164
17:26 164
17:36 164
17:45 164
20:6 47
20:29 47
24:27 37
24:41 37
25:24 37
25:25 37
25:28 37
25:31 37
25:39 174
25:41 37
27:12 309
28:21 37
28:22 37

2Sam.

5:13 90
6:20 37
6:22 37
Ch. 13 100
13:1 110
13:13 164
14:7 37
14:12 37
14:15 37
14:16 37
14:17 37
14:19 37
16:21 100
16:21-22 90, 99
17:19 169
20:17 37

21:11 89
21:16 68
21:18 68

1Kings

1:13 37
1:17 37
2:22 99
3:20 37
3:26 68
3:27 68
11:3 90

2Kings

4:2 37
4:16 37
5:2 37
5:4 37
5:26 36, 37
14:9 58
16:15 176, 177
19:22 163

Isa.

4:1 164
8:3 321
13:16 320
14:2 36, 37
24:2 36, 37
37:23 163
43:9 249
45:18 301
47:3 164
54:4 164

Jer.

2:4 64
2:14 62
3:2 320
5:11 145
6:10 164
16:5 48
23:32 193
Ch. 34 273
34:9 36, 37, 45
34:10, 11, 16 36, 37
35:5 80

Ezek.

Ch. 16 13
22:10 100
Ch. 23 13, 101
23:20 90, 91, 100, 101, 102
23:30 98
34:11 176
34:11-12 176

Hos.

2:7 150
12:15 164

Joel

3:2 36, 37

Amos

6:7 48

Micah

7:20 331

Naḥum

1:1 97
2:8 37

Zeph.

2:10 163

ZeCh.

14:2 320

Mal.

2:11 145

Ps.

Ch. 16 59
27:4 176
45:10 320
55:13 163
68:5 330
68:22 158
Ch. 86 59
86:3 59
86:11 59
86:16 59, 60
96:13 330
98:9 330
116:10 59
116:16 59
120:34 333
123:2 36, 37

Prov.

14:31 163
20:25 176
27:22 169
30:21-23 4
30:23 37, 43, 227

Job

1:3 157
14:1 68
15:14 68
19:5 37, 163
25:4 68
27:6 165, 170
29:4 180
31:13 36, 37

Cant.

6:8 90

Ruth

2:13 37
2:14 106
3:9 37
4:11 315
4:22 115

Lam.

3:30 164
5:8 341

Eccl.

2:7 36, 37
8:1 86
9: 7-8 150

Esth.

7:4 36, 37

Dan.

5:2 95
5:3 95
5:23 95

Ezra

2:58 221
2:65 36, 37
4:4 238
10:2-3 9
10:14 238

Neḥ.

2:6 320
3:26 221
7:67 36, 37
13:23-24 9

1Chron.

1:31 99
1:32 89, 90
2:1-2 316
2:46 90
2:48 90
5:1 105
5:1-3 106
7:13 316, 340
4:18 86
14:4 68
20:4 68

2Chr.

9:18 347
28:8-10 21
28:10 36, 37

2. Bible Translations

Septuagint (LXX)

Gen.

15:2 79
15:3 79
21:10 54
21:13 54
30:23 164
35:22 89, 105, 106,
38:10 106
49:4 106, 109

Exod.

21:7 43, 227
21:10 150
21:26-27 43

Lev.

19:20 43, 152, 160, 172, 227
25:44 227

Deut.

15:12 227

Ezek.

23:20 102

Dan.

5:2-3 95, 319
5:23 95, 319

Peshitta

Gen.

15:2 79

Samaritan Pentateuch

Gen.

15:3 79
49:4 106, 109

Exod.

21:4 122
21:8 122
21:9 122
21:10 122
23:12 60

Lev.

19:20 151, 153, 161
25: 44 125

Vulgate

Gen.

35:22 89

Lev.

19:20 173

Ezek.

23:20 103

Jewish Bible Translations

Targum Onkelos

Gen.

15:2 80
22:26 320
31:33 318
32:23 318
33:1-2 318
33:6 318
35:22 89, 324
36:12 323

Exod.

21:6 123, 309
21:10 150
22:26 320

Lev.

18:9 68
19:20 152, 161, 275
25:45 238

Deut.

15:17 309
23:18 269, 325

Targum Pseudo-Jonathan

Gen.

15:2-3 80
20:17 324
21:12 56
29:24 343
29:29 343
30:3 317
30:9 317
31:33 318
32:23 318
33:1-2 318
33:6 318
35:22 110
37:2 317

Exod.

12:36 320
14:21 331
21:6 309
21:10 150
22:4 192
23:11 192
23:12 62

Lev.

19:20 161, 172, 275
25:45 238

Deut.

25:5 192

Targum Neofiti

Gen.

22:24 109
31:33 318
32:23 318
33:1-2 318
33:6 318
35:22 109, 324
37:2 317

Exod.

22:4 192- 193
23:12 62
23:24 192-193
32:2 192-193

Lev.

19:20 162, 172, 275
26:30 192-193

Deut.

15:17 309
25:5 192

Samaritan Targum

Gen.

15:3 79
21:10 43

Exod.

23:12 60-61

Lev.

19:20 162, 172

Targum Jonathan

Judg.

9:4 193

2Sam.

3:7 323

Jer.

23:32 193

Fragment Targum

Gen.

15:3 79

Targum Ps.

40:17 165
71:24 165

Targum Eccl.

2:7 80, 87

Targum Job

27:6 165

3. New Testament

Luke

2:1-4 371

4. Dead Sea Scrolls

4Q252 107
4Q215 334
11QP5a 105

5. Apocrypha, Pseudo-Epigrapha & Judeo-Hellenistic Works

Aḥiqar

58, 322, 323

Joseph and Aseneth

Ch. 24 56, 316

Josephus Ant.

1:78 65
1:303 317
4:244 325
5:142 90, 114
5:233 249

Jubilees

13:25 64, 79
14:2 79
34:15 340

Letter of Aristeas

323

Philo

On Mating 325, 340
On the Virtues 249, 325

Pseudo-Philo

58, 114, 115

Testament of Naphtali

336-338

Tobit

1:1 339
1:3-5 339

6. Mishnah

mArakh.
6:1 193, 195, 198, 210

mB.Bat.
3:1 30
8:4 278

m.B.Metz.
1:5 28, 45
4:9 30
7:6 30

mB.Qam.
8:3 28
8:5 28
9:2 30

mBer.
2:7 327

mBikk.
1:5 30
2:8 305

mEdu.
1:13 300, 302

mGitt.
1:4 311
4:4 306
4:4-5 274, 302
4:5 280, 300, 302, 304, 305
4:6 51
7:3-4 311
8:2 305
9:3 274, 278, 311

mKer.
1:1 284, 292
1:2 284
2:2 284, 292
2:3 284
2:4 172
2:4-6 251, 252, 300, 304
2:5 152
5:5 271

mKet.
4:4 225
4:8 341
9:1 201
11:2-4 193
11:4 196
11:5 191, 193, 194, 195, 196

mMak.
3:12 173
3:14 173

mMeg.
110, 111
4:10 109, 324

mNid.
5:4 263
5:5 p 262

mPesaḥ.
8:1 31

mQidd.
1:1-3 5,
1:2 26, 27, 30, 62, 219, 222, 234, 267, 309
1:2-3 13, 28, 220, 222, 275, 278
1:3 30, 78, 223, 274
1:5 30, 210
1:7 19
3:12 8, 30, 160, 219, 220, 301, 304, 314, 317, 346, 350
3:13 1
4:3 256

mSheb.
6:5 30

mShevu'ot
7:8 82

mSotah
3:4 19

mSukk.
2:1 326
5:4 333

mTa'an.
3:8 83

mTer.
3:4 82

mYev.
4:10 300
4:13 1
7:5 8, 30, 220, 245, 346, 350
9:5 75

mZev.
5:5 165

7. Tosefta

tArakh.
4:1 211
4:3 191, 210, 211

tHor.
1:1 211

tKer.
1:16 165, 255
1:16-18 251, 256, 265, 304
1:19 165
1:18 152 (.n)
4:5 165

tKet.
11:3 191, 193, 195

tMeg.
3:35 110

tQidd.
5:11 245, 246, 248, 250, 257-260

8. Midreshei Halakha

Mekhilta deR. Ishmael (ed. Horovitz)
Neziqin, par. 3 144

Mekhilta deR. Ishmael (ed. Lauterbach)
Dibaḥodesh (Ex. 20:10) 61
Neziqin par. 2 226, 227, 304
Par. 3 (Ex. 21:7-11) 225, 226, 227, 228
Pisḥa (Ex.23:12) 61, 62

Mekhilta deRashbi ed. Epstein&Melamed

Mishpatim
21:7 228

Sifra (ed. Weiss)
Metzora
pereq 6:1 262
6:7 262, 263
7:1 262, 264

Aḥarei Mot
7:9 270
9:8 104
12:1 270
13:18 269

Emor
par. 5:4-5 75

BeHar
par. 6:2-3 240, 126

Qedoshim
pereq 5 172, 260-262, 267, 269, 272, 274, 275, 279-284, 286-291, 294, 295, 298-302, 304-306, 312
5:2-4 152
5:10 165
9:13 270
9:14 265
10:13 270

Ḥova
pereq 21:7 165

Sifrei Deut.
pisqa 118 229, 231, 236

Sifrei Num. (ed. Horovitz)
pisqa 78 86
pisqa 117 85

Sifrei Zuta (ed. Horovitz
Num. 12:5 89

Midrash Tannaim
230, 236, 237

9. Minor Tractates

Semaḥot
1:13-14 326, 332, 344

10. Jerusalem Talmud

yBer.
9:1 13a 85

yGitt.
4:5 45d 215, 216
4:5 46a 276

yKet.
5:2 29d 50, 92, 93
11:6 34c 199

yNaz.
8:1 57a 165

yQidd.
1:1 59a 152, 165, 168
1:2 59c 144, 145
1:2 59d 43
1:3, 60a 30
3:13 64d 246, 247

ySan.
1:2 19b 199
10:2 28d 86

yShevu'ot
7:8 38a 82

yYev.
6:1 7b 165
7:4 8b 75
9:5 10b 75

11. Babylonian Talmud

bBekh.
34a 145, 147

bBer.
16b 327, 332

bGitt.
6b 118
38ab 215, 216
39b 280, 281, 282
41b 273, 276
42b-43a 76
43a 165

bHor.
13b 298

bKer.
9a 285
10b 255
11a 152, 165, 169, 251, 279, 293, 299, 303
11ab 288

12b 165
25b 165

bKet.
99b 194, 198
100b 198

bMeg.
25ab 100

bSan.
21a 92, 93
31b 86
103b 114

bShab.
55b 110
72a 165
135b 76, 77

bShevu'ot
48b 82

bSotah
3b 242
21b 19

bYev.
23a 9
48b 62
55ab 165
78b 241-243
99a 245-247, 249

bQidd.
6a 160, 165, 300
14b 27
16a 234, 274
16b 241, 243, 244
17b 268
18ab 141, 148
18a 145, 230, 231, 233-236
18b 146, 147, 148
19a 147
20a 234
69a 325

bZev.
48a 165
54b 165

12. Midreshei Aggadah

Ber. Rab. (Theodor-Albeck)
52:1-2 56
66:4 326
84:2 317

Gen. Rabbah (Rom)
44:11 79
45:2 170
47:5 55
61:4 90
62:3 54
66:4 326
70:7 331
71:9 342
74:14 343
84:11 340

Bereshit Rabbati
(29:24) 334, 336, 337, 338, 339, 341, 342, 343

Lev. Rabbah (Rom)
1:13 91
12:1 84

VaYiqra Rabbah (Margoliot)
12:1 84
29:11 329

Eccl. Rabbah
7:3-4 77

Esther Rabbah (Rom)
1:12 329, 330
5:1 84

Exod. Rabbah (Rom)
15:18 85
35:6 85
40:4 318
43:6 83

Midrash Leqaḥ Tov (Rom)
Lev. 19:20 173

Midrash Sekhel Tov
Gen. 35:22 97

Midrash Tehilim
24:2 85
4:3 85

Midrash Tehilim (Vilna 1891)
2:13 85

Num. Rabbah
4:1 85
10:1 157
14:11 328, 333
21:15 85

Pesiqta deRav Kahana
1:3 85
12:1 85
26:3 85
Num. 7 pisqa 1:7 329

Pesiqta Rabbati
(parshat 27,3) 64

Pirqei de R. Eliezer
pereq 37 344

Sefer ha-Yashar
341

Song of Songs Rab.
6:4 329, 330

Song of Songs Zuta
1:15 328

Tanhuma

Vayeshev 2 114
Ki Tissa siman 13 318

Yalqut Shimoni

remez 320/Ex. 21 146
Mishpatim Ex. 22 232
Re'eh remez 88/Deut. 15 232

Midrash HaGadol

Exod 12:36 241, 244, 260, 261, 262, 290

13. Commentators

Abarbanel 93
Ibn Ezra 160, 169, 239, 267
Malbim 273, 280, 283, 285
Maimonides (Guide) 16
Magid Mishneh 264
Metzudat David 59
Moshe haDarshan 314, 328, 332, 334, 342, 343
Naḥalat Ya'aqov 332
Naḥmanides 55-57, 93, 94, 169, 174, 333
Penei Moshe 82, 216
Rabad 94, 95, 260, 261, 263, 279
Rabbenu Baḥya 333
Rabbenu Hillel 260, 261, 269, 279
Radak 60, 102
Rashak 255
Rashba 146, 147, 231, 235
Rashbam 239
Rashi 59, 67, 86, 92, 93, 101, 103, 116, 126, 145-148, 161, 173, 198, 242, 244, 267, 285, 325, 327, 342, 343
Qorban Aharon 289
Qorban HaEdah 75, 216
Tosafot 20, 301
Tosafot HaRosh 148
Yaqub al-Qirqisani 249

14. Posqim

Mishnah Torah

Avadim

7:1-2 278
7:6 281
8:13 251
9:3 244

Ishut

4:16 161

Issure Biyah

3:13 161
3:14 173
3:17 263
12:11 325
12:13 325
12:25 240
15:4 9, 325

Malveh veLoveh

12:11 197

Talmud Torah

1:13 19

Yam shel Shelomo

Qiddushin 38

15. Ancient Law Codes and Texts

Aramaic Documents (Porten/Yardeni)

2.2, 11 202
2:B.3.3 320
B.2.2 321
B.3.5 321
B.3.6 310, 320, 321
B3.11 80, 323
B.3.12 320

Aramaic Papyri (Cowley)

63 322

ABL

3 167
99 73
311 168
1164 167
XII 1239 51

ADD

1041 72

Aug. 65

187

BE

9 14:6 81
91:20 80

BU

89-4-26,6 167

CH

171 50

CT

6 26a 117
II. 9-12 117
II 39 185
VIII 22b 313
VIII 28b 69
33 34 138
47 40 138
48 53 140
53 21 73

Cyr.

332 188

Dar.

212 187
537 187

Hittite Laws

31-33 140

HSS

V 57 141
IX 145 138
XIX 37 141
XIX 39 141
XIX 40 141
XIX 45 141
XIX 49 141

JEN

572 141

Justinian

C7.7.1.1 277

K

492 167
630 168
958 72
1097 73

Keret Epic

K III iv 13 319

Ki

1902-5 73
1902-10 73
1902-13 73

LE

31 154, 158, 217
42 164

LH

9-13 11, 184
114-116 66
115-119 162
116 67
117 136, 183
117-119 66
118 180
125 11, 184
129 13, 264
146-147 57
150 180, 185
155-56 139, 149
170-171 57, 140, 185
175 140
179 180, 185
185 180, 187
187 180, 187
188 180, 187
196-201 12
202-5 164
278 187
279 180187
280-281 51

LL

25-28 140

LU

5 140

MAL

A 43 139
A 44 66

MSL

1, 80, 18 179

Nuzi

N. 432 140
NII, 120 140

PSBA

6:102 187

SAA

I, 99 73, 74
5, 199 168
X 316 73
10, 191 167
XI 72, 73

SAAS

V 16, BM 103206 308
V 72

TCL

1 29 70
133 71

TD

133 187
156 187
232 185

UAZP

29 278
77 313
82 71, 187
84 187
85 187
262 185
265 185
288 69

VAB

6 143 70

VAS

16, 4:25 69

VS

V 73 187
V 85 187
V 126 187
VII 50 187

16. General Index

actio in personam 182
actio in rem 155, 178, 182-184, 190
adulterer/adulteress 14, 155, 249, 264
adultery/adulterous 4, 6, 10, 13, 33, 39, 96, 117, 151-156, 158, 162, 174, 175, 183, 217, 267, 280, 348, 349, 350

aḥ 13, 21, 125, 127, 221, 222, 224, 347
aḥim 28
amah 4, 5, 12, 16, 21, 26, 29, 33, 36- 46, 48-62, 66, 68, 80, 87, 90, 94, 95, 96, 98, 109, 116, 121-125, 127-128, 129, 130-136, 142, 148-150, 152, 219, 220, 222-225, 226, 227-231, 237, 249, 250, 267, 269, 310, 315, 317, 318, 320, 328, 343, 344, 345, 346, 347
amtum 46, 57, 69, 70, 154
avadim 37, 61, 122, 126, 134, 226, 227, 228, 229, 336
awīlu 12
ba'al marriage 45, 94
beena 45, 46, 58, 94, 116, 117
begged 145, 146
begidah 145
ben amah 33, 53, 54, 55-60, 62, 87, 90, 94, 249
ben bayit 33, 53, 65, 78-80, 82-87, 238
ben ḥorin 4, 26, 31
Bilhah 34, 36, 40, 41, 43, 56, 89, 90, 95, 98, 99, 100, 101, 104-111, 118, 249, 313-319, 324, 326, 328-330, 332-344
biqqoret 14, 33, 151-153, 155, 158, 160, 161, 162, 171-175, 177, 178, 181-184, 191-200, 202, 203, 205, 208-212, 216, 217, 279, 285
BQR/PQR 33, 138, 152, 157, 174, 175, 178, 179, 181, 183-185, 187, 188, 190-192, 213, 216, 217
Canaanite slave 28, 38, 161, 223, 226, 239, 244, 256, 266, 267, 274, 275
cessio in iure 277
common law 5, 6, 7, 17, 20-23, 32, 155, 348
comparative law 16, 347
concubine 4, 33, 35, 36, 39, 40, 41, 50, 52, 53, 89, 90, 91-96, 98, 99, 101, 102, 103, 104, 110, 113, 114, 115, 121, 150, 170, 300, 315, 318-320, 323, 343-345
concubinage 5, 38, 39, 89, 91, 92, 95, 96, 103, 104, 121, 162, 319, 325
Decalogue 36, 60-62, 133
Eshnuna 23
eved 4, 5, 12, 16, 21, 26, 28, 30, 31, 36-38, 42, 44, 50, 52-54, 57, 59-62, 64, 66-68, 80, 82, 90, 122, 123-127, 128, 130-136, 140, 223, 224, 226, 227, 229, 230, 237, 269, 299, 304, 309, 346, 347
eved ivri/Hebrew slave 122, 123, 132, 223, 224, 226, 229, 230, 233-235, 297, 347
eved kena'ani/Canaanite slave 28, 229, 259, 304
eved olam 21, 122, 124, 128, 132, 133, 135, 136, 140, 221, 226, 309
free man 299
freedman 247
functional equivalence/ equivalents 15-17, 26, 33, 62, 132, 137, 139, 150, 155, 347
gentile/s 8, 9, 78, 127, 245-48, 250, 270, 301, 350
ger 61, 214, 247
ger tzedeq 61
ger toshav 61
Hagar 36, 40, 41, 54,

56, 90, 98, 99, 105, 170, 313-315
Haggada 326
half slave-half free 268, 276, 279, 303, 305
Hammurapi 10, 12, 17 23, 50, 56, 57
Hand wahre Hand 11 184
hapax/es 13, 14, 33, 41, 152, 155, 159, 163, 172, 177, 217
heqdesh 191, 210, 211
heres 277 292
hevqer/hefqer 192, 212, 213, 217
ḥofshi 4, 26, 31
Holiness Code 128, 156
iggeret biqqoret 175 191-200, 202, 203, 208-210, 211, 212
iggeret mazon 192, 199, 206
inter vivos 277
ishah 4, 36, 37, 54, 90, 91, 94, 97-99, 105, 111, 112, 116, 119, 162, 315, 317, 345, 348
ishah pilegesh 90, 111, 112, 116
Josephus 44, 65, 90, 114, 228, 249, 317, 324, 325, 344
Jubilees 64, 79, 340, 344
Juridicization 15
LB 81, 167, 179, 187, 188, 308
LE 155
lectio difficilior 142, 147, 232, 235, 236, 249, 288, 332
lex talionis 11
LH 66, 190, 191
mamzer/mazerut 8, 9, 220, 245, 247-250, 350, 351
mār ālim 81
mār bīti 80, 81, 87
mār bītim 71, 81
mār ekallim 71
māru/ mārū 57, 81
matrilineal 7, 9, 34, 53, 121, 150, 158, 219, 220, 237, 245, 250
matrilineal principle 6-10, 30, 33, 34, 52, 127, 152, 158, 218-220, 314, 346, 348, 349, 350 352
matrilocal 45, 46
meshuḥrar/reret 4, 26, 30 31, 247, 349
MB 178, 179
NA 51, 57, 72, 73, 167, 168, 201, 308, 313
NB 66, 72, 81, 137, 179, 201, 308
Neo-Sumerian 308
neḥerefet 10, 13, 33, 41, 151-153, 155, 159-161, 162, 166-170, 183, 217, 251, 252, 265, 267, 280, 284, 288, 290, 297, 299, 300, 301, 304, 350,
netinim 221
Nuzi 22, 23, 24, 137, 138, 139, 140, 141, 179, 201, 308, 341
OA 178
OB 24, 69, 71, 72, 78, 81, 138, 140, 152, 178, 179, 184, 185-187, 278, 313
Philo 249, 250 261, 325, 340
pilegesh 4, 33, 35, 50, 57, 58, 89-109, 111, 112, 113, 114-119, 170, 315, 318, 323, 324, 344
PLḤ 141, 309, 310
qiddushin 8, 92, 93, 142, 170, 225, 245, 301, 304, 314, 348
qinyan 5, 95
qinyan kesef 75, 76, 78
Qumran 5, 34, 105, 107, 334, 335
sakhir 238
Sarah 54, 56, 101, 313, 326-330, 332, 333, 340
sex right 4-6, 10, 32, 34, 251, 345, 348, 350, 352
shifḥah 1, 4, 5, 10, 16, 26, 27, 28, 30, 33, 36-41, 42, 43-46, 47, 48, 52, 54, 56, 77, 82, 89-91, 94, 95, 96, 109, 142, 151, 152, 153, 157, 158, 161, 162 163,

169, 170, 172, 217, 218, 224, 227, 251, 252, 254-256, 258, 259, 263, 265, 267- 270, 280, 282, 284, 288-294, 297, 299, 301-304, 314, 315, 317, 318, 337, 338, 342, 344- 346, 350
shifḥah kena'anit 1, 28,
shifḥah neḥerefet 10, 13, 41, 142 151, 161, 162, 169, 170, 251, 252, 265, 267, 280, 284, 288, 290, 297, 299, 301, 304, 350
shinnui ha-itim 352
talion 11, 12, 13, 68, 123, 226, 350
Targum 34, 39, 43, 54, 56, 60, 62, 79, 80, 87, 89, 100, 102, 106, 109-111, 116, 150, 160-162, 165, 172, 176, 192, 193, 238, 269, 275, 309, 314, 317, 318, 320 323, 324, 325, 331, 333, 343, 344
terumah 8, 75, 76, 82
toshav 61 126, 127, 221, 237-244
vindictam imponere 181
virilocal 45, 46, 116
wilid bītim 63, 68-72, 78
wildum 69
yelid bayit 33, 53, 57, 59, 60, 62-66, 68, 69, 71, 74-78, 87
Yizkor 326
Zilpah 34, 36, 40, 41, 43, 56, 98, 105, 109, 249, 313-319, 324, 326, 328, 329, 330, 332, 333, 335-344
zonah 116, 117

CPSIA information can be obtained at www.ICGtesting.com
230247LV00002B/3/P

9 781934 843482